# AMERICAN COMMUNISM IN CRISIS, 1943-1957

This study was prepared under the auspices of the Research Institute on Communist Affairs, Columbia University.

# AMERICAN COMMUNISM IN CRISIS, 1943-1957

## JOSEPH R. STAROBIN

Harvard University Press, Cambridge, Massachusetts, 1972

To our dear Bob

Unhappy warrior for great causes,
who did not want to stay the course

# CONTENTS

# PREFACE

This book has to do with the political experience of several hundred thousand Americans who gave the attempt to build a revolutionary community in a nonrevolutionary situation their best years, their immense energies, and highest hopes. The community was a political party which they tried to make into a fraternity of comrades, animated by the great ideal of human brotherhood and the aim of making the whole society conform to such brotherhood. It was a community that went beyond national boundaries and differences of race and creed: it was driven by the certainty that man's sojourn on earth could be happier if only his social relations were transformed from competition to cooperation. These Americans were sure that a universal strategy for creating a new society had been found in the experience of Russia and China, even though these were less productive, less democratic societies than their own. The notion that a universal formula existed, and needed only to be applied in concert with revolutionary parties elsewhere, proved most tenacious. Under the impact of mistakes and failures, it took a long time, at least in one man's mind, to sort out what had really been at stake in the matter.

The outcome in this book is given from the start. The actors in the drama did not know what history's verdict of their behavior would be. They were never fully aware of the contradictions on which their actions were impaled, even though they boasted of an ideology which claims to give its adherents a maximum of self-consciousness, and therefore of control over events. Here were a group of men and women who believed they had found the assumptions and allegiances that would enable them to "make history." Yet because they could never bring themselves to re-examine these assumptions and allegiances, they became history's victims. Their familiar self-criticism, presumably the rule by which they lived, proved superficial. Trying to fuse the experience of a rich past and confront the urgent issues of their time, they built what was by far the most powerful and pervasive radical movement in American life and then helped to shatter it. The record shows, beyond dispute, that it was shattered as much by their own behavior, their inability to choose between the antagonistic strands in their own movement and their impotence to change their course, as it was by the formidable power of their opposition. This book, in its structure and underlying theme, conforms to the model of tragedy. The tragic mode was chosen because it seemed most honest and appropriate.

My intention was to follow the analytic method, working backward from what was known in order to establish why things happened, not massing great detail except as it contributes something essential to understanding. This book is therefore not a history. Given the time available, with the material accessible, and my own temperament and stance, a true work of history seemed impossible. Perhaps the high standard set by Theodore Draper's two volumes on the origins of American Communism had something to do with this decision. What I have tried to do forms a sequel to the two volumes on the thirties which he has been preparing. The works of many others have been helpful. Irving Howe and Lewis Coser, as well as David A. Shannon, Daniel Bell, Daniel Aaron, and Earl Latham have contributed historical essays which deal with the period covered here, the forties and fifties. At times too polemical, even exasperated with the subject, some of them reveal the absence of intimate experience. Although I have appreciated the force of the argument in these essays, my effort has been to submerge the intimate experience in as reasonably a detached and scholarly fashion as possible.

For me, this analysis of the rise and decline of American Communism required a long interval of reflection and the perspective of political distance, even a certain loneliness. There is a deliberate coolness here, which is only in part in keeping with my own participation in these events and my character. Although there is little that is autobiographical in this book, except between the lines and in some footnotes, and only occasionally do I draw on personal recollection, subjective judgments will surely be found, for whatever they may be worth. This book is, after all, the effort of one who was not a stranger to the drama nor a bystander. Any real autobiography, if it can be done at all, must be left for another occasion. A shattering turn in our lives, as will be explained shortly, now makes such autobiography seem very important.

One major consideration in determining the treatment of the subject matter chosen here was that many prominent individuals who were active in the American Communist Party and its sphere of influence are not at all eager to discuss it. Most of them were not avowed Party members, and some have achieved eminence and a degree of security in other fields. They do not appreciate identification, even for archeological purposes. They could not be expected to contribute to this analysis. Others, who were Communists and never concealed the fact, have had to remake their lives; in some cases a certain allegiance lingers on. Many have faced all kinds of public and private persecution; most of them have been treated with hostility by one-time associates. Without denying their past, these former Communists feel no need to recall it. Thus, it was difficult to find even the minimal cooperation needed for this study.

Moreover, a surprising number of individuals, intimately involved in all these events, suffer from a certain amnesia which may be characteristically American. (So much has been forgotten by the whole nation, perhaps because forgetting is easier when dealing with neuralgic matters, that the forgetfulness of a few is not surprising.) There has been, in addition, a real problem of adequate documentation. Radical movements, intending to "make history," are extraordinarily indifferent about records of themselves. They are rarely self-contemplative. They seem to assume that history will be self-explanatory with ultimate victory. There may be dossiers, files, and documents in quarters which are professionally hostile to Communism, but none were available to me.

Other writers, among them many of the key actors in this drama, have tried to recapture and understand the past, some through analysis, others by autobiography. Books have been written by William Z. Foster, Elizabeth Gurley Flynn, Benjamin Davis, Jr., Steve Nelson, William L. Patterson, and John Williamson: they all threw some light on their times. Some of these books have deeply authentic passages, but their apologetic character detracts from their value. It was always interesting to me, as I came to know Earl Browder during the preparation of this book, that he, too, began an autobiography in the early fifties. Perhaps the chief reason it was never finished is that he recognized how useless apologetics would be and how difficult it would be to establish the truth. Men of the same generation — Herbert Benjamin and Samuel Darcy — are said to be writing autobiographies. A huge opus, revealing and stimulating, remains in the files of Alexander Bittelman and awaits a sympathetic publisher.

Aspects of the Communist story have been told by still another group of men who were members of or close to the Party but not in its inner sanctum. For example, Len DeCaux has written an honest, if hardly very analytical, account of the great days when America's workingmen in the mass production industries built their unions. Harold Cruse has given us tormented but serious insights into the contradictions facing American Communism in its dealings with the world of black Americans. And there are now younger scholars, too young to have lived through some of the experiences related here, but increasingly attracted by them. I have tried to help these younger men and women, many of whom have asked for assistance. Perhaps others will be helped by what they find in these pages.

There may be some revelations here, matters about the politics of the forties and fifties not generally known. But there are not the recantations so often encountered among former Communists. The lament about lost opportunities and impossible choices will be found here without the suggestion that it was all a wasted effort. Few were wise before the event and there was enough fault to go round in all the contending positions, and for everyone involved in political combat. Among the opponents of American Communism, there were a few who proceeded from serious principle; they were wiser at the time and must be respected. Yet was there not also a basic fault in the visceral anti-Communism which refused to see a movement of genuine Americans engaged in trying to square a circle? Has not the public record of a great many of Communism's opponents on the critical issues of the sixties — the enormity of the outrage and disaster of Vietnam, for example — proved that having been right at certain times is not assurance against ghastly mistakes at others? The problem in American life with regard to the subject matter of this book was always one of *understanding* a political movement that was in the impasse resulting from its doctrinal ambiguities and its successes as well as its failures. I do not invoke the French proverb: *Tout comprendre, c'est tout pardonner.* Many matters described here were unpardonable. The problem remains one of making them understandable.

The question remains: To what purpose? Why address oneself to a subject which evokes such a fugitive moment in the nation's experience, distant in time and experienced by only a handful? A case can be made that I should have stayed away from my subject entirely and let others, less committed, probe its mysteries. Many friends urged this course. Yet there was a justification which, when frankly faced, reveals how tenacious are the earlier hopes of men like myself, even after more than a decade of political detachment. Although I wrote this analysis so that many tens of thousands like myself might have a better clue to our past, and wrote it also for as large an audience as may be interested in "dead-sea scrolls" or fossil drawings in obscure caves, I also wrote it for a new generation.

All movements try to overcome the inherent mortality of their participants. Radical movements are no exception. In fact, radicals may be driven more than others by the hope that somehow the movement which engages them will achieve something more lasting than any individual can: this is the rationale for the community they try to build. In addition to all the obvious motives for writing this book there was the hope that a succeeding generation, the generation of our son, Bob, might benefit from a sober reassessment of the American radical past as seen by someone who believed in socialism, never concealed this belief, tried to make a go of achieving it, and was defeated by the inability to distinguish between what *could* be accomplished and what *could not* be.

The new left which arose in the sixties thinks of itself as a break from the past, especially from the old left. It believes it is rediscovering America as no previous generation has. This phenomenon has been extraordinary — these millions of sensitive, courageous young people with so much to their credit within a few years. They have confronted the nation with its most profound failings: the stupidity and inhumanity of its priorities of placing private accumulation of wealth ahead of public needs; the intolerable burden of racism; the cost of trying to hold back the revolutionary transformation of underdeveloped peoples by frightful military power, an attempt which has boomeranged upon America and revealed its utter impotence. The new left has made radical ideas legitimate in the land, something which older radicals never quite succeeded in doing and because the democratic roots and processes are alive and operative, this legitimated radicalism has already diffused itself throughout the society and transformed the way of life of millions of Americans. No other country has made so severe a self-criticism nor has attempted so ambitious a self-correction as America is attempting now. The issue vibrates and pulsates throughout the body politic: at the height of the greatest fever the processes of healing are at work.

Yet this same new left hardly recognizes where the "revolution" is. All the historic weaknesses are present in a fashion heartbreaking to anyone with a historical experience and perspective: the belief that change must be instant, the impatience with concrete achievements, the attempt to demand more of any situation than it can give, the hallucinatory fascination with revolutions among less-developed peoples as though these can be imitated in more complex societies or hold any universal lessons, and thus the suicidal alienation from one's own society. This new left, when confronted by setback or the slowness in the diffusion of its message among the less swiftly moving mass, looks for the explanation within itself, as though the cure lies in self-purification and as though by some heroic voluntarism, some great act of will, the process of historical change can be forced forward. The result is a terrible factionalism, a self-destroying narcissim: have we not seen all this before? The new left's impatience with humble and ordinary people, engaged in the everyday work which sustains their lives and which they try to make satisfying and creative in contradictory circumstances becomes a form of elitism, because the new left believes that everything can be accomplished by self, by a heightened sensibility, and by a defiance of history. This elitism is all the more alienating because it speaks in the name of those humble and ordinary people.

All these matters were part of the dialogue over the past decade with our Bob — our son, Dr. Robert Saul Starobin — who went from his Cornell undergraduate work to become a leader in Berkeley's "free speech movement," and then, with his pioneer graduate study of *Industrial Slavery in the Old South* became an able professor, first at the University of Wisconsin, and then at the State University of New York at Binghamton. Author of several books at the age of thirty-one, a rare teacher (his students and colleagues tell us), Bob struggled to learn from the experience of the decade, contrasting his own convictions with those of his parents and their friends; he was more and more driven to explore for himself, in a book which he had outlined, his own origins as an activist of the new left out of a particular heritage of the old left. At times he gave every evidence of achieving a synthesis. Yet he was also humiliated by the collapse of his own illusions, for example, about the Black Panthers, as well as contradictions of a more personal character arising out of a broken marriage. Our Bob took his own life on a bitter mid-February morning as these very pages were being revised by me, hundreds of miles away and unable to help him.

This failure, arising out of the impulse to "do it," that terrible slogan which one of his Berkeley colleagues has now made into a career as well as a species of anarcho-syndicalist ideology, would be only our private grief were it not as well the political failure of a much larger number of his friends and associates. Once again, this most corrupting variety of impotence that tries to hurdle the barriers it has itself erected by violent voluntarism — which has plagued the American left for generations — demonstrates its folly: to us a tragedy without measure — unbearable, unforgivable, irreversible. What is the meaning of this collapse, this denial of those personal-political obligations, those ties of regard for parents, children, friends, students, colleagues which alone can be the foundation of a genuine radicalism — in the name of selfish, demonstrative, "doing-it" wrapped in Guevarist, Fanonist, or Maoist robes? It is the repudiation of history. It is the terrible price of historical discontinuity.

Would it have helped Bob if this book had been written, as it should have been, a dozen years earlier? Could some saving, healing transfer have been made from the tragic remnant of the past? Could a more cohesive, really loving, less quixotic revolutionary community in the new left have saved the life of one of its most representative members? I stagger with these questions now that so much is changing in the world, now that so much that Bob and so many others have fought for is being achieved, now that the inevitable self-criticism and self-examination is being made by his white and black friends alike, all so predictable to men and women of my own generation who went through it all before.

This is, therefore, also a book of culpability, of acute mourning. It is once again the recognition of the ultimate illusion that something could be passed on, and once again the admission of defeat. Having been unable to say in time what was to be said, and having been unable to communicate with our own son and generation, this book is a testimony to the defeat of both generations — granted that for Bob's friends, his colleagues, his students, and his millions of contemporaries unknown to us the issue remains undecided. I am not comforted by those who insist it was his *own* responsibility, just as I am not moved by any facile optimism that the issue for the new left will be favorably decided.

This volume is my own responsibility in conception and execution. But many individuals and organizations must be thanked for their help in making it possible. Thanks must go first to my two advisers at Columbia University — Dr. Alexander Dallin and Dr. Wallace S. Sayre. Important encouragement came in the later stages from Dr. Harvey O. Mansfield. Dr. Marshall D. Shulman was especially demanding in his critique, which I took as a much appreciated measure of his confidence. Also at Columbia University, the Research Institute on Communist Affairs was generous with an eighteen-month fellowship; its chairman, Dr. Zbigniew Brzezinski, showed great understanding, all the more remarkable since this book is surely a maverick contribution to the research fostered under his leadership. Thanks must also go to the Hoover Institution, at Stanford, California, for its hospitality in the summer of 1966. I am in particular debt to Phillip J. Jaffe, who not only made useful criticisms but also made his extraordinary library available to me as he has to so many scholars on so many subjects.

Many friends, both in and out of the academic world, gave me much time and frank opinions. Among these are Theodore Draper, Robert C. Tucker, James A. Wechsler, Milton Meltzer, Victor H. Bernstein, John Gates, and Max Gordon. Old and new friends gave of their ideas and recollections. Mention of them in no way suggests their agreement with my conclusions. Among these are Earl Browder, Alexander Bittelman, Samuel Darcy, Rexford Guy Tugwell, Judge Robert W. Kenny, Michael Straight, Hugh Bryson, Doxey A. Wilkerson, George Charney, Joseph Clark, John Caughlan, Carl Dorfman, Eleanor Abewitz, Rob F. Hall, Roy Hudson, Sidney Roger, Samuel Coleman, Harold Simon, Louise Lambert, Dorothy Healy, George Watt, and Saul Wellman. The temptation must be resisted to mention those who declined to be helpful for reasons best known to themselves. That, too, is part of what must be understood, and perhaps forgiven.

The librarians of Columbia University, especially the guardians of its Oral History Project, and of Syracuse and Berkeley were most gracious; a special salute must go to the Bancroft Library at the University of California which was wise enough to come into possession of the excellent collection of Oleta O'Connor Yates, an old colleague, to whom I owe special homage. Warm gratitude, also, to Mrs. Edith Howard, of Toronto, and to Mrs. Ruth Griffin, secretary of the Department of Political Science, Glendon College, York University, Toronto, for their tolerance and persistence in the preparation of this manuscript. Embraces to my brother, Herman, for his immense comfort, and to my wife, Norma, for her endurance under these unendurable circumstances.

# PART I    THE BACKGROUND

# I  THE HARD LOOK BACK-
# WARD OVER THE DIFFICULT
# DECADE

Eugene Dennis, the general secretary of the Communist Party of the United States of America (C.P.U.S.A.), opened his report to an "enlarged meeting" of his organization's most authoritative body on April 28, 1956, with the words: "Five years have gone by since the last full meeting of our National Committee." To the assembled men and women, who comprised the major part of the leading corps that had directed American Communism over the past quarter century — with some important absentees — this was an extraordinary and fateful occasion. They were surveying the entire decade since their Party's reconstitution in July 1945 after it had experimented with another type of movement, the Communist Political Association. In a sense they were obliged to look much further back, over the entire decade of the thirties when they had built the strongest, most influential radical movement in American history. Now they were examining its disaster. Inevitably, the debate of 1956 anticipated the grim struggle of the next two years which would tear this political organism apart, turn comrades against each other, and witness the flight from Communism of most of the remaining twenty thousand members and the withdrawal from political life of the most tested, most trusted cadres. American Communism would again become the sect it had been in the twenties and which it has remained since 1958.

Dennis entitled his report *The Communists Take a New Look*.[1] It was a look backward, and two dates came into focus with special sharpness. Five years before, almost to the month, the Party's main leaders had dispersed; some to serve jail sentences under the Smith Act,[2] others in an ambitious attempt to guide their movement from an "underground". The latter group had been joined by some of the second echelon leaders, as well as by several thousand other cadres. (No such effort at a dual — and in fact triple — leadership had been attempted since the formative days of this movement thirty-five years before.)[3] By April 1956, many of those who had been imprisoned were free on parole, and many of those who had gone underground had returned from five years of hiding. Had it all really been necessary?

This was a tense weekend. Many ghosts were present, uninvited. Political skeletons from a tormented history rattled in the hall. Sharp words were to be exchanged, disclosing a state of factionalism in the very highest ranks such as had been taboo for this particular radical movement since the bitter experience of the twenties. This was an "enlarged" National Committee meeting and many were present who had not been elected at the Party's previous convention, in December 1950. But noticeably, those cadres whom the Communists considered most precious, the "influentials" operating in the trade union movement and in a galaxy of left wing organizations under the Party's aegis, were absent. It was essentially a meeting of "functionaries," that is, "full-time" cadres responsible for the Party's mechanism and political policy.

Eugene Dennis considered his report an account of a ten-year stewardship of the Communist Party's top post. Dennis had been groomed for this post by two different leaders: in July 1946 the Party's chairman, William Z. Foster, had nominated Dennis as general secretary, citing his decisive role in steering the movement through the crisis in which the Party had repudiated its former general secretary, Earl Browder; the latter had kept Dennis close to him over the decade prior to 1944. (Browder's name was not mentioned at the gathering, although he was surely the chief ghost present.) Although the main thrust of the Dennis re-examination was to admit collective responsibility for the disaster facing the Party, the chief target was the most eminent leader, William Z. Foster. He stood alone that April, voting against the Dennis report. Thus, within one decade, American Communism saw its two foremost leaders repudiated.

Six of the original Smith Act defendants, all important veterans of this movement, were absent. Henry Winston, the organizational director and one of the most influential Negroes in the Party, was in hiding, as was Gilbert Green, secretary for Illinois, who previously had led the Party's organization in New York State and had directed the Communist youth movement in the thirties. Both Winston and Green had had the deepest influence on the younger cadres who had come to Communism. A veteran of the heyday of the Young Communist International, Green's preeminence had been rewarded in 1935 by his election to the executive of the Communist International, the highest body in the international movement. (He was the youngest of the American contingent on that body.) Both men were key figures in the underground. In April 1956 they had not yet emerged from it.[4] Also absent were two men who, by their decision to evade the Smith Act prison term, were intended to play the core role with Green and Winston among the "unavailables." These were Gus Hall, who had come from the Ohio organization to be Dennis' deputy in the early fifties, and Robert Thompson, who had succeeded Green at the head of the New York State party. Thompson had been a member of the triumvirate, with Dennis and Williamson, which supervised the ouster of Browder; he had been the man closest to Foster during the late forties. Both Hall and Thompson had gone into hiding and had been caught. They were now serving not only their original terms, but additional years for contempt.[5]

Since the underground forms such an important backdrop to the April 1956 conclave, something must be said of it here, although a much fuller treatment of its make-up and its implications will be required.[6] Three levels of leadership had functioned simultaneously during the first half of the fifties — an unusual and complex situation which made this reunion of men and women from all three levels particularly tense. During the period of the underground, formal leadership still rested with the National Board that had tested the Smith Act, the men who had led the Party since the war. Their ability to give this leadership was, however, hampered. Dennis tried, through letters to his wife, and by instructions to her during their prison meetings, to keep a hand on the helm.[7] The second, and most important, level of leadership consisted of the unavailables. This level had been assembled for the express purpose of giving emergency leadership in the expectation that the country faced world war and military dictatorship. The four leaders who had evaded jail, plus several thousand cadres carefully selected from across the country and from various functional levels, made up this level. The American Communists did not establish two parallel parties — one public, another secret. They established parallel structures within the existing party. The third level of leaders functioned above ground, and was composed of cadres who either had not been indicted or were at liberty on bail and who functioned openly under the Party's chairman, William Z. Foster (his case on the Smith Act charge had been severed because of his heart condition). The underground was an experiment in trying to deal with all high policy matters as well as membership and financial details by a cumbersome remote control. There was an inevitable clash between the functions of the underground leadership and the third level leadership.

The attempt to mesh all activities would have caused frictions in any case. But these were intensified because the cadres in the underground, almost as soon as they removed themselves from daily contact with the Party as they had known it, began to question matters of basic policy. They began to reflect on the past. These reflections inevitably cast doubt on the competence of Foster as ideologue and leader, since it was under him that the entire previous system of Party thought and practice, under Browder until 1945, had been overthrown.

Another aspect of the drama lay in the fact that the re-examination at the National Committee meeting made public in April 1956 had begun much earlier. Indeed it had begun before the 20th Congress of the Soviet Communist Party in February 1956 where the allusions to Stalin's "cult of the personality" were given substance and elaboration in the sensational report of Nikita Khrushchev and the remarks of Anastas Mikoyan. The American Communists had begun independently to ask where they and the international movement were going. But because of a peculiar set of circumstances as well as their own difficulty in cutting through to the heart of their problems, an independent re-examination — though they badly needed it and were later to lament their dependence on Moscow — was exactly what did not take place. The men who entered prison in July 1951 were at liberty by March 1955 but still on parole; the terms of parole forbade them to engage in political activity until January 1956. They hesitated to jeopardize their freedom. In 1955, intensive conversations took place among them and with leading figures by then returning from "unavailability" and from abroad. The dimensions of the Party's crisis were growing and were openly discussed among leading cadres, if not among rank and file members. But no public intimation of the crisis came until an anniversary meeting of the *Daily Worker* in January 1956.

At this meeting, both Dennis and the Party paper's editor, John Gates (who had been in Atlanta Penitentiary with Dennis), spoke in "re-examinationist" terms. Gates revealed in his book, two years later, that throughout 1954 and early 1955 he and Dennis were able to exchange opinions about the need for a complete overhaul of their Party's course. They tried at times to share these opinions with Thompson, who was sent to Atlanta after his capture.[8] The term "new look" was first used by Dennis at this January anniversary meeting. Gates deliberately emphasized the Party's commitment to a "constitutional path to socialism." He surprised his audience by declaring that American Communists would support any government in Washington that abandoned McCarthyism, seriously enforced civil rights, and based itself on the principles of coexistence. Gates omitted any reference to the Soviet Union and the mysterious events there since Stalin's death — a fact that his more perceptive colleagues noted and for which some criticized him.[9]

Both Gates and Dennis, and through them many others, were groping for a new course. To be sure, it was the publication on June 13, 1956, of Khrushchev's secret speech which opened the floodgates of the re-examination for the Party's membership and its larger audience. But a summary of the speech arrived at the April 1956 meeting and its implications immediately confirmed for the top leaders the depth of the Soviet crisis, and therefore of the international Communist crisis. This served to underline the sweeping conclusions and self-criticism which Dennis had already prepared.[10] Paradoxically, the fact that the Soviet re-examination overtook, in its public form, the re-examination which the American Communists had begun on their own undermined whatever might have been fertile in their autonomous effort. Once again, it proved impossible to establish the Party's independence of Moscow although the convention of February 1957 would try to do so. Because the American Communists, in probing what had happened to them, were forced inevitably to do so on the terrain of an international development which had its own dynamic and pace, the lineup within the Party leadership soon changed — in tune with what was happening abroad. This doomed the entire process of re-examination.

A more general background, less immediately connected with the Communist Party's inner life and fortunes, is required at this point. Contrary to expectations when the leaders went to jail, world events had not moved toward a cataclysmic clash between the United States and the Soviet Union. The Korean War, which had appeared to be the opening round of such a clash, had ended in truce. This truce was followed within a year by the Geneva conference terminating the French phase of the Indo-China war. A "thaw" in the Cold War was everywhere in evidence. Khrushchev and Bulganin were travelling to India and Britain, a new style for Soviet leaders. Communist China entered the international arena by participating in the Bandung parley, pledging support for the "panch shila," the five principles of coexistence, Asian-style. A treaty neutralizing Austria was at last signed. And in the summer of 1955, Soviet foreign minister Vyacheslav Molotov spoke at the United Nation's tenth anniversary meeting in terms that made for an unquestionable *détente*. Even Marshal Tito's Yugoslavia was included in the thaw; Khrushchev had made a pilgrimage of apology to Belgrade. In the light of how readily Communists everywhere had accepted Stalin's charge that Tito had been a "spy," a heretic within the Communist fold (in the name of fighting "Titoism" many trials had wracked the Eastern European countries and introduced a Communist version of McCarthyism throughout the international movement) the question arose that if the campaign against Tito had been wrong, then *what* about Stalin had been right? It was the most difficult question a serious Communist could contemplate.

But were all these great changes in world affairs simply tactical, and perhaps deceptive in character? Had the turn to coexistence been the result simply of the victories of the "peace forces"? This explanation was not satisfactory. It made the receding danger of world war the responsibility of only one side. On the other hand, once a Communist began to allow that there might be forces at work within American capitalism favorable to peace, and that representatives of the most decisive capitalist circles were also favoring a truce with the Soviet Union, a Pandora's box was opened. The prospect of a truce between the systems did not preclude the possibility that the truce might only be temporary. But suppose it were durable? The possibility of a durable truce might alter the prescriptions for social change which were at the heart of Communist doctrine. If American capitalism could envisage peace with a rival social system, then what became of the thesis that war was inherent in the system? This thesis had been converted over the previous ten years of American Communist thinking into a serious anticipation of early war, an anticipation on which the whole future of the movement had been planned. If American-Soviet war was not in the cards, then the forces making for the system's inevitable collapse had to be sought in other realms. Was it by inevitable economic crisis? Or might there not be factors of reform, of peaceful evolution at work in the direction of qualitative changes? Here, too, fundamental aspects of doctrine were at stake.[11]

Domestic changes had taken place simultaneously with events abroad. In November 1952 the Communists had judged General Dwight Eisenhower's accession to the White House to be proof that the "decisive and most reactionary circles of American monopoly-capitalism" had at last put their man-on-horseback in a position to impose militarization and fascism. Yet it remained to be explained why under the first Republican president since Herbert Hoover one war — in Korea — had been ended and another — in Indochina — had been refused, and why the ambitious Republican senator from Wisconsin, Joseph McCarthy, had been cut down by the secretary of war under Eisenhower. The Supreme Court, headed by a California Republican, Earl Warren (whom the left had so bitterly opposed ten years before), now pronounced decisions so favorable to social reform that they could not be explained simply as the result of popular pressure, surely not pressure brought by the left. The McCarran Act would have forced the Communist Party to register as a "foreign agent" and would have set up "star chamber" proceedings against any group accused of being "Communist-controlled"; the Act was now returned to the lower courts. The Fifth Amendment, whose use by witnesses caused so much controversy, had been upheld. The State Department's passport limitations on Party members and non-Communists of the left — causing so much anguish — were now being whittled down as the judiciary maintained its countervailing role. And the Court was pondering the California Smith Act verdict, which affected important C.P. leaders.[12]

Even more fateful for the nation's future was the Court's ruling in 1954 rejecting separate but equal educational facilities for Negro children and undercutting the premises of second-class citizenship for blacks in the key realm of education. The N.A.A.C.P., a middle class organization, had revived to fight and win that case. This went contrary to the Communist conception that only black workers, organized as a separate force, could spearhead the Negro people's movement. A new voice from a hitherto muted quarter, the black churches, was now defying white supremacy in the heart of the former Confederacy. Martin Luther King's nonviolent leadership of the Montgomery bus strike not only captured the imagination of blacks and gained important white support, but also called into question what had been since 1946 the chief trend in the Communist analysis of the "Negro question." In re-establishing the "Negro question" as a "national question" the Communists had been ambiguous about integration as the way forward. Within their own ranks the concept of "black power" had taken hold. In the years of the Party's greatest crisis, these ideas caused a schism between blacks and whites who had been proud of building an integrated movement which championed the Negro cause as a nationwide, all-class responsibility. Now the civil rights movement was taking on unexpected importance as a movement of unity, a movement for drastic change and sanctioned by the government.

Moreover, the cyclical economic crisis which the Communists had envisaged as an inevitable development that would accelerate the turn to fascism and war had not materialized, despite the recession of 1954. Was this attributable solely to the boom accompanying the Korean hostilities? Or were more fundamental stabilizing factors at work within capitalism? How did these factors bear on Foster's philippics against the fallacies of Keynesism, the illusion that capitalism could be made to work?[13] In the late forties, Gilbert Green had tried to express his embarrassment with the political sterility implicit in the Party's grim prediction of imminent economic disaster combined with the hesitation to put forward positive programs against this disaster.[14] Green had proposed the slogan "a welfare, not a warfare state." But this formula had been withdrawn. It implied that a welfare state could be made to function, an impermissible illusion which contradicted the doctrine that only fundamental inroads on monopoly capitalism merited Communist support. By 1956 the possibility that Green had been right in his initial impulse and wrong in his subsequent retreat confronted the Party's leadership.

In 1956, the two main wings of American labor reunited. Labor unity, so long a leftwing objective, had now become a fact. Yet the left had not played much of a role in bringing this unity about. The left within the C.I.O., as late as 1949 a united bloc of left wing trade unions and the product of fifteen years of the most difficult, self-sacrificing effort, had fallen into disarray in the early fifties. Some local left wing unions, notably the turbulent New York District 65 (long a Communist stronghold), had made a separate peace with the C.I.O. leadership. Sections of the Farm Equipment and Electrical Workers in the Midwest had rejoined the "main-

stream" from which they had walked out in 1949. The Fur and
Leather Workers Union, the only union headed by avowed Communists, had merged with a major A.F.L. union, and at a minimum political price. On the other hand, the major left-led unions,
the United Electrical Workers (U.E.) and International Longshoremen and Warehousemen's Union (I.L.W.U.), were contemptuous of their former comrades, scorning the idea of re-asso-
ciation of any kind with the mainstream labor movement; the
same was true of the even more beleaguered Mine, Mill and Smelter Workers. Part of the left wing flirted with the older ideas of
"dual unionism" and tried to link up with trade unionism's loner,
John L. Lewis, who held his United Mineworkers aloof. In the
halcyon days Lewis had not hesitated to use every left winger, but
now he had little incentive to cater to their idea of a third labor
federation. The Party's writ on strategic matters no longer carried
weight with those who had been its most cherished and trusted
influentials.[15] And the Party's own strategic view was blurred.
Was the A.F.L.-C.I.O. nothing more than a "labor front" for Wall
Street? Were there possibilities that within the apparent unanimity of such diverse figures as George Meany and Walter Reuther
there might be useful leverage for progressive advance? It was
striking that Reuther's closest associate, Emil Mazey, was consistently calling for a new approach to ending the Cold War, and
reminding organized labor of its international responsibilities.[16]

In the political field, the Communists were faced with almost
complete isolation from the real political forces in the country.
The most important repercussion of the 1948 adventure of the
Progressive Party persisted in that the myriad ties between progressives and the main arteries of Democratic Party politics
remained ruptured. The bitterness of these ruptures, the vindic-
tiveness of the Americans for Democratic Action, who were in the
saddle after 1948, inhibited political activity by the left. The Progressive Party became no more than a reunion of defeated fellow
travellers. In the 1952 campaign, the presidential ticket of Vincent Hallinan and Charlotta Bass had gotten a vote no greater
than the Communist vote itself two decade before. In the 1954
gubernatorial campaign in New York, the American Labor Party
(the A.L.P.) failed to receive the necessary fifty thousand votes
to qualify as a party: to stay in politics it would henceforth need
to collect signatures locally. Four years earlier, the A.L.P. had
delivered half a million votes to Wallace.[17]

The crisis on the left was dramatized by two different tendencies among those who had previously respected the Communist Party's advice. For example, John McManus, an editor of *The National Guardian* at that time, and Clifford McAvoy, another important figure in the non-Party left, were increasingly involved in the will-o-the-wisp of "independent" election campaigns in association with the Trotskyists. To the Communist Party this activity was anathema on many grounds. On the other hand, Vito Marcantonio, having lost his congressional seat against the overwhelming strength of a combined opposition, found himself searching for some way to return to politics. Although he was head of the A.L.P. he realized that this party was an obstacle to his ambitions. "Marc," who owed much to the Communists and who had been helpful to them without ever sharing their ideology, now assumed an increasingly anti-Communist attitude. Recriminations, characteristic of movements in decline, were destroying relations between people who had been friends.[18]

At the same time, the Communists had to ask themselves why a stauncher morale prevailed in other wings of the left and the capacity for mutual aid seemed stronger. In 1955, a centennial meeting took place in Chicago at which prominent labor leaders who had never concealed their continuing Socialist faith joined Norman Thomas in honoring Eugene Victor Debs. Would the labor leaders of Communist persuasion, now holding their private forts in virtual isolation, have participated in an analogous gesture? All the underlying problems of ethos and morale weighed heavily on the left in those years. Among the staunchest opponents of both the Smith Act and the McCarran Act were Norman Thomas, the Socialist, Rev. A. J. Muste, the independent radical pacifist, and Eleanor Roosevelt — each of them long maligned by the Communists and now so helpful. Whereas in the grim days of ostracism and loneliness, the families of the Smith Act victims had great difficulty in marshalling help from among fellow Communists, these non-Comunists proved most compassionate. They took part in committees of financial support and indicated their sympathy. Weighty implications of these contrasts tormented the Party's leaders and ranks.

## Personification of Failure

Eugene Dennis was the most authoritative Party spokesman, yet the least known and the most enigmatic. At first glance, he gave the impression of an ideal American Communist leader. Of Irish-Norwegian extraction, born in Seattle, Dennis was tall, of handsome build, with a high forehead mantled by a shock of black hair greying at the temples. The details of his upbringing were shrouded.[19] Nobody knew who his parents were, nor his whereabouts when other Communist leaders were establishing public records. This shroud gave him a particular aura for he had obviously been abroad in the service of the International. A Party member by 1926, Dennis had been arrested at the March 6, 1930, unemployment demonstration in Los Angeles (part of the nationwide action that had placed Communists at the head of the movement of the jobless). Thereafter he disappeared. The flyleaf of a later book says that "he was closely associated with the national liberation movements in South Africa, the Philippine Islands and China."[20] There is indirect evidence of his presence in Moscow as late as 1937.[21] He reappeared briefly as the Party's organizer in Wisconsin; shortly after he became one of Browder's closest aides at headquarters, then a Party lobbyist in Washington, and soon after in charge of much of the "political action" work.

Dennis was American Communism's "organization man." He does not seem to have had any intellectual training or organizational experience outside the Party, and his activities had been confined to its uppermost echelons. Although chief Party spokesman, his forte was the inner conclave, the interminable meeting, the confidential lobbying, the "correct formulation." He was not, in Party parlance, a "mass figure." Few members had met him on a picket line or at a branch meeting. Dennis had enormous difficulty with public appearances, even in front of Party audiences. His voice was strangely weak, and he continually interrupted himself by throat clearing; this habit was often concealed by a Stalinesque deliberateness, a weighing of words and silences that gave an impression of greater wisdom than his opinions conveyed. He had no taste for the rough-and-tumble of either public or private debate.

Thus he came to personify political indecisiveness.[22] All his political instincts ran in the direction of making his party a genuine, native political force; all his own characteristics negated these instincts. The central reasons for this contradiction lay in his tropism for Moscow, his Comintern training. Even in face-to-face conversation he seemed to believe that each "rounded-out" phrase was being weighed in some distant balance. His indecisiveness and his Comintern mentality guaranteed that the attempt by Dennis in 1956 to rejuvenate the Party on a new basis — which was the main thrust of the April 28 report — would also cause him to retreat before its own implications, to suffer the fate of the "centrist." Those colleagues who in April saw him as the exponent of basic change were appalled when — by the time of the Hungarian events half a year later — he had swung behind Foster's orthodoxy in response to clear signals from abroad. Foster's contempt for Dennis, however, for having opened the floodgates to "revisionism" only increased when they were subsequently thrown together in the receivership of political and organizational bankruptcy.[23] The April 1956 report became the basis of the Party's Draft Resolution in September which opened an acrimonious debate and resulted in unprecedented decisions at the 16th National Convention the following February. In the ensuing year, however, the Party fell apart. Dennis was one of those who defied the "revisionist" convention.

Although the precise formulations of the Dennis report seem rather pallid in retrospect, the men and women assembled that April felt that something radically new was being said. The explanation of what had happened to the Communist Party, Dennis began, could not be found in the "adverse, objective factors," that is, in the "sharp, costly and continuing political attacks and repressions" which the movement had endured. To be sure, the heavy repression had to be taken into account. But the real problem lay within the Party itself, in its "basic, deep-seated and long-standing weaknesses and shortcomings" which had "come home to roost with a vengeance." Among other major faults, the American Communists had been "afflicted with a deeply-ingrained left-sectarian approach to united front relationships and tactics," becoming a "prisoner" of the left wing centers of their own fabrication. Even more crucial was "the strong and persistent tendency in the Party to apply the experiences of other Communist parties and the science of Marxism in a mechanical and doctrinaire fashion — all of which inadvertently gave aid and comfort to the slander that [Communists] were 'foreign agents'."[24]

The Party's failures were not due "merely or chiefly to the general shortcomings . . . inherited from the past, or even to the mistakes that [the Party itself] made in previous periods." This was a delicate rebuttal to the proposition, widely held since 1945, that

"Browderism" had been the ultimate source of all the Party's troubles. Dennis noted drily that the crisis of the previous ten years was rooted in "decades-old weaknesses."

The Party's general secretary then took up the long catalogue "of erroneous judgments and tactical mistakes of this specific period in the context of the given time, place and concrete circumstance."

"While we repeatedly asserted that World War III is not inevitable," Dennis declared, "the fact is that we frequently tended to evaluate certain war preparations and threats of Washington as if a new world war was not only possible — but almost imminent." Confusing intentions with reality, the Party had been "unable to distinguish between the imperialist aims of U.S. monopoly capital and its inability to realize its predatory objectives."[25]

"The fact is that even as late as the middle of 1955 our Party still found the thinking of many of its ranks based on an analysis which saw the only major difference in the camp of U.S. monopoly capital as that between 'those who want war now, and those who want war when ready'."

This was a direct reference to William Z. Foster's acute embarrassment with the thaw in the Cold War. When the war he had expected had not materialized, Foster gave a purely subjective explanation — unreadiness of the capitalists.[26] But if, as Dennis insisted, peaceful coexistence was possible "under existing conditions," namely the continued rule of American capitalism, then the Party's postwar slogan of "pulling the teeth of U.S. imperialism" had been unsound.

The same doubts were expressed about the judgment of the "fascist danger" which had served as the rationale for evasion of prison terms and for the underground. Implicitly that entire strategy was being questioned. "For instance, in our statement on June 4, 1951, while we stressed that World War III and fascism were not inevitable, actually we placed things as being a few minutes before midnight. Certainly the statement of the National Committee that the Vinson decision signified 'a wholly new situation' was open to misinterpretation."[27]

If protective measures were required at that time, "it did not flow from this, nor was it correct, that the Party take such drastic measures as it did in regard to most of its leadership. Certainly it was incorrect to have maintained this system of leadership, without any modification, for such a prolonged period. Equally it was wrong that the Party adopted such arbitrary and undemocratic measures as it did in 1951 in the process of verifying the Party cadre and membership — measures, by the way, that reduced the Party membership by one-third."[28] Referring to the new program issued in 1954 by the underground, Dennis took issue with the thesis that with the easing of international tensions, McCarthyism was bound to become more acute. The opposite had been true. It had been "incorrect to lump the Eisenhower forces and McCarthyism together."

Equally bedeviling was the "repeated over-estimate of the imminence of a new cyclical economic crisis," which, according to Dennis, had misled the Party in 1945, again in 1949, and once more when the new program argued that the recession following the Korean truce would "inevitably give rise to a major economic depression in 1955-56." Such a prognostication had also been combined with the notion that the oncoming crisis would "confront the country with the immediate threat of fascism and war." Here Dennis touched on the influence of foreign Marxists. He questioned the wisdom of the international movement and the Party's reliance on its infallibility. "One of the lessons that has to be learned from these repeated mistakes in the last decade — and I do not speak of previous periods — is the necessity to judge economic and political facts and trends factually and objectively, not to be swayed by other opinions, including those of diverse Marxist economists who have not made a thorough study of economic facts and trends in the United States. . . ." This was as close as Dennis came to questioning Moscow's competence, with all that such questions entailed.[29]

What were some of the practical political consequences of these errors? The most painful reference was to the labor movement, into which the Communists had put many hopes and able cadres. The left wing in labor had not really tried to prevent its ouster from the C.I.O., Dennis decided, nor had it undertaken "to repair the damage of that event." Prior to the expulsions, the left approached the struggle in the labor movement against the Marshall Plan and the Truman Doctrine as if war were virtually around the corner. And the Party compounded this mistake by continuing a "very harmful, untenable and sectarian policy," failing to take into account "the level of understanding of the workers" and making "foreign policy issues the acid test of all united front relationships." Indeed, the left wing had "aggravated the sharp breaks and ruptures" in its relations with the "center forces," that is, with the Sidney Hillman and Philip Murray leadership of the C.I.O., failing to realize that "much of its mass influence derived from its participation in broad left-center coalitions." Even the left-led unions were coalitions, Dennis reminded his audience. The left had no strong base of its own in the labor movement. The Party's operatives, it appeared, had not been simply the victims of conflict with opponents and potential allies. They had precipitated such conflict. They had been insensitive to the strategic requirement of coalition.

As for electoral policy, the particular domain of Dennis himself and his closest co-workers, the record was no better. The admission of failures in electoral strategy evoked the memory of enormous projects carried out at immense cost. Formation of the Progressive Party (P.P.) in 1948 had "widened the cleavage in the C.I.O. and weakened the ties between the Left Wing and the mainstream of the labor movement." Was the Progressive Party venture necessary?[30] Might there not have been a Democratic Party "peace ticket" in 1948, an attempt to project Henry Wallace's ideas and his presence within the Democratic Party. Dennis now admitted that it had been "erroneous and harmful to support the formation of the P.P. *as a third party*" (italics in the original). Then carefully skirting the implication that the decision to form a third party had been a Communist decision, he suggested as much. "Insofar as the position of our Party on the question is concerned, I assume a particular responsibility." Given the verdict of November 2, 1948, which had "clearly revealed that the P.P. had no promising future in the policitical life of the country" why had the left continued to support the Progressive Party after 1948? "Not to recognize this then, and to entertain the illusion that the contrary might be the case, was not only a mistaken political judgment per se, but also made it increasingly difficult for the Left to reorient and to forge a broad democratic people's coalition which it advocated." The attempt to force a basic political realignment when this realignment had proved impossible had "retarded the efforts of the Left to influence the course of the Administration and to effectively influence developments in and

around important sectors of the Democratic Party on key issues."
The long detour from 1944 was coming to an end. The necessity
for American radicals to take part in politics within the two-party
system was now being realized again.

How were these grievous mistakes, these expensive misjudg-
ments which had affected the lives of tens of thousands of people,
to be explained? At one point, Dennis touched gingerly on one
explanation, the failure of the American Communists "to understand the differences between that which is universally valid in
Marxism and that which is peculiarly applicable to one country
or another." If logically extended, this explanation opened the
way to "polycentrism," a concept which at that moment had not
yet gained the currency it would soon have. At bottom Dennis fell
back on the familiar distinction among Communists between
"Left sectarianism" and "Right opportunism" — the Scylla and
Charybdis between whose shoals Communists had to steer in
rough waters. It appeared that "most of the erroneous analyses
and tactical mistakes" the Party had made since 1945 had been
"chiefly of a *Left sectarian character*" (italics in the original).
Yet why had this left sectarianism been possible, in view of the
Party's self-assurance about its course since 1945?

Dennis gave two reasons. It would appear that with "the determination to give no quarter" in the face of mounting opposition,
setbacks and defeats, the Communists "frequently became impatient and forgot that it is the task of the vanguard to lead and
mobilize broad masses; and that the independent activity of the
vanguard and its supporters, no matter how brave and heroic,
can never be a substitute for the concerted activity of the masses
and their decisive organizations." The Party had run far ahead of
the American people. It had substituted its own "voluntarism"
for the objective development of the struggle, and had tried to
force the pace of history. In response to what had become known
as "Browderism," the "Left danger" had become more pronounced, and many had "tended to blunt [the] struggle against
[Browderism] by waging a 'balanced' struggle on 'two fronts', an
'even-handed' struggle against both Right and Left opportunism."
But in reality the Party was always way over to one side of the
road, unable to find its bearings.[31]

Dennis added an underlying reason why the collective intelligence of so many men and women with such tough, practical expe-

rience and armed with the presumed science of Marxism-Leninism had not sufficed to keep the Party on a proper course. This reason, which was the crux of the problem but had been known to only a small part of the cadres and unknown to the members, was that the top leaders had been profoundly divided since 1945. Despite all the stress on "collective work" and genuine "self-criticism" and the painstaking search for unimpeachable proletarian credentials — all of which were to guarantee against the Browder heresy — the facts were "that as the attacks on [the] Party mounted and the unity of the Party itself was at stake, sharp political differences which arose in the leadership were often temporized and left unresolved for long periods, and inner-party democracy and the corrective influence of the collective views of the membership and sympathizers was narrowed."

Thus, the American Communist leaders had been at loggerheads for years. "Democratic centralism" had failed to function. The men who had been staunch supporters of Browder had turned against him, and had tried to run the movement at Foster's behest. They had had bitter differences as to where all this was taking them. Some had known it would lead to ruin. Because they were in terror of being accused of Browderism, however, and were unable to distinguish the needs of their Party in a country so different from those in which Communism held sway, they could not withstand the dynamism of their own mistakes. Nor would they take counsel with their own members and good friends. Their doubts, their divisions, and their difficulties had been concealed from their own constituents. Two rival leaderships had gravitated around two different political lines which seemed to rise from within one movement. No one had been able to break the Gordian knot which all of them had tied. In this peculiar paralysis, men who were otherwise "activist" had been unable to continue their course or to change it. And now it had ground to a halt.

# II  REMEMBRANCE OF

# THINGS PAST:

# THE THIRTIES TO THE WAR

In its stocktaking and search for a path forward out of crisis, the American Communist leadership turned to its past, but there were different attitudes toward this *recherche du temps perdu.* Two different generations were involved. Despite the influx of many hundreds of thousands of members and the emergence of native-born cadres who had sparked the Party's revival in the thirties, the levers of control always remained in the hands of those who had become Communists in the early twenties. These old-timers had never yielded power. In their opinion, no contemporary crisis was as great as the ones they had lived through before; no period of their lives could be considered misspent. No twist or turn in Communism's vicissitudes could shake their conviction that a Leninist party was necessary, and that Marxism-Leninism was a coherent doctrine, indeed a science.[1] Although Eugene Dennis, among the youngest of this stratum, seemed to be questioning some fundamental parts of this conviction, nothing really fundamental was questioned by the older functionaries.

It would not be quite fair to place these long-time Communists in the category of true believers who, having decided that the world was coming to an end on a given day, prepare for it, and then go on believing when their prophecy has failed.[2] For them, the perennial problem was how to apply their science more adeptly. The basic premises had been established by a world movement whose wisdom and unity could not be questioned. Paradoxically, this type of Communist rejected the chief characteristic of science, which is to place its own hypotheses in doubt and either prove them again or discard them.

For the younger cadres, who had for twenty years done the Party's spadework, the crisis of 1956 coincided with the midpoint in their lives. Most of them were about the age of forty. Many had fought in Spain, and the Second World War; they had made the great changes of 1944 and 1945 in good faith and had persevered stubbornly for the next ten years. Few of them had any personal experience with Moscow or the Communist International; they had accepted a great deal on the word of others. At their age, they were neither callous nor cynical in examining what they had done with their lives. They were young enough to contemplate a drastic change, a renovation, in their movement in 1956. It would take another year before their confidence in that prospect collapsed.

Neither group should be confused with the rank and filers who came and went through Communism's revolving door, illustrating Emerson's wisdom about the "perpetual mobility of American institutions." To this category, a political movement was a vehicle, an instrument, to be repaired when it functioned badly or abandoned when it had been wrecked. The Party experience need not be exaggerated nor wholly disavowed.[3] This was a comforting view, and rarely involved deep soul searching. Mild or even strong nostalgia, hardly touched by the agony of examining premises, is still typical of the mood of the former Communist rank and file, which is perhaps one reason why a new generation could learn so little from them. The older functionaries could remain in a sect, working to revive it. It held the "franchise," the Holy Grail. The greater part of Communism's one-time members and sympathizers could not understand the trauma of 1956-58 at the time, and remained indifferent to it. But those who won the ideological and organizational battle of those two years soon realized they could do nothing with their victory: it was Pyrrhic. Perhaps in humility in face of this fact, they had hesitated to raise their voices and make themselves heard in the turbulent, terribly promising, and terribly frightening sixties.

The long look backwards was complicated by difficult questions which touched on the nature of Party organization, the implications of Communist doctrine, and the whole historical trajectory. It was not easy to decide where things had gone wrong and what part of the Party's heritage could be accepted without qualification. By the midpoint of the Second World War, American Communism had reached its zenith in numbers, and its influence far exceeded its own strength.[4] From 7,000 members in 1930, the Communists could point to nearly 100,000 members, which included some 15,000 in the armed forces (many of them former members of the recently-dissolved Young Communist League. Only the Socialist Party (S.P.) prior to World War I, in a totally different political era, had had a larger membership in proportion to population.[5] But the Socialists, proud of 750,000 votes which Norman Thomas had received as presidential candidate in 1932, could claim only a quarter of that vote four years later. The Communists did not measure their success by votes in elections. The Socialist cadres were dispersing and were riven by opposing tendencies, whereas the Communists took many of the former S.P. members and even some of its leaders: the C.P.'s corps of activists was increasing, becoming more native, more cohesive.

In the fierce competition among diverse radical groups, the Communists had defeated challenges from its own offshoots, the Trotskyists led by James P. Cannon and Max Schachtman, and the former "right opposition," the followers of Jay Lovestone and Bertram Wolfe. Each of these groups had the allegiance of talented intellectuals, many of them to figure importantly into our day. Each had a base in the trade union movement: the Trotskyists among the auto workers and teamsters, the Lovestoneites among the auto workers and in the garment unions. In 1934-35, the nonconformist churchman, A. J. Muste, tried to realize Edmund Wilson's old dream of "taking Communism away from the Communists" and formed the American Workers' Party, attracting many members of these dissident groups as well as other left wing socialists.[6] This ambitious group did not prove durable, soon being riven by factions and impotence, but the Communist Party learned something from the challenge. The C.P. moved quickly to attract important figures out of all the other radical groups, and to give them more than symbolic posts.[7] At the same time, it attempted to present itself as the inheritor of the entire previous radical tradition, as a movement above petty factions. Thus it claimed descent from William Sylvis, of the Knights of Labor; Eugene Victor Debs, the humanitarian Socialist unionist; Daniel De Leon, the sectarian syndicalist; Frederick Douglass, the Abolitionist; and "Big Bill" Haywood, the Populist-become-Wobbly. To this panoply of ancestors was added Marx, Engels, Lenin, and Stalin; later, the venerables of the democratic tradition, Jefferson, Jackson, and Lincoln were included. Such a bizarre spectrum revealed how anxiously the Party sought to find the most diverse and secure roots. It sought to project American Communism as the inheritor of the radical and the democratic traditions, and to portray its framework for postcapitalist America as an integration of these two traditions. The attempt was attractive and ambitious, but also pathetic.

As all observers and historians have noted, the Communist Party in the twenties was largely foreign-born and working class in composition (the American working class of that time was largely foreign-born). In the following decade this composition changed drastically. Communism attracted the older stock of Anglo-Saxon and Nordic background, especially in the Rocky Mountain states and the Far West. Many of those who had abandoned the Socialists and the I.W.W. in the twenties and were now returning to the left, as well as their offspring, joined the Party in the thirties. In the first three years of the Depression, Nathan Glazer reports, the C.P. doubled its membership. It doubled again in the first two years of the New Deal, and once more in the next two years. By October 1936 "an important watershed" had been passed: "the majority of its members were native-born."[8] Even in New York State, with its particular character, this change occurred by September 1938.

Thus the American Communists had become a melting pot of their own. Second generation Americans found the Communist movement a channel for their rebellion, a cure for their anomie, a vehicle for ambitions to make their mark in the country adopted by their parents. Sons and daughters of the "new Negro" who had come up from the South found equality in the Party which was denied them outside of it, and a chance for leadership and self-expression which few other movements offered to blacks as well as to whites. Children of the disintegrated "middle border" of Hamlin Garland's day, the uprooted Populist farmers, as well as young people of a more Brahmin and "eastern" tradition (in revolt against Puritan narrow-mindedness or in search of the progressive impulse of the Protestant élite) also sought to resolve their rootlessness in a changing America by the camaraderie and the apocalyptic hope that Communism offered. Thus an "un-American" movement turned out to be the vehicle of Americanization.[9]

The C.P. was always keenly conscious that its geographical distribution was abnormal. Half its members were in New York State, with comparatively large blocs located in the industrial East and Midwest; an effective group existed in Minnesota and in the state of Washington, but only a smattering of members in the South and in the farming communities. In California, both north and south, the membership level was comparatively significant.

In addition, the Party was never satisfied with the composition of its membership — the balance of workers, blacks, women, and youth. By the middle of the war, the character of the membership was changing, with a significant influx of white-collar workers, professionals, and even business men, together with an increase in the working class membership, which the Party deemed essential and distinctive.[10] Some characteristics of the fifteen thousand new members who came in during 1943 are worth noting. Whereas at the end of the previous year, 43 percent of the Party's membership consisted of industrial workers, 62 percent of the 1943 recruits were in this category. In 1942, half of the membership had been trade unionists; in 1943 this number rose to 56 percent. Just below a quarter were in "basic industries." And whereas at the end of 1942, 10 percent of the members were blacks, of the new recruits a year later one third were blacks.[11] All this was reassuring. The fact that middle class Americans were also adhering in significant numbers — 10 percent of the 1943 recruits — was not necessarily cause for concern considering the changes that were taking place in the work force and the Party's goal of influencing the whole of American political life.

The Party's growth did present problems — how to turn new members into "real Communists," how to shift from the older corps of cadres to the new. At the close of 1944 — by which time the Party had become the Communist Political Association (C.P.A.), a change which requires separate discussion — it was reported that no less than two-thirds of the Michigan membership was new.[12] Less than 10 percent of the Party's members in this crucial state had been in the organization for more than a few years. Half of the officers of the Political Association's clubs (the new name for branches) were women; only one-fifth of the officers of these clubs had ever held the post before. Fifty-four percent had not read the proceedings of the May 1944 convention which had made the change from the C.P. to the C.P.A. Organizational secretary John Williamson expressed the leadership view of this situation: "We cannot expect to be the same well-knit organization that we were when we were smaller and composed of a group of conscious and tested Communists." Yet he also complained that in operating a looser, more popular, less Leninist organization than the Communists had been, "a small handful of loyal comrades" tended to "jell into an ever tighter group" and "without rest, [kept] going themselves, trying to carry the entire load."[13]

In 1938, the circulation of the Party's Sunday paper exceeded

100,000; it remained above the figure during the war. In San Francisco, a daily paper with a "broader," less authoritative line, the *People's World*, had built an influential following. The *Midwest Record*, launched in Chicago, was striving for a similar influence. *International Publishers* not only reprinted Marx, Lenin, and Stalin, but also was able to distribute, through the Party, half a million copies of the Dean of Canterbury's eulogistic *Soviet Power*.[14] Drawing on the influence of more than a dozen foreign-language dailies and weeklies, inherited from the foreign-language federations of the twenties, the Communists had succeeded in creating a powerful left-wing fraternal society, the International Workers Order.[15] The I.W.O. grouped those sympathizers who still clung to ethnic allegiances. This agency proved to be an important adjunct, serving as a reservoir of finances and a custodian of Party funds. Headed by the Communist leader, Max Bedacht, it gave shelter and an arena of activity to older cadres and to some important anti-fascist refugees. With the rise of the Nazi threat and the mobilization of the "national groups" for the war effort, the I.W.O. with its summer camps, schools and political activities in its own name served to enlarge the Party's contact with trade unions and Democratic Party politics.

The Party did not concentrate on electoral activity because its chief intention was to influence the existing two-party system. Nevertheless, the Party did put candidates forward at times and with some success. In New York City, two Communist councilmen, Peter V. Cacchione in Brooklyn and Benjamin J. Davis in Manhattan, rolled up impressive first choice votes under a system of proportional representation. In Cleveland, San Francisco, Los Angeles, Boston, Detroit — even in Richmond — the party gave certain of its popular leaders repeated chances to run up impressive results in local balloting.[16]

Finally, the Communists commanded a system of popular, labor-progressive educational institutions, centers of adult training and discussion, which were distinct from its own inner-Party "training schools." Among these were the Abraham Lincoln School in Chicago, the Samuel Adams School in Boston, and the Labor School in San Francisco. In New York there was the Jefferson School of Social Science, an ambitious venture with its own building and at one point an enrollment of nearly ten thousand.

Yet the characteristic feature of the American Communist Party, that which distinguished it from other radical groups, was the

*outward* thrust of its activity — the political influence it wanted
to exert, and the energy it devoted to the world of politics outside
of its own immediate structure and ideological orbit. To build a
community of like-minded people who would attract followers by
the nobility of their dream and by the quality of their communal
life, did not satisfy the American Communists, although they did
try to build such a community. The task they set themselves,
however, was much more ambitious: *to propel the whole country
forward*. Having floundered as a sect in the twenties and conscious
of the doom of other radical sects, the Communists searched for a
different formula: this formula was found in Leninism, in the idea
of a vanguard party which is so intimately connected with the
struggles of millions of non-Communists that it is capable of leading them to ultimate social change.

Neither mere education nor exemplary action, the techniques
of a lower level of the class struggle, would suffice. The Communists constructed their organization on the assumption that if
"the masses" could be led in struggles for the relief of their most
elementary grievances, their "immediate demands," they would
accept left wing and even Communist leadership in a fight for
total social change[17]. Yet the struggle for immediate demands had
its perils. It could lead to the reform of the system, and not necessarily to its revolutionary overthrow. Thus the Communists led
actions for the redress of immediate grievances at the same time
that they argued that the system was actually beyond repair, that
its malfunction could be cured only by socialist change. The
masses were supposed to learn by experience that capitalism could
only be modified to a constantly unsatisfactory extent. As a result
of the confidence of the masses in trustworthy leaders, the private
views of these same leaders would somehow rub off on their followers. In any case, revolutionary consciousness would be confirmed by the ever more desperate, ever more visible crisis of
capitalism.

In this elaborate theory, there were deep tensions and uncer-
tainties. Activizing the masses for immediate reforms without
concealing ultimate objectives, without concealing one's own banners, was not easy. Establishing organizations in which the rank
and file could not be expected to share the views of leaders ran a
certain risk. Leaders might themselves be influenced by the comparative political backwardness of members, by their reformist
tendencies. Leaders might face competition from ideological oppo-

nents and ultimately be defeated because of their views (despite the service of such leaders in founding these very organizations). Or else left wing leaders might be obliged to conceal their views, running the risk of duplicity. They might also be forced to weaken their own ties to the Leninist vanguard.

What if the masses, in motion for a given historical period, were to be satisfied with reforms, at least for a time, and thus the revolutionary crisis were to be delayed, even postponed? What if the capitalist system were more elastic than brittle? Could left wing leaders ride out the temptations of the prolonged period between reform and revolution? What if the struggle for reform did not lead to revolution at all? How could a party with revolutionary aims, which had assembled a tough, self-sacrificing corps, maintain itself as a community without degenerating into a propaganda sect, or without accepting the logic of reform at the expense of revolutionary ideals? And how could the Leninist equilibrium be sustained in a country so different from Lenin's? The question itself led to heresy.

Three particular circumstance — within American life and in world affairs — had a decisive bearing on these dilemmas. The first circumstance was the organizational *tabula rasa* of America. In the beginning of the Depression, the period that Edmund Wilson has called the great "American Earthquake," people were crying for leadership, for almost anyone to organize them. This gave Communists, like other radicals, an exceptional chance, and favored them in a way that would not be true once the thirties had taken shape. The second circumstance was the profound division that polarized the American ruling elite. Those traditional "free enterprisers" who rejected reform and were prepared to repress it were opposed by the Burkean conservatives, those who wanted to reform in order to conserve. In 1932, the same year that Hitler turned Germany to facism, Roosevelt turned America toward reform. This contrast would determine the fortunes of the country, indeed of the world, as well as the fate of American radicalism. The third circumstance was the growing coincidence of interest between the Soviet Union and the United States in the face of the consolidating German-Italian-Japanese Axis. Antithetical as were the Soviet and American civilizations, in their systems and their history, they were driven ineluctably to stand together for self-defense. Within the decade the fate of humanity's subse-

quent evolution would be decided and all relationships transformed by this De Tocquevillean juxtaposition.

All of these circumstances favored the American Communists.
They acquired a reputation for organizational expertise which was
merited.[18] They were accepted, however reluctantly, as a wing of
the democratic movement. They were legitimized by the cautious
respect and ultimate bargain between Stalin and Roosevelt. Yet
all three circumstances had their perils. Although the sanction for
pressing forward with an American version of the Popular Front
was given by the 7th (and last) congress of the Communist International, the very successes of the Communists strained their
ties with the international movement. Working exceptionally
well, they confronted the risk of an "American exceptionalism"
which would tear at their ideological anchorage, with all this implied.[19] Moreover the Soviet Union, in its pell-mell industrializa-
tion, the precondition for meeting the Nazi attack, underwent
frightful internal convulsions. In the early thirties the Soviet
model could be hailed as relevant to the planlessness of America,
floundering in crisis. By the end of the decade American Communists had to answer for the hollowness of Soviet democracy, for
Stalin's perversion of what the West had believed socialism to be.
The U.S. Party defended Stalinism. Failure to have done so
would have been unthinkable, given the dynamic and the cohesion which arose out of its own concept of internationalism. Yet
the defense was costly. The hold which the Communists had acquired in American life, especially in intellectual and cultural life,
became tenuous and uncertain. The protestations that American
socialism could be constitutional, democratic, and consonant with
the historic American heritage were hard to believe. No matter
how nimbly the Party leaped from projecting "collective security"
in 1937 to the isolationism of the "phoney war" period in 1940
following the Soviet-German Pact, then to "national unity" on
behalf of defending America in concert with Russia in 1941, and
finally to the desperate projection in 1944 that the Cold War
could be avoided, the American Communists could no longer
claim that their hard work in helping to organize America was
proof of their integrity as socialists; this integrity had been undermined.

Looking backward from 1956, the survivors asked themselves
why they had been unable to convert their advantages into dur-

able achievements. Why was every achievement alloyed by dross? Was there something they had failed to understand about their own country? Was there something within Communism, as a system and a doctrine, that was self-contradictory to the point of dooming to failure the efforts of its most well-intentioned adherents?

In its outward thrust, the Party began in 1935 to popularize the need for collective security against the fascist menace. This was not easy in a country whose isolationist tradition had merged with the disillusion of radicals after the First World War, and the record of imperialist adventures during the decade of "normalcy." One of the most successful organizations in the campaign to "defend America by quarantining the aggressors" was the American League against War and Fascism, which at one point had perhaps five million members. Late in the thirties it acquired a more positive name, the American League for Peace and Democracy. This organization offered a platform for personalities from the most diverse walks of life to express themselves.[20] Another organization formed to oppose fascism was the North American Committee to Aid Spanish Democracy, which enlisted all those who supported the Spanish Republicans in their battle with the fascists (and who saw a Republican victory as crucial for Europe's future). Independently, the Communists had given their best cadres the task of building the Abraham Lincoln Brigade. (This was the U.S. contingent in the international volunteer force, the International Brigades, which became a factor in the European Resistance, and a tragic legend.[21] Vincent Sheean, in his *Not Peace but a Sword*, exalted the American young men confronting the fascist offensive at Teruel, or at Jarama, and described some of them swimming the Ebro in their shorts, arriving on the safe shore to resume their posts with a matter-of-fact common sense and tragic humor. The saga of these American youngsters, without previous military experience, became a heartbreaking drama for millions, and a red badge of courage and honor for American Communism.)[22]

In another dimension of American life, the special problem of the South, the Communists were sure they had pioneered: they had built separate movements of both black and white southerners, and had achieved a special influence at the point where both orbits met. In Communist theory, the American black population was a nation within a nation. Borrowing heavily from concepts arrived at in Moscow, American Communists postulated the liberation of the Negro as the result of agrarian revolution and separate nationhood, possibly necessitating the recasting of state boundaries in the South to correspond to the Black Belt. [23] However mechanical and unreal either in essentials or details, this stance enabled the Communists to make the routine effort at judicial hanging of the Scottsboro boys into a national, even international, *cause celebre*. Out of the confrontation of the country with the reality of repeated lynchings of blacks, absence of federal standards of nondiscrimination in employment, and abridgment of voting rights by sheer terror or the poll tax, the Communists sparked important new movements, replacing their own paper organizations. The most successful and ambitious of such movements was the National Negro Congress, which for a time challenged the National Association for the Advancement of Colored People and the Urban League.[24] Another was the Southern Negro Youth Congress (the S.N.Y.C.'s patron was W.E.B. DuBois, of Niagara movement fame and a founder of the N.A.A.C.P.). This organization educated and activated a whole black generation. Out of it came some of the Party's most effective figures. (In the S.N.Y.C. they had mingled with Negroes who were to take a different ideological path, who were to become the presidents, deans, and professors of the major Negro universities, heads of church movements, directors of the fraternal and insurance societies, and civil rights leaders.)

Less dramatic but no less meaningful was the Communist contact with Southern Conference for Human Welfare (S.C.H.W.), the organized expression of liberal white opinion on which President Roosevelt relied as a partial counterfoil to the conservative grip on the Solid South's Democratic Party. In this lively group of liberal and maverick Southerners were the experts who conceived the T.V.A., who sparked the revival of regional music, and who awakened Appalachia to unionism. Led by Frank P. Graham, president of the University of North Carolina, the S.C.H.W. had connections with Texas liberals such as Homer Rainey of the National Youth Administration, and the courageous Aubrey Williams. In this circle, black and white radicals were something of a leaven, sometimes too yeasty for their friends, too doctrinaire, yet almost always given hospitality.[25] The Communists also played a part in sparking all sorts of campaigns: to inaugurate Negro History Week in the public schools; to persuade Branch Rickey to hire the first black baseball players for the Dodgers (this was the almost singlehanded work of the *Daily Worker* sports editor); to protest the "darky" dolls and chauvinistic figurines in local neighborhood stores. How much had been done, and how little was later acknowledged, either by whites or blacks!

Historians have noted, often with intense exasperation, the particular success of the Communists in the field of communications (a field which the Communists rather superciliously termed the "cultural front"). Nathan Glazer has cited the special susceptibility of librarians and social workers to Party influence. Eugene Lyons became indignant at the virtual dictatorship which the left wing established in the publishing field during the "Red Decade" (the thirties), and Daniel Aaron has chronicled the same phenomenon with more understanding and compassion.[26] Arthur Schlesinger, Jr., expressed contempt for the quasi-intellectual professionals whom the Communists enrolled.[27] (Murray Kempton wondered why such a national paranoia developed about Communist influence in Hollywood, supposedly the undefiled fount of the country's virtues and moral standards; Kempton's examination of the films written by left wing writers suggested that these hardly exuded socialist ideology. They were as mediocre as the work of their political opponents.)[28]

As for the Party, however, its impact on the world of communications was in some ways less a matter of a conscious, direct concentration in this field than an offshoot of its labor organizing activities. The upheaval which produced a Newspaper Guild[29] and related unions of white-collar and professional workers soon set a progressive standard in publishing. It was the ricochet effect of labor's organizing drive that pushed screen writers and screen actors to form guilds in which left wing leaders came to the top as they did elsewhere. Yet the Party had made a conscious effort to break from the earlier bohemianism and avant-garde character of the small left wing groups of the early thirties. This effort bore fruit in newer, more representative bodies. The days were gone when vigorous young women had concluded the performances of the New Dance League by waving *Daily Worker* in exhortation to proletarians (who despised modern dance). The John Reed Clubs, the New Theatre League, the Film and Foto League, the Union of Technical Men, and the International Juridical Association — all seminal but very limited bodies — were soon superseded, especially as the Works Progress Administration gave funds to Hallie Flanagan's Federal Theatre and the Writers'

Project. Experimental talent nurtured in Party circles took the center of the stage in such legitimate and influential agencies as Group Theatre.[30] The American Artists Congress, like the Congress of American Writers, replaced what the far left had built and became an arena for leading figures associated with different traditions, not all of them radical. Much the same could be said of the Hollywood Anti-Nazi League, or the National Lawyers Guild, a genuine united front of the most active, socially minded lawyers and jurists, or Physicians Forum, which sparked a new view of social medicine for thousands of students as well as for eminent figures in the health professions. The relatively modest but influential Washington Bookshop enabled Supreme Court Justices to rub shoulders, while browsing, with left wing New Dealers, clerks, and middle echelon officials at the most effervescent moments of the New Deal. The Communists had mixed feelings about this spectrum of new organizations because they had to share influence in them with a membership that was considerable and sophisticated: self-satisfaction was mingled with a certain intellectual inadequacy.

*New Masses* (which had been started as a monthly in 1926 and became a weekly in 1934) never became what the old *Masses* had been in another time, in that heyday when Debsian socialists and I.W.W. iconoclasts taunted disenchanted Wilsonians as they emptied glasses in the salon of Mabel Dodge.[31] The *Masses* then had been a center for rebels and iconoclasts, many of them major talents in varied fields. Certainly after the ouster of Joseph Freeman, the magazine hardly reflected the heady moods and diversities among left intellectuals. Party orthodoxy inhibited serious inquiry and *New Masses* could not match the freewheeling of the *Nation* and the *New Republic*, or the searching inquiry of *Partisan Review*.[32]

It was in the cultural domain that the Party had the most difficulty riding out the storm over the Moscow Trials of 1936-1938. At the next great turning point, the Soviet-German Non-Aggression Pact of 1939, a large number of those intellectuals who had begun the decade in support of the Communist Party left it — sometimes abruptly, sometimes reluctantly — with such bitter disillusion that not even the new relationships wrought by the war would reconcile them to the Party.[33] The C.P.'s cultural luminaries and commissars were to discount these losses somewhat frenetically (as Mike Gold called his onetime friends "hollow men"), but the impact of the Trials and the Non-Aggression Pact was eventually muted in the national unity of the war. As late as 1944, the Hollywood Writers Mobilization could hold an impressive conference on the U.C.L.A. campus, chaired by university president Robert Sproul. The wide spectrum of esteemed professionals that gave learned papers included scenario writers who three years later were accused of Party membership. The White House sent a warm greeting. In Franklin D. Roosevelt's fourth-term campaign much of the revived left-progressive influence was crystallized through the Independent Citizens Committee of the Arts, Sciences and Professions, staffed by a band of young women of exceptional expertise. This movement was to contribute importantly to the 1948 Wallace campaign. In 1949 it was still vigorous enough to sponsor the Waldorf-Astoria peace conference.

In no field, with the exception of labor and the "Negro question," did the Communists feel they had done so well, and achieved such pervasive results, as among the student and working youth. The upheaval of the thirties had expressed, after all, the search, the protest, and the unbounded energy of youth. From the members of the Young Communist League the Party had drawn a solid segment of its middle echelon leaders: a few of these had been integrated alongside the old-timers in the Party's very "top leadership." Among the students, a close relation had developed between Socialists and Communists; the merger of the Student League for Industrial Democracy and the National Student League to form the American Student Union (A.S.U.) coincided with the Popular Front which had been sanctioned by the Comintern's 7th Congress. The A.S.U. led a series of antiwar strikes each spring throughout the middle thirties which changed the academic climate. Opposition to the R.O.T.C. as the symbol of militarization and imperialist war reached a height which was not regained until the sixties.[34]

The youth movement, however, went beyond its student component. The American Youth Congress, a clearing house of organizations as diverse as the Young Communist League and the Young Women's Christian Association, became, with Mrs. Roosevelt's patronage, the expression of youth rebellion. Its legislative proposal, the American Youth Act, put on the nation's agenda for the first time the special needs of a younger generation which capitalism-in-crisis had discarded.[35] This movement soon acquired international form. A World Youth Congress at Vassar College in August 1938 attracted an internationally wide spectrum of young people. Many returned home with a new image of America which was to shape their attitudes as they became leading figures in the wartime Resistance.

The war brought this phase of the Communists' youth activities to a close. The armed forces now constituted a "youth movement" with a special and fateful historical function. Service in the war involved vital cadres, "several thousand Communist leaders, 86 full-time officers, hundreds of full-time Communist trade union or other mass organization leaders."[36] The Party exalted its heroes: Herman Boettcher, veteran of the Spanish war, who died in the South Pacific; "Hank" Forbes, the popular New York leader who fell on the Anzio beaches; Robert Thompson, who went from Spain to win a Distinguished Service Cross for exceptional heroism in New Guinea. Scores of Communists won their spurs not only on the battlefields but also as seamen in the National Maritime Union, who were responsible for passing the ammunition to beleagured Europe and the Far East. When "Wild Bill" Donovan established the Office of Strategic Services, the first U.S. experiment in counterintelligence and counterinsurgency operations, he recruited scores if not hundreds of Communists and their close sympathizers.[37] Many of them, just returned from Spain, were able at the climax of the war to assist leaders of the Resistance in almost every Western European country. Yet even during the war the Communists never quite achieved that acceptance which had been their goal in peacetime. At first the War Department placed restrictions on Communists; men with valuable Spanish war experience were refused as candidates for the Officer's Training Corps and confined to routine tasks in Alaska or Panama. Not until the war was almost over, on February 27, 1945, was the ban on Communist officers lifted.

In retrospect, the war had been for thousands of Communists a great turning point. Many from the cities came for the first time to grasp America's magnitude, the immense political space between the labor-democratic-progressive milieu in which the left had been sheltered and the real level of consciousness of the millions who were recruited to fight for flag and country. A good part of the Party's cadres never returned to its life and orbit. The war was a caesura, a break. Many migrated to other parts of the country, many began to build families and change their lives.

Communism became a warm memory for some; for others it was a past mistake.

Six months after the July 1945 upheaval in the Party, only 30 percent of the Communists in the service had been demobilized, but one report complained that "a large percentage of these already-discharged Party and Y.C.L. veterans were not being reached in the re-registration drive." The reasons given were revealing. "Among a small proportion of our returning veterans, including a few former leading Party *actives*, there exist attitudes of reluctance to accept quickly Party responsibilities. In such cases, because such comrades have been for a considerable period detached from the life and problems of the Party, very often such underlying attitudes are doubts about the correctness of the Party's role, underestimation of the urgency of the problems confronting our Party and the labor movement."[38]

The Party's outward thrust had been most dramatic in the twin areas of political action and the labor movements, although the fragile results there were perplexing for its self image as a Leninist vanguard. Mention has already been made that the Party's electoral successes were not the chief measure of its political impact. For a brief moment, just before President's Roosevelt's 1936 campaign, emphasis was placed on an old slogan, "A Farmer-Labor Party." Negotiations took place to achieve a united front with the Socialists and with the important Farmer-Laborites of the northcentral states where the Non-Partisan League of an earlier day had nurtured a radical tradition. But on closer examination, the Party realized that the idea of a Farmer-Labor Party was an oversimplified transference of the European model — the model of a pact among distinct parties had little promise. Only in New York State had anything comparable to a Farmer-Labor Party developed. The American Labor Party had grown out of the cooperation of independent Republicans (led by Mayor Fiorello La Guardia), the Amalgamated Clothing Workers, the International Ladies Garment Workers, and the newer unions (transportation workers, seamen, white-collar workers) emerging from the C.I.O.'s organizational drive. Successful as the A.L.P. was in projecting a nonpartisan reform program, it also served as an adjunct to the Roosevelt wing of the Democrats. The Communists were never represented as a distinct constituent.[39]

The unwillingness of the C.I.O. to enter politics as a separate force turned the Party's thrust to infiltrating and winning influence within the two-party system. Through Labor's Non-Partisan League, the C.I.O. preferred to bargain with both parties as an independent. This preference reflected the distinctive character of American labor — it preferred to be a nonpolitical pressure group throwing its weight around without becoming, like the British unions, the backbone of a separate political party. The Communists had seen this plainly in 1936 and 1937. In the 1936 election, the Party's presidential candidate, Earl Browder, had run as an independent under the slogan: "Defeat Landon at all costs." Browder's aim was less to win Communist votes than to demonstrate the indispensability of the Communists to the democratic movement, enabling Roosevelt to disavow the Party's support while relying on its mobilizing power.[40] In June 1937 Browder explained the limits of the Party's independent electoral activity as well as the futility of projecting a Farmer-Labor Party in the circumstances of the acute split between Roosevelt and his "Liberty League" opposition. "We will be utterly unrealistic if we expect a Farmer-Labor Party of serious consequence in Pennsylvania until the C.I.O. is convinced that such a party will immediately exert as much political power as the C.I.O. already exerts through the Democratic Party."[41]

The Communists also discovered that they could exert political power through local Democratic (and sometimes Republican) parties far better than they could in their own name. The American political system's amorphous character, its direct primaries, and the absence of a really cohesive national party made this possible. Thus, in Minnesota, the Communists could parley with the Farmer-Labor governor, Floyd Olson, without embarrassment; they were instrumental in achieving the fusion of the Farmer-Laborities and the Democratic Party in that state. In Washington and Oregon, it was the left, including publicly known Communists, who built the "Commonwealth Federations" that became powerful ginger groups within the formal Democratic structure. In Philadelphia, the Communists connected themselves through local reform movements based on the citywide C.I.O. councils (whose flexibility and autonomy of action the Communists were quick to appreciate and exploit) in such a way as to exert powerful leverage on the Democrats. So successful was this strategy that the Party's ideological opponents, both the Social-Democrats and the Trotskyists, tried the same tactic, in the Michigan Commonwealth Federation for example. Well known left wingers were soon being elected as congressmen, and a well defined progressive bloc was emerging both in the Senate and the House to which the left had access.[42]. In the early thirties, Communists had led the unemployed into the seats of city and state government, clamoring for the satisfaction of immediate needs; in Trenton, New Jersey, the state house had been occupied. By the late thirties, they no longer had to break down doors nor come in by the back door. It was not unusual for Communist Party legislative directors or state secretaries to be given cordial attention in the offices of senators, congressmen, mayors, governors and intermediaries of the White House. Communist political activity was still considered not completely legitimate, but the Party was no longer politically ostracized.[43]

The increasing acceptance of the left in the political arena reflected what was happening in the Party's chief area of concentration, the trade union movement. The working class was, by definition, the motive force of ultimate social change. Organizing labor was, in the Party's eyes, the chief task. In the early thirties, several thousand Party cadres in the Trade Union Unity League (T.U.U.L.) had cut their eyeteeth (and broken their backs) trying to stimulate independent unions. (The Trade Union Unity League replaced the Trade Union Educational League in 1929. The latter had been an attempt to build an opposition within the American Federation of Labor. The former was frankly a dual union effort, justified on the grounds that the A.F.L. could not be moved to tackle the unorganized, mass-production industries.) Few solid results could be tallied by 1935, when the T.U.U.L. was dissolved, but fertile seeds had been sown. Once the Roosevelt administration, zigzagging its way through the N.R.A. period, encouraged unionization, millions of hitherto unorganized workers streamed into both A.F.L. affiliates and into "company unions"; the latter had been encouraged by antilabor employers to resist unionization and find some "corporativist" form which they might control. Left wingers moved with this stream and when section 7A of the National Recovery Act was upheld by the Supreme Court and was followed by the Wagner Act, unionization took on tidal wave proportions. In Nathan Glazer's phrase, the Communists, like many other kinds of radicals, were carried "like corks in a flood" to strategic positions.[44]

When the A.F.L. Executive Committee underwent its famous split, and a formidable group of ten major leaders formed the

"Committee for Industrial Organization," the left wingers came to the surface as local and national leaders. Thousands more turned to this most dramatic and characteristic mass movement of the thirties — from the colleges and from the unemployed. Nor was the left's activities confined to the C.I.O. Those unions which remained with the A.F.L. (after the "Committee" became the "Congress" of Industrial Organizations) also experienced a sharp rise in membership. In the independent International Typographical Union and in the Railroad Brotherhoods, the left had maintained nuclei from that period of the twenties when both these independent centers had had a strong progressive contingent. Within a short time, the political complexion of American labor's leadership changed.[45] One third of the C.I.O.'s executive committee, leaders of well over a million workers (a quarter to a third of the C.I.O. as a whole) were identifiably of the left, if not members of the Communist Party.

### Peculiar Problems: Inner Structure, the Moscow Tie

Two aspects of these comparative successes presented tantalizing challenges to the American Communists, and can be used to explain the changes with which they were wrestling at the midpoint of the war. Neither aspect was ever satisfactorily resolved by the Party, neither the genuine legitimacy within U.S. life or the categorical imperative of keeping pace with the international movement.

The problem of "citizenship" or "full legality" had nothing to do with those members who were aliens;[46] these were few after 1940. Nor did it pertain to "legality" in the technical sense. Although many state laws banned employment of Communists in the civil service, and many trade union or other public organizations had constitutions which barred Party members from office or even membership, these legal prohibitions were not the major reason that so many C.P. members were obliged to conceal their political affiliation. Formally, the American Communists were legal. They had headquarters, published periodicals, held meetings of branches or leading committees, ran candidates, and staged often spectacular conventions. What undermined the movement's legitimacy was the inability of thousands of leaders of public, civil, political, and trade union organizations who privately adhered to Communism to make this adherence publicly known and to participate openly *within the Party*, leaving no doubt as to who they were and what they were. This situation had come about because in the Party's outward thrust two categories of Communists had arisen: those members who were known as such, never denied it, and were largely involved in the inner functioning of the Party; and those who lived in a political limbo, who blurred their political affiliation and did not participate in the Party's structure except on a semiclandestine level. To avow their private faith openly would jeopardize their leadership in exactly those organizations and areas of public life on which the Communist Party had concentrated for a decade. These unavowed Communists might be called the Party's "influentials." In the Party's own argot they were known as "submarines."

No deliberate conspiracy was involved. The Communists had taken the line of least resistance. A gap had arisen between their ability to gain leadership positions in huge organizations and their ability to build within those organizations a solid corps of left wingers. It had proved easier to become a leader of "masses" than to build a "mass base." In part, this situation was explained by peculiarly American reasons. In the labor movement, the rank and file strongly separated "politics" from "pork-chops." Political conviction was a man's private affair, and the Communist convictions of a particular leader did not matter much provided he "delivered" on "bread and butter" issues. It seemed a dubious proposition to most rank and filers that a leader was doing a better job because of the unique qualities of his private political faith. After all, leaders of the most varied faiths were doing good jobs.

Moreover, the Party's own decision in the late thirties to abolish its "fractions," or caucuses, within the labor movement had the paradoxical effect of widening the gap between union members in the Party and secretly affiliated leaders. Until the caucuses were abolished, all Communists in any given group or in any campaign would map out strategy and tactics together, and a common discipline would be binding on everyone no matter what their echelon or particular task. The American Communists were seeking to break away from this Leninist form, suitable to quasi-military purposes;[47] their object was to obviate the suspicion of conspiracy, and to give their influentials leeway to behave as organizational leaders with no strings attached to a hidden center. Yet this very dissolution of fractions operated to remove the influentials from the discipline of Communist rank and file in their organizations. At the same time, it relieved them of the obligation to "build the Party'" within these organizations.

In this way, the revolutionary community tended to become a pseudo-community: it became flawed at both ends of the gap that grew between the leadership and the base. As Communists participating in the wider world of public life, they became subject to all its temptations. They were now responsible for budgets and programs that had to command allegiance from a nonleft rank and file. Rivalry with hard-bitten ideological opponents increasingly led them to use techniques of control that relied less on persusasion and more on bureaucratic devices, political machines, even strong-arm squads. Try as the influentials did to make their organizations paragons of democratic procedure — and they often succeeded — they were also prone to "cults of the personality" and to wheeling and dealing. And although they continued to accept the authority of the Party, they left its operation to functionaries.[48]

The influentials tended to live a life apart, however much they felt, as many did, that this separation from the Party contradicted their private political commitment. They tended to take little responsibility for the Party "line," and became concerned only when the line intersected their particular sphere of interest. The separation of the influentials from the Party had a serious effect on the Party itself. Few of its public leaders were "mass figures." Foster had been one, but his reputation was based on achievement of an earlier time; the same was true of Elizabeth Gurley Flynn. Others, such as Benjamin J. Davis and Cacchione in the electoral field achieved a certain public standing, and Browder made a serious effort to talk to the nation as such. Yet on the whole the Party's functionaries became a political caste. Some acquired the special skills of Talmudic exegesis, becoming the guardians of the precious and obscure language of Marxism-Leninism. Others became excellent brokers, messengers between the Party's inner sanctum and its operatives in every phase of Communist interest. The corrupting character of this system spiraled as it continued. Although it was true that in publicly revealing themselves, many Communist influentials risked political decapitation, it is also true that in failing to do so they undermined those bonds of confidence which it was in their interest to establish with the democratic-progressive world in which they wanted respect. This happened between the Youth Congress leaders and Mrs. Roosevelt.[49] It was to happen within the C.I.O. between the left and Philip Murray.

The influentials were thus living in two worlds, and whereas in favorable times they seemed to have the best of both worlds, they were also contributing, in times of stress, to saddling the Communist Party with the worst of both worlds. The influentials were functioning according to what Max Weber has called "the ethics of responsibility," that is, in the realm of pragmatic effort to achieve real aims. At the same time, they were enjoying the comfort of the "ethics of ultimate ends," the certainty that they were achieving a revolutionary goal. They did not choose between these ethics: they followed both and straddled both.[50] In effect, two trends of experience were at odds within the same political movement. Many of the Party's influentials wanted a sanction for their social-democratic attitudes and activities (social-democrats had always allowed for a certain autonomy of their partisans in public or parliamentary or trade union life). Living with the ambivalence of being leaders of important organizations while privately Communists, the influentials wanted the Party to do nothing adventurist or unrealistic which would make their lives difficult. They rationalized their compromises as essential to the Party's growth. Had not Lenin, after all, been the master of compromise?

On the other hand, many of the influentials began to combine a growing doubt about the wisdom of the Party's leadership with a certainty that if only the management of the left wing were left to them, it would prosper. Their tendency was toward intransigence. In part, they reflected an anarcho-syndicalist tradition which tried to make the political party and the trade union *into one and the same organism.* Dissatisfied with their own ambiguous position, and privately assuring themselves of their revolutionary commitment in the most vehement and self-persuasive terms (for the very reason that they could not avow it in public) these influentials were often most impervious to the Party's advice of caution and patience. Because they held power in significant organizations, they were tempted to view these organizations as surrogates for the Party, especially once the latter was in trouble. In this segment of the American radical world, it became fashionable to disparage the Party as incompetent, and indeed to look abroad for greater wisdom.[51]

All these matters were involved in the attempted transformation of American Communism in 1944-45, including the change from a Party to a Communist Political Association. Although couched in terms of response to projected postwar developments, this transformation was also a response to a deep organizational crisis.[52] It was an effort to "legalize" a Marxist movement which had burst through the framework of the Leninist model but whose very growth, by its pecularities, had not served to remove the stigma of "conspiracy." In some ways the problem resembled what confronted the Western European Communists after the Resistance when they had become mass parties at the cost of their Leninist character. In Western Europe, however, Communism was in reality a subculture, with deep roots in the radical movements that have existed in those stratified societies. In the United States the phase equivalent to the Resistance had come earlier, prior to the war, and the Communists were faced during the war with its consequences and its dilemmas. Both their organizational forms and their doctrine were incapable of meeting the new and unprecedented needs created by the Party's growth and success. And they had no real roots in a radical tradition to draw upon.

The U.S. Party also faced perplexing difficulties because of its ties to the international movement, especially to the Soviet Communists. No special or obvious problem existed here for the older Communist generation. Their support for the Soviet Union was not, as is widely believed, the result of the large number of foreign-born in that generation (although to many of these immigrants the tug at the heart of the wondrous things that were said to be happening in "the old country" was a real one). This explanation would not account for the large number of native-born Americans who had come to American Communism from the Socialist Party and the syndicalist groups. For them the wonder was the Russian Revolution itself, the fact that it had succeeded, that the Bolsheviks were personally creating socialism as the social-democrats had failed to do, and thus ushering in the world revolution.[53] In this stance there was a universalism, a Whitmanesque assumption that all men were brothers and by this fact all revolutions were part of one another, regardless of the Marxist distinctions between levels of development. After all, it was a largely native-born, peculiarly American, revolutionary force which had called itself "The International Workers of the World." In this atmosphere, it was easy enough to build a movement on the *non sequitur* that because Lenin and his friends had succeeded, they must have the solution for everyone else's problems. In this regard, the American radicals out-Lenined Lenin.[54] Two other typically American motivations help to explain the deference of American Communists to their Soviet counterpart. Both a deeply ingrained inferiority complex which assumed that beyond America's barbarian shores was an "Old World" — wiser, nobler, more experienced — and the American worship of "success" played their part. Had not Lincoln Steffens assured the world that in visiting Russia he "had seen the future, and it works"? If indeed "it worked," Russia must have the universal prescription for socialism.

Thus, the idea of the Communist International (C.I. or Comintern) as the "general staff" of world revolution appealed to American left wingers, who felt the need for an international organization more tightly structured and more effective than the Socialist International. None of the subsequent bitter experiences with the parochialism, the Russian-centeredness, and the cynicism of power struggles in which the interests of all the detachments under the lead of the "general staff" were subordinated to "bolshevization" could damage this appeal. When the Lenin School was founded in 1926 as a training center for promising cadres, the U.S. party sent its contingents as a matter of course and with pride. Its graduates of the school later occupied the Party's key posts. And postgraduate training in the Lenin School could mean for American Communists, as it did for Dennis, missions in the most diverse areas of the world. It was taken for granted that the Intenational could intervene in even the most minor aspects of the American Communist Party's operation, just as it was taken for granted that the Russian Communist Party was the logical leader of the International. All American groups and factions took their cases to mixed commissions in Moscow, which included in addition to Russians a motley collection of experts: Japanese, Germans, Hungarians, Englishmen. These were assumed to be experts not because of any firsthand knowledge of the United States, nor on the basis of any careful differentiation of the situation in America from that in other lands, but by virtue of their presence at the Comintern's headquarters, in Moscow. Indeed many of them had been failures in making the revolution in their own countries, but were judged competent to tell the Americans how to succeed. Thus, emissaries, telegrams, cables, "reps" (C.I. representatives), and delegations supplying plenty of dollars on both sides of the Atlantic, went to and fro.[55]

Ironically, one of the reasons Comintern intervention was warmly supported by Americans was the Comintern's own emphasis on "Americanization." The demand that the U.S. Communist Party cease its dependence on the foreign-language federations which had played such a large part in its earliest years came from the foreigners in Moscow. They insisted upon the publication of an English-language newspaper, a daily, which at last appeared in Chicago in 1924, assisted by a subsidy from the International. There is evidence that these same foreigners, in the Comintern's highest councils, had their private doubts about the capacities of the Americans with whom they had to work. But there is no evidence that anyone asked himself whether the whole project of trying to build a U.S. party on the Soviet model was not a complete impossibility.[56] To question the universality of the Leninist model, to admit that the United States might not fit the mold of Leninist thought, was too heretical, because if there were no universally valid model then the basic premise that all parties had to accept Russian pre-eminence would collapse. Stalin, combining an important insight with a good deal of guileful flattery, had said in 1929, "The American Communist Party is one of those very few Communist parties of the world that are entrusted by history with tasks of decisive importance from the point of view of the revolutionary movement."[57] For the comparative "rubes" who came to Moscow from America this was heady stuff.

During the thirties, it was still exciting to read *Inprecorr*, the weekly bulletin of the International, printed on thin paper which in itself connoted something confidential; this bulletin quickened the heart beat of American Communists with its reports of the sufferings of nameless comrades in far-off dungeons and the great projects of foreign revolutionaries. In those years, Party members affixed special red stamps in their membership books each month, signifying their solidarity with the persecuted Germans, the encircled Chinese. These stamps were sacred twenty-five cent special assessments; they symbolized the bonds which gave Communism its special appeal. Young Communists demonstrated in front of consulates of semifascist regimes and fought with police over the treatment of Cubans or Filipinos. Probably no other Party was so involved in a series of friendship organizations, each with their own publications, in solidarity with Communists of all continents.[58] Throughout the decade, the masthead of the *Daily Worker* proudly proclaimed it to be the organ of a Party which was "a section of the Communist International." Nobody thought this strange. It required no explanations or apologies.

Yet during the thirties, this older, simplistic internationalism gave way to a new relationship between the different Communist Parties. This change coincided with a sanction from abroad, but it also represented a changing composition within the American C.P., and a new domestic emphasis. The Comintern's 7th Congress, in August 1935, called on all parties to defend democracy against fascism, to find the link between Marxism and the democratic tradition. The Popular Front was intended to prepare a defense of the Soviet Union. Having failed to find that defense in proletarian or colonial revolutions, and having been forced to base their self-defense on the "building of socialism in one country," the Soviet leaders were anxious to make a capitalist united front against them impossible. This required a new strategy for the left in the West. The net result of this new strategy was to transform the left in the West, and in the United States in particular.

Imperceptibly at that point, yet implicitly, the basis was being laid for polycentrism, for the disappearance of those forms of solidarity that had become outmoded with the growth of the movement. The Party's meetings in Madison Square Garden now opened with the singing of the Star Spangled Banner (somewhat self-consciously, to be sure) and closed with a slight but significant change in the last line of the traditional anthem, *the Internationale*—the song no longer said that the "international soviet" would be "the human race."[59] The U.S. Communists were now motivated by what they believed was an authentic national purpose, to save America by moving it toward alliance with Soviet Russia. This national purpose in itself would end the Party's dependence on the Russian Communists, and encourage it to be autonomously creative, imaginative, and effective. True, the slogan blazoned on the Party's banners, "Communism is 20th Century Americanism," had disappeared, somewhat mysteriously by 1939.[60] But its impact lingered on. This slogan signified the Party's desire for legitimization, countering the charge of its opponents that it was an alien force. At the end of 1939, the C.P. decided to disaffiliate from the International. This decision was accepted in Moscow and caused no protest within the Party's ranks.[61] A maneuver? Perhaps. But in a deeper sense, it was the expression of a reality that within a few years would be acknowledged internationally. In the libraries which thousands of members and sympathizers were accumulating, alongside the classics of venerable Germans and esteemed Russians and the books about prestigious Chinese (such as Edgar Snow's *Red Star Over China*), there was now a slim paperback by a New Hampshire-born product of Harvard, Granville Hicks, epitomizing the era. It was entitled *I Like America*.[62]

Looking backward (and each group of Communists departing from the movement at critical turns asked these questions, and they arose, in a muffled way for all those who remained) there was still a problem. The plant which had grown from all these roots was not exactly a weed, as opponents charged, nor was it a flower, as Communists wanted to believe, yet why had it wilted on the vine?

All memories had a bittersweet quality. Many Party members could recall the picket lines at dawn in front of steel mills and coal mines when men risked their lives to distribute leaflets prepared in shanty town huts the night before. Who had ever chronicled the story well? Yet might the pits and mills have been organized more swiftly and longer-lasting recruits brought to the Party if the leaflets had not "linked up" the persuasive simplicities of wages and hours with dubious claims about the wonders of far-off Russia? The Communists had built unity movements with the Socialists well before this unity was developing abroad. Yet had they not broken up mass meetings which the Socialists called to mourn their martyrs after the attack on Socialist Vienna in 1934? Were these not their own heroes and martyrs just a few years later? The Y.C.L.ers (fresh from the colleges) had helped the dust-ridden, desperate farmers of Nebraska to shoulder rifles against the sheriffs at the mortgage foreclosures ordered by bankers. (The farms were bought back when everyone present would bid no more than a penny — the famous "penny-sales.") Yet years later the Communists would reread what they had written in *Farmer's Weekly*, edited by their authentic American heroine, Mother Bloor, and their hearts would be heavy. So much of it, appearing in America's heartland, read like a translation from the Russian.[63] During the war itself, the government had placed a group of American Trotskyists on trial for conspiracy under the same Smith Act which in 1949 would be used against the C.P. The Stalinists then had cheered the government on. They supported the prosecution of political opponents on charges which, when used against themselves, they would denounce as without substance.

What, after all, had it all been about? The passion of a few Americans for Trotsky conflicted with the passions of a few Americans for Stalin, neither of whom had the slightest reality for most Americans. Yet the failure to make civil liberties a principle, the failure to abide by principled behavior, cost the Communists dearly.

American Communism's international ties represented its Achilles heel. It paid a heavy price for a conception of international obligations which was neither reciprocated nor respected by Moscow. During the war, the prestige of the Russians and the necessity of American-Soviet cooperation made these ties an asset, but both the prestige and the cooperation were short lived. By 1945, the American Party's attempt to build a large, successful American left wing on the basis of American-Soviet understanding would be undermined on all sides, including the Russian. Try as the American Communists did to create an autonomous and effective American Marxism, in the spirit of Stalin's judgment that they had been "entrusted by history with tasks of decisive importance," they found themselves considered expendable by Moscow. The very international movement which they wanted to help, in unique ways related to their unique circumstances, "pulled the rug" from under them. This was the humiliation of 1945, and it requires examination in detail.

In the days when the Communists filled New York's Madison Square Garden: (left to right) Earl Browder, general secretary; James W. Ford; William Z. Foster; and Elizabeth Gurley Flynn. In the background, Robert Minor. (Wide World Photos)

# PART II    FROM WAR TO
# THE AMBIGUITIES OF PEACE

# 3  TWO LEADERS FACE

# THE UNKNOWN

Almost the entire leadership and most followers of the American Communist Party supported its unorthodox course in 1944 and its return to orthodoxy within one year. Almost without exception, the same men who had made what they considered a bold and breath-taking departure in political judgment and organizational structure — an experiment in "creative Marxism" — made within twelve months an about-face and abject self-criticism. The chief objection to the new course in 1944 came from the Party's chairman, William Z. Foster.[1] Perhaps "hesitation" is a better word to describe his conduct. One year later, the major architect of the policy that Foster had criticized — Earl Browder, the Party's general secretary — came under attack. After some hesitation, Browder took the unexpected path of refusing to abandon his views, despite repudiation by his associates and denunciation from abroad. The issue between the two men was not personal, although there had been profound antagonism between them for a decade.

Even before becoming Communists, Browder and Foster enjoyed a close relationship distinguished by a common experience in the trade union field. It was this interest that brought them both through the Socialist Party (and in Foster's case via a considerable experimentation with syndicalism) to the Communist Party. Browder, who was ten years Foster's junior, stood for a long time in the latter's shadow. He was Foster's chief lieutenant in the attempt to make their Communist careers dovetail with their trade union concerns, and was a member of the latter's faction within Party politics. Their clash was between men with a similar heritage and a distinct intimacy, one of whom outstripped the other in power and prestige. Foster made his comeback in 1945 as the avenger of political orthodoxy, but his preoccupation with "Browderism" throughout the next decade revealed such an intensity of feeling that the aspect of personal revenge cannot be denied. Although Browder attempted in both 1944 and 1945 to place the issues on the level of strategy and theory, his contempt for Foster was obvious. Foster was, in Browder's eyes, an "eclectic" and an "anarcho-syndicalist", harsh terms in the Marxian lexicon. In later years Browder could hardly conceal, especially in private, his deep personal resentment of Foster's role in their common debacle.

Browder, of English stock which could be traced back to Revolutionary times, was born in rural Kansas in 1891. His father had been a Populist and a Unitarian. By the First World War, Browder had taken part in Socialist Party activities in Kansas City, Missouri. He then turned to trade unionism and cooperatives. During the war he and his two brothers, William and Waldo, went to prison for opposing the draft. Browder then turned to the Communist Party, and was a member of the Party by 1921, when he was invited to organize an American trade union delegation to the first congress of the Red International of Labor Unions (the R.I.L.U or Profintern).

Foster, not yet a publicly avowed Communist, joined the delegation on Browder's urging. Of Irish stock and raised as a Catholic, Foster was born in 1881 in Taunton, Massachusetts. His *Pages from a Worker's Life* reveals an authentic, spirited, restless workingman.[2] He went from the Socialist Party to anarcho-syndicalism (he founded his own Syndicalist League for a time), and was deeply impressed by the French and German labor movements, which he studied during pre-World War I travels.[3] He rose to eminence in the Chicago Federation of Labor, having decided against "dual unionism." Foster was one of the few syndicalist-minded trade unionists who insisted on working within the existing labor movement. Foster achieved national attention as leader of the dramatic and difficult strike of the steel workers in 1919.[4] His major achievements thus antedated his adherence to Communism.[5]

Both men were key figures in the Trade Union Educational League,[6] which attempted to become a radicalizing center for unionists inside the American Federation of Labor and the Railway Brotherhoods; Foster was its chairman, and Browder the editor of its *Labor Herald*. Disparaging critics have spoken of Browder as "Foster's man Friday" and the latter never quite accepted Browder as more than his subordinate.[7] In the euphoric period of May 1944 Robert Minor was to suggest that Browder had been less occupied by the infighting among the Communists of the twenties and had acted as a bridge between the Ruthenberg and Foster factions;[8] yet all the evidence places Browder in the latter group. Browder took part in the international labor delegation that went to China in the last phases of the Kuomintang-Communist alliance and he resided in China from 1926 to 1928 as the executive officer of the Profintern's Pan-Pacific Trade Union Secretariat. He was thus at a distance from the American scene when the struggle between Lovestone and Foster was reaching a climax.

When the Comintern sought to bring some order out of the American Party's chaos in the late twenties,[9] it chose Browder to lead the Party, partly because of his comparative remoteness from the scene, partly because of his proven trustworthiness to the Comintern, but also because of his trade union background and link with Foster. Even then, Browder was for several years only a member of the Party's secretariat. He did not assume full control of the C.P.U.S.A. until its Eighth Congress, in Cleveland in 1934. By then, Foster's comparative eclipse was well under way. Foster had been the Party's presidential candidate in 1932 (the Negro leader, James W. Ford, was the candidate for the vice-presidency) but retired that summer because of *angina pectoris* and resided for the next several years in Moscow. His two volumes *Towards a Soviet America* and *From Bryan to Stalin* reflected the Party's oversimplified imitation of the Russian experience in the years prior to the Seventh Congress of the Comintern and before the Party's "Americanization." Both books were embarrassing to the younger generation of Communists and were disavowed at the Smith Act trial.

Foster and Browder were present at the Seventh Congress of the Comintern in Moscow, August-September 1935, but it was Browder who made the chief address for the American delegation. Both were elected to the Executive Committee of the Comintern (E.C.C.I.), but Foster's role was henceforth almost an emeritus one. The Party chairmanship did not compare in power with the position of general secretary. In 1936 Browder was the Party's presidential standard-bearer.

Both were self-made and self-educated men — deeply influenced by the Russian Revolution. They soon learned the peculiar Esperanto of the Comintern.[10] Although by the midthirties Browder had begun to shake off this language and to acquire a style appropriate to a serious effort to impress his Party's views on all segments of American life, Foster's manner remained an amalgam of his trade union origins and his "fundamentalist" understanding of Marxism.

Browder became a national spokesman, familiar on a wide variety of platforms, the object of a hero worship typical of the Stalin era, and unquestionably one of American Communism's few effective figures. Within the Party, Browder's leadership appeared to be undisputed. But there is evidence that in 1936 he had disagreed bitterly with Foster over the way the Communists should support President Roosevelt.[11] And again in 1939 — when the Communists had to make an abrupt turn from the People's Front tactic and proclaim that the war was imperialistic on both sides — sharp disagreements arose; Foster was dissatisfied with Browder's political behavior. While in the Atlanta Penitentiary in 1941, Browder named as acting secretary his close coworker, Robert Minor.[12] (This unusual figure was the son of a Texas judge, a recruit to Communism from the anarcho-syndicalist variety of radicalism, who had left a great career as an artist to become one of the most Browderist and then anti-Browderist figures in the American movement.) By this time, the Party had limited Foster's activity to agitational writing, even in the trade union field.[13] (The Party had by then a new breed of specialists in trade union work as in other realms of activity.) Browder acknowledged his debt to Foster in the most formal terms.[14] Foster had been outdistanced by his junior, and felt this lapse in status keenly; he also felt his own intellectual attainments to be deeply inadequate.[15] In the crisis of 1945, both men were to say things about each other which only an older generation could hope to understand.[16] To newcomers and outsiders the spectacle was bewildering.

Anticipations of Browder's 1944 ideas can be found in his 1942 booklet, *Victory and After*.[17] It has already been shown that the Party's wartime recruitment, its renewed respectability, and the inner strains between its structure and its influence operated in favor of basic changes. Many of the Party's wartime conceptions can be traced to the sanction of the Comintern's Seventh Congress in 1935. But the dissolution of that organization in May 1943 had enormous meaning to the American Party leaders. It seemed to them that their own creative thinking was now being validated in Moscow. In the autumn of 1943 new signs appeared — Churchill's visit to Stalin and preliminary agreements with respect to postwar relations. In December 1943, Roosevelt, Stalin, and Churchill met together for the first time. Their apparent harmony exceeded the most optimistic expectations. Browder, speaking in Bridgeport, Connecticut, on December 12, 1943, hailed the accord at Teheran, Iran (where the Big Three had met) as a sign of a new world approaching.

At the Party's National Committee meeting on January 7-9, 1944, Browder outlined his wartime conception of the postwar prospects with boldness and confidence. Something new was taking place in world affairs. The prospect of banishing "the scourge and terror of war for many generations" and the vision of an "enduring peace" were no mere diplomatic phrases. Nor were these pledges of agreement intended simply to facilitate cooperation in concluding the war.

Something more fundamental was happening. "British and American ruling circles had to be convinced that their joint war together with the Soviet Union against Hitlerism would not result in the Soviet socialist system being extended to Western Europe under the stimulus of the victorious Red armies. The men who determine Soviet policy had to be convinced that the Western capitalist circles had finally learned that the Soviet Union is in the world to stay, and that hostility to it can only bring disaster to themselves as well as to the rest of the world. Upon this basis, both sides could then come to an agreement as to how all the particular problems should be solved by conference, conciliation and agreement, without either immediate or ultimate resort to the arbitrament of war."[18]

In brief, Browder declared: "Capitalism and Socialism have begun to find the way to peaceful coexistence and collaboration in the same world."

Browder described this collaboration further in discussing the inter-Allied agreements on Italy and Yugoslavia. Stalin's willingness to acknowledge "the basic principles of private property" relieved the "fears of British and American ruling circles," while Roosevelt and Churchill were committed to "freeing the forces of the democratic people's revolution, and sweeping away all forms of absolutism, thus relieving the anxiety of Soviet statesmen over the possible re-emergence of the old anti-Soviet forces." The European policy indicated by the Moscow meeting of foreign ministers in October 1943 was premised on "minimizing and if possible eliminating the use of violent struggle for the settlement of inner problems." This suggested that on a world scale "a broad, all-inclusive anti-fascist democratic camp must be established, within which all relations are determined and problems settled by free discussion, free political association and universal suffrage. Such a democratic camp, of necessity, must include the Communists. . . ."[19]

These were not matters of abstract speculation. Projecting a new course for world history was related to immediate issues. Would the policies associated with President Roosevelt continue into the postwar period? Or would a Republican victory in the 1944 presidential elections come before the war's end, and thus alter the wartime course? Might this imply a swing to the right, such as had happened after the First World War? In January 1944 it was not at all certain that Roosevelt would try for an unprecedented fourth term. The Republican Party was expressing the fear prevalent in important capitalist circles that the United States was being taken in a "socialist" direction as a consequence of F.D.R.'s wartime policies. How could the Communists help to dispel these myths, assist Roosevelt, and by the same stroke contribute to a durable postwar American-Soviet harmony? Such objectives clearly preoccupied Browder.

No one can suspect me of holding any prejudices in favor of capitalism, whether in America or elsewhere. I have been an advocate of socialism during all of my adult life, of socialism for America. The Communist Party is the only party of socialism in this country. But I have not the slightest hesitation in declaring that any plans for American postwar reconstruction which are based upon the introduction of socialism are in effect a repudiation of the aim to unite the majority of the nation behind the Teheran policies.

It is my considered judgment that the American people are so ill-prepared subjectively for any deep-going change in the direction of socialism that post-war plans with such an aim would not unite the nation but would further divide it. And they would divide and weaken precisely the democratic and progressive camp, while they would unite and strengthen the most reactionary forces. In their practical effect they would help the anti-Teheran forces to come to power in the United States.

If the national unity of the war period is to be extended and even strengthened in the post-war period, then we must recognize that in the United States this requires from Marxists the reaffirmation of our war-time policy that we will not raise the issue of socialism in such a form and manner as to endanger or weaken that national unity.[20]

The American Communist leader acknowledged that things might be different in other countries, although earlier in the same address, he had placed his own Party's perspectives within a "broad, democratic world-wide front." But, clearly, it was now possible and permissible to differentiate between circumstances abroad and in the United States where, after all, "even the most progressive section of the labor movement is committed to capitalism, is not even as vaguely socialistic as the British Labor Party." The strategy of defeating the ultraright required not only agility on the part of the left but clarity about essentials. The Communists were not going to become involved in a defense of the Roosevelt administration as socialistic while its opponents affirmed the virtues of free enterprise. As Browder, sarcastic, but pursuing his main point, put it, "If any one wishes to describe the existing system of capitalism in the United States as 'free enterprise,' that is all right with us, and we frankly declare that we are ready to cooperate in making this capitalism work effectively in the post-war period with the least possible burden on the people." In Browder's view, all the sloganizing about free enterprise obscured "the central fact that all Roosevelt's policies have been designed for the preservation of capitalism ['free enterprise'], have in fact strengthened capitalism, whereas the policies of his reactionary opponents would have brought capitalism very quickly into as deep a crisis as that of Hoover's administration."

The truth, as Browder saw it, was that even in wartime Roosevelt's policies had involved a minimum of government intervention. Roosevelt had not even availed himself of the possibilities of "state capitalism," as developed in Great Britain and elsewhere. As though replying to unnamed critics within his own Party, Browder insisted that there had "never been anything of socialism in Roosevelt's policies" and "every suggestion to the contrary, no matter from whence [sic] it comes, serves only to falsify the problems and confuse the issue."

Contrary to what these unnamed critics implied, the task in 1944 and thereafter would not be one of "breaking monopoly capital." In his Bridgeport address a month earlier, Browder had attracted national attention and evidently aroused "some very sharp objection" within his own Party by offering to shake hands with J. P. Morgan if the financier would "go down the line" for the Teheran policies. He now tried to explain this bizarre image. "In order that we waste no time quibbling, I now make explicit what is inherent in the thought expressed, namely, that I was not making a verbal abolition of class differences, but I was rejecting the political slogan of 'class against class' as our guide to political alignments in the next period. I spoke of Morgan symbolically as the representative of a class, and not as an individual, in which capacity I know him not at all."[21]

The Communists expected that the American ruling class would remain divided on basic policy. This division had existed throughout the New Deal and even during the war. That Browder expected this division to continue did not mean that he was "relying on the capitalists" — as the debate a year later suggested. The problem was to unite the left with as large a spectrum of nonleft opinion as possible in the hope of continuing and deepening the division of the right. Browder was not sure this could be done, but felt it was worth trying. Implying that doubts prevailed in his own ranks, he declared: "I have been challenged to produce a list of the big capitalists on either side of the issue and evaluate their relative weights in political matters. I have no such lists, nor can I make my political judgment on such a basis. Of one thing I am sure: that part of the bourgeoisie which supports Teheran *can be the decisive part* — provided it joins effectively with the whole democratic-progressive camp. The policy of supporters of Teheran must be to seek and facilitate support from all classes and groups with the working people as the main base, from the big bourgeoisie to the Communists." [Italics in the original][22]

Again, the tactic was not certain to succeed. It was, however, worth the political attempt on the following assumption: "not only the workers, farmers and middle classes are the supporters of Teheran, but also among the big bourgeoisie, the monopoly capitalists, there are those who will be our allies. Such an approach is correct even if it should turn out that we find no allies there. For should there be no allies, let the fact be established without confusions about the threat of Communist hostility having driven the poor fellows into their reactionary stand." At another point, again hedging his bets, Browder projected his postwar readiness for national unity in another way. "We Communists are opposed to permitting an explosion of class conflict in our country when the war is over. If it happens, it will not in any way be our responsibility, but that of men who did not know how to use their power in the national interest and who abandoned the nation for private greed."

There were pressures on the Communists to abandon a strategy based on national unity. Within the labor movement two powerful forces had opposed the wartime stabilization of wages. One of these was led by John L. Lewis (at that time standing outside both the A.F.L. and the C.I.O.), whose United Mine Workers had not hesitated to strike the coal fields at the most critical moments of the war. The Communists believed that these tactics flowed as much from the association of Lewis with the "America First Committee," the impressive isolationist united front, as from a regard for the miners' wages and hours. Large sections of the C.I.O. which were not, however, supporters of Lewis were also restive about the wage stabilization policies. The Communists did not deny that the workers were getting the short end of the stick. But they opposed the adherents of Walter Reuther in the United Automobile Workers (U.A.W.) union who were threatening strikes in the war industries. Late in 1944 they opposed the U.A.W.'s referendum with respect to maintaining the no-strike pledge. This nonmilitant stand was maintained even though the war was clearly approaching a favorable outcome, at least in Europe.[23] The Party sided with Philip Murray, Sidney Hillman and other center leaders who in the spring of 1945 were to meet with the United States Chamber of Commerce to formulate a Labor-Management Charter, premised on the prospect of avoiding sharp class battles in the reconversion period. Left wing labor leaders — Harry Bridges, for example — took their cue from this policy position, although both Browder and his trade union expert, Roy Hudson, did not go as far as Bridges in projecting an absolute no-strike policy for the post war period.

The Communist leadership was extremely apprehensive about postwar relations for at least one other reason. This flowed from its own past. Having been formed in the early twenties, most Communist leaders remembered the antiunion offensive of the employers at that time and the inability of the trade unions to withstand that offensive. Labor had been weakened by the 1921 economic crisis, by the Red Scare of that era, and by management's refusal to accept the wartime gains. How to avoid a repetition of that experience was a factor in their thinking.

A prerequisite of national unity was economic prosperity, which in turn required the development of postwar markets that could absorb the increased output of an economy immensely expanded by the war. The government had been underwriting the annual production of eighty-five billion dollars' worth of war goods, and the country's productive capacity had doubled. What would happen when seven million men returned from the armed forces and when the twenty million workers engaged in production of war goods had to be reintegrated into a civilian economy?[24]

In Browder's view, "some extraordinary means must be found to double the buying power of the individual consumer." Browder favored the prospect of expanded foreign markets to absorb American goods, but he pointed out that "huge foreign markets were unthinkable except under stable conditions, without international or civil wars of major proportions." Without such markets abroad there would be "no possibility" of finding "an economic foundation for national unity within the United States." Interesting in all this was the Communist leader's assumption that U.S. participation in world development was necessary and beneficial to the recovery of a war-shattered world, and that because such markets required world stability, some compact with socialist and revolutionary forces was essential. Recognition of stable prospects for development would in turn be a platform for a compact of intelligent capitalists and a nonsocialist but militant working class.

In his initial projection, at the National Committee meeting of January 7-9, 1944, the Communist leader was reticent and circumspect about those areas of domestic and foreign economic policy which touched on delicate aspects of classical Marxist theory. But he attempted to square his previous acceptance of free enterprise with the obvious need for governmental intervention. "As to the degree of governmental intervention in guaranteeing full employment, this most disputed point of all must be resolved somewhat along the lines of agreement that it shall be limited to that margin by which private enterprise fails to measure up to the standard of one hundred and fifty billion dollars annual national income or thereabouts."[25]

Browder then turned to the problem of equipping the Party for the task of implementing the new strategy. There was almost no self-critical or apologetic note in his treatment of past Party policy. He did not disavow the Leninist concept of the party as a vanguard of a special type.[26] The Party would change its name to the Communist Political Association (C.P.A.). Although some consideration had been given to dropping the word "Communist" the final decision was negative.[27] "It is conceivable that a situation might exist in which another name would be practically more expedient, and in several countries that has been found to be the case by the Marxists of such lands. It is our considered judgment that there is nothing in the situation of the United States which makes such a change from the name "Communist" to something else an expedient one. It might even be detrimental, in giving an opening to our enemies to create more confusion in the country by spreading the suspicion that the new name is a camouflage to cover direly sinister conspiracies. At the same time, the very name itself has the highest prestige in its history, and is not to be discarded lightly and without the most serious necessity." Thus, the American Communists had not embarked on a "dissolution" of a Marxist organization as such, despite the currency given to this charge a year later, both by Jacques Duclos in his April 1945 critique of Browder, and by Foster himself. They were dissolving the Party *structure,* but intended to remain as an organized force. As will be seen, Foster did not view the proposal to convert the Party into a "Political Association" as a matter of fundamentals at that time.

What concerned the Communists was to give their organization — which was already penetrating and influencing a wide variety of existing institutions —a certain legitimacy and a greater flexibility that would enable it to do more of the same. The problem was to make an adaptation to the American political system whereby the Communist impact in politics, in the labor movement, and in everything else could be increased without leaving the Communists any less a cohesive, a purposeful force. They wanted to be both a revolutionary community within themselves, and a pervasive, coherent influence in the real world where revolution was not the order of the day. Trying to overcome the inner tension between ideological commitment and the necessity for changes arising from his Party's own growth, Browder was led to re-examine the character of the Republican and Democratic parties and the American electoral system. "These parties are parties only in a formal and legal sense; they are not parties in the sense of representing well-defined alternative policies. They are coalitions of local and regional interests, diverse tendencies of political thought, and institutionalized politics from which national policy and national interest come forth in a distorted way, with much confusion and with a maximum dependence upon the personality which emerges as leader."

By contrast with Europe, this curious two-party system was specifically American. "It is an old tradition . . . which recognizes as a party only that particular combination which is in power and the combination of the opposition which is the immediate alternative to take power. All lesser political groupings are contained within the two-party system which are in fact coalitions of many groups that in most other countries would be separate parties; if the lesser group takes the name of party and becomes one of the so-called minor parties it is regarded as a sect which has withdrawn itself from the practical political life of the nation." All of this, Browder continued, had been "tremendously strengthened and buttressed against the storms of constant political changes that go on within it, by the system of direct primaries which gives all voters the opportunity to enroll under one or another of the two major parties and participate in choosing its candidates as well as the party committees and delegates to conventions.[28]

Most Americans believed that such a system guaranteed democracy. In 1940, when the Communists had been deprived of a place on the ballot in many states, there had been little significant opposition by defenders of this system. Not only the left but the Bull Moose movement of 1912 and the La Follette movement of 1924 had, as Browder put it, "bruised their heads against the stone wall" of this specifically American political structure. Only where state and local laws allowed proportional representation, as in New York, could independent candidates and minor parties play a direct role in electoral politics. The American Communists now proposed to abandon the word "party." This would be a demonstrative indication that they did not want to be a sect, and they did not believe the issue before the country was "Communism." They wanted to dramatize their commitment to something far less than an immediate socialist program at least for the United States, fearing that the alleged danger of socialism would be the main rationale for a return of the right wing to political power. Browder put the matter as follows. "Obviously, to realize the promise of Teheran the broader democratic-progressive united front must be maintained in the United States. Equally obviously, the Communists will be a part, and a small minority part, of that united front. The Communist organization will be in a long-term alliance with forces much larger than itself. It follows that in the peculiar American sense of the word the Communists will not be operating as a party, that is, with their own separate candidates in elections, except under special circumstances when they may be forced to act through 'independent candidates'."[29] In his summary of the discussion, Browder spelled out how Party members should behave in the proposed Political Association as clearly as could be done without indiscretion. "We are not, in our new course, entering any other party. The Communists are not joining the Democratic Party; the Communists are not joining the Republican Party. We are not endorsing either of the major parties. We are taking the line of issues and not of parties, and of choosing men as they stand for or against issues without regard to party labels. When I say we are not entering parties or endorsing parties, I don't mean we have any objections to our individual members registering in one or another of the parties when their local community life calls for it and their associates and fellows are following that course. But I mean that the Communist movement and our organization is not committed to any party label or any party organization. We are independent, in the same way as the great bulk of America's independent voters who make up fully one-third of the total voting strength of the country and who are not committed to either of the major parties, though most of them are registered in one or the other."[30]

Before turning to Foster's rebuttal of Browder's views, one final aspect of this ambitious political architecture requires comment. Browder was conscious that the new strategic perspective and even its tactical aspects had to be justified in terms of the underlying, classical ideology. In this regard he was rather careful, remarkably pragmatic, even tentative. Only by implication did he suggest that his strategy would serve the Soviet interest, for he presented the new strategy as being in the interest of both capitalism and socialism. Some of his listeners undoubtedly felt that the Soviet Union was so badly damaged in the war that a long period of peace with the West was indispensable. A world revolutionary crisis was held to be harmful, and Browder was able to appear, in this sense, as favoring a policy which the "land of Socialism" desperately needed. But since no full-fledged analysis of the changes within capitalist society was ever made, Browder did not advance any full-blown revisionism in this sense.[31] Browder did, however, appeal to a theme which had become characteristic of the American Communists, namely that their relative success entitled them to do some pioneering along the Marxist frontiers. In subsequent years this theme reappeared in Foster's thinking.[32]

Browder struck notes of both modesty and theoretical daring. At one point, the accent was all pragmatic. "We are not prepared to give any broad, theoretical generalization for this period," he declared. The coexistence of rival systems, he continued, had been no more than a possibility until the summit meeting of Roosevelt, Stalin and Churchill. "We could not unconditionally throw our forces into this new period while it was still merely a possibility, but now that this possibility has been confirmed by the agreement of Teheran, we know we can feel absolutely certain that we have crossed the borderline from the past and have definitely entered the present." Browder was quite explicit in denying that the Party's new policy could be achieved without militancy or struggle. "It will require political struggles, but these will be struggles for unity in the nation, not struggles that will break that unity; struggles against the enemies for which we will have to find new means and forms; of unity and for uniting with everyone who recognizes, even indistinctly, but enough to take the first steps, the need of going along the road of the Teheran conference."

Yet an unorthodox path had been charted. The unknown was exciting. And here Browder said some curious things.

> For the first time we are meeting and solving problems for which there are no precedents in history and no formulas from the classics which gave us the answer. Perhaps we could say that our Party is standing on its own feet for the first time. Marxism was never a series of dogmas and formulas; it was never a catalogue of prohibitions listing the things we must not do irrespective of new developments and new situations; it does not tell us that things cannot be done; it tells us how to do the things that have to be done, the things that history has posed as necessary and indispensable tasks. Marxism is a theory of deeds, not of "don'ts." Marxism is therefore a positive, dynamic creative force, and it is such a great social power precisely because it takes living reality as its starting point. It has always regarded the scientific knowledge of the past

as a basis for meeting the new and unprecedented problems of the present and the future. And the largest problems today are new in a very basic sense.

True, according to all of the textbooks of the past, we are departing from orthodoxy, because none of our textbooks forsaw or even predicted a long period of peaceful relations in the world before the general advent of Socialism. But now we are setting our course to realize the possibilities inherent in the present situation of what would have been described in the past as an evolutionary development of the transition period — provided of course that we can successfully meet our responsibilities.

Then, adding a more philosophical fillip, he concluded . . . "History has never yet been known to follow anyone's private blueprints. The great turning points of history are in this sense always unexpected; there is always something fresh in them that has to be fundamentally evaluated. We are in such a period today."[33]

At the January 7-9, 1944, meeting, the challenge to most of these propositions came from Foster, and from the Philadelphia organizer, Sam Darcy. [34] Ten days later, the National Committee met again. By this time Foster had put his views down in a letter to every Committee member. The rank and file was not to read the letter until a year later, when it was made public after the Duclos article gave excerpts from it. The full weight and flavor of Foster's views cannot be appreciated without going back to his writings of 1941, at the point when the "war had changed in character." In March 1941 Foster had made the following analysis. "The world capitalist system is much weaker internally, and consequently it is less able to stand the shocks of war and revolution than it was at the inception of the world war. There are four basic paths along which the world's anti-capitalist forces are now developing — the expansion of the Soviet Union in power and world influence, the spread of the national liberation movement in the colonial and sem-colonial countries, the growth of an explosive national indendence movement along the conquered peoples and oppressed nationalities of Europe, and the development of a revolutionary, anti-war, anti-imperialist, anti-capitalist spirit among the workers and toilers of the warring capitalist empires. These four great anti-capitalist world streams beat against a common enemy, the capitalist system itself, and as the war advances they are certain to converge more and more towards one great irresistible anti-capitalist river."[35]

This language was modified once the Soviet Union became allied with the United States and Great Britain, but the basic concept of a cataclysmic crisis and a multipronged advance of socialism did not change in Foster's thinking. Nor did the experience of the wartime alliance alter Foster's apprehensions about the postwar period. Writing in *New Masses* on December 14, 1943 — just when Browder was making his Bridgeport speech — Foster envisaged a danger from the right wing of American politics, a right wing which was, for him, the political expression of a "rampant American imperialism." These circles were challenging Roosevelt's conduct of the war on both the domestic and foreign planes. If they came to power they would necessarily reverse the whole course.

In his critique of Browder in the letter to the January 20, 1944, meeting, Foster alluded to his *New Masses* article and cited his own concept of a rampant American imperialism, stemming from what Foster believed were the main circles of American capitalism.[36] Such a formulation was more accurate, he felt, than the one put forth by Browder. But his critique was more trenchant and specific. "In attempting to apply the Teheran decisions to the United States," Browder had been mistaken in drawing "a perspective of a smoothly working national unity, including the decisive sections of American finance capital, not only during the war but also in the postwar." In this picture, Foster complained, "American imperialism virtually disappears, there remains hardly a trace of the class struggle, and socialism plays practically no role whatever."

In Foster's view, Browder had underestimated "the deepening of the crisis of world capitalism caused by the war." Indeed, he suffered from the illusion that capitalism had "somehow been rejuvenated and was entering a new period of expansion and growth." Foster admitted there might be a "temporary postwar economic boom in some countries and possibly also an increase in the productive forces." But central to his analysis was the concept of a "badly-weakened world capitalist system whose weakness would also be felt in post-war United States." And, as he was to emphasize throughout the next twelve years, this weakness could operate only to enhance American imperialist aggressiveness. It could not be expected to facilitate any compromise with Socialism.

To Foster, even more grave was "the idea that the main body of American finance capital" was then or could be "incorporated into the national unity necessary to carry out the decisions of the Teheran conference in a democratic and progressive spirit." Foster found it most disturbing that Browder was "making policy calling for new relations between two whole classes, the working class and the capitalist class." It was "unfounded" optimism to believe that big business could take a progressive stand either in winning the war or in leading postwar reconstruction. "The plain fact, and we must never lose sight of it, is that American big capital cannot be depended upon to cooperate with the workers and other classes in carrying out the decisions of Teheran, much less lead the nation in doing so."

Foster's view of the "decisive sections of finance capital" was plainly different from Browder's. Foster and Browder differed also in judging the Roosevelt administration. The Communists must not, in Foster's judgment, "trail after the decisive sections of capital." The task was to "rally the great popular masses of the people and resist the forces of big capital now, during the war, and also to curb their power drastically in the post-war period." As for Roosevelt's administration, its progressive military and political policies "had come, not from the main forces of finance capital, but from the broad masses of people" and there was "no reason to suppose that this situation would alter in the foreseeable future." The Roosevelt administration was "in fact, if not formally, a coalition among the workers, the middle class elements and the more liberal sections of the bourgeoisie." Thus, while Browder saw the Roosevelt regime as essentially the expression of "intelligent capitalists" Foster saw it as a type of Popular Front.

Roosevelt was opposed by the big monopolists, who were relying on a return to power of the Republican Party to "get rid of the government and trade union hindrances that irked them so much under the New Deal, so they could branch out into the active imperialist regime they had in mind." Foster continued: "The United States is not Czechoslovakia or Greece. It is not Great Britain. Despite its war injuries, which are more serious than appears at first glance, it will nevertheless emerge from this war by far the most powerful capitalist nation in the world. And its great industrial rulers will not be inclined to make such concessions as is now being done by the capitalists of some occupied countries, who are even accepting Communists in the cabinets. American finance capital has not been seriously chastened by the war. It does not consider this war as a world defeat for monopoly capital (which it doubtless is) after which its job will be to assume a responsible attitude toward the world capitalist system and to work out a progressive domestic program with democratic forces. It is strong, greedy and aggressive."[37]

Foster's essential conclusion was summed up in the statement: "Comrade Browder goes too far when he says that world capitalism and world Socialism have learned to live peacefully together." It was a mistake to suggest, as the Bridgeport speech had done, that "Britain and the United States had closed the books, finally and forever, upon their old expectation that the Soviet Union as a Socialist country was going to disappear some day."

The future would prove otherwise. "In my judgment," Foster commented, "it will be quite different from the long period of peaceful class collaboration and social advance, in which the monopolists are progressively collaborating that Comarde Browder seems to envisage. The gravity of the world's post-war reconstruction problems, which our country will also feel, and the sharp contradictions in class interests involved, will not permit such harmonious progress."

Foster expected that the decisive sections of capital, hostile to the Roosevelt administration, would also be unreconciled "to the far-reaching economic programs, including government intervention in industry on an unprecedented scale" that would be "necessary to guard our country from an economic collapse worse than that of 1929." Indeed, "Big Business could not be expected to tolerate a repetition of the New Deal. It could therefore be expected, what with the growing fascist spirit in its ranks and the tricks it has learned from Hitler, that the monopolists would adopt, if necessary, the most drastic means to clip the strength of labor and to prevent the return of any popular, progressive government."

Quite in distinction to Browder's view that the Communists should propose only such measures as the most decisive segments of capital would swallow, Foster drew upon the Populist and earlier Socialist concepts in his thinking, heavily influenced as it was by the experience of the immediate post-World War I era. "The counter-program of the progressive, win-the-war, win-the-peace

forces to the reactionary 'free enterprise' or unrestrained monopoly program of the reactionaries does not now contain demands
for nationalization of the banks, railroads or other industries, and
it will not in the immediate post-war situation. But the grave
difficulties that will confront capitalism all over the world after
this war, not excluding American capitalism, will surely eventually raise the need and popularity of such demands."

The Communist Party chairman concluded his letter with a
few passages on the two-party system and socialism. He agreed
with Browder that the situation was "very much not ripe for a
new political party line-up in the United States," but he felt that
this could "by no means be excluded permanently." The concept
of a Political Association, functioning as an independent non-
party factor within the existing system, was faulty mainly because it left "the impression that the Communists no longer look
beyond the present two-party line-up even in the most eventual
sense." Such a position underestimated "the political initiative of
the democratic masses" and was an "overestimation of their acceptance of the bourgeois leadership of the two main parties."

Granted that socialism would "not be a political issue in the
United States in the early post-war period," Foster thought it
would "nevertheless be a question of great and growing mass interest and influence." The reasons Foster gave for this view disclosed the wider aspects of his thinking. He spoke of the "possibility that some countries of Europe might adopt Socialism at the
close of the war." Beyond that consideration, he also believed
that "a mass interest" in socialism would be generated by the
"world-shaking demonstration of the power and success" of this
system and what he expected would be the "miracles" of Soviet
reconstruction. Moreover, with the "world capitalist system badly injured," there would be definite tendencies for the peoples in
all countries to learn from the Soviet regime and to adapt to their
own problems such features as they could from the obviously successful and flourishing Socialist Soviet Union. The whole question
of the advance to Socialism "would be in for a fresh discussion in
the new world conditions."

It is noteworthy that Foster took no exception to the change in
name and structure which Browder had proposed for the Communist Party. Fifteen months later Duclos was to take Foster,
as well as Browder, to task for this change. Foster clearly viewed
the move neither as a "dissolution" nor as a "liquidation" (as he

was later to charge), but as a "reorganization of the Party." He was to explain in a curious appendix to his own letter when it was finally published — after his triumph over Browder — that "when Comrade Browder proposed his liquidatory step several members of the National Board raised objections to it, and, of course, I opposed it and voted against it."[38] But, he argued, things had proceeded so far by January 20, 1944, "that I considered the reorganization of the Party into the C.P.A. as a virtually accomplished fact. It had already been publicly announced and endorsed . . . and in fact, the Party was already in the preliminary stages or reorganization. Consequently, I felt that further agitation of the matter was hopeless for the time being and could only cause useless strife and confusion in our ranks. So I left the whole question out of my letter to the National Committee. The immediate task, as I saw it, was for me to help keep the C.P.A. in fact, if not in name, the Communist Party."

This explanation is not the whole truth, but it brings us to the hidden history both of Foster's acceptance of the main trend of Communist political development (and his acceptance of the chairmanship of what was to become the Association at the May 1944 convention) and of the mysteries of the Duclos article which triggered Browder's overturn.

# 4 SANCTION FROM DIMITROV AND DOOM BY DUCLOS

The American Communists went through the first months of 1944 to the convention in May, which transformed their Party into a Political Association, with great dynamism. They were possessed by a sense of traversing the frontiers of "creative Marxism." Their new policy caused a genuine discussion throughout the left. Many left-liberal opponents shook their head in sarcastic disbelief.[1] There were many doubts about the new policy in the Party's own ranks, but these were dispelled by the recruitment of new members, the striking improvement in what the Communists considered a satisfactory membership "composition," and the signs of their increasing acceptance in American political life. The doubts were all the more easily overcome because the fundamental objections which William Z. Foster had voiced in the January and February leadership meetings were kept from the rank and file.

In April 1944 issue of *The Communist*, a vivid picture of the recruiting campaign was given by the Party secretary for Ohio, Arnold Johnson.[2] He reported that 1,233 new members had joined in twelve weeks. The Cleveland organization, with 669 new members, now had the "largest membership in its history." The same was true in Youngstown and Toledo, where recruitment, having doubled in 1943 over the previous year, had doubled again early in 1944. Earl Browder spoke to a Cleveland meeting at which Democratic and Republican city councilmen shared the platform and "a number of leading Negro Democrats and some Negro Republicans joined" the Party's ranks "after they read Browder's report and the decisions of the National Committee." Johnson was optimistic because, whereas in 1943 only 30 percent of the previous year's recruits had been retained, by the beginning of 1944 as many as 85 percent of the members gained the year before had been re-enrolled. "We have brought into our ranks a far larger number of trade union leaders, especially local officers, shop stewards and others," the Ohio secretary continued. "In the course of all these discussions we have heard of only isolated cases of those who did not fully agree with the new policies proposed by our National Committee. Of the several thousand who were visited, only a handful of 'professional sympathizers' shook their heads in skepticism." It was Johnson's judgement that the new policies had "tremendous support among the masses, particularly among those who are active and are concerned about public policy."

The inaugural convention of the new organization, for which Browder produced a full-length book elaborating on his January report, came on the eve of the major developments in the war itself — the arrival of the Soviet armies into eastern Europe and the Anglo-American landing in Normandy. The latter event eclipsed the "second front" issue. It heightened the universal sense that a new era was in the making. By this time, moreover, President Roosevelt had overcome his initial reluctance to run for a fourth term, partly as a result of the initiative taken on his behalf in the labor movement. The Communists felt they had contributed to this initiative.[3] Moreover, the sharp antagonism to Roosevelt's policy, expressed in the Republican's choice of Thomas E. Dewey as their presidential candidate, confirmed the Communist judgment that a profound rift on both domestic and external policy was manifest in the ranks of American capitalism.[4] The Communists threw themselves wholeheartedly into the campaign.

They were so singleminded in support of Roosevelt that in the disagreement between the C.I.O. and the top level Democratic Party leaders over the selection of a new running mate — which produced the candidacy of Harry Truman, of Missouri, at the expense of Vice-President Henry A. Wallace — the Communists did not side with Sidney Hillman and Philip Murray, the C.I.O. leaders, who favored Wallace. In justifying their acceptance of Truman, Communist spokesmen argued that a less controversial figure than Wallace might consolidate national unity around the Teheran policy.[5] They worked to maintain such unity because they feared it would not survive in the postwar period, and because it was the basis of their entire strategy.

A critical factor in the upswing of the Communist movement throughout 1944 was the outward harmony of its leadership. The membership knew nothing of the crisis among their leaders. Foster had opposed the Teheran projections at the January 7-9, 1944, meeting of the Political Committee, but had been dissuaded from pressing his views. On January 9, Foster spoke on a nation-wide radio hookup, advertising Browder's policies, although the record shows he had disagreed with them that very weekend.[6] On January 20 he drew up a letter to the National Committee out-lining his opposition in detail; it was this letter which most Na-tional Committee members saw for the first time at the February 8, 1944, meeting. On this occasion, Foster received support from no one except the Party's secretary in eastern Pennsylvania, Sam-uel Adams Darcy. The latter, a veteran of Party activities in Minnesota, California, and Massachusetts and a member of the Party's delegation to the Comintern Congress in 1935, accepted the political implications of Browder's proposals but questioned their economic foundations. He was not prepared to say that be-cause the American economy had greatly expanded its productive capacity during the war, American capitalism would necessarily seek, in the interest of stable markets, a new relationship with the Soviet Union.[7] Foster himself did not press his views. To one re-porter who evidently had access to the Party's inner sanctum, Foster denied any differences with Browder's policy.[8] Foster not only assumed the chairmanship of the newly formed Communist Political Association in May but he presided over the commission which examined Darcy's insubordination and decided upon Darcy's expulsion.[9]

A year later, in response to the widespread query in Communist circles as to why he had concealed his own views, Foster was to argue that if he had not done so, he might have faced disciplinary measures, and these would have precipitated a profound Party crisis. Bearing in mind the long history of the Foster-Browder antagonism and the fact that they had been at loggerheads at key points of policy since the midthirties, Foster's apprehensions were probably well grounded. Browder was on the verge of cutting down his opponent without mercy. The transcripts of the January-February meeting reveal a tone very hostile to Foster.[10]

Yet the basic explanation for Foster's reticence lies on another plane: it will be found in the interpretation which the American Communist leaders placed on the development in the internation-al Communist movement and the signs which both Browder and Foster were receiving from abroad. At that moment, Browder had no opportunity for direct consultation either with the Soviet leadership or with his close friends in the caretaker apparatus winding up the affairs of the Comintern. After all, Moscow was preoccupied with the war. But there is particular evidence — as will be indicated shortly — that Browder had direct signs from Moscow approving his course. Browder also seized upon general political evidence, stemming mainly from the dissolution of the International, in support of his outlook. Foster was aware of the signs Browder was receiving, which explains his conduct.

For example, Browder early in 1944 received a congratulatory letter from André Marty, the French Communist leader who had only a short while before gone from his wartime refuge in Moscow to Algiers where the French Communist leaders had by then come to terms with General Charles de Gaulle. Marty's prestige was considerable. He had been commissar of the International Brigades during the Spanish Civil War and was a signatory of the final declaration dissolving the Comintern the previous June. In his letter, Marty praised Browder's January 7, 1944, address to the Party's Political Committee as a "beautiful speech," and added "We are publishing it in our theoretical magazine."[11]

Once the controversy with Foster sharpened Browder gained still another reassurance. This reassurance not only explains his self-confidence in proceeding with the transformation of the Party but is also the key to understanding why Foster did not press his differences and why Browder took no disciplinary action against Foster, despite his threat to do so. It is also one clue to the mysteries of the Duclos article a year later.

In one of his extensive interviews with me in August 1965, Browder declared that he had sent the transcript of the January and February 1944 discussions to Georgi Dimitrov, former Comintern general secretary who was then still in Moscow.[12] Such action conformed to long-time Comintern practice. Deep divisions of opinion in any Party were normally submitted to the central organization with as full a documentation as possible. Browder shrugged off my question as to why he felt obliged to send the Party's documents to Moscow *ten month's after the Comintern's dissolution.* He implied that habits of a lifetime persisted. Browder further declared that he received support for his own policies in the form of the advice from Dimitrov to Foster that the latter should not press his differences. When I asked Browder how he knew this to be true, he replied that he had the radio code permitting communication with the former Comintern chief, and he personally communicated to Foster the cabled message from Dimitrov.

If true — and there seems no reason to doubt this account since it is so much in harmony with the record of the men involved — this episode shows why Browder believed he had Moscow's sanction for his course. Foster was being advised by Dimitrov not to press the argument with Browder. This is also why Browder did not press Foster to the point of "organizational measures," although such measures had been threatened. Browder's admission of reassuring contact with Dimitrov also explains Foster's effort to support Browder's policy while cautiously proposing what he believed were necessary modifications. Foster, like Browder, knew from bitter experience that Dimitrov's advice was not lightly to be dismissed — even though the Comintern had been dissolved.

Browder's testimony also explains where Duclos got the documentation that was so authentic that it astonished the American Communists in May 1945. Foster himself did not press his case abroad, as many Party members assumed. His views had been made known to Dimitrov, to Dimitri Z. Manuilsky, and to other leaders of the dissolved Communist International *by Browder*, who had sent the most intimate American Party documents to Moscow. This explains why Foster was obviously as much surprised by the Duclos article as everyone else in the Communist ranks.

In the autumn of 1944, the American Communists received evidence in addition to Dimitrov's apparent approval to justify confidence in the validity of their new policy. On the eve of the successful re-election of President Roosevelt, the most authoritative figure in the Communist world, Marshal Stalin, made a triumphal address on the occasion of the annual celebration of the anniversary of the Russian Revolution. By this time, Stalin had met with Churchill and had reached what both leaders believed was a satisfactory division of the European and Mediterranean spheres of influence.[13] Although sharp divisions among the Allies persisted over the structure of the United Nations, then being debated at the Dumbarton Oaks conference, and over the political settlement in Poland, Stalin's review of the military and political scene contained the following judgment. "Differences do exist, of course, and they will arise on a number of other issues as well. Differences of opinion are to be found even among people in one and the same party. They are all the more bound to occur between representatives of different states and different parties. The surprising thing is not that differences exist, but that there are so few of them and that as a rule in practically every case they are resolved in a spirit of unity and coordination among the three great powers."

The Soviet leader then dealt with the future of the Anglo-Soviet-American coalition on precisely that wave length to which the ears of the American Communist leaders were attuned. "The alliance between the USSR, Great Britain and the United States is founded not on casual, short-lived considerations but on vital and lasting interests. There need be no doubt that, having stood the strain of over three years of war and being sealed in the blood of nations risen in defense of their liberty and honor, the fighting alliance of the democratic powers will all the more certainly stand the strain of the concluding phase of the war."[14]

Was this but an understandable reassurance to the war-ravaged Soviet people? Was there in Stalin's phrase "the concluding phase of the war" the implicit suggestion that something else might happen in the postwar period? If such subtleties engendered doubts among American Communist leaders, they showed few signs of it. On the contrary, the perspective which had been advanced as a purely pragmatic matter, without any theoretical pretensions, almost as a political ploy in January, became by the end of 1944 a prognosis of the course of history. In his book *Teheran*, Browder had by mid-May ambitiously undertaken to work out the modalities whereby both American and British capitalism could resolve their antagonisms in the development of the underdeveloped areas. The *possibility* that America *could* develop the domestic and international markets required by the greatly expanded economic capacity both by assisting the reconstruction of Communist-led states and by a vastly increasing domestic living standards soon came to mean that all this *would of necessity* come about. At the outset, Browder's projections implicitly and explicitly included the necessity of great political struggle if these possibilities were to be realized. But by the end of 1944, the tentative and possible aspects of his projections became certain and inevitable in the popularization of his concepts. Some of Browder's closest co-workers, notably Robert Minor, soon converted the whole proposition into a dogma of a new kind in the name of abandoning dogma.[15] Those Communist commentators who by virtue of having to make daily comment on changing realities were inclined to be more realistic, together with some of the more intellectually mobile Communist leaders, felt the deep need to find a more satisfactory theoretical basis for the Teheran policy. It could not be simply a tentative projection of transitory political utility, but had, in Communist eyes, to be *theoretically* grounded.[16]

By the winter of 1944-45 it was plain that, although some satisfactory trends were at work, perplexing clouds also hung over the dawn of the new day. The Communists derived great satisfaction from the London meetings at which the leaders of the C.I.O., the British Trades Union Congress, the French and Italian Confederations of Labor, and the Soviet Trade Union Council met to work out the terms of a new international labor center. On the other hand, within the C.I.O. itself and within the American labor movement generally, there was intense dissatisfaction with the "Little Steel" wage stabilization formula. Walter Reuther became president of the important United Automobile Workers (U.A.W.), a C.I.O. affiliate. Although still surrounded by an executive board of political opponents, Reuther became a serious power because of his championship of the rank and file's dissatisfaction, The U.A.W. almost abandoned the no-strike pledge during the "Battle of the Bulge" in December 1944. The Communists were furious with Reuther, but the auto workers liked his militancy.

Although the leaders of both major American labor organizations were able to work out with the Chamber of Commerce a Labor-Management Charter, premised on avoiding sharp class battles after the war — a move which the Communists hailed — reconversion was bound to be a stormy process. Was it not illusory to imagine that the American working class would forego the use of the strike weapon after the war? The Communist leaders were themselves divided on the emphasis that should be placed on the avoidance of strikes. Both Browder and his chief trade union specialist, Roy Hudson, had strong doubts about the validity of the postwar no-strike pledge which had just been advanced by the leading left wing unionist, Harry Bridges. Neither Browder nor Hudson was prepared to recommend such a pledge. But they had implied as much and had sanctioned the idea. If they were embarrassed when Bridges made the pledge on the basis of his understanding of Communist policy, they did not say so.[17]

In April 1945, at the Communist Political Association's first

National Committee meeting since the previous May — a ten-month interval — proposals were made for a general review of policy. On the day of Roosevelt's death, April 12, 1945, Browder was quick to issue a statement expressing the hope that the new president would carry out "Roosevelt's legacy." The fervent wish for continuity of policy hardly concealed the fear that the successor might not continue on Roosevelt's course.

It was evident in the weeks preceding the San Francisco meeting of the United Nations which opened at the end of April, 1945, that deep, unsettled problems existed between Moscow and Washington. Widely divergent interpretations of the Yalta agreement were separating Russia and America. The chief mover of a sharp change of tone toward Moscow on the eve of the UN's founding session was Ambassador W. Averell Harriman, whom the American Communists had hitherto included within the pro-Teheran segment of the ruling class, indeed had considered one of Roosevelt's decisive aides.[18] Were these but passing storm-clouds? Or was a change taking place in American-Soviet relations of so fundamental a kind as to make a fresh look at the assumptions of American Communist policy necessary?

By this time, Browder had intimations that the French Communists were not in agreement with his course.[19] Then the lightning struck: the famous Duclos article appeared in the French Communist monthly magazine, *Cahiers du Communisme*, for April 1945.[20] In its opening passages, it feigned to be merely an informational essay directed to those French readers who had inquired as to what was happening in American Communist ranks. The views of Browder, Foster, and Darcy were presented as though only factual matters were involved. But the inner structure of the article and the source of the factual evidence made it plain that a political judgment was being made. Browder's conception of international relations was being challenged, and so was the internal course of the American Communist movement. In this sense, the Duclos article is one of the crucial and most mystifying milestones of wartime and postwar Communist policy.

It was the central judgment of the Duclos article that "Earl Browder declared, in effect, that at Teheran capitalism and socialism had begun to find the means of peaceful coexistence and collaboration in the framework of one and the same world; he added that the Teheran accords regarding common policy presupposed common efforts with a view to reducing to a minimum or completely suppressing methods of struggle and opposition of force in the solution of the internal problems of each country. The Teheran agreements mean to Earl Browder that the greatest part of Europe, west of the Soviet Union, will probably be reconstituted on a bourgeois-democratic basis, and not on a fascist or Soviet basis."[21]

With respect to these matters, and with respect to his domestic propositions, Browder was then declared to have drawn "erroneous conclusions in no wise flowing from a Marxist analysis of the situation;" he had made himself "the protagonist of a false concept of social evolution in general, and in the first place the social evolution of the United States." Evidently, Duclos did not approve of the reconstitution of Western Europe on a "non-Soviet basis," which, in the light of French Communist policy, was puzzling. The Duclos article concluded with the following summary. "By transforming the Teheran declaration of the Allied governments, which is a document of a diplomatic character, into a political platform of class peace in the United States in the postwar period, the American Communists are deforming in a radical way the meaning of the Teheran declaration and are sowing dangerous opportunist illusions which will exercise a negative influence on the American labor movement if they are not met with the necessary reply."

The Duclos article took particular exception to the purely internal, American, aspect of Browder's policy — the transformation of the Party into the Political Association. The criticism of this transformation, was stressed by its selections from Foster's January 20, 1944, letter to the Party's National Committee. The article took issue with Foster because he had not seemed to realize that the change in name and structure of the American Communists was not merely a change in form, but "ended in practice in the liquidation of the independent party of the working class in the U.S." In Paris as well as Moscow, Communist leaders clearly believed that the American Communists had dissolved as an organized force. There could be no more grievous sin.

The Duclos article went further. "Despite declarations regarding recognition of the principles of Marxism, one is witnessing a notorious revision of Marxism on the part of Browder and his supporters, a revision which is expressed in the concept of a long-term class peace in the United States, of the possibility of the suppression of the class struggle in the postwar period and of the establishment of harmony between labor and capital." The article adduced evidence that thousands of Party members had not re-registered in the spring of 1944. Here Duclos was using altogether interim figures — and this was one reason why the article proved so astonishing to the American Communist leaders. Important gains, particularly among industrial workers, were ignored by Duclos. Moreover, the article alluded to the antimonopoly posi-tion of the former vice-president, Henry Wallace, in laudatory terms. This contrasted strongly with the lack of enthusiasm for Wallace as a person and as a representative of a political trend which the Communists had shown the previous summer.

In these respects the article seemed to be arguing that the French Party's attack on the "men of the trusts" was a model for the American Communists — as though the role of American big business in the course of the war could be equated with the collaboration of French big business. The essential differences in the relationship of class forces between American and Europe was being denied. Even if it were argued that the American Com-munists had not conducted a vigorous opposition to the advan-tage which big business had taken of the working class, it could not be argued that in the United States the capitalists as a class had betrayed the nation. In France they had. Thus, the Duclos article called into question exactly that adaptation of Commu-nist policy to particular national conditions which, in the eyes of the U.S. Communist leaders, had been sanctioned by the dis-solution of the International.

Because the American Communists had not, in their own minds, dissolved their party simply by the act of giving it an-other name and by declining to use it as a distinct electoral force — and this was plain from Foster's own view of the matter — the Duclos article was ambiguous. It was factually inaccurate. And it lacked comprehension of the U.S. scene. It could be ac-cepted only in the sense of forecasting an era of "class against class" confrontation in the postwar period. Duclos was demand-ing that the American Communists return to a political posture which had not served them well in the past and which they were trying to avoid in the future in order to build a more effective American Communist movement and thus contribute to inter-national Communism in terms of what they believed was its new strategy.

The international implications were, therefore, even more

mystifying. Duclos was denying the prospect of peaceful co-existence as a new stage in the struggle between two systems. He was denying the validity of seeking to avoid civil war. By stressing the purely diplomatic character of the Teheran accords, he was suggesting that a polarization between the Soviet Union and its Western allies had been in the cards throughout the war and would dominate the postwar period. He was suggesting, if taken literally, that the whole of Europe was bound to be the arena of Soviet as well as native Communist ambitions.

All this had been put down on paper between February and April 1945, when only the proponents of an immediate "get-tough" policy in the United States and Britain were projecting such a perspective. No one had done so on the Communist side, at least in public. The difficulty for the American Communists in comprehending the Duclos article was enhanced by the fact tha no Communist party, including the French, was making such propositions the basis of policy at that time. The French Party itself had just taken great pains to avoid civil war. The avoid-ance of civil war was also the theme of all the Communists who took up positions of relative importance in Eastern Europe, among them men who had been in Moscow during the war. Few in the international Communist movement were talking civil war at that point. One exception was the Yugoslav Communist Party, which believed it had found in the framework of national liberation precisely the way to destroy bourgeois political forma-tions. The Greek Communists offered the other exception, but the first round of civil war in Athens, in December 1944 and January 1945 had come to an uneasy halt, partly because the Soviet Union had indicated its unwillingness to support a civil war.

Was this article then the expression of a particular viewpoint, peculiar to the French? Browder tried for a time to sustain this view. The difficulty with this assumption was twofold. Nothing in the experience of the American C.P. leaders suggested that so authoritative a party as the French would make a public crit-icism of another party without clearance in Moscow. Abstractly considered, the dissolution of the International made such bilat-eral criticism possible. Yet all the actors in the drama were still fresh from a tradition which precluded such an interpretation. Moreover, the internal evidence was confusing. Whereas in some respects the Duclos article had domestic French references (for example, in its allusion to "men of the trusts") certain documentary evidence in its critique was unlikely to have been available in Paris. Allusions to the Proceedings of the May 1944 convention raised no questions since these Proceedings had been sent far and wide; the same was true for the references to Browder's January 8, 1944, report and his book, *Teheran*. The difficulty lay with citations of articles which appeared in the American Party press early in 1944, when Duclos was still in hiding in a Paris suburb and when the French Communist press was illegal, indeed, before Paris had been liberated. The article cited by Duclos could have been available only from one news-gathering organization, the Soviet agency TASS. Moreover, the Foster letter to the National Committee of January 20, 1944, and the debates in the Political Committee of January and February 1944 had been communicated only to Dimitrov in Moscow. They must have been made available to Duclos, if in fact he was the author of the article at all.

Some American Communists speculated that Foster had by devious ways gotten his case abroad. But Browder and Foster and the men closest to them in the American Communist leadership knew that this was not the case. Bearing in mind that the documentation of the January 1944 differences had gone to Moscow, Duclos had to be viewed as a spokesman for powerful men in Moscow. But were these men the former secretaries of the International, or was the C.P.S.U. directly involved? On all the assumptions of past experience, the Soviet Communists themselves were involved.[22] This gave the matter a totally different dimension.

Had Stalin early in 1945 changed his view expressed in November 1944 or was the Soviet commitment to a new world relationship, implied in his statements in November 1944, and indeed from 1942 onwards, nothing but a ruse? Was a struggle between opposing tendencies going on within the Soviet party and the international movement? If Moscow had sought no more than a correction of American Communist policy, then why was the criticism made publicly? And why was it peremptory and sweeping?

At that time, nobody asked still another question, one based on a scrutiny of the exact timing of the article and the strains in the relations between Moscow and Washington; namely, whether the article was a "diplomatic document." It had been written, as is clear from the references to the Yalta agreement and to President Roosevelt, between February 1945 and April 12, 1945. The article may have been a Soviet blunderbuss in the delicate post-Yalta bargaining. The threat of a more militant posture by the American Communists conceivably was being used to put pressure on Washington. So cynical an explanation could not recommend itself to such true believers as the American Communist leaders, despite the many instances they had known of such behavior by Moscow toward foreign Communists.

### Initial Reactions — Pained and Uncertain

The members of the C.P.A.'s National Board — the equivalent of the Political Committee, or the "Polburo," in the Party's nomenclature — had the Duclos article in front of them at least as early as May 16, 1945. At that point it had not yet been published by the *New York World-Telegram*. The Communist leaders were discussing how to present the article to party members. The evidence — which comes from the stenogram of the Board's meetings of May 22-23 — confirms that Earl Browder with Dennis and Foster, had already met with two important French Communist leaders in Washington, both of whom were en route to San Francisco for the founding session of the United Nations and of the World Federation of Trade Unions. Both French leaders had confirmed that the Duclos article presented a serious challenge to the American Communist leadership.[23]

It is exceptionally interesting and important to study the next three meetings — the National Board meeting of May 22-23, the Board's meeting on June 2 (at which time the first votes took place), and the first and enlarged meeting of the C.P.A.'s National Committee on June 18-20, 1945. At this last gathering, the leaders of the state organizations and prominent "influentials" in the American trade union movement were present and participated in the discussion of what course American Communism should take. At these three meetings, the small group who made up the Communist leadership made the crucial decisions about the course of the American Communist movement for the next twelve years. These policy decisions were made by mid-June — well before the membership began to discuss future policy in the light of Duclos article. The subsequent upheaval was anticlimactic.

Earlier, at the May 16, 1945, meeting the American Communist leaders were by no means agreed that Duclos was entirely right, nor that Foster had been sound enough in 1944 to be upheld a year later. They did not feel that the Party's dissolution had constituted the liquidation of the Communist vanguard. Most important, all of them — including Foster — wanted Browder to lead their movement through reasonable self-examination and a safe passage into the new political situation. Foster proposed a telegram to Duclos saying that the American comrades agreed with and accepted the basic content if not all of his criticism, but assuring Duclos that the American Communist forces were "solidly united and functioning actively politically." This phrasing of the proposed telegram suggests that Foster was himself astonished by the scope and force of the Duclos article, and unprepared to accept it *in toto*. Other leaders were even more astonished. The telegram was held in abeyance.

At the May 22-23 meeting, the veteran leader and organizational director, John Williamson, complained: "A year and a half went by without any indication of other Marxists having different opinion from ours and then we receive an article which is a political blast." Williamson noted that the peremptory way in which the Duclos article was written was "the way you deal with a leadership in the last stage of political struggle against it, and not as though raising criticism in the initial stage of trying to correct it." Moreover, Williamson could not accept Foster's attempt to make his proposals of January 1944 appear retroactively justified. Williamson told Foster: "I don't think your position was basically the same as the Duclos article."

Elizabeth Gurley Flynn had come to Communist leadership, as she herself lamented, "from the top," having been recruited in the midthirties because of her great fame as a onetime "Wobblie" (I.W.W.) leader and without any experience either within the American movement or in the Comintern. She now felt that "Duclos did something catastrophic." She was not going to be convinced, she said, simply because the criticism came from the French comrades. "I must be convinced on the merits of what I read and the sense it makes to me." She took issue with the idea that the movement could dispense with Browder; this thought had already been advanced by Robert Thompson, the war hero who, during his convalescence from malaria contracted in the South Pacific, had been functioning in the top leadership. Elizabeth Gurley Flynn felt "nothing would be so disastrous as having Earl Browder's leadership called into question." Her remarks showed an interesting association characteristic of the atmosphere in Communist circles at that time. "After Willkie and Roosevelt, now Earl Browder . . .," she sighed. In her mind, the crisis in Communist leadership was of a piece with the national crisis in leadership caused by the deaths of Willkie and Roosevelt.

Benjamin J. Davis, Jr. — the outstanding Negro Communist and at that time a city councilman in New York — also paid tribute to Browder. Contrary to what would become stock in trade of the hysteria against Browder within a few weeks and contrary to the mythology which Davis himself would inspire in the next ten years, Davis affirmed that Browder had saved the Communist Party from underestimating the Negro question at an earlier phase of the war. Only when Browder returned from jail in May 1942 had the Party's backsliding on Negro rights been corrected, said Davis.

Roy Hudson, a former sailor with unimpeachable proletarian credentials, made a long review of Communist trade union policy. While he had an open mind on some of the Duclos criticisms, Hudson said he did "not have an open mind on the leadership of Earl Browder." Hudson insisted that Browder had helped him to oppose the oversimplifications of Communist policy in which some left wing labor leaders were engaged, for example, with regard to the no-strike pledge in the postwar period. Hudson was not for rushing into anything that might disorient the trade union cadres: steering their course was a difficult job in any case.

Most remarkable about the May session was the behavior of Foster. The previous evening Browder had spoken in defense of his basic position. He granted that exaggerations had beset his policies, and he admitted that the European Communists might have had problems in their own countries because of the distinctive difference between their own and the American Communist line and its influence on them. In Browder's view such differences were inevitable, since the circumstances were different. On the other hand, the large outlines and purpose of all policies, European and American, were based on something new and central, namely the transformed relationship of the United States and the Soviet Union. Foster took exception to this speech, but in a moderate spirit. He believed that if his colleagues had not been harsh and stubborn the year before, if they had listened to his criticisms, the crisis could have been averted. Whatever the aberrations of the American Communists during the war, their line had not been dangerous; it had only become dangerous, Foster believed, by the war's end. Foster now proposed that Browder take the lead in admitting his errors, especially as regards the nature and role of American imperialism. "If we do this in the Marxian spirit in which we were trained and all grew up in," he appealed to Browder, "I think everything will be all right." But if not, "we are in deeper trouble."

At another point in the free wheeling exchanges, Foster returned to this theme. "I think everybody in this room wants Earl to continue as the head of our Party but if he goes to the Association with such a line as he presented last night, he is jeopardizing his leadership in the Association." Browder remained unyielding, without revealing his intentions. Eugene Dennis and Gilbert Green returned to the question as to what Browder intended to do. The latter denied he would form any faction, but neither would he accept criticism with which he disagreed. He would not, he said, abandon the conviction that "an American program cannot be a reflection of the Communist movement in Europe." American Communists had to think for themselves. Sarcastically, he derided his own colleagues. "I get the impression that most of the comrades are not thinking; they are making demonstrations of faith and when thinking breaks down perhaps that is the best substitute." As for himself, he had no intention of becoming "a political zombie." Dennis asked what a "zombie" was. Browder replied sharply: "A zombie is a modern myth about a dead person who has been raised by some magical process and walks around under the control of another mind."

Browder made his own mood clear. "And when our Association is having a basic political discussion I am going to say nothing which is an echo of somebody else's thoughts. I am going to speak my own thoughts and nothing else because that is all I have to contribute to this movement." The meeting ended in only one agreement, namely, that the Duclos article would be published in the *Daily Worker* as quickly as possible with an introduction by Browder of a character that would give guidance to the membership.[24]

Ten days later, on June 2, 1945, the National Board met again.[25] This time additional leading Communists took part — Morris Childs, the state secretary for Illinois and a veteran C.P.

leader; Robert Minor, who had been the chief expositor of Browder's ideas and his stand-in during the latter's absence in Atlanta Penitentiary early in the war; James W. Ford, the veteran Negro Communist leader with Comintern experience, and vice-presidential candidate on Foster's ticket in 1932; and finally someone identified only as "Comrade J.," clearly a very prominent trade unionist whose name could not be entrusted to the stenogram.

Friend and foe had by then acknowledged that the Duclos article had created a new situation for the American Communists. The entire leadership was conscious of confronting basic choices. Three main problems dominated the discussion — (a) a precise definition of the differences, (b) what should be done in political and organizational terms, and (c) what role Browder would play. Before this meeting, a subcommittee had drafted a resolution which combined an endorsement of the main import of the Duclos article with a program of action relating to problems of the prosecution of the war in the Pacific and reconversion of industry. Browder restated his basic view that "it would be the grossest error" not to realize that the Teheran agreement had been much more than "a diplomatic document," although it was that, to be sure. "If an enduring peace for many generations is possible we must be able to understand fully what makes it possible. It has never before been possible for Marxists to declare that there is such a possibility, short of the time when socialism will replace capitalism in at least the major nations of the world. If we cannot define the objective factors which create this possibility then we are departing from Marxism. Any perspective that admits of the possibility of a durable peace without defining the change in the relation of world forces that makes it possible can be nothing but harmful Utopianism or arrant opportunism. Is there such a change in the world relation of forces? I think there is such a change, and it is not in the class character of the bourgeoisie, or in the imperialist nature of the capitalist system of the United States; that remains the same, as I have emphasized time and again in every major document that I wrote."[26]

What were the "objective factors" that now entered in this unprecedented fashion into the "change in the relation of world forces?" Browder's argument in mid-1945 (before the advent of either nuclear military power or mutual deterrence) was similar to the Soviet Union's rationale — twenty years later — for peaceful coexistence, when its policy was challenged by Maoist China.

He listed several factors: the emergence of the Soviet Union as a victorious world power; the deep-going challenge to the colonial system arising on a scale and with a force that could not be met by the classical methods of repression; the democratic upsurge in Europe which now gave the Communist movements a pre-eminent association with bourgeois-democratic forces that no longer considered the Communists as outside the nation; and finally, the emergence of the United States as a world power with its productive capacity doubled and with the necessity, in order to maintain a viable welfare state, of enormously expanding its domestic and world markets within the context of altered world relations in which Communism was now a major factor.

Browder pursued this argument.

The question becomes whether it is possible for the greatest capitalist, imperialist power — America, the land of highest degree of concentration and centralization of capital, i.e. of monopoly capitalism, capitalism in its imperialist stage of development — whether it is possible for such a country to find the way of peaceful coexistence and collaboration with the Soviet Socialist Republics within one framework, within a single world order of nations which they jointly sustain.

I know there is a widespread negative opinion among Marxists, among leading Marxists, men whose opinions we must respect, who hold that this possibility is theoretically excluded and that to admit this possibility as a factor in our thinking in itself constitutes revision of Marxism.

It must be acknowledged that this pre-established Marxian view, established on the basis of the previous relation of forces, is firmly buttressed not only in theory but in facts of life as they were experienced throughout the past decade by hundreds of millions of people throughout the world. It requires weighty factors now to enable one to conclude that what proved impossible in the past has now become possible.

In Browder's view, these weighty factors could not be found in the general coincidence of interest between the peoples of the U.S.A. and the U.S.S.R. This coincidence had been unable in the past to exert its influence "upon the bourgeois class which dominated America and determined its policy, the class which has an innate hostility to the Soviet Union and a class which came to the war coalition only under the stress of direst necessity." Some new rationale would be involved henceforth. "Only if the bourgeoisie has a class interest which coincides to some degree with the national interest does the possibility exist that the policy of long-term collaboration with the Soviet Union can be realized without a basic change in the class structure of state power in America."

Browder believed that short of a change in class relations, that is, short of revolution within the United States which would of itself alter the entire problem, there was a prospect for American capitalism, in pursuit of its *class* interest, to fulfill *national* interest. *America's necessity to survive in a constricted and altered world market while its own productive power had expanded would compel it to overcome its "innate hostility" to socialism.* It was not axiomatic that this hostility would be overcome. Nor would it be overcome without great effort. But if Browder's analysis were deemed theoretically admissible, it would require a new approach by American Communists to those elements of the capitalist class who had enough intelligence to realize the necessities under which their own system would henceforth function.

What, he asked, were the real alternatives? The first was an "immediate transition to war against the Soviet Union." He ruled out such a prospect on the grounds that when the Western powers had "failed to save and take over the armies of Hitler," this alternative had been precluded. Such a course would have meant, in his view, a turn toward domestic fascism and America's political isolation. In June 1945 all this was unthinkable.

The second course he called the "road of armed peace" or the carrot-and-club policy."[27] Superficially, this course was attractive to American capitalism, Browder admitted. Indeed, it would be a "hypocritical and masked form of the first course, the path of war, and more dangerous" because it would create "the conditions and the atmosphere in which its innate tendencies could lead the American bourgeoisie on to the path of war without a conscious decision based on cold calculation." But in Browder's view, this alternative would not solve the problem of markets. Without probing the matter in great depth, he believed that it would lead to a devastating economic crisis that would then "force a decision under much more unfavorable circumstances between war and a long-term peace of collaboration which had been postponed by this policy." To Browder, an era of "Cold War" was inconceivable as a prolonged era of U.S.-U.S.S.R. relations. His thinking telescoped events into an immediate choice between war and coexistence. Ruling out the former he projected the latter as the stage worth fighting for in practice because it could now be admitted in theory. He argued that American Communist strategy demanded "a serious effort to mobilize all the forces that could be mobilized to realize it, to form a bloc, an alliance with that section of the bourgeoisie which saw its true class interests, fighting with them for its realization and bringing the power of labor and the democratic mass movements to bear upon the more backward and reluctant sections of the bourgeoisie, therefore reinforcing the more farsighted leaders of the bourgeoisie."[28]

The discussion remained only briefly and intermittently on the level where Browder had placed it. He tried to epitomize his position by asking whether Communists could "pose a workable economic program short of the abolition of capitalism." That was "the essence of the problem." Gilbert Green replied, "You are right." And then Green gave his view that Communists could *not* take the line of "trying to make capitalism work." They could *not* abandon the classical proposition that capitalism was unable to avoid economic crisis.

William Z. Foster believed that Browder's error was in taking what was the Party's "immediate program of demands under capitalism and transforming it into an ultimate program and thereby seeking to solve all the contradictions of capitalism." The idea of finding foreign markets on the scale of ten or fifteen or fifty billion dollars a year was not only illusory but an improper function for Communists.[29] "So far as working out a coherent policy," Foster said, "we cannot do it short of socialism. And we cannot do it at the present time."

Thus two views of correct Communist strategy were presented — one made a fundamental critique of capitalism but sought to enlist people in the struggle for partial demands which if realized could not change the system's character; the other projected what today would be called "structural reforms" (to use the Italian Communist phrase) which were realizable short of the abolition of capitalism but which facilitated the transition from capitalism. The fundamentalist and revisionist variants of Communism thus wrestled in debate.

Foster also challenged Browder's concept that a coincidence

of interest between opposing systems was the key reality of the war. At best, the pressure of democratic forces had compelled the wartime relationship. No fundamental change in the U.S. attitude toward the U.S.S.R. was involved. "I have not the slightest doubt that if these democratic forces relax their pressure in the United States and other countries the bourgeoisie would be at war with the Soviet Union in six months," Foster declared. "That's what their coincidence of interest with the Soviet Union amounts to." Foster's key concern of the next decade — sudden war between the two powers — was mirrored in this remark.

Two of the participants veered away from discussion of basic theory in a way which perplexed and exasperated their colleagues. Elizabeth Gurley Flynn again proposed a "basic discussion" of the Duclos article, as though no one was satisfying her need; again she lamented her own inability to take part in it on the level required.[30] Robert Minor, whose initial remarks seemed to support Browder, took fright at the prospect of being associated with a man who was grievously and stubbornly sinning, and proceeded to attack Browder bitterly and personally. Minor was again making a turn of 180 degrees. On the other hand, Roy Hudson was still unconvinced on the evidence of his own experience. He refused to leap on any bandwagon. Hudson repeated that he had prepared an article criticizing the postwar no-strike attitude of Harry Bridges and had received Browder's support. It was also untrue, Hudson said, that the Communist attitude toward the Labor-Management conference that spring had been euphoric and uncritical. Foster interrupted to declare that Browder could not escape responsibility for the exaggerations of Communist policy expressed by Bridges, whose views were not an aberration (as Hudson was trying to make them appear) but the logical consequence of Browder's line.[31]

Soon the organizational dilemma took the floor away from policy questions. John Williamson gave figures to show that the Duclos article had been inaccurate; the C.P.A. had a membership of 63,000 with 10,000 in the armed forces, that is a 25 percent increase over the 1944 figure. Foster spoke up to declare that although it had been "a mistake to change the Communist Party into the Communist Political Association" the problem now was not necessarily to admit that this had been a mistake, and not necessarily to change back from an Association to a Party. Thus he did not at the beginning of June favor a reconstitution of the Party. In Foster's mind, this was a secondary matter.

Browder offered to vote for the draft resolution in so far as its immediate program of action was concerned, but he would not vote for any judgment upholding the Duclos article as such. When the vote came, Browder stood alone, opposed to Foster, Ford, Williamson, Childs, Minor, Thompson, Green, Dennis, and Flynn. "Comarde J." (who evidently did not have more than an *ex officio* status) voted with the majority. Roy Hudson abstained, and also proposed that he and Browder be given more time.[32] "Comrade J." agreed that it was the duty of the National Board to meet with Browder and "help him find his position." Under questioning, Browder made it clear that he would vote for the action program, provided that it included a reference to the problem of markets, thus suggesting that his intransigence could be overcome. He proposed to await a full meeting of the National Committee before deciding on his own course.

At this point, Foster's tone began to change. Whereas at the May 22-23 meeting and even earlier, Foster had been appealing to Browder to help lead them out of their dilemma by appropriate self-criticism, now the prospect of a leadership minus Browder loomed up, and Foster's reasoning illuminated the entire tradition, the all-or-nothing standard, of Bolshevik conduct. "I don't think we should take 50-50 votes. Earl is a veteran in the labor and Communist movement and such a vote as that in the old C.I. would not be tolerated; it would be thrown out of the window. I think Earl must make up his mind and say 'Yes' or 'No,' and the comrades here are not afraid to fight you in the Party, Earl. If you vote against this resolution, you commit political suicide in this Party. Pay attention to what the comrades here are saying; they are not going to allow you to disorient this Party."

In the voting on various amendments, Browder continued his dissent. He appeared to take special umbrage at the charge which his long-time associate, Eugene Dennis, had made privately that he, Browder, was trying to "mobilize American Marxists against the European Marxists." Everyone appeared to reject the logic of a polycentrism that underlay the American Communist dilemma.

The National Committee of the Communist Political Association met in a three-day session beginning June 18, 1945. Fifty-

four members were present, including prominent trade unionists. It was the first conclave of the Association's highest body
since the Duclos article and the publication in the *Daily Worker*
of Browder's viewpoint as expressed at the National Board on
June 2, whose main passages have been cited here.[33] The Draft
Resolution had also been published. C.P.A. members were already reacting by letters and articles. The American Communists also had to reckon with the first observations of liberal and
conservative opinion-makers.[34] What the Association would do
had become a matter of national attention and no doubt was
being closely watched abroad. A close reading of the mid-June
transcript discloses all the dilemmas which American Communism had inherited from its past. The problems for which solutions were sought in the next decade lay exposed in the June
18-20 debates.

The mid-June meeting was dominated by the gulf between
Browder and his colleagues. If in the previous month, the top
Communist leaders entertained some hopes that Browder would
lead them out of their common difficulty, by mid-June this hope
had disappeared. Browder himself addressed the gathering with
extended quotations from his books and articles, as though making a lawyer's brief for his leadership, as though establishing the
record for the sake of history, and thus admitting that his power
was gone. One National Committee member observed that Browder had behaved like a schoolmaster to difficult pupils. After
Browder's initial address, he refused to take part in the meeting, except to cast the sole negative vote. Only one trade union
leader (identified in the transcript as "Joe. S.") tried to argue
with Browder. One of the Communist old guard, Alexander
Bittelman, tried to get him to come to the meeting.[35]

The discussion was monopolized by the older leadership, men
who stemmed from the twenties, some of whom had Comintern
experience and all of whom had known the factional fights of
that era. This group now turned fiercely on Browder. All manner of charges against him, previously unvoiced, were now heard,
and history was recalled and re-examined to make the contemporary charges credible. Foster observed that in 1944 (that is,
at the beginning of the previous year when his own challenge to
Browder had gone unheard) "it was widely believed both within
the Party and outside of it Browder was taking into consideration the points of view of other C.P.'s of other lands. He did noth-

ing to correct this false impression which came in so handy for him." Foster was suggesting here that Browder had not had the sanction of the key men in the International, that Browder had deliberately misled his own colleagues. This is in striking contrast to Browder's evidence that it was the International's caretaker committee, via Dimitrov, which had approved Browder's policies and had urged Foster not to press his views.

Foster suggested — echoing the idea which Eugene Dennis had put forward privately and which so exasperated Browder — that the latter had really been engaged in an ambitious effort to deflect a large part of the international Communist movement. He had been trying, Foster said, "to shift the international line." Thus, Browder's heresy was given an international dimension.

Others joined in this retrospective and retroactive attack.[36] Max Weiss, who had been in Moscow in the late thirties as a delegate to the Young Communist International, now recalled that in 1939 the chief Soviet figure in the Comintern, Dmitri Manuilsky, had criticized the American comrades for "glossing over the character of bourgeois-democracy;" evidently, Browder had been considered too zealous in applying the ideas of the Comintern's Seventh Congress. Browder was also accused of having lagged behind the rest of the leadership in accepting the implications of the Soviet-German nonaggression pact. Pat Toohey, another old-timer with experience in the struggles in the coal fields in the twenties and in the Comintern, recalled that "leading comrades elsewhere" had been obliged in 1938 to reject Browder's slogan, "Communism is 20th Century Americanism."[37]

For the first time, important Negro leaders voiced views which contrasted with Councilman Benjamin J. Davis' affirmation early in May of Browder's staunchness on the Negro question. It was now suggested by James W. Ford, by William L. Patterson, and by the lesser but important figures, Audley Moore and Rose Gaulden, that Browder had been cool to them as individuals and *ipso facto* had been guilty of profoundly underestimating the Negro question, and its importance as a revolutionary factor in the postwar period. Davis did not repeat his defense of Browder but joined the attack.

The leading trade unionist at this gathering, identified as "Joe. S.," tried to stem the tide of near-hysteria. He recounted his own effort to persuade Browder to take part in the meeting.

It was urgent, he thought, "to avoid the mistake of jumping on a bandwagon without understanding the issues, and to join a 'lynching party.' " In the opinion of "Joe. S." there were unfortunate "manifestations of this" in the Communist ranks and the Communist leadership. Andrew Onda, another old-timer with long service in the coal and steel area of Pittsburgh, warned that the "membership did not want Earl Browder to be made the goat."

The stenogram of these proceedings reveals that one group of the participants — the older generation who had led the movement since the twenties — was most keenly hostile to Browder because he refused to give them leadership now that they desperately needed it. This sentiment of helplessness coincided with an acute sense of their own responsibility, as though men of such sterling Communist character who had to admit their own flaws were thereby being humiliated. For leaders who were supposedly selfless in serving their cause, they exhibited a curious vanity.

What also stands out is the profound inadequacy which everyone felt in the essential nature of their movement, although no one dared to trace this to any shortcoming in Marxism-Leninism. Outwardly the exponents of the brotherhood of man, they had all been living in a sort of jungle. Pat Toohey recalled that he had had the courage to defy John L. Lewis in the bitter battles of the United Mine Workers in the midtwenties; yet in 1944 Toohey had hesitated to give Foster support "for fear of reprisals." Bittelman argued that the American Communists were witnessing "the collapse of Earl Browder." He reminded his audience with consummate cynicism that "as long as Browder was enabling the movement to make such major achievements, the question of methods of leadership were secondary." Their remorse at the undemocratic atmosphere of Browder's rule was hypocritical, Bittelman implied. So long as it worked they had not objected.

Steve Nelson, a popular commissar in Republican Spain with meritorious prior service in the Comintern, revealed that although he had known Earl Browder for 20 years, he had "never had a conversation with him." Nelson continued: "If we had a Comintern now, this organization would be in receivership." Turning to men and women who had prided themselves on building a movement based on the unique virtues of democratic centralism, Nelson cried out: "We are good wheel-horses; we are good 'yes-men.' " Then touching a very sensitive nerve, he ex-claimed: "Of course, it should not be carried to the other extreme of developing an adulation for Comrade Foster." Foster then in-terjected, recognizing that he had just been accorded the crown, "That will never happen." To which Nelson replied: "Yes, but Browder had a way of saying that he was nothing but modest." At this point the transcript records: "Laughter." This was the only moment which provoked such emotion.[38]

Equally striking in the mid-June meeting was the role of the trade unionists, who gave evidence of acute dissatisfaction with themselves and with their relation to the Party, and received clear indications that Party leaders and members held deep-seated grievances against them. It would appear that the Com-munist movement, proud as it was of its members who had achieved leading positions in unions, also doubted their integrity. And the union leaders wondered whether they were being good Communists.

Few of the union leaders taking part in these sessions dealt with the issues confronting Communist policy as such or as a whole. With the exception of "Joe S." who tried to deal with Browder's future and was unhappy that a "lynching party" might be taking place, each of the unionists described the local and immediate situation of his or her union or industry. Few said anything about the destiny of the movement, which was, after all, the real issue. They had long been accustomed to think of themselves as operative leaders of a particular sector, but not as leaders of the entire movement. This shortcoming now seem-ed to rankle them. It contradicted the implicit assumption that a leader of working people, a unionist, was *ipso facto* the most desirable and authentic candidate for political leadership.[39]

Thus, "Ruth Y." (not otherwise identified) spoke of this meet-ing as an occasion for pride. At last "we have a feeling we are Communist trade unionists, not simply trade union Commu-nists."

On the other hand, one union leader (identified only as "Lew") made the following complaint. "In the main the trade union leadership is an underground Party leadership and so if the Com-munists make a mistake they simply shrug their shoulders, and say 'what's that got to do with me?,' thus strengthening the whole idea of their remaining underground." In "Lew's" opinion the time had come to "make a sharp break in this practice. Communists in the trade unions have got to take responsibility and the best way to indicate this is for a number of people like myself to come out openly as Communists. Actually I do everything now except call myself a Communist [publicly]," "Lew" reflected. "I think it is necessary to come out openly." Then came the afterthought that he, "Lew," represented the "white-collar workers," who were hardly the most crucial elements in the working class. "It is important that this, the legalization of Communist cadres, take place among the leaders of the industrial workers. Unless we are ready to do this, then I say the discussion will have failed."

"Joe S." observed that he was "tired of being needled on the question of legality." He explained that he had been constantly in touch with Roy Hudson in this matter, and evidently had been exploring the advisability of "legalization" for many years. Clearly the Communist unionists had been involved with the pros and cons of the matter ever since they had come to lead large bodies of workers most of whom either did not know their leaders were Communists, or did not care so long as they did their jobs. But the hidden Communist unionists feared that these workers might reject their leadership if they now avowed Communist membership. The loss of strategically-placed power might be more grievous than the loss of integrity. "Joe S." argued that the time had not yet come to make the step of avowing Communist affiliation in so far as his own union was concerned.

Peter V. Cacchione, one of the two Communist councilmen in New York, spoke heatedly on this matter. "If the trade union leaders have not come out openly as Communists in three and a half years of easy sailing," it was "idealistic" to believe they would do so "in the next period." Cacchione warned his listeners that the Communist rank and file was critical of the unionists who had become the leaders in the mass organizations. People were now asking about "the salaries of the paid officials." He spoke contemptuously of those "who make $100 a week, who contribute nothing to the C.P.A., who do not even attend meetings."

In this castigation, he was joined by one of the few labor leaders whose full name is given in the transcript, David Davis of Pennsylvania, long a figure among the electrical workers. As Davis saw it, bureaucracy was widespread, above all in the left-led unions. "I have found cases where there is a complete disregard for the feelings and needs of the members of unions where comrades are leaders in these unions."

One of the most plaintive speeches came from Bella Dodd. She had made a significant career as the leader of the New York Teachers' Union; she had been one of the few union leaders to accept the rationale for converting the Party into a Political Association the year before, and to disclose her Communist affiliation; she had become an acknowledged C.P.A. leader, representing it in New York state and municipal legislative affairs. She was familiar and influential at City Hall and the State House in Albany. Like many of the union leaders, Bella Dodd was extremely reluctant to renounce Browder and was appalled by the ease with which his long-time associates were evidently able to do so. "He is and has been a great man," she declared. "He got rid of the leather jackets and the low heels" in the Communist movement.[40]

But she also disclosed her dissatisfaction with the way she had functioned as a Communist leader in the past fifteen months. The National Committttee had met only three times since the C.P.A.'s founding convention in May 1944, and her own contribution had been a "five minute speech." There was something wrong with the way Communist policy was discussed and decisions were made. If Mrs. Dodd's case was typical, it was revealing. She had made the step which others were pondering and resisting, and her experience had not been satisfactory. Somehow neither a shift in personnel nor the open leadership by people closer to the masses than the Party functionaries seemed to resolve the American Communist dilemma.

One other problem came out in the discussion, namely, the relation of Communists to those movements in which they were working intimately with non-Communists. This was illustrated in an anecdote by Anita Whitney, daughter of a much-respected West Coast family, who had been tried on criminal syndicalism charges and had won her case.

Miss Whitney told of a meeting of precinct workers of the Democratic Party in Los Angeles, over which a certain Mrs. Eliel had presided. The C.P.A.'s leadership discovered that "nearly everyone in the local Democratic Party was a Communist." Had Mrs. Eliel known this to be the case? it was asked. "No, of course not," was the reply. Miss Whitney did not spell out any conclusions from this anecdote, but plainly it troubled her. The American Communists had evidently succeeded, in the fluid politics of California, in becoming the prime movers of local Democratic Party organizations: to do so had been the "line" of the Political Association. Yet the Communists were embarrassed by the problems arising from their very success. The Los Angeles instance may not have been so widespread, but it posed a dilemma. If they were to reveal their Party membership, what would happen to the organization, in this case a local Democratic Party club which they were loyally trying to build? If they did not reveal their membership they might — at some turn in the political road — find themselves open to the charges of deception from good people like Mrs. Eliel.

In New York, a dilemma of another kind existed. Benjamin J. Davis, Jr., who had won his seat as councilman almost unchallenged in Harlem, had by mid-1945 registered in the local Tammany Hall Club, and at the same time was seeking the American Labor' Party's endorsement. In the latter organization, the left wing (often made up of concealed Communists), was in alliance with what were known as the "Hillman forces," that is, the non-Communists of the Amalgamated Clothing Workers. Davis was hopeful of becoming the unchallenged spokesman of the entire Negro community, the successor to Adam Clayton Powell, who had just gone to Congress; Powell supported Davis' ambition.

But the Hillman forces did not wish to endorse a Communist in the autumn 1945 elections. They saw the chance of electing a Manhattan councilman of their own. Davis demanded that the Communist Political Association use its power and influence to get him the A.L.P. endorsement — alleging that the failure of the Hillman forces to endorse him disclosed anti-Negro prejudice. The C.P.A.'s state secretary, Gilbert Green, spoke to this point and explained his differences with Davis in a revealing passage: "I want to say that if we cannot convince the Hillman forces of the need for that [endorsing Davis], I am still absolutely opposed to using any mechanical majority, and I don't know if we have it or not, but if we do have it I would be opposed to using it. I think what is involved is not the Negro question but maintaining an alliance with those forces we have to work with more closely in the future than we have in the past, and I think that is the heart and spirit of the Duclos article as well."

Green was supported by the legislative secretary, Bella Dodd, and by the state chairman, Israel Amter. Davis returned to the argument. He observed, with sarcasm, that Tammany Hall was more receptive to his position than his own comrades, pointing out that he was being considered by the Manhattan Democrats as their Harlem nominee to the City Council.[41] (The wide, cross-party support which emerged in Harlem for Davis was an anticipation of what today would be called black power.) To Gilbert Green, the issue was whether the new policy stemming from the Duclos discussion meant that the Party was "going to declare organized warfare against all of its allies in the labor movement and elsewhere." Green argued that it should not. The Negro question was not at issue, however much Davis tried to make it so.

Another phase of the June 18 discussion centered on Communist organization, and was discussed in the report by the organizational secretary, John Williamson. The statistics given in Williamson's report were the first since early 1944.[42]

Forty-three percent of the Association's members in 1945 were industrial workers; the figure had been 46 percent the year before in 1943. One-quarter of the members were in "basic industry"; this figure had varied only slightly throughout the war, showing a rise to 27 percent in 1944. Just about half of the membership was in trade unions. One-quarter were housewives, and this number had risen significantly from less than a fifth at the beginning of the war. Roughly another quarter were "professionals," meaning essentially lower middle class, self-employed, and other than industrial workers; distinct from this category, Williamson gave a figure of 5 percent for members engaged in "business," which had risen from 1 per cent in 1943. Ten percent of the members were black, but no occupational breakdown was given. The value of these figures can be disputed in the sense that the wartime work force was a fluid one; housewives, who could not be considered part of a continuing industrial proletariat, entered the labor force in large numbers, as did farmers. In terms of the Communist standards in 1944, a high percentage of "industrial workers" did not mean a stable workingclass base.

Williamson expressed great dissatisfaction with the trend of the Communist membership in industry although his own report in January, 1945 had boasted of a rise in these categories. Yet the actual figures were impressive. The predominantly working class character of the Communist movement was clear. Although half of the Party's members were housewives, professionals and even business men, nevertheless given the wartime absence of working men, the Political Association was a potentially viable organization in terms of the objectives it had set itself. Any movement that was striving to influence other political forces and make its impact within the existing formations of society would have been well served to have such a balance between industrial and nonindustrial workers.

A similar point can be made with respect to Williamson's complaint that the dues payments of the Political Association had declined. Whereas payment of dues had been 85 percent "years ago," he declared, the C.P.A. had averaged only 71 percent in 1944, and in the first five months of 1945 payments had only reached 58 percent. The sale of Marxist classics had fallen off. From 1938 to 1943 (for all the state organizations excluding New York), Williamson reported, annual sales of Marxist-Leninist classics averaged 34,000 copies, whereas in 1944 this figure had declined to 19,000 copies. But if, as the Communists believed in 1944, the Marxian classics gave no clear guidelines for policy, the decline in such sales was not surprising. Similarly, a looser, less-than-Leninist organization could not expect the same level of dues payment as a tightly knit, quasi-military body. The same could be said about the C.P.A.'s recruitment. In 1945, the transformed organization had enrolled 63,000 members — an increase of 25 percent over 1944.[43] This figure represented 82 percent of the former Communist Party membership, not counting those in the armed forces. It meant that large groups of new members had flocked into the C.P.A., and only a relatively small number had rejected the new organizational-political form — contradicting the allegation by Duclos.

True enough, the rate of recruitment had declined. In the first half of 1943 the average monthly recruiting had been 3,615 members. One year later, during the enthusiasm for the new course, it had risen to an average of 4,275 recruits per month; in the first half of 1945 this figure had dropped to 1,185. Williamson made the important qualification, however, that the Association had decided against a recruiting campaign in 1945. This would suggest that, whereas in earlier years it took a mobilization of the membership to gain new recruits in large numbers, by 1945 they were coming at a rate of almost 15,000 a year without any membership drive. It could be argued from the change in the dues payments (now annual rather than monthly) and from the more stable if less spectacular growth in membership, combined with changes in the character of the Communist Political Association branches which had ceased to be "cells" and had become neighborhood institutions, open to a general public, that the Communist movement was transforming itself. It was losing its character of a Leninist vanguard. It was becoming something which approached more nearly an American political lobby.

Williamson's lament about the changing occupational structure of the membership and the decline in literature sales and in dues had meaning in mid-1945 only on the assumption that what had taken place organizationally was an unexpected consequence of the changes initiated by Browder, whereas he himself had observed in January, 1945, that the Party could not "expect to be the same well-knit communist organization" that it had been when it was "smaller and composed of a group of conscious and tested Communists."

The question might have been asked whether the French Party (with a membership of almost a million) or the Italian Party (enrolling more than two million) were not experiencing an analogous transformation. Although the American Communists could not stand comparison with their French and Italian counterparts, they had built something approaching a mass movement with all the problems this entailed. But their achievement was fragile. The Party was undergoing a change. Its own leadership had proclaimed the change as desirable but had no experience with it, and recoiled from its implications. Thus steps to carry it out were hesitant and transitional. Williamson expressed it this way: "Equally decisive as these figures is the fact that our ability to convince the trade unions, including the C.I.O., of the correctness of our policies is far from fully established. We do not have so deep-rooted an influence or organized strength that we can influence and continue to lead decisive sections of the labor movement, irrespective of what any leader inside or outside the trade union movement, may do at a critical moment."

This was the nub of the real state of affairs. The Communists had gained members in large numbers, more than any other radical group, and had not retained them. Their influence depended on strategically placed operatives who came to their movement, or came out of their movement without, however, having a secure base even in the organizations they controlled. Given a longer period of time than a single year, the Communists might have changed this state of affairs in their favor. But they could do so only by becoming something else than they had been. Just at the point when they were beginning to become a different kind of political formation, they reversed the effort, and went back to the classical pattern.

By trying once again to straddle the dilemmas of a closely knit revolutionary community operating in an atmosphere quite inhospitable, and by trying to keep in step with a world movement whose needs and objectives were quite contradictory to those of an American left wing, the Communists would lose by 1948 even the uncertain hold which they still held within American life in 1945. This would turn them — despite their intentions to thrust outward — even more inward in the hope that by sustaining their own community they might survive. By the mid-fifties, having barely survived, they were faced with their own irrelevance and their inability to rebuild.

The final — and decisive — aspect of the June 18-20 enlarged National Committee meeting was the issue of leadership. When matters once again came to a vote, Browder stood alone against the 53 members of the National Committee. He refused to accept the Draft Resolution unless it were amended on the basis of his line. From this point forward, Foster held command, but having acquired it in a rather ambiguous way, the ambiguity would haunt him. Foster's own earlier hopes that Browder would lead the movement were abandoned.[44] In mid-May Browder might have been the savior. By mid-June, he had become an obstacle, the heretic. Yet Foster could only rule by co-opting the men who had been Browder's closest aides. An interim secretariat was elected: Foster and the two men who had been thoroughly "Browderist" — John Williamson and Eugene Dennis.[45] How comfortably would they live under Foster's wing? Would not the two traditions within Communism clash again?

The immediate problem was less speculative, namely, to stem the near-hysteria which swept through Communist ranks as one leader after another made abject apology for political misdemeanors. The spectacle gave rise to a mood within the membership for a clean sweep of the leaders, although where such new men could come from — given the standards of loyalty and experience — none could say. Obedient to the concepts of democratic centralism, the Party really had no other leadership unless absolute novices were to be entrusted with power, and that was unthinkable. Browder's rout was made all the easier because he himself did not fight for views. At the June 18 session, he simply defended his policies but refused, as we have seen, to attend the rest of the meeting. His own address did not appear in *The Worker* until July 20, 1945 — a full month after its delivery. By that time the membership had already gone through county and state conventions condemning Browder with striking unanimity but knowing his views only from the article of June 8.[46]

Browder's defiance of the leadership (when unanimity was the ultimate value) much more than his arguments in themselves turned the membership against him. Communists were accustomed to the complete subordination of differences in the interests of unity. Browder would not, however, recant. On the other hand, although defying the views of his colleagues, Browder did not propose to leave the movement. Nor did he lead any grouping against the new (essentially old) leadership. He was not a delegate to the New York state convention. His behavior was contradictory, which blurred his image and reduced the little sympathy he enjoyed. On the eve of the Emergency National Convention he pledged to support the Resolution which he had until then opposed.[47] But at the Convention proper he outraged and worried Foster and Dennis by suggesting that it was "a very naive view that this convention of the Communists of America would decide and close the discussion of all these questions." The deposed leader continued: "This is not a simple American discussion of American issues; it is an international discussion of international problems which was internationally initiated and will continue for some time on an international scale. It will be finally decided and closed only by an international consensus of opinion of Marxists of all lands. If this Convention should make decisions or prohibit expressions of differing opinions hereafter, that would only mean to withdraw America from the international discussion that continues. That would be American exceptionalism with a vengeance."[48] Eugene Dennis took the floor immediately thereafter to denounce Browder bitterly for the implication that there was some kind of "Supreme Court" which had powers over the American Communist movement. The Dennis rebuke was entirely hypocritical. His political behavior and that of his colleagues since the arrival of the Duclos article was premised on this very conception to which Browder now made appeal, namely the policies of the American Communist movement were assumed to be valid only if they corresponded to the policies of the international movement. Browder was invoking this same conception and speculating that the basic issues were yet to be decided. He was reminding his colleagues that in the history of American Communism the last word had always come from abroad. Were the C.P. leaders so certain that international trends would validate the Duclos line? Browder was, with a stubborn desperation, counting on those whom he had known as powerful friends.[49] He was gambling also that Foster was misjudging the polarization between the two systems. As it turned out, Browder misjudged both the tactics of American capitalism and Soviet Communism in the short run, although he grasped that something new had happened to both. Foster, who judged more accurately in the short run, clung to an apocalyptic view which history eventually rejected.

Browder's only other intervention in the discussion came equally late — a polemical article of July 24, 1945, to which Foster made an immediate rebuttal the next day. This exchange revealed clearly the gulf between the two conceptions of Communist policy the two men personified. To Browder, his course in 1944-1945 was part of a new departure in world Communist policy. He proposed that American Communists strive for the widest possible unity together with those sections of American capital who would, out of their own profit interests, be animated in the direction of averting an economic collapse and finding some basis of cooperation with the Soviet Union and the forces allied with it. The alternative, in Browder's view, was a species of anarcho-syndicalism, premised on the assumption that world peace was impossible without a fundamental change in American class relations.

Foster derided Browder's conception. He argued that it was illusory for Communists to project any strategic program which had at its premise the supposition that the contradictions of capitalism could be surmounted. Any such view represented a concession to the concept that American capitalism could be anything but reactionary and that anything less than an American-Soviet confrontation was to be anticipated.

The Emergency Convention, unanimously ratifying Foster's views of both world and domestic developments, reconstituted the Communist Party of the United States. A leadership was elected which, with few exceptions, was composed of the same men and women who had throughout the previous years operated this movement. They now set forth with a deep sense of returning to basic verities. Alfred Wagenknecht, the veteran from Chicago who had been a leader of the old Socialist Party contingent in the founding of the American Communist movement in 1919, expressed the view that the American Communists had "at last come home." The sense of homecoming after dangerous excursions into perilous temptations, indeed into the swamps of revisionism, now animated this movement and pervaded its intellectual and spiritual life for the next three critical years. What did coming home mean, however, in the cyclonic period from 1945 to 1948? Whether the old homestead would prove comfortable with the particular ideological and organizational furnishings which the C.P.U.S.A. brought with it was a large question.

# 5 THE PARTY RESTORED

If the American Communist Party had been simply one of these sects, so plentiful in the turbulence of American life, which advanced a particular cause and disintegrated under the impact of changing circumstances or superior odds, no particular problem would arise in the analysis of its decline. Movements that shoot up and then disappear have long fertilized the American soil. Their trajectory is remembered by some with nostalgia and by others with pain; bystanders have been indifferent to their demise and opponents have derived satisfaction from it. The Non-Partisan League which swept through the Dakotas and Minnesota during and after the first World War has been given a sympathetic epitaph.[1] The Old Age Pension crusade of Dr. Francis Townsend has had its chroniclers.[2] And there has been a revival of interest in the International Workers of the World, a mighty movement which contributed members and ideas to American Communism. The I.W.W. — the terror of its time — is now remembered almost benignly by one time opponents, and with envy by present-day imitators of its policies of confrontation.[3] Viewing the American Communist Party as a party which reconstituted itself in mid-1945 and came to grief by 1949, which resisted persecution in stubborn bewilderment and then exploded by 1958 like a delayed Roman candle, one is tempted to dismiss it as having fought against great odds and lost. According to one's lights, the failure was honorable or pitiable.

Yet can one make so pragmatic a judgment of the American Communists? Does not their own definition of their *raison d'être* require a more rigorous standard? Unlike other movements of faith or protest, this particular party claimed to have been guided by a special doctrine, Marxism-Leninism. This doctrine was not an assumed truth nor a revelation but supposedly a science of history, a political science. The Party boasted a knowledge of the laws of historical development which presumably had been tested in the experience of great nations and the cauldron of world-shaking events. If in 1945 the American Communists were lamenting what they considered to have been their wartime errors, Marxism-Leninism itself was not thereby called into question. They had simply departed from its straight and narrow path. They had made an injudicious application of this science and in the nick of time had returned to a correct understanding of it. Because the Communists denied that their "ism" could be a dogma and yet the record showed that by 1949 their failures had multiplied, one must conclude either that something was faulty in this science or else that they were a particularly inept group of adherents, unusally prone to the erroneous application of propositions which should not have led to disaster.

In one of the few instances in which postwar Party leaders found an epigram from the treasury of American history to illustrate a point, Eugene Dennis had declared in February 1946: "If we but knew where we stand and whither we are tending, we should then know what to do and how to do it" — a phrase from Abraham Lincoln's "House Divided" speech. His Party, Dennis insisted, knew where it stood and where history was tending and hence knew what to do and how to do it. Ten years later, Dennis admitted that exactly the opposite had been true. Exactly how this self-deception operated for Dennis and his associates needs investigation.

For the span of 1945-1949 as a whole, it is striking how many conditions could have been considered favorable to American Communism. It was a time of considerable class struggle, a situation in which the Party presumably felt at home. As the United States armed forces were quickly demobilized[4] and the economy went through rapid reconversion, two huge waves of strikes — one in the winter of 1945 and another in the summer of 1946 — swept almost every segment of the trade unions. In the first autumn of peace, the C.I.O.'s Automobile Workers struck General Motors for 118 days; very important unions, the Steel Workers and the Electrical Workers, were involved in the settlement. The Communists controlled the latter union and had considerable influence in the auto and the steel unions. In the spring of 1946, major confrontations took place between the government and the C.I.O.'s packinghouse workers, in which the left wing was strong. Almost simultaneously the Railway Brotherhoods had to face a government takeover of their industry, which raised the most acute problems of the nature of relations between unionism and society. Later that summer, it was the turn of the coal miners. This strike brought into play another independent union, headed by the prestigious John L. Lewis. The entire labor movement appeared to be on the move.

Much more was involved than the issue of wages and the ability of the unions to galvanize their new members recruited during the war. Political relations were being tested. After a decade of close association with the Democratic Party, the unions now had grievances against President Truman in an atmosphere of rising Republican demands for antilabor legislation; in the fall of 1946 this disaffection expressed itself in a Republican sweep in the congressional elections.[5] New problems arose. To what extent should government interfere with collective bargaining? And if it were to break strikes by obliging the workers to stay on the job because it controlled the industries, how did this bear on a theme which had not been heard in a generation — the nationalization of key industries? Short of nationalization (which was attracting some interest at that moment as the newly established British Labour government experimented with it) the question of what role the trade unions ought to take in national economic affairs, such as price controls, came to the fore. Related to these matters was the problem of how the trade unions could exert an independent influence in politics, bringing pressure to bear on a Democratic administration which needed labor's support and had enjoyed it in the past but was now favoring measures hostile to labor or was not exerting its full strength to head these measures off.[6]

For the first time in two decades voices were heard in favor of an independent political party based on the labor movement. In response to Mr. Truman's takeover of the railways, A.F. Whitney, the Railway Brotherhoods' chieftain, pledged his whole union treasury to defeat the Democratic President in the next presidential election. This evoked memories of the 1924 campaign, in which Whitney himself, the Railroad Brotherhoods, and the American Federation of Labor had supported the independent ticket of Senator Robert LaFollette. Although by 1948 the third party championed by Henry Wallace had strong Communist support — indeed, Communists had a lot to do with launching it — it is often forgotten that many trade unions headed by anti-Communists adopted third party resolutions in the spring and summer of 1946. Much of this activity could be interpreted as a form of pressure on the Democratic administration. But a great deal of it expressed the reality that the labor movement no longer enjoyed priority consideration in the White House. It was confronted with the inadequacy of its traditional and automatic reliance on the Democratic Party.

Both the magnitude of the strike movement and its political

implications recalled to the older generation of Communist leaders that period following the First World War in which they had gained their first experiences (and in which William Z. Foster had gained his reputation). But the aftermath of the Second World War had novel features. The trade unions were neither defeated nor weakened. On the contrary, they grew in membership and power. The Party's trade union specialist, Hal Simon, noted that the scope and success of the strike actions were without precedent. In the spring of 1946 two million workers had engaged in strikes and "not a single strike had been lost."[7] Cooperative actions of C.I.O. and A.F.L. unions grew on a local scale, bidding to overcome the split in labor and having a marked impact on elections. In many municipalities from Connecticut to California labor-supported tickets won in 1946. The returning veterans did not act as strike breakers, and often formed the backbone of the picket lines. However dissatisfied the Communists might be with the protection which the new contracts gave to the war time gains of Negro workers (they were now a distinct and powerful force, especially in the C.I.O.) nothing analogous to 1919 took place. Black workers could not be used to break strikes as had happened a quarter of a century earlier.

Equally strong were the prevailing winds among the variety of organizations which expressed the heightened participation of the middle class in politics. The increasing proportion of white-collar, professional and technical people in the population made its impact on political life, and among these sectors the Communists had gained a significant influence.[8] Although by early 1947 the Americans for Democratic Action had been formed on a platform which precluded cooperation with either Communists or their sympathizers, the A.D.A. did not, at its inception, make such a stand prevail in public life.[9] In the first three postwar years middle class political activists opposed discrimination against the far left; they regarded attempts to isolate the Communists as "red baiting," as antithetical to the war's aims and hardly in keeping with the experience of wartime cooperation among Americans of diverse ideological persuasions.[10]

Two of the most distinctive and influential middle class political organizations were the National Citizens Political Action Committee (N.C.P.A.C.) and the Independent Citizens Committee of the Arts and Sciences (I.C.C.). The N.C.P.A.C. was an offshoot of the C.I.O.'s Political Action Committee. The I.C.C.

had rallied outstanding figures in the professional world on behalf of the fourth term campaign of President Roosevelt. Late in
1946 these committees merged to form the Progressive Citizens
of America (P.C.A.). Well into the next year this organization
included on its leading committee important New Dealers, outstanding intellectuals, and prominent men and women in many
walks of life alongside well-known radicals. It was to this body
that former vice-president Henry Wallace turned once he left the
cabinet in the autumn of 1946. Out of it came the chief impetus
for an independent Progressive Party.

At that time there still existed a wide spectrum of organizations which the Communists had helped form in an earlier era:
the National Negro Congress (for a while a serious competitor
of the N.A.A.C.P.); the American Slav Congress; the American
Youth for Democracy; and the National Lawyers' Guild. Some
groups of this general derivation were only paper committees or
*ad hoc* formations. They were later to populate the pathetic
graveyard of radical initiatives when the Attorney General proscribed them in the famous list of "subversive" organizations. But
some were genuine enough. And they were sufficiently representative to give the Communists within them serious leverage in the
nation's political life. Because the chief Party objective was to
"forge an anti-monopoly people's coalition" the existence of this
gamut of movements and the acceptability which the Party still
had within them must be reckoned as a plus on its side.[11]

From 1945 to early 1948 the Communists were not swimming
against the tide. They were swimming in turbulent waters —
quite another matter. It seems unreasonable to view the increasing hostility toward them and the serious measures to isolate
them legally and politically as the basic reasons for their failure.
The government's decision to institute "loyalty" procedures in
public employment and later in a sweeping group of defense industries did not come until March 1947.[12] The indictment of the
twelve top Party leaders was not handed down until July 1948;
the trial itself did not begin until the following year. Most significant about the proposals to outlaw the Communists — for
instance that of Secretary of Labor Lewis Schwellenbach in
March 1947 and the Mundt-Nixon bill of the following spring —
was the strongly negative response from political circles with
whom the Communists were already in deep conflict on all other
issues. Mrs. Eleanor Roosevelt personified this trend. She op-

posed anti-Communist legislation while combating the Communist position, politically and intellectually. The Communist Party did not lack for funds or political support when it made "defense of the Party" the urgent issue. In response to the Schwellenbach threat, the Communists launched a financial and political campaign which, on the authority of organizational secretary Henry Winston, reached no fewer than ten million citizens.[13] A quarter of a million dollars were raised for the national organization within 25 days. Winston indicated that perhaps four times as much money went into the Party's coffers on the state and local level. In 1948, the threat of the Mundt-Nixon bill brought the Party a defense fund of half a million dollars — an impressive figure when it is realized that this came on top of the annual Party-Press Fighting Fund Drive, which had just brought in a quarter of a million dollars, and when it is recalled that by the spring of 1948 the Progressive Party's electoral campaign, competing for some of the same sources of funds, was already underway.

The uphill character of the immediate postwar period for the C.P. cannot be adduced as the fundamental explanation of the Party's disasters. The Communists had maintained growth in adverse circumstances at many earlier points in their career even if their growth was always fitful and their successes relative. The battles for unionization and social security, the struggles of the unemployed, the dramatization of Negro rights — all in the early and midthirties — were difficult campaigns. So were the Party's effort to mobilize a predominantly isolationist America for collective security against fascism, and the movement to aid the Spanish Republic. From 1940 to 1942 the Party had weathered astonishing reversals and had landed on its feet in the political arena. After all, a Communist Party is supposed to prosper by giving battle in an unfavorable climate.

An examination of the Party's membership and the condition, at least the outward condition, of its leadership does not give evidence of a physical decline. The membership figures show a steady inflow of new members to the Party ranks; the new members were undeterred by the exodus of an almost equal number. Despite the characteristic turnover, there was a slight net gain. In terms of what Philip Selznick has called the "deployable" membership, that is, the cadres organized to be available for any given campaign, the Party's power of effective mobilization was at its peak after the war.

The first figures for the post-Browder period were given by Eugene Dennis in a report to the National Committee in February 1946: nearly 50,000 members had left the organization since mid-1944 when the Political Association had been formed.[14] (To be sure, this did not mean that all who left the Party were the same ones who had joined in the "revisionist" period. It has already been shown that important cadres and members of the thirties left at the close of the war, taking advantage of the mobility which the war offered or reacting with disenchantment to the 1945 changes.) Yet 50,000 remained in 1946. In August 1948, Henry Winston the organizational secretary, reported a membership of "over 60,000," which confirms that recruiting drives of the previous two years had resulted in a small gain. Winston complained: "in the last three years the industrial composition of our Party has increased only slightly"; even so, some 51 percent of the Communist Party's membership was made up of industrial workers of whom only 11 percent were unemployed. The proportion of unionized members had declined only slightly from the wartime peak — from 46 to 44 percent. Somewhat more than a quarter of the unionists (28 percent) were in C.I.O. unions; 13.5 percent were in the A.F.L.; 2.5 percent were in the independent unions (such as coal mining or railroads); and 7 percent of the working class members were not unionized at all. Translating these percentages into figures on the basis of 60,000 members, this meant a Communist Party of some 30,000 industrial workers, of whom perhaps 3,000 were unemployed as of mid-1948. Close to 9,000 were in the C.I.O., with perhaps 5,000 in the A.F.L. As for the South, where the Party had supposedly been dissolved by its transformation into People's Educational Associations, the enormous emphasis on "reconstitution" had borne fruit. By the beginning of 1946, it was reported that "the Party in the South has at present a membership already equal to that at the time of its liquidation a few years ago."[15] By October 1947 this membership was said to be 2,000, "the highest ever attained."[16]

All these figures reveal the C.P.U.S.A. as a small group, a handful in relation to the population. The figures also suggest that the great effort to recruit was constantly undercut by the departure of both new and old members. Yet the Communists were still the largest of the radical parties. In terms of "battle readiness" — the Party's chief objective in re-establishing a "Marxist-Leninist vanguard"—the figures are not unimpressive. Changes of structure also increased the "deployability" of members. Compared to some 800 community clubs which existed during the last phase of the war, the Party now had 1,700. Winston also reported that the Party had 3,425 industrial clubs.[17] Of these, 300 were "shop branches." The existence of 200 professional and 200 student and youth clubs was also disclosed. In widespread areas of the country the Communists had no membership at all — "not even a foothold" as one leader lamented.[18] Yet the Party did exist in 600 cities, towns, and rural communities. If half its members were not workers, this did not necessarily militate against their effectiveness, in view of the coalition political strategy. All in all, it was not because of a lack of members that the Communists ran into trouble.

As for the Party's leadership, it had undergone important shifts of personnel and by 1947 had also been redeployed. Unlike previous periods of sharp ideological dissension and the expulsion of prominent leaders, no rival party or formally organized opposition to William Z. Foster took shape.[19] This contrast with the past should have favored the Party. After 1929, the Lovestone faction maintained itself for an entire decade. The Trotskyist opposition under James P. Cannon and Max Schachtman, however minuscule, continued to exist as a coherent force. Both these groups had taken out of Communist ranks a significant corps of unionists, organizers, writers, and speakers; each had its own publications and a certain influence. Nothing of the kind happened with Browder's expulsion. Despite the drumfire of criticism against him by Party pundits and the "ism" which now bore his name, it cannot be said that the American Party's problems stemmed from the existence of a competing force led by Browder. He did not organize such a force.[20]

The critics within the ranks whom the Foster-Dennis leadership took seriously enough to expel came from the left, long-time opponents of Browder. They were treated so harshly that by the end of 1946 one would have expected that this opposition had been crushed. The most prominent figures who came under attack in 1946 were Samuel Adams Darcy and William F. Dunne. The former, expelled by Browder in 1944 and then vindicated by the Duclos article, was apparently unwelcome to the one time

Browder men who surrounded Foster after mid-1945.[21] Yet Darcy attracted many admirers. (Two of these were the husband-wife journalistic team of Ruth McKenney and Bruce Minton, both editors of *New Masses*.) Dunne, a former *Daily Worker* editor and also a one time Comintern delegate, had a legendary stature from his days as a leader of the Butte, Montana, copper workers (his two brothers, both Trotskyists, had been key figures in organizing the Minneapolis truck drivers). Dunne was under a shadow during the Browder regime, partly because of chronic alcoholism. In mid-1946 both Darcy and Dunne were charged with having formed a leftist faction. Darcy, never having been "rehabilitated," could not be expelled; but Dunne was ousted along with others. Related to this grouping were two veteran West Coast Communists with an I.W.W. background, Harrison George and Vern Smith, both editors of the *Daily People's World*. Their expulsion was part of a bitter inner-Party battle among left wing unionists who led the machinists' strike in the Bay area.[22]

Neither oppositions of the left nor of the right can be cited to explain the Party's troubles. There were, however, significant changes within the leadership. A serious effort was made to promote younger men to the top levels, and prominent Communist unionists were advanced to leading positions on the assumption that men in touch with the working class would be comparatively immune to "revisionism."

One of the three chief figures of the youth movement of the thirties who came to play major roles in the postwar period was Henry Winston.[23] He was a self-tutored, former bootblack from Hattiesburg, Mississippi, a Negro whose winning personality and intelligence made him one of the Party's most attractive younger cadres for many years. Winston took the post of organizational secretary in mid-1946 (when John Williamson replaced Jack Stachel in trade union responsibilities) and was to figure prominently in the underground of the fifties.

The second major recruit from the youth movement was John Gates, who at the age of twenty-five had been the political commissar of the Abraham Lincoln Brigade; he had left college to organize the unemployment movement in Ohio for the Young Communist League in the early thirties. By 1946, Gates became the key figure in what the Party called its "political action" work. He was also to hold the most trusted posts in the Party's "security" structure. In mid-1947, he was named the editor of the *Daily Worker*, a post he held for the next ten years.[24]

The third important figure among the younger men promoted to top leadership was Robert Thompson, who had joined the Party in Oakland, California, to which he had wandered from his native Grant's Pass, Oregon, in the early thirties. Thompson's record as a one time commander in the Lincoln Brigade and a Distinguished Service Cross winner in the Second World War has been cited. Less known was the fact that early in his Y.C.L. career he had been sent to the Lenin School in Moscow, and went from there directly to Spain. He became secretary of the most important and numerically the largest Party organization — New York's — replacing Gilbert Green, who had shifted to his native Illinois. Having won his spurs as a close associate of Foster's in the emergency secretariat which presided over the mid-1945 crisis, Thompson was to become the chief agent of Foster's policies, formidable because he commanded the New York Party. He was joined by Benjamin J. Davis, the Party's city councilman and most prominent black leader.

A second group of new leaders, some old-timers, some comparatively new to Communism, came out of the trade union movement. They appear for the first time as top Communist Party figures in the first National Board (the equivalent of the "Polburo") immediately after the Emergency National Convention of July 1945. They included Louis Weinstock, of the A.F.L. Painters' Union; Frederick N. Myers, secretary of the National Maritime Union; Irving Potash, the chief figure (along with Ben Gold) in the Furriers' Union; and Josh Lawrence, a Negro seaman. Bella Dodd, who had been the leader of the New York Teachers' Union (only to retire from that post when the Communist Political Association was formed), remained after 1945 as the New York State Party's legislative director. On another echelon, John Steuben, the veteran trade union Communist, came from the Hotel and Restaurant Workers' Union to assume the important post of organizational secretary in New York.[25] Comparatively prominent unionists held leading Party positions at the state level. For the first time men such as William Sentner, leader of the United Electrical Workers in Missouri and Indiana, appeared not only in the roster of the Party's National Committee but in local organizational posts.[26]

Yet within two years few of these figures remained in the leading committees. The effort to integrate the unionists into the Party's leadership came up against a variety of obstacles. Only Irving Potash (perhaps because his position was secure within a union having a large number of left wing workers) could afford full identification with the Party, and he was to be one of the first eleven Smith Act defendants. The departure of the others from the National Board can be explained either by their unsuitability for political leadership or by the pressure of specific union circumstances which made it advisable to remain in a union despite the Party's own needs. Thus, the gap between the Party organization and its most important influentials was not bridged, after all. Neither Browder's attempt to make this possible by changing the Party into an association nor Foster's vow to guarantee the Party's proletarian integrity by having unionists at the helm overcame the dichotomy that had plagued the American Communists for so long.

Shifts within the Party hierarchy reflected Foster's basic dilemma, namely, that he inherited a leadership which had been entirely pro-Browder. The fact that older cadres were usually "leftist" while the indispensable leaders had been "rightist" (no matter what penance they now did or how they were reshuffled) made for an equivocal leadership situation. The former Browder men were increasingly unhappy with Foster's ideas, yet they dared not explicitly oppose them. Even when it became obvious that the Party might be driven into a *cul-de-sac*, they could never shake themselves free of these policies for fear of being tarred with the "Browderist" brush.

Two of the most important casualties in the 1945 changeover were the long-time spokesman, Robert Minor, and the veteran trade union expert, Roy Hudson. Both were viewed either as too compromised by Browder's ideas or as having accepted the repudiation of Browder too reluctantly. Minor, a native of Texas, tried to do appropriate penance by becoming the Party's expert on the South — in a sense he was seeking a return to his native roots after much wandering. From the autumn of 1945, he operated from Washington as a special correspondent for the *Daily Worker* but took an insignificant part in the chief postwar decisions. Hudson, the chief architect of the Party's trade union affairs in the thirties, was relegated to a secondary post in Pittsburgh, after which he went to San Francisco where he was quietly expelled in 1951. This was partly because of a suspicion that his wife of that time was a government agent.[27] Less well known among the casualties was Rob Fowler Hall, a native of Alabama, a founder of the left wing student movement at Columbia University in 1932, an organizer of the farmers' movement, and the Party's most authentic figure in the South until midway through the war. He then became the *Daily Worker's* Washington correspondent, a post for which he was exceptionally well suited but where he was always insecure as Party politics became increasingly chaotic.[28] Jack Stachel, the *éminence grise* of the thirties, headed trade union work until the upset in the U.A.W. in mid-1946 was blamed on him. He became the Party's educational director for a brief time and then returned to his earlier post as the ex officio commissar for the *Daily Worker* until the appointment of Gates in 1947.[29]

All these figures operated under the cloud of a generally rightist past, but the most characteristic and revealing drama was personified in Gilbert Green. His instincts were always toward a broader, more native, and more effective policy, and yet he condoned the ultraleftist course in 1949 and paid the heaviest price for it. As the chief architect of the Party's youth movement in the thirties and therefore the mentor of most of the thousands of second-level cadres, Green had won enough esteem to be named a member of the executive of both the Young Communist International and of the Comintern. One of Browder's closest coworkers, Green also felt the deepest need to give the wartime experiments an ideological underpinning. Uprooted by the critique from abroad, and stricken with remorse, he returned to his native Chicago after 1945 on the assumption that this would give him closer contact with the presumed healing qualities of the industrial working class than was possible in cosmopolitan, "petty bourgeois," New York. By becoming the Illinois secretary, Green opened the way for Robert Thompson's accession to a power position in the sophisticated politics of New York for which the latter was hopelessly unprepared by personal or political training.[30] Green remained, however, a key Party leader. He was constantly involved in trying to strengthen the vacillating Dennis and to minimize the damages of Foster's doomsday drive. Yet, plagued by the memory of his Browderism, Green's own course vacillated. In 1950-51, he was the chief architect of the underground and its most authoritative leader after evading jail under the Smith Act. When he finally gave himself up in September

1956, he had to serve an additional term of almost four years. This removed him from the Party's great crisis, whose depth he could not understand. In particular, he could not grasp why almost all his protégés left the Party in 1956-1958. All told, the Illinois Communist leader endured separation from both his family and his organization for ten years, thus paying the heaviest penalty for the political irresolution of a leadership in which he was the most talented figure.[31]

Finally, in judging how the American Communists applied Marxism-Leninism after their postwar reorganization, some account must be taken of their relation to the international movement. If contact with the Soviet Union and the Communist movements had broken down during the war — this breakdown was advanced as one reason for Browder's grievous errors — the same argument could not hold between 1945 and 1949. The mounting difficulties of this period could not be ascribed to lack of contact abroad. True enough, a direct and formal tie with the Soviet Party was not established until early in 1951 — which was late indeed; that contact hardly dealt with strategic questions, and it disclosed that the Soviet leaders had no particular wisdom to offer.[32]

But as soon as the war ended, important exchanges *did* take place between the C.P.U.S.A. and many other parties, including spokesmen for the Soviet Party. Late in 1945 one of the most distinguished (although least sophisticated) Party leaders, Elizabeth Gurley Flynn, visited Western Europe, where she attended the congresses of the French and British parties. With her was Fred Fine, one of the younger leaders who was soon to be entrusted with the position of assistant organizational secretary and who was later a key figure in the underground. In the spring of 1947, the editor of the *Daily Worker*, Morris Childs (an old-timer who had served as Illinois secretary until mid-1945, and was then charged with the Party's "political action" work until early 1946) covered the Moscow meeting of the Council of Foreign Ministers as a correspondent. Sidney Stein, second in command to Williamson for trade union affairs, attended important meetings of the World Federation of Trade Unions in Budapest at the same time. In the autumn of 1946 I visited most of the Latin American countries as the *Daily Worker's* foreign editor, and attended a congress of the Venezuelan Party and sessions of the Confederation of Latin American Labor. This visit opened contacts with the most prestigious Latin American Communists — such as Victorio Codovilla of Argentina, Blas Roca of Cuba, and Luis Carlos Prestes of Brazil — for the first time in a decade. Apart from trips to Canada, Cuba, and Puerto Rico (with the New York leader, George Blake), the Party's chairman, Foster, travelled to Western and Eastern Europe in the winter of 1946-1947. This trip was another occasion for exchanges of opinion at a moment of great uncertainty for the international movement and the results of these exchanges figured heavily in the most vital Party decisions in the United States.

Top-ranking American Communists were also able to meet foreign Communists of great prestige at the United Nations. One such contact was made between Eugene Dennis and the Hungarian leader, Matyas Rakosi, in the spring of 1946, and another between Dennis and Juliusz Katz-Suchy, the Polish U.N. delegate. Finally, the late Pierre Courtade, the foreign editor of *L'Humanité* (the French Communist paper) accredited to the United Nations, met with all the leading U.S. Communists privately during his first visit in 1947 and again in 1949.[33]

Yet all these contacts proved of little value in guiding the C.P.U.S.A. What these exchanges revealed, taken as a whole, was that the Party in the U.S. was almost always out of step with its friends abroad, and always anxious to stay in step. To get into step meant to make those moves that would prove costly, if not disastrous, in the United States. To survive as a movement required a degree of independent judgment and critical analysis of the American scene and a frank recognition of how different the terrain of European political action was. Yet this independence and critical judgment was exactly what the American comrades did not have and were never permitted.

The American Party's inability to apply Marxism-Leninism successfully, or the crucial inadequacy of the "ism" itself when applied, requires a closer examination of the Party's strategic and tactical judgments. Nothing that has been suggested so far explains in itself why a movement which apparently was restored and operating in favorable circumstances, had so much difficulty.

# 6 QUESTIONS IN SEARCH OF ANSWERS, 1946-47

The leaders of American Communism in the postwar period made little systematic effort to decide what was new in American capitalism, or what the mixed economy and the welfare state might conceivably mean for earlier analyses, and what new relationship might be developing between the United States and a war-ravaged world in which the Soviet Union was now a major power and revolutionary forces were plainly changing the physiognomy of politics. The Communist daily press and periodicals contain detailed factual data and reports on a wide spectrum of events which are invaluable to the historian. But little systematic analysis is found there of what was new about American labor, or of what the New Deal had been (although the departure of Franklin D. Roosevelt made retrospective insight all the more necessary).[1] Only with regard to the character of the Negro rights movement did the Communists do some deeper thinking and contribute to the national debate. Yet all the while the Communists insisted that they had returned to Marxism-Leninism, a doctrine said to be indispensable to political creativity.

The attempts to find a Marxism-Leninism appropriate to the postwar world was accompanied by organizational measures, the redeployment of leaders, and more active participation in the great upswing of the class struggle; the Party's policy stands, however, were basically a refurbishing of older positions. The American Communists were gripped by a desire to re-establish that purity of commitment, that militancy, and that clarity which they believed had been eroded by their wartime errors and by the corruptions and enticements which the wartime policies had imposed. Inevitably they looked toward the past. They turned toward those forms and that definition of the "party line" which seemed in retrospect to have been clear, simple and effective in the thirties.

As early as September 1945, Foster had formulated an overview of world affairs which stemmed from his wartime view, and which he would express throughout the next year in increasingly strident form. (He took this view with him on his visit to Europe early in 1947.) At the Madison Square Garden rally celebrating the Party's 26th anniversary, Foster affirmed that the rulers of the United States, having grown relatively more powerful in a war-shattered world, fully conscious of their superior position, but fearful of revolutionary change, were "determined to subordinate so far as they could the peoples of the world to the economic and political will of American capitalism."[2] What could stop this inherent drive of "the reactionary monopolists," who were "heading the world toward a fresh debacle of economic chaos, fascism and war?" In Foster's view, the Soviet Union and the revolutionary forces which it would seek to associate with it were the chief obstacles to American world domination. In this polarization, what of the U.S. Communists? Their task was to generate a political struggle whereby the "democratic forces" would "pull the teeth of American reaction." This was as ambiguous as it was ambitious.

These ideas were given fuller, less agitational treatment in the February 1946 issue of *Political Affairs* as part of a re-analysis of the Leninist heritage.[3] As Foster saw it, the basic premises of Lenin's analysis of imperialism were as accurate in 1945 as they had been in 1915. Nothing in Lenin's theory needed to be changed even if imperialism as a system had been shattered and the Soviet state was now backed by revolutionary forces of enormous power. Foster believed that an inherent drive to world domination was the main characteristic of American imperialism, even if that imperialism had many peculiarities, had undergone great expansion, and stood in a new relationship to world politics. All political wings of the American system were equally involved in this drive. Foster admitted that there were some differences between the American political parties; the clientele to which they appealed was not the same. Yet the drive to dominate the world, which, he believed, had "proceeded even under the checks of the liberal Roosevelt regime," was "more militant and dangerous under Truman and under a regime dominated by Hoover, Vandenberg and Dewey, etc., it would quickly create a fascist war threat throughout the world."

How was all this to be blocked? In Foster's view, the problem was not to rely in any sense on any wing or part of American monopoly capital. This had presumably been the core of Browder's mistakes. Yet no single force could oppose monopoly capital head on. Evoking the skill with which Lenin had employed class alliances, admittedly in circumstances quite different from those prevailing in America, Foster agreed that an alliance of different classes was required. A coalition would have to be created whose function would be to "pull the teeth of American reaction." Foster envisaged an alliance going "beyond anything in Roosevelt's time." The alliance that had enabled the country to emerge from the worst of the economic crisis, to head off fascist tendencies, to encourage and integrate the organization of labor and finally to win the war — an alliance which included the Communists — was no longer adequate. Foster called for a new alliance. "First, the workers should enter into organized co-operation with the poorer farmers, the Negro people, with the progressive professionals and middle classes, with the bulk of the veterans in joint political action against the common enemy, monopoly capital, in such forms as to culminate eventually in a broad third party movement, and second, this great political combination must be led by the workers, by the trade unions."[4]

Exactly what the political form of such an alliance would be, given the rigid character of the American electoral system, was not at all clear. It is noteworthy that for the first time in a decade the Communists were projecting or rather reviving the concept of a third party. True, this was viewed as a long-term goal. "Eventually" was the operative word. Ten years of experience had demonstrated that much headway could be made by the left within the two-party system. Foster's own experience in the early twenties with the La Follette movement had been catastrophic, in that trying to "go it alone" had set back the left of that time. Yet none of these experiences seemed to enter into Foster's analysis and the projections in 1946. The Communists were abandoning the lessons of that part of their past in which they had been comparatively successful and adopting a prior strategy which had been a failure.

As for the organized workers, to what extent were they prepared to assume the responsibilities which Foster assigned them? In this regard, his article was exceptionally interesting. The American Communist leader granted that American labor had not turned to socialism as a faith and a movement in the sense that European labor had. But American workers had learned through hard experience that the so-called "free enterprise" system could not furnish jobs without government intervention. This lesson in itself "constituted a diminished mass faith in the capitalist system and was a political fact of major significance." Unwilling to leave matters at that, or to draw the conclusion that new initiatives in government intervention were necessary, Foster then foreshadowed what would become over the next several years a prolonged polemic against the ideas of John Maynard Keynes.

Foster admitted that the American trade unions had absorbed Keynesian ideas, meaning that "by government assistance to 'free enterprise,' the breath of life can be breathed into the whole economic system, full employment can be achieved, economic crises overcome or minimized and the ailing capitalist system put on a working basis indefinitely." To the American Communist leader, this working class consciousness, which he considered "a political fact of major significance," was, however, entirely inadequate. It did not "constitute a sound economic or political perspective" and did not allow for "an effective struggle against imperialism."[5]

Thus, the basic forces with which Foster hoped to engineer an antimonopoly coalition were, by Communist definition, unreliable. Their unreliability lay in their belief that capitalism could be reformed. Yet they were indispensable to blocking the drive to war. Without them, so ambitious a task as "pulling the teeth" of American reaction could not be entertained. On the other hand, for the Communists to attempt to forge "a working-class imbued with the spirit of Marxism-Leninism which alone could possibly understand the complex character of the general issues presented by obsolete capitalism" was at best a long-term task. Despite the Party's reconstitution, despite its influence and its membership, one could hardly say as of 1946 that much headway had been made in forging this class consciousness. It was unlikely that the American working class would develop socialist convictions in time to prevent the approaching economic chaos, fascism, and war.

The problem was further complicated by Foster's conception that in standing up to the threat of American imperialism, the Soviet Union would be seeking to lead a world-wide coalition. In Foster's words, such a coalition would encompass "the organized workingclass in the capitalist countries, the peoples of the colonial and semi-colonial countries and the new democratic governments in various parts of the world." The alliance which the American Communists projected as their contribution to the issue would necessarily have to be part of a larger coalition, led by Soviet Russia. Yet acceptance of Soviet leadership was a tall order for a working class woefully Keynesian in its thinking and lacking any faith in the Soviet Union, or for the middle classes, professionals, poorer farmers, and the Negro people who were inherently unreliable except as led by the trade unions. For the antimonopoly movement in the United States to keep in step with a world-wide coalition headed by the Soviet Union and by mass Communist parties in Europe and Asia would require extraordinary political footwork.

Before much of 1946 had gone by, the American Communist leaders introduced in their speeches and writings a note of urgency, a sense of approaching apocalyptic doom. This was summed up in the concept of a growing, ever more acute "war danger." At the Party's National Committee meeting in February 1946, Eugene Dennis suggested that the Party was "in a race with time" and had to "act with dispatch to win, to secure the peace."[6] The Communist leaders were not concerned about wars within the capitalist world or conflicts between the metropolitan powers and colonial peoples. Of course, the increasing assistance by the United States to Chiang Kai-shek, and the conflict between the returning Dutch and the Indonesian nationalists worried them. What they feared was a direct military confrontation between the United States and the Soviet Union. They did not distinguish between the inherent propensity of capitalism toward war (a doctrine which needed re-analysis) and the war danger in the sense of an imminent reality. Despite many indications in their own writings of a recognition that some progress was being made in reaching postwar settlements, the war danger was presented as menacing and ever more imminent.[7]

In an ambitious article for *Political Affairs*,[8] appearing promptly after the important July 1946 meeting of the C.P.U.S.A.'s National Committee, Foster tried to define what was now in the world situation. He began by indicating that the defeat of the Axis had resulted in a "very changed world setting"; nonetheless, the "reactionary manifestations were now more pronounced than they had been in 1919." American policies threatened to "produce an economic breakdown that would arrive more quickly and have far more disastrous consequences than the one which followed the first World War." Whereas the contradictions of imperialism took two decades after 1919 to mature "and it took the war-mongers almost 15 years until they had the world definitely on the way to another world slaughter, World War II is hardly over when the world reactionaries, led by American monopoly-capital, are already beating the drums for a new war. Only in the sense of war preparations against the USSR can one understand the present huge imperialist peacetime military program of the United States, the violent anti-Soviet campaign now raging in the American press and on the radio, and the State Department's officially-stated policy of 'getting tough with Russia.' The danger of war is rendered all the more acute because of the need of haste that the reactionaries feel to make use of the atomic bomb before the Soviet Union can acquire for itself this lethal weapon."[9]

The urgency of an antimonopoly coalition was still very much in the forefront, but the suggestion also crept in that continued defensive action was no longer adequate. Foster came close to adopting the classic Trotskyist position, namely, that peace was not possible without the overthrow of American capitalism. "The axe must be applied to the root of the evil," he thundered, and "the power of finance capital, the breeder of economic chaos, fascism and war, must be systematically weakened and eventually broken." The way forward, he believed, was for the United States not only to take the path of the People's Democracy, as in Europe, but ultimately to achieve socialism. "In no country have the workers and other democratic forces so great a responsibility in the present world crisis as here in the United States."[10]

Along with this judgment of international relations, an estimate of the probable course of the economy which was equally apocalyptic appeared in American Communist thinking. This estimate was largely the work of an eminent theoretician, Alexander Bittelman, who for more than a quarter of a century had been one of Foster's closest coworkers.[11] The Truman administration, Bittelman believed, was yielding to the big monopolists on the question of the rate and scope of reconversion and the dismantling of price controls. The government was not intervening in the economy in defense of the "people's needs." Bittelman set out the consequences if this state of affairs were not changed. "Something else is bound to materialize. That is, an economic catastrophe, within the next three to five years, the likes of which we have never seen before . . . it is generally agreed that the next cyclical economic crisis is about to break out some time between 1948 and 1950. The only question is: if the monopolists have their way in the next three years in domestic and in foreign policy — as they are having it virtually now — then the economic crisis will break nearer to 1948 than to 1950, and will assume a depth and proportion which will dwarf the economic catastrophe of 1929-33."[12]

By November 1946 — that is, three-quarters of a year after the above prognosis — Bittelman became even more specific and his tone more urgent. The sharp fall in stock exchange values that September was seen as a "storm signal." On the other hand, production was plainly on the upswing and the first phase of reconversion as well as the major round of strike actions (which resulted in significant wage increases) had passed. Weighing all these factors, Bittelman made his predictions very concrete: "We must expect a more rapid tempo in the maturing of the economic crisis. Without projecting any definite time forecasts, but merely by way of orientation, it is possible to say that we shall continue to have a rising curve for the next six months to one year, following a similar period of leveling out, followed immediately by the outbreak of a crisis. The question is: will it be a crisis of the type of 1921 or 1929, or some other type in scale, depth and severity?"[13]

The Party's expert noted two elements which entered into the answer. First, there was the growth of war preparations — "faster war preparations, larger war orders." He granted that this development might slow down the tempo of the oncoming crisis, but it would make only for a "more catastrophic crash" later on. Second, "the struggle of the masses," that is, the wage gains and the checking of price rises (requiring a measure of both private and governmental action), might offset the tendency to crisis, but only to a limited extent. Bittelman was quick to qualify both factors. "Without removing any of the elements of basic importance that are responsible for the maturing of the economic crisis, let alone 'abolishing' the causes of the crisis as projected by some bourgeois economists (Keynes) and in part by Browder revisionism, the struggle of the masses against the reactionary offensive and for the maintenance of living standards may slow down the tempo of the maturing economic crisis, may equip the masses economically to withstand with less suffering the impact of the crisis and also narrow the scope of the crisis."[14]

Thus, their analysis convinced the Communist leaders that a crisis was coming. Practical policy dictated the development of a program to alleviate, offset, or delay the crisis. Such a program, however, could not be presented in such a way to foster "illusions" that the "anarchy of capitalism" could be overcome or that the system could be made to work. The Communists therefore raised the alarm over an approaching crisis and indicated a readiness to support proposals to alleviate the effects of that crisis, but never attempted to convince any one of the efficacy of such proposals. Crisis was ineluctable unless serious inroads were made upon monopoly capitalism itself. The job of making these inroads was immense. It could only be effectuated with allies who, by the very fact that they were not Communists, were full of Keynesian illusions, believing in the possibility of making capitalism — and democracy — work.

The Party was placed by its own doctrine in the position of proposing economic measures which could only slightly affect the course of events short of a drastic change in class relations. Furthermore, if these measures were taken seriously as being able to affect the course of events, they might blur the distinction between the Communists and their allies — a distinction which had to be maintained at the risk of falling into "revisionism." Yet the strategic objective of "curbing monopoly capitalism" demanded the help of these very allies. The desired alliance between the Communists and the center-left was thus constantly in jeopardy, or at least always subject to a serious inner strain. The Communists could go along with sorely needed allies only in the conviction that even mutually agreed-upon proposals were no more than illusions. The Communists wrestled with the dilemma that their own proposals would overstep the limits of ideological purity as soon as these proposals were entertained at all seriously.

At the December 1946 plenary session of the National Committee the problem of economic outlook was broached by Dennis himself. It was essential, he thought, "to pay more attention to the question of economic perspective." Then, acknowledging Bittelman's memorandum to the National Board and his article the previous month, Dennis argued as follows. "Insofar as 1947 is concerned, this much is already certain; there will be an economic recession that will take place either in the late spring or summer. This may be followed either by a short period, lasting six to nine months, of a leveling off, so to speak, or it may be followed by a precipitate drop in production and employment, by the development of a full-blown cyclical crisis."[15]

The Dennis formulation was unusually precise, virtually a flat prediction. It dovetailed with the views expressed by Eugene Varga, the leading Soviet economist. Varga's clearest prediction of an early crisis was contained in an article for *Pravda*, November 27, 1946, in which he said: "All this indicates that in the near future, probably not later than 1948 and perhaps even sooner, the outbreak of a new economic crisis can be expected in the United States. Definite, although quite different factors, such as large expenditures on armaments, considerable loans, extended to certain countries, wide and prolonged strikes, can only slightly delay the crisis." Six months later, in an article entitled, "The Coming Economic Crisis in the United States and the Marshall Plan," Varga again voiced the belief that economic crisis would come "not later than 1948."

Whether Dennis, speaking in December 3, 1946, had seen Varga's article of the week before or whether, after making his November 1946 predictions, Varga was reinforced by the opinions of Dennis which were made public in January 1947 is a fine point: a certain interaction of American Communists and other Communist views was probable. In any case, imminent economic crisis was predicted.[16]

To ward off such a prospect, Dennis called for a program that would "help to impede, however slightly, the outbreak of a crisis and above all to safeguard the interests of the people from the ravages of the crisis." The phraseology, which both predicted the crisis and yet sought a program to impede it "however slightly," reflected the basic paradoxes confronting the American Party.

Dennis struck two notes, however, that had not been heard so clearly before. In asking for a "more extensive program for curbing the monopolies" he projected "a more developed program of "nationalization under democratic controls." The slogan of "nationalization" was combined with "the idea of struggle for a new democratic alignment and for the election of a progressive presidential ticket and congress in 1948." The second theme was as ominous as the former was ambitious. "The next cyclical economic crisis in the United States — whatever its special features or length — will enormously accentuate the danger of fascism in the United States which already today is the main center of world reaction." The 1948 elections were therefore viewed in terms of a race against the possibility of a "reactionary, pro-fascist victory." Such an eventuality was situated within the prospect of a full-blown economic crisis, which had already been forecast for the same fateful year, 1948.

Another example of the Party's turn to battle readiness involved its redefinition of the "Negro question" — a subject that was always central to its policy. The debates began early in 1946 and took place at every National Committee meeting until a definitive stand was adopted in December 1946; a specially formed National Negro Commission was occupied with the matter all year.[17] If there was any policy concern on which it can be said that contrasting views were presented and the semblance of a genuine debate achieved, it was the Negro question. Nothing touched so many of the Party's passions, hopes, and calculations as its attitude toward the Negro, and the matter went far beyond championing an oppressed and neglected minority.

This concern with the Negro question had, to be sure, a long history. At their inception in 1919, the American Communists shared the prevailing attitude of the Socialist Party and the I.W.W. that the Negro was part of the oppressed population as a whole. It sufficed to oppose discrimination on grounds of race or color, and it was assumed that racial antagonisms would come to an end when the contradictions of capitalism were overcome by a new social order. Any special program for the Negro was viewed as "reverse racism."[18]

But few Negroes came into the early Communist movement. Those who did soon showed that they were nationalists even more than socialists. They conceived of the American Negro as a colonial entity within the nation. Theodore Draper has shown how the African Blood Brotherhood group was formed quite independently of the Communists but ultimately joined with them and influenced their political position.[19] By the midtwenties, the American Communists were deeply impressed by the Marcus Garvey movement. This was the Universal Negro Improvement Association which championed Negro self-help and self-advancement as part of "a return to Africa." Garvey's popularity revealed a tremendous nationalist potential, and the Communists were intrigued by how they might exploit this potential.[20]

In the late twenties, the Comintern assisted the American party in reaching a vital doctrinal change. American Negroes came to be viewed as a distinct people, as an oppressed nation within the United States, conforming in all essentials to Stalin's definition of oppressed nations which was derived from the experience of Eastern Europe and the tsarist empire.[21] The American Communists declared that the Negro majority stretching throughout the Black Belt — a contiguous section of the South cutting across existing state lines — had the right of self-determination. That is, this majority was entitled to the functions of sovereignty, including the reorganization of state lines to make possible a Black Republic. The Party did not propose *secession* of this conjectured Republic but emphasized its *right to secede* if the Negro majority so desired; the exercise of this right would depend on the level of cooperation between the white minority and the black majority and the level of political advance in the United States as a whole. Negro self-determination was thus seen as being possible before the establishment of socialism. It was granted that the Negro nation could make headway even though capitalism persisted, but increasingly the Communists came to believe that the struggle of American Negroes for equal rights and for changes in the predominantly agrarian structure of the South would bring them into such basic conflict with monopoly capital that they would constitute a powerful ally of the white workingclass.

Strategically, then, the issue of democratic rights for the Negro became a central ingredient in the overturn of capitalism. This issue came to be viewed as a galvanizing force not only for black people but also for the white majority. "Negro rights" became the touchstone of the devotion of whites to the realization of unfulfilled democratic aims as well as an explosive force assisting the white majority in the struggle against the system. As Harry Haywood, one of the original architects of the concept, put it, "The full unleashing of the struggle for Negro liberation" meant "bringing up the strategic reserve of democracy and socialism" and striking at the "Achilles heel of American imperialism."[22]

The Party's considerable impact on the Negro community during the thirties had little to do with the self-determination concept, and indeed it could be argued that the Party had made headway *despite* the Black Republic concept. The Communists had won adherents because they had championed immediate, simple, and practical issues comprehensible to the Negro at a time when few other political forces paid him any attention.[23]

But the idea of self-determination was so powerful that even when Earl Browder proposed to abandon its most negative implications early in 1944 he did so in the form of paying it tribute. Browder argued that wartime experience had shown integration to be the most desirable and effective course. Browder asserted that abolition of discrimination and the achievement of equal rights were possible as part of the antifascist and democratic struggle, but he did so on the grounds that the Negro people had in fact exercised their right of self-determination by opting for integration. Browder was trying to minimize those aspects of Communist policy which smacked of separatism; he hoped to offset the hostility of many Negro leaders, especially A. Philip Randolph, whose March on Washington Movement for the attainment of a national Fair Employment Practices Code in 1942 had been opposed by the Communists (while Browder was in jail) as a blow at the war effort. The Party's opposition to the main Negro organizations had been painful and costly; in 1944 the Communists believed that a wide front in support of the Teheran perspective required making peace with the integration movement. Browder was attacked by mid-1945 (although not at the beginning of the Duclos discussion) as having postulated that the Negro question could be resolved under capitalism. Once the C.P.U.S.A. had decided that nothing in American life could find a solution without a head-on opposition to monopoly capital, it was inevitable that the Negro question would be reopened.

It is significant — and the key to later developments — that in reaffirming the "national character" of the Negro movement the post-Browder leadership tried to shy away from the self-determination concept. It wanted to avoid a separatist approach. Yet the more the Negro question was postulated as "national" in character, the harder it became to offset separatist tendencies. Curiously, the two spokesmen who warned most vigorously against separatism were Southerners — Dr. Doxey Wilkerson, a leading black educator who had contributed to the Gunnar Myrdal report, *An American Dilemma*, and Francis Franklin, a white educator of Virginia Calvinist background. Their sharpest critics were James S. Allen and Max Weiss, both ideologists of the first rank and both trained in the Comintern.

Wilkerson argued that the "separatist implications" of the self-determination slogan were not only "theoretically incorrect" but also a "source of irritation to the Negro people, serving only to alienate from the Communist Party many Negro workers and intellectuals" who would otherwise have been among the Party's "staunch supporters."[24] In his view, the Party's popularity among Negroes in the early 1930's was not based on this slogan "which, fortunately, relatively few Negroes knew about anyway, and fewer still understood." Wilkerson gave two reasons for the comparative success of the Communists; first, their militancy on immediate issues at a time when no one else championed the Negro and second, the prestige of the Soviet Union's nationalities policy. Discrimination had presumably been overcome in the U.S.S.R.

Wilkerson granted that the Negroes constituted an emergent nation, but argued that nations could decline as well as grow, and envisaged the Negro people becoming a "national minority," at least in the North. He also stressed that the Black Belt was diminishing in economic importance and he foresaw the possibility of a growing integration movement among the Negro people as part of what he felt would be possible progressive social development. Not all things in American life must necessarily be thrown backward by capitalism. It could not be assumed that advancement for the Negro was impossible short of the overthrow of capitalism. Doxey Wilkerson felt that progress in the realm of Negro life was possible, even if it were improbable in the nation as a whole.

Two months before Wilkerson's article appeared, the other Southerner, Francis Franklin, argued that Stalin's definition of a nation had been misinterpreted.[25] With a flair for almost theological distinctions, Franklin declared that "Stalin specifically warned against thinking that what may be a correct program for an oppressed nation in one country is necessarily correct for other oppressed nations in other countries." To Franklin, the Negro people in America had gone through an ambiguous evolution. They were "halfway in the American nation, halfway out. Belonging to one nation, they . . . simultaneously developed separate national characteristics of their own." He advanced the rather heretical thought that it was "childish nonsense to say that every statement Browder ever made is false and that every statement that Browder ever made must be automatically rejected merely because Browder said it." In Franklin's opinion, the Negro people were in "a transitional state of flux" and might develop either "toward further separate national development or toward complete voluntary amalgamation on the basis of equality. . ."

Wilkerson was refuted in two articles by James S. Allen, one of the Party's most eminent theoreticians and himself a pioneer in Communist writing on the subject.[26] Allen challenged the statistical evidence that the Black Belt was declining in importance. In his view, wartime Negro migration out of the Black Belt did not significantly reduce the Black Belt's size or the Negro population within it. Moreover, it was "illusory to expect decisive expansion of machine-production in the plantation area under present conditions." Therefore the growth of capitalism could not be a factor in resolving the problem. Wilkerson was prone to accept the possibility of a solution to the Negro question under conditions of monopoly capitalism, Allen charged, and this was, at the least, a Browderist illusion.

A related charge, this time against Franklin, was contained in another closely written article by Max Weiss, then editor of *Political Affairs.*[27] To Weiss, the existence of the Negro nation was the basis of the Party's position. It did not matter, he argued, whether the Negro was conscious of his nationhood. "It would be incorrect to draw the conclusion that, since the Negro people in the Black Belt are not conscious of being a nation, they are therefore not a nation." The substance of race consciousness and pride in being a distinct entity within American life was "national" in character, whether expressed in these terms or not. Moreover, Franklin's argument that as discrimination disappeared — and Franklin also had insisted that this might be possible under capitalism — the Negro nation would take the path of integration, was also unsound. The Negro people were a nation, whether oppressed or not.

Weiss also argued at length the importance of finding those forms which would achieve Negro political power, whether or not this involved a change in federal-state relations or territorial changes within states. He came close to reaffirming the idea of a separate Negro republic within redrawn state lines — the concept which had troubled the two Southerners in the discussion. But Weiss also left himself and the Party a loophole. "What is decisive is that without advancing any specific or concrete demand at this moment, we establish the principle involved."

This approach ultimately prevailed. The Party re-established its concept of the Negro question as a *national* question, thus refurbishing a policy position which had been attenuated in the war years. But in doing so, great emphasis was placed on avoiding anything which smacked of separatism. In the concluding remarks of Eugene Dennis to the December 1946 plenary session of the National Committee, praise for resolution reaffirming the Negro's right to self-determination was balanced by the warning to avoid past errors, namely the "academic debate or fruitless speculation on *when* and *how* this right will be realized and precisely *in what form*" (italics in the original).[28] In contradistinction to the past, said Dennis, "we do *not* present the slogan of self-determination as an immediate slogan of action, but as an affirmation of a historic right which guides and establishes the direction of all our work in the South." A similar balancing of the issue was spelled out in Foster's remarks to the same session.[29]

The decision to redefine the Negro question as "national in character" contained an underlying ambiguity which soon had deep consequences. Once the Negro question was so defined, the Party became more active in this field, but also laid itself open to deviations of "petty-bourgeois nationalism." If integration was no longer a satisfactory answer for the country as a whole, could a political party founded on integration maintain its inner unity once the theoretical premises of integration were abandoned? The crisis that began to wrack the organization in 1949 was due, as will be shown, to the general circumstances of failure and defeat. But it was also due to the contradiction between a movement based on integration and the search for the national essence of the Negro situation. In facing this contradiction, the American Communists were to anticipate by twenty years the experience of the new left of the sixties with the disintegrating force of black nationalism. Yet the Communists can also claim to have pioneered; they had grappled with the "black power" concept since the twenties.

Before turning to Party policy in the unions and in the field of political action, where all the contradictions of battle readiness came into focus, it is useful to pause on one episode which, on the surface, had to do with a secondary matter — culture. (Culture is one of the many fields of Party activity which can only be mentioned, and not deeply explored, in this study.) In general, the Party's leadership shared the anti-intellectualism of the American labor movement, and intellectuals — although deeply attracted to Communism — had difficulty integrating themselves into its activities and leadership. While Communism presumably embraced all aspects of the human experience, most of its leaders had little interest in cultural issues, and were not men of any breadth of culture. It is not surprising, then, that their reaction to the famous "Maltz affair" was strictly political. Yet the affair itself revealed how far the emphasis on battle readiness could take the movement pellmell in a leftist direction, and how costly this could be.

The matter began with a rather innocuous review by the *New Masses* literary critic, Isador Schneider, a novelist of stature who had been part of the distinguished group of American men of letters residing in Paris in the period just after the First World War; he was one of those who had turned most wholeheartedly toward Marxism in the early thirties.[30] Schneider's essay on postwar problems provoked an article by Albert Maltz, one of Hollywood's leading writers and author of the successful wartime novel, *The Cross and the Arrow.* In the February 12, 1946, *New Masses,* Maltz posed the question: "What Shall We Ask Of Our Writers?" He admitted from the outset that some of his statements were "too sweeping, others badly formulated," but he urged that "the attention of readers, however, be directed to the problem itself, rather than to formulations which may be imperfect."

Reviewing the previous decade, Maltz came to the conclusion that many of the problems of the left resulting in "wasted writing or bad art" had been *"induced in the writer by the intellectual atmosphere of the Left Wing"* (italics in the original). He took issue with "the vulgarization of the theory of art" which lay behind left wing thinking: namely, that "art is a weapon." This concept had caused the left much embarrassment. For example, Lillian Hellman's anti-Nazi epic, "Watch on the Rhine," had been criticized by *New Masses* in 1940 (at the time of the German-Soviet Non-Aggression Pact) but was hailed in 1942 when the play reappeared on Broadway unaltered. "This work of art ," Maltz argued, "was not viewed on either occasion as to its real quality — its deep evaluation of life, character and social scene — but primarily as to whether or not it was the proper 'leaflet' for the moment." Maltz then broached the cases of James T. Farrell and Richard Wright, both of them former Communists. In his view, they were writers of talent whom the Communists were inclined to denigrate as writers simply because of their political stance. (Farrell had become an avowed Trotskyist and Wright stepped away from left politics.) Maltz insisted that "writers must be judged by their work, and not by the committees they join. It is the job of the editorial section of a magazine to praise or attack citizens' committees for what they stand for. It is the job of the literary critics to appraise the literary works only."

Maltz' rejection of the concept that "art is a weapon" immediately caused a storm, a veritable furor. Mike Gold, at one time one of Communism's most promising writers and more recently an embittered and unfulfilled columnist for the *Daily Worker*, assaulted Maltz in the coarsest terms, suggesting that he seemed "to have let the luxury and phony atmosphere of Hollywood at last to poison him."[31] One year later, Maltz was to be among the Hollywood Ten who defied the House Committee on Un-American Activities and went to prison for this defiance, unaffected by the poisons of Hollywood. But Gold's attack was hardly a serious rebuttal. This was left to Dr. Samuel Sillen, a professor of English who had been the *New Masses* literary critic and then the *Daily Worker's* literary commentator. He analyzed the Maltz heresy in a series of six articles (February 11-16 and February 24, 1946) thoroughly damning the Hollywood writer. The Sillen articles were a literate presentation of what was to become known in the next years as the *Zhdanovshchina*, (the crackdown on dissident Soviet writers and the subordination of art to politics). All this took place in New York before it began in Moscow.

Schneider was obliged to beat his breast in regret. Joseph North and A.B. Magil (at that time, the chief editors of *New Masses*) joined in the *mea culpa*, since Schneider's initiative and Maltz' article, were felt to be *ipso facto*, a sign of their poor editorial vigilance. Although many letters to the *Daily Worker* showed considerable sympathy for Maltz, he was so roundly condemned that he himself subsequently recanted.[32] The entire episode had a great deal to do with the Party's increasing isolation from many writers.[33] But the only observation from the Party leadership came as a phrase in the report by Eugene Dennis to the mid-February 1946 meeting of the National Committee. He remarked contemptuously that the indulgence of the *New Masses* editors toward a "bourgeois-intellectual and semi-

Trotskyist article" in their pages was a warning to the Party as a whole. Nothing more than this appeared necessary.

At the July 1946 session of the National Committee, at which Foster nominated Dennis to become general secretary, Dennis surveyed the problems of trade union policy and political action against the background of the Party's judgments on international affairs and economic prospects.[34] It was a sobering portrait of the Party's real problems. Serious strains were developing between the Communists and the allies they considered indispensable. The left wing both in the C.I.O. and in the field of political action was having great difficulty implementing a united front policy which Dennis projected in the same breath as he stressed the "war danger," the "maturing economic crisis," and the "enormously-accentuated danger of fascism."

Urging his listeners to stand firmly for a united front with non-Communists, Dennis declared: "Unfortunately, not everyone in the Left Wing grasps this. Unfortunately, there are even some Communists who have a cavalier attitude with respect to relations between the Center — the Murray-Hillman forces — and the Left Wing in the C.I.O. Unfortunately, even some Communists in the C.I.O. misjudge and distort the middle-of-the-road though generally progressive position of the Murray-Hillman forces. Instead of seeking to resolve tactical and similar differences in a friendly fashion as between allies, some Leftwingers are frequently inclined to blow up each point of disagreement and every divergency of view into a major conflict, into a head-on collision with Murray and all non-Left forces in the C.I.O."[35] Dennis made an emphatic rejection of such tendencies. "This meeting of our National Committee must declare war against such attitudes. We affirm that the C.I.O., headed by Philip Murray, is the most progressive union center in the U.S. We affirm that the basic policies of the C.I.O. are progressive and today are vital to advancing the struggle for economic welfare, democracy and peace. We declare that the relations between the Left Wing and the Center are decisive for the future of the C.I.O. and our relations with the Murray-Hillman forces are not temporary, are not based on transitory considerations but are based on a long-range perspective of friendly collaboration for progressive aims, without which there can be no substantial progress of the C.I.O., the American labor movement and the developing unity of action of Communists and non-Communists."[36]

Equally emphatic was the treatment which Dennis gave to problems of political action. By mid-1946 the Democrats had suffered serious setbacks in primary elections in California, and the left had contributed to these setbacks.[37] The disunity among the Democrats, who were increasingly divided over the policies of the Truman administration, favored a Republican comeback. Dennis sounded the alarm against this trend. The Communists, he insisted "must work hard to bring about even temporary and limited alliances and cooperative relations with all peace-loving elements, no matter how unstable and vacillating they may be, but who, for one reason or another, desire to advance the cause of peace and democracy. For example, . . . the Communists must not hesitate to develop joint action with numerous groups and individuals who still support the Administration. . . . Furthermore . . . the militant workers must enlist the aid of certain political figures and groups who also happen to support various features of the Administration's imperialist foreign policy. This tactic is an anti-fascist axiom which now, particularly, must be utilized and brought into practical operation."[38]

Thus, while reaffirming the post-Duclos concept of an independent Communist position on all issues, Dennis warned: "In doing this we must reject the sectarian concept and practice that the maintenance of our independent position means or must result in our self-isolation, the separation of the Communists from the mass of the workingclass, or the alienation of us Communists from our progressive non-Communist allies, especially in the labor movement."[39]

Yet this alienation seemed to be taking place. As he struck the political balance sheet, Dennis was alarmed. He admitted the Communist responsibility for the ebbtide among the Democrats.

The adverse results in many of the primaries were due, furthermore, to the sectarian and one-sided position which sections of the progressive labor movement, including certain Party forces, developed toward all Democrats, including progressives like Kenny and Patterson in California, and toward other and more conservative, middle-of-the-road or wavering pro-labor Democrats.

Increasing indignation toward, and correct opposition to the reactionary course of the Truman Administration . . . blinded certain labor and progressive groups to the need for simultaneously unmasking and opposing the vicious political spokesmen of the N.A.M. [the National Association of Manufacturers] gathered around the reactionary Republicans. It also resulted in a confused state of thinking on the part of many progressives. They failed to differentiate between the Farleys and the Kennys, and lost sight of the urgent need for the labor-progressive coalition to influence, win over and give critical electoral support to certain wavering, pro-labor elements in the Democratic Party.[40]

What strategy, then, did Dennis advise? It was essential, he thought, that "while pursuing an independent workingclass policy and expanding its independent political organizations and activity," the labor movement "help influence a progressive regrouping within the Democratic Party." The left wing had "to achieve a working agreement with these forces" for the November 1946 congressional elections. This strategy was admittedly "fraught with many difficulties." The "Murray-Hillman forces," with whom the Communists wanted a long-term relationship, were "prone to drag themselves after the Democrats, to adjust themselves to the Democratic Party organizations and decisions, to follow the electoral pattern of '44."

The left wing had to push for an independent policy. But in doing this, it had to remember the following. "The decisions and the blessing of the Left Wing are not only prerequisites for the successful running of independent candidates and tickets. ...What is also required is the collaboration and active support of the Murray-Hillman forces and other progressive elements, including the cooperation of certain conservative-progressive groupings now associated with the Democratic and Republican parties."

As for the idea of a third party which had been broached by Foster the previous January, Dennis entered strong qualifications. "By and large conditions have not yet matured at this time for crystallizing third parties organizationally on a state or local scale." Admitting that among the allies whom the Communists considered indispensable, "a trend of opinion is coming to the fore which challenges the basis and outlook for new party alignments," Dennis advised that the Communists ought not to clash directly with such trends. Instead, he counselled patience. He urged the Party to occupy itself with "preparing the way" and "laying the foundations" for grass roots movements out of which a third party might someday emerge.

Wallace and Ickes, as well as certain C.I.O. Political Action

Committee (P.A.C.) leaders, represented points of view opposed to a third party, Dennis noted. "They recommend increased progressive political action . . . but solely within the framework of the two-party system. They consider that a third party would *ipso facto* become a minority party and would inevitably ease the way for the coming governmental power of the most reactionary forces." To Dennis, "such viewpoints were based on the status quo" and not the dynamics of American life. But he felt constrained to warn his listeners that the left wing could "neither ignore nor dismiss the viewpoints of such honest, though confused, progressives. Least of all [could the left wing] develop a head-on collision with the leading spokesmen of such outlooks. . . ."

Clearly, Dennis groped for a formula whereby those who wanted to remake the Democratic Party, in the mistaken but honest hope that this could be done, would be assisted by the Communists. At the same time, the latter would advance their own perspective of a third party without trying to precipitate such a party prematurely, even on a local scale. And in employing these two tactics, Party members must not allow them to clash. "In no case should the struggle for a third, people's party be developed so as to weaken the cooperation of all progressives in the 1946 elections or so as to launch a major, and frontal attack against the advocates of limited independent political action, such as the Wallaces and the Ickes. Serious and legitimate differences regarding the future course of labor-progressive political action must not divert the Communists and other militant workers either from advancing a new progressive party alignment — based on the trade unions and other mass organizations of the people — or from cooperating with, or seeking out and cultivating, allies and associates from the followers of Wallace, Ickes, and other independents."[41]

These were difficult tactics to implement. The Communists found themselves impelled in two directions at once. Two different conceptions were at work. Dennis personified and expressed the Party's misgivings as it plunged from one to another.

### Zigzag in a Critical Autumn

In the autumn of 1946 three events — each bearing on a different phase of Communist policy but all interconnected — took place which revealed that the overall program of achieving battle readiness had run into serious difficulties. The close of 1946 is thus the crucial moment in the American Communist Party's new course. A political movement had readied itself for battle. Suddenly there were doubts as to where the battlefield lay.

The first problem involved the Party's attitude toward Henry A. Wallace, at that time Secretary of Commerce in President Truman's cabinet. He was the man who might have succeeded Franklin D. Roosevelt if the Communists had been as enthusiastic about him in 1944 as they were to be in 1948. The Communists, it will be recalled, did not mourn when Mr. Wallace was passed over by the Democratic Party's 1944 convention in favor of Harry Truman. Wallace missed the presidency by a matter of months. But he remained with Mr. Truman's administration, and not until 1946 did he begin to criticize its course. At a Madison Square Garden rally in September 1946 Wallace gave his views on foreign policy, proposing in effect a delineation of spheres of influence with the Soviet Union and taking strong exception to the "get tough" diplomacy of both the American and the Soviet governments as their differences escalated. Mr. Wallace presented his remarks in the framework of support for Mr. Truman. The latter had received a memorandum from Wallace the previous July outlining views which Truman approved, and the speech itself had the President's approval as well. The predominantly left wing audience did not appreciate Wallace's remarks except as they were critical of United States policies and could be interpreted as a difference of opinion with Secretary of State James F. Byrnes, who was at that moment negotiating with the Russians in Paris. As for those passages in which Wallace took exception to Soviet policy, the audience responded with hisses and boos.

The next morning the *Daily Worker* was critical of the Wallace speech, arguing that by his failure to disassociate himself from Mr. Truman's policy he was actually giving it support. The former vice-president was accused of seeing Soviet policy in terms not too different from Mr. Byrnes and Senator Vandenberg. In the hectic week that followed, Mr. Truman at first supported his Secretary of Commerce and then, after a long transatlantic teletype conversation with Mr. Byrnes and a bitter analysis from Bernard Baruch, decided to dispense with Mr. Wallace's services.[42] A few days after having assailed Wallace, the Communists found themselves obliged to support him. What had been brought to the surface was a major rift within the Democratic administration along precisely the lines that the Party found desirable but for which it was unprepared. The Communist paper's chief editorial writers had failed to grasp what Dennis had taken such pains at the July meeting of the National Committee to emphasize, namely, that rifts within the Democratic Administration could materialize even among those Democrats who, for reasons peculiar to their history and their limitations, had not until then been ready to break with Mr. Truman and who did not hold opinions about Communism to the liking of the Communists. The Party's editorial writers had been unable to implement the line which Dennis had projected.

The second problem that autumn concerned the maintenance of alliances. This problem emerged very acutely in the trade union field, and, called into question the whole nature of the American Party's relationships in the labor movement. As has been shown, the left wing held a minority position in the C.I.O., but an important one. Several key unions were under its control. Perhaps the most important was the United Electrical, Radio and Machine Workers, with contracts in the most vigorous and developing parts of American industry. Another much smaller union of strategic importance was the American Communications Association. A third was the United Public Workers, which during the war had made considerable headway in the federal as well as state and municipal civil services. In a series of secondary unions — the fur and leather workers, the distributive trades, and the furniture workers — the left was strongly entrenched. And it was the predominant influence in the Mine, Mill and Smelter Workers of the Rocky Mountain area as well as in the International Longshoremen and Warehousemen's Union on the West Coast. From mid-1945 on, the left was on the defensive within the National Maritime Union which it had done so much to build, but it had not yet been routed there. As for the United Automobile Workers, Walter Reuther, the arch enemy of the Communists, had gained the presidency, but he was still hemmed in by an executive board in which the left wing had a definite influence as a result of its alliances with the Addes-Thomas faction.[43] In the Transport Workers' Union of New York, which also had contracts in other cities, the left held undisputed sway, having built the union from scratch.

But the left wing strength did not depend only on control of separate unions. The left dominated a variety of city and state industrial union councils which in the C.I.O. were the counterpart of the Central Trades and Labor councils of the A.F.L. And at that moment — toward the close of 1946 — the left wing was extremely influential in the C.I.O's national office, thanks to the reliance which president Philip Murray placed on his chief legal counsel, Lee Pressman, and the editor of the *C.I.O. News*, Len DeCaux. Both men had been inherited from the earlier regime of John L. Lewis.[44]

The left wing had played an important part in bringing to life the World Federation of Trade Unions, a new world body that rivaled the moribund International Federation of Trade Unions to which the A.F.L. still adhered. Through the World Federation and also by direct relationships, the C.I.O. was connected with the Confederation of Latin American Labor (the C.T.A.L.) in which Communist-led union federations had full citizenship under the presidency of the Mexican quasi-Marxist, Vicente Lombardo Toledano.

A decade of hard work had gone into securing all these positions. From the tumultuous midthirties, the Party's activities and influentials had come a long way. Whereas all earlier ideologically motivated unionists, for example, the socialists and the syndicalists, had not been able to achieve a durable place within American unionism, the left wing of Communist persuasion appeared to have succeeded.[45] The socialists had fought Samuel Gompers for control of the American Federation of Labor and, except for a brief and fugitive victory, had lost. Another variety of socialist then attempted under Daniel De Leon to build a dual union apparatus intimately tied to the Socialist Labor Party and that had failed. In the I.W.W., all kinds of radicals tried to build trade unions which would at the same time be political instruments, but this synthesis of the union and party had come to naught. During the twenties, the most politicized of the unionists had attempted to find their way back into the mainstream of the official labor movement through the Trade Union Educational League (in which both Browder and Foster had taken part) and by the early thirties had turned in desperation to another round of dual unionism in the form of the Trade Union Unity League. The cadres who had their baptism in these experiences found themselves, after the Wagner Act and the sanction of the New Deal, in the leadership of a new wing of the House of Labor. The maintenance-of-membership clauses, which the War Labor Board accepted as the key to industrial peace, had operated to strengthen the unions and bring into them millions of new workers, most of whom had not had the experience of the organizing drives of the thirties.[46] This new membership not only swelled the union coffers but gave labor enormous economic power and made it a factor in the politics of both the Republican and Democratic parties.

It appeared that, for the first time in 75 years, left wing unionists had been able to integrate their trade union activity with the political movement which had given them their original impetus. But they were unable to maintain influence simply by their reputation as union leaders, and only in a few unions did they have a strong rank and file of left persuasion. They were able to lead because of a carefully nurtured alliance with what they called the "Center" leaders, personified by Philip Murray and Sidney Hillman. (In the earlier period, the alliance had centered on John L. Lewis.) These men were disposed to respect the individual political views of the left wing leaders, provided these did not jeopardize the C.I.O. as such. Indeed, only by this alliance was the left able to fend off the hostility of its ideological opponents.

Well before the war, the Social Democrats (also entrenched in important unions) and the Association of Catholic Trade Unionists (A.C.T.U.) had challenged the left wing and tried to balance or whittle down its influence. Although a large proportion of American workers were Catholic and so were many trade union leaders (in particular, Philip Murray), the appeal of political Catholicism made little headway so long as the C.I.O. existed as a center of diverse opinions which no single group attempted to monopolize. Melting-pot trade unionism, reflecting the melting pot of the society as a whole, could hold the movement together, provided that all groups were prepared to subordinate their special interests for the sake of this unity.

But if the Communist Party were to demand of its members things they could not do as unionists, then it could easily be accused of wanting to use the union for ulterior purposes. The pro-Communist left had either to try to win support on the merits of the argument and abide by the decision of the majority if such support could not be won, or to provoke a bitter, fratricidal battle in which it was strong enough to make a fight but not strong enough to win. If it abided by the relationship of forces, it could retain trade union positions. But increasingly these positions might demand support of policies divergent from the aims of the Party. The Party could accept this state of affairs only if it accepted an essentially non-Leninist relationship between Party and union, giving each autonomy.

But if it made a fight to politicize its union positions, the left wing would be returning to a syndicalist conception, the notion that the Party and the union were interchangeable and indistinguishable. With such a concept, the left wing of the mid-forties hardly had a better chance of maintaining itself than its predecessors had. To adapt itself to the separation between Party and union meant to follow the logic of the success of the unions which had become autonomous and institutionalized forces within the society, whatever the private views of their pioneering, crusading founders. Many a left wing unionist in fact accepted the compulsions of this institutionalization as a matter of day-to-day practice.

But for the very reason that the Communist influentials had not legitimized their political convictions, they tended in private to rationalize their roles by assuming that they were better revolutionaries than the publicly avowed Communists; often they tried to use their union positions to support these private opinions. Many adherents of the left wing were thus disposed, as Dennis had noted, to break the discipline of the center-left alliance, and to let political differences intervene in the union balance. The peculiar sociology of the concealed Communists and their close supporters thus fed all sorts of rivalries, factionalism, and political maneuvering within the C.I.O. at a moment when the Party was being pressured by its battle readiness to encourage such tendencies even as it recognized their dangers.

Without understanding the dilemmas of the left in any such terms, Philip Murray was being impelled in the summer of 1946 to seek a formula of his own to keep his organization intact. His formula was to reject "outside interference" in the C.I.O. and keep the C.I.O. as separate as possible from the crisis of the Democratic Party without, however, losing the advantages of the C.I.O.'s influence in politics. Murray had taken part in the Chicago meeting of the "Conference of Progressives."[47] This gathering brought a wide variety of the most prominent New

Dealers as well as left wingers of both union and middle class derivation together to consider how the Roosevelt heritage could be carried forward under changing postwar circumstances. Once Wallace (who was present at Chicago) had been ousted from the cabinet, Murray declined to make this Conference a continuing affair. During the following winter, he tried desperately to preserve the unity of the C.I.O. in other ways. For example, he forbade members of the executive board to join either the Americans for Democratic Action or the Progressive Citizens of America. As early as May 1946, Murray declared to the convention of the United Steelworkers (of which he was president): "This union will not tolerate efforts by outsiders — individuals, organizations or groups — whether they be Communist, Socialist or any other group — to infiltrate, dictate or meddle in our affairs." Yet he also made it plain at both the Conference of Progressives and in a subsequent speech to the United Electrical Workers' Convention that he did not want a witchhunt. "I am not a very good hunter," he told a reporter who specifically asked whether the "Reds" in the C.I.O. would come under attack.[48]

It was understandable, then, that on the eve of the C.I.O's eighth national convention in Atlantic City in November, Murray insisted that the executive board adopt the following resolution. "We resent and reject efforts of the Communist Party or other political parties and their adherents to interfere in the affairs of the C.I.O. This convention serves notice that we will not tolerate such interference."

This declaration was adopted almost without debate. It had been prepared by a subcommittee which included prominent left wingers, among them Michael Quill. Certainly these left wingers did not act without prior consultation with the Party.[49] The question arises — and this is what makes the entire incident an important turning point — as to whether the Party and its trade union supporters were fully conscious of what was at stake. For if the acceptance of this declaration was more than a maneuver, it signified that the Party was consciously accepting a departure from doctrine. It was recognizing the autonomy of its members in their trade union activity. Abiding by the logic of this stand, the Party could not ask the same unionists to place the Party ahead of the union at some future point (especially for trivial reason). On the other hand, such a social democratic stance might not give a long-term and loyal character to the relations between the left wing and the center, as Dennis had demanded in his July 1946 National Committee report, unless the Party's own unionists fully accepted the logic of this stance. There was always the possibility that *they*, not the Party as such, would exacerbate relations with the center on the private assumption that in so doing they were advancing the revolutionary cause. In this respect the essentially syndicalist background of the most important left wing labor leader, Harry Bridges, chief of the West Coast longshoremen, must be taken into account.[50] Bearing in mind that the Communist unionists were either unavowed or were linked with quasi-Communists of a syndicalist stamp, such as Bridges, it was entirely possible that merely accepting the "resent and reject" declaration would neither ease the C.I.O.'s crisis nor guarantee its unity.

If the acceptance of the declaration were a mere maneuver, it could boomerang in another way. Devoted Communists among the unionists would see in it an unprincipled compromise. The readiness of the Party to accept this device would compromise the Party in their eyes. Opponents would feel that the Communists were on the defensive; and therefore, it would be only a matter of time before the pressure on the left wing would grow. Time would have been bought at the expense of integrity. With integrity gone, time would run out.

The third, and gravest problem that autumn resulted from an interview by Joseph Stalin with correspondent Alexander Werth, during which the Soviet leader denied that the world stood in danger of early war. Stalin also denied that Anglo-American ruling circles were planning war. After a year of increasing tension with his former allies (Stalin had himself in February 1946 declared that wars were inevitable so long as the imperialist system prevailed)[51] and half a year after attacking Churchill for the bellicosity of his Fulton, Missouri, speech, Communism's most eminent leader now deflated the talk of war. He dismissed it as a species of blackmail related to the internal politics of the Allied countries. Stalin's statement came, it should be noted, after a year of an increasingly shrill emphasis by the American Party on the war danger, and thus it represented a rather bewildering challenge to Foster. Did Stalin's statement mean literally what it said? If it did, the American Party was out of line, not only in judging the actual danger of war, but also in its interpretation of American life. Or was Stalin's statement intended to have a specific diplomatic effect? Did it reflect a specific Soviet internal need? A case could be made that the Soviet leaders were demanding such an extraordinary mobilization of their own peoples for reconstruction that they had to give them assurances of a long period of peace. None of these latter considerations seem to have entered into the American Party's reaction. As was its custom, it took Stalin literally and assumed that his declaration had a universal significance.

In the November 1946 *Political Affairs,* ideologist Max Weiss devoted an article to the Stalin declaration. He carefully avoided any explicit self-criticism or any strictures against his own Party's leadership: this would have opened a Pandora's box. But he did say the following. "An estimate that the outbreak of war is imminent, under conditions in which this is not so, makes it more difficult to mobilize the masses for struggle around the concrete issues which are involved in the present reactionary foreign policy of the Truman Administration. The fight for peace is not advanced one iota by shouting that war is right around the corner when in actual fact it is not."[52]

The intellectual challenge of Stalin's interview went much deeper and Weiss could not deal only with its tactical or diplomatic purpose. The Soviet leader could not be interpreted as having made a "repetition of the Soviet Union's diplomacy of peaceful coexistence." A mere propagandistic purpose was "not sufficient to justify a declaration that there is no imminent danger of war. If the ruling circles of American or British imperialism planned an attack on the Soviet Union in the immediate future, there would be a real danger of war despite the Soviet desire for peace. Hence Stalin's reply to Werth is based on a realistic estimate of the present relations of all world forces. It takes into account not only the policies of the Soviet Union, but the present policies of the ruling circles of American imperialism as well."[53]

But if the "present policies of the ruling circles of American imperialism" were *not* oriented toward war, then what happened to the basic outlook of the American Party? Weiss was aware of the dilemma. He could not countenance any suggestion that the United States, with all the power which its imperialist ruling class exercised, might not envisage any military conflict with the Soviet Union. Such a view would open the gates to Browderism. Nor could it be postulated that the Cold War had its limits, that it would not necessarily lead to full-scale war-fare; this was too subtle a view and would invalidate much of the American Party's tactics. Doubt could not be cast on the war-making character of capitalism, for this would upset the conceptions of Marxism-Leninism on which the Party's reconstitution was based. Weiss fell back on the distinction between subjective desires and objective reality.

Weiss argued that the American ruling class, which definitely *did* want war, was encountering obstacles in trying to change the unfavorable relationship of world forces in its favor. Weiss did not go into the logical question of why, if the obstacles to a world-dominating policy were removed, the United States would at that point need war at all; it would be having its way without war. But the distinction did enable him to define the Republican Party as "the main vehicle and center of reaction and fascism," whose coming to power would heighten the war danger. "If (the reactionary) forces are not identified, isolated and defeated, and if they are allowed to come to power in our country then the present talk of war will soon be converted into an actual danger of war." Thus, the danger lay in a Republican victory in 1948.

The question which followed logically was whether the antiwar forces should not, as a consequence of this danger, do everything in their power to block a Republican victory by supporting the only feasible political alternative to the Republicans, the Democratic Party? Yet a basic Communist thesis was that the Democratic administration was yielding to the Republicans and in any case represented a wing of American imperialist interest on whom no reliance could be placed. The thrust of the Weiss analysis placed the Party's electoral tactics in doubt. His article ended by attempting to square the circle. He reaffirmed the need for an antimonopoly coalition which would emerge in time to stop the inherent danger of war that a Republican victory would represent, and at the same time rejected the alternative of re-electing the Democrats.

All these matters came up for review at the Party's National Committee meeting in December 1946. In a groping somewhat bewildered fashion, several Communist leaders revealed their dissatisfaction with the Party's line. But no one challenged its premises. William Schneiderman, the California secretary, moved to censure the *Daily Worker* on the grounds that its fumbling treatment of the Wallace-Truman affair had helped to disorient the entire movement. Dennis replied that the editors of the *Daily Worker* were "largely on their own, by a decision, and a correct one, of the National Board." In discussing the *Daily Worker*, however, Dennis lifted the veil on deeper problems of the Party's leadership. For he spoke of "a two-way vendetta and factional attitudes which have been developed on the part of some comrades in New York and the *Daily Worker* editors."[54]

Dennis, who had become general secretary at the previous National Committee meeting, could not let the responsibility rest with the *Daily Worker*. He admitted that the Party's leadership had failed to achieve "full clarity, a solid viewpoint . . . on a number of questions." And he spoke of

> serious errors committed in the direction of misjudging the relationship of international forces, in underestimating the world forces and factors that have been operating to prevent the outbreak of a new world war in the immediate future. Furthermore, those tendencies which did exist to regard World War III as imminent, as something that might break out any day or month . . . were not sufficiently combatted. From this there developed certain sectarian attitudes towards forces, people and movements in the labor movement as well as in the broad democratic coalition who, for one or another reason, have been slow in publicly breaking with the Truman administration and its reactionary policies.

> It was in part because of such tendencies that the first editorial in the *Daily Worker* on the Wallace speech adopted such a completely negative attitude toward Wallace's position. That is why some comrades—and not only those on the *Daily Worker*—could not see the woods for the trees and were disoriented by the unjust and harmful remarks by Wallace on the Soviet Union and the Communists. Because of this, the comrades failed to grasp the fact that Wallace, in his own way and within the limitations of his position, was challenging the main line of the Byrnes-Vandenberg policy.

> This is why some comrades who had excluded the possibility of any cracks, rifts or fissures in the Administration or the Democratic Party circles, no matter how small or lim-

ited, were misled in their first estimate of Wallace's speech because at that time he had not yet left the Cabinet, had not broken formally with the Administration. Suffice it to say that we must still be on guard against such attitudes and tendencies and must eradicate them from our thinking and work.[55]

What we have spanned in this chapter, then, is a year in which the Party prepared for battle in favorable circumstances, but without a clear understanding of what was happening and why. It had painted itself into an ideological corner, and it was now facing the test of its actions in the year of decision, 1947.

# PART III  WHEN A MOVE-
# MENT HAS LOST ITS WAY

Arraigned in 1948 under the Smith Act, some of American Communism's top post-war leaders: (left to right) William Z. Foster, chairman; Jack Stachel, educational director; Henry Winston, in charge of organization; Benjamin J. Davis, Jr., city councilman; Eugene Dennis, general secretary; and John Williamson, trade union director. Missing from this photo are John Gates, *Daily Worker* editor; Robert Thompson, N.Y. state secretary; Gus Hall; Gilbert Green; and Carl Winters, the Party secretaries for Ohio, Illinois, and Michigan, respectively; and Irving Potash, leader of the Furriers' Union. (Wide World Photos)

# 7 DUBIOUS BATTLES AND

# CRUCIAL DECISIONS, 1947-48

The decisions for which the American Communist Party had been preparing came earlier than had been expected. In 1947 the Party made the basic decision which led to catastrophe one year later with the failure of Henry Wallace's campaign for president. The major analytical problem is to determine the meaning of the contradictory trends that were at work within the Party that year, and to understand why, after strong hesitation in the first half of 1947 with respect to the third party, the Communists went ahead by the end of the year to endorse Henry Wallace's decision to form a new organization. The problem is to establish what elements caused them to hesitate, and what new factors caused them, in the late autumn of 1947, to override their earlier misgivings and gamble their entire political capital on the antimonopoly coalition which they assumed the new party to be.

In the early days of 1947, William Z. Foster made a trip to Europe. This trip came after mounting evidence of what Dennis called the absence of "full clarity, a solid viewpoint" in the Party's top leadership. It was Foster's first visit abroad since before the war, and came 18 months after his accession to power following the Duclos article. Foster's immediate destination was the conference of the Communist Parties of the British Empire countries, which met in London from February 26 to March 4, 1947. This gathering was followed by the congress of the British Party. Afterward, Foster visited the chief capitals of Eastern Europe—Prague, Sofia, Belgrade, and Warsaw—and conferred there with men he had known from the Comintern days, such as Klement Gottwald and Georgi Dimitrov. (The latter, as mentioned, had harbored strong doubts about Foster's outlook in the late thirties and therefore the encounter must have had special drama.) Foster also visited Paris and Rome, stopping in Switzerland and Trieste. Whether he went as far as Moscow is doubtful. It would, however, have been natural for him to confer with Soviet Communist leaders somewhere in Eastern Europe, although no evidence exists that he did so.

Foster's book, *The New Europe*, which appeared in mid-1947, is characteristically propagandistic.[1] It does not describe his conversations in any political depth, nor does it identify all those with whom he met, not even Western Communists. Foster does not seem to have confided completely to his own colleagues the substance of his agreements or disagreements with the most prestigious Communist figures in Europe.[2] Yet we do know from Foster himself (at a later date) that these disagreements existed. And there is important indirect evidence from the Canadian Communist leader, Tim Buck, that the American Party's outlook and emphasis was criticized during an encounter with none other than Jacques Duclos.

The evidence from Foster that the American Party was quite out of step with most of the other parties in 1946-47 came a year later, after the Cominform had been organized and after the Cold War had developed to an acute stage. Speaking to the Party's 14th National Convention in August 1948, Foster made a curious reference to the state of affairs early in 1947. "I attended the London Conference of the Communist Parties of the British Empire, as well as the Congress of the Communist Party of Great Britain. At these gatherings I listened to the reports of delegates from thirty-four Communist parties and very few of them indicated any sense of the real danger of war and fascism from American imperialism. It was only later, and especially after the announcement of the Truman Doctrine regarding Greece, that these parties, which had undoubtedly previously under-estimated the role of American imperialism, brought themselves up-to-date on this question."[3]

The other evidence of Foster's dilemma abroad appears in a book by Tim Buck, who attended the same conferences as Foster and toured much of Eastern and Western Europe with him. Buck did not have the same reticence as Foster in naming the distinguished Communist leaders with whom they talked. The Canadian tradition was more open and the atmosphere less charged. One passage portrays Foster, Buck, and Jacques Duclos in conversation. Quite fascinating is the clear rebuke by Duclos to Foster over the latter's fixation with the war danger. Moreover, Duclos' own treatment of world issues suggested the nascent polycentrism of that period. Said Buck: "Jacques Duclos summed it up when he said to Bill Foster and me: 'The most decisive question today is not "is there or is there not a war danger." The decisive question for individuals, parties and governments is: "Where do you stand?" Two great bodies of opinion are competing for men's support. It is not true to say that this is a contest between the Soviet Union and the United States because it is going on in every corner of the civilized world. It is true, however, that this contest comes into focus and is more obvious between the new democracy of which the decisive center is as yet in Europe and the struggle to stabilize imperialism, of which the decisive center is now in the United States. It is quite clear that the one means whereby the danger of a third world war can be eliminated is by giving us in Europe time to show that the tremendous human advance achieved by the peoples of the USSR on the ruins of Czarism can be surpassed by the peoples of Europe building on the ruins of Hitlerism.' "[4]

Shortly after Foster's return from abroad, the Cold War intensified. General George C. Marshall, at a meeting of the Council of Foreign Ministers in Moscow, concluded that, for the time being, no bargain could be struck with Stalin. This meeting in May 1947 came just before the Secretary's famous address at Harvard University on June 5, 1947, announcing the readiness of the United States to underwrite the rehabilitation of Europe. Later that month the Communists in Prague, Warsaw, and even Moscow were at loggerheads as to whether to accept what soon became the "Marshall Plan." In the period between Foster's trip and the Council of Foreign Ministers meeting much had happened to worry the American Communists acutely, and at the same time a great deal was going on which gave them hope.

The declaration of the Truman Doctrine in March was followed by a vast outcry against Administration policy. The trial balloon of Secretary of Labor, Lewis Schwellenbach, on March 11, 1947, proposing to outlaw the Communist Party also provoked widespread protest. Little protest, however, met the Administration's decision on March 23, 1947, to require a loyalty oath of all civil service employees. This was Executive Order 9385, later extended to all workers in defense industries. At the same time, the new labor legislation introduced by Senator Robert A. Taft and Representative Fred Hartley brought about an unprecedented negative reaction from all wings of labor, and a personal meeting of Philip Murray, John L. Lewis, and William Green (hitherto a most difficult thing to achieve).

To the Communists and their friends in the labor movement,

the provisions in the Taft-Hartley bill for an 80-day cooling-off period and a ban on secondary strikes, and the other clauses in the bill hampering the trade unions were not as important as Section 9H, which required that all trade unions who wished to avail themselves of the Labor Board's procedures for determining the collective bargaining agent would have to file non-Communist affidavits. In other words, a union whose officers failed to file affidavits attesting that they were not Communist Party members could function only if it could enforce contracts with employers without necessarily taking part in elections in the plants. Certification of a union for Labor Board election procedures now depended on the signature of affidavits.

The vital question arising out of the Taft-Hartley law — once it was passed by the Senate over the President's veto — was whether the heads of the labor federations would contest the law's validity; whether they would abide by this affidavit clause, or whether, in defying it, they could persuade the National Labor Relations Board not to enforce it.

The left wing leaders of important unions were faced with a Hobson's choice. If they refused to abide by the law and were not supported by the top leadership of their federations, they would need total support from their rank and file. If they abided by the law, they would have to either deny membership in the Communist Party or give up such membership. It was a rare left wing union in which the leaders had total support. Thus, for most of the Party's influentials, the choice was to sign the non-Communist oath or resign from the Party. The former course led to the possibility of perjury proceedings by the government. The latter meant that the Party would lose important union leaders. Whichever choice the left took, the Taft-Hartley law favored anti-Communist opposition within the unions and encouraged interunion "raiding."

In June 1947, however, the Communists could take encouragement from the extraordinary response to Henry Wallace's first transcontinental tour, made following his winter visit to Western Europe.[5] Everywhere the former Secretary of Commerce drew large crowds. The Gallup Polls showed him to be a magnetic vote getter, an important factor in American politics either within the Democratic Party or on an independent ticket. As of that summer, Mr. Wallace had by no means decided to form a third party, and important advisors were urging him to fight for the Democratic presidential nomination.

As of that same June, the Communist Party's leadership was not at all decided on what would become within a few months the main themes of its policy. Foster showed some signs of having absorbed the impact of the different opinions about the war danger which he had found in Europe. With respect to a third party, important Communist leaders went on record as opposing any initiative unless it had the support of major elements of the labor movement. They were echoing the notes of caution and hesitation which had been struck by Dennis in his review of policy at the end of 1946. In the face of strong impatience with President Philip Murray felt by C.I.O. social democratic and A.C.T.U. leaders because he did not favor a witchhunt against the left wing (this impatience was manifest at the Massachusetts and New Jersey state conventions of the C.I.O. that summer), the main trend of Communist policy was to try to find a meeting ground with Murray.[6] Yet this attempt to maintain some basis of understanding with Murray was contradicted by many of the left wing influentials within the labor movement. They wanted a showdown within the C.I.O. At the same time, middle class progressives were becoming impatient with Mr. Wallace. They wanted him to take decisive steps at the peak of his popularity in the direction of a third party.[7]

The Party's National Committee, meeting in June 1947, heard its political action report from John Gates, who was shortly to be named the *Daily Worker*'s new editor. The Gates report advised a dual approach — fostering all expressions of popular opinion in favor of a third party while bearing in mind that such a party could not be successful without the unfolding of a genuine trend toward it within the Democratic Party and the support of unions beyond the control of the left wing. Gates frankly doubted that a Wallace candidacy was possible. But he believed it could become possible if the Democratic leaders who favored it had the backing of a third-party groundswell powerful enough to constitute a "sword of Damocles" over the Democratic politicians. Then, stepping back to ponder the subtleties and complexities of such a dual tactic, Gates declared:

It is not possible at this moment to make the final decision as to the presidential ticket, nor to state definitely whether a

third presidential ticket or a third Congressional ticket will
be formed in time for the 1948 elections. But regardless of
whether or not a third ticket can be formed, the movement to
build a third party must continue and be accelerated. The formation of a third party is possible even without a presidential
ticket. Such a party must be broadly based if it is to be effective. The decision to form such a party does not lie only in the
will of the Communists, Leftwing forces and all others who
favor a third party at this moment. Much broader forces than
are now committed to a new party will have to join the movement to make it possible for it to come into existence in 1948.
Practically, this means that such unions as the United Auto
Workers and the Amalgamated Clothing Workers must favor
it. It is not necessary that the entire top leadership of the
A.F.L. or/and the C.I.O. favor a third party before active
steps are taken to form it, but certainly more substantial sections of labor must favor it than do so at present. Furthermore, there can be no third party without a significant breakaway from the Democratic Party, and the winning of the support of large sections of farmers.[8]

At the same National Committee meeting, Foster returned to
the problem of the war danger which clearly had haunted him
ever since his trip abroad. His report is exceptionally interesting
because he attempted to combine his earlier analysis, namely,
that American imperialism was actively preparing war, with a
recognition of many countervailing factors.[9] "We should not
reduce the war danger to a theoretical abstraction," he argued,
"nor should we paint the picture that would make it appear war
was just around the corner." He pleaded for a "sober Marxian
analysis" that would "dialectically weigh the factors that are
making for and against war."

On this occasion, Foster spoke of real differences within the
American ruling class, asserting that the "largest and most decisive section," although "bent on eventual war equivocates on
the actual question of war." Among the equivocators he placed
all the leading political figures from Herbert Hoover to George
C. Marshall, including President Truman, Thomas Dewey, and
John Foster Dulles. If this group was not at the moment plotting
war, under what circumstances might the war danger increase?
Foster now arrived at a formula which he was to repeat over the

next several years. He spoke of "moods of desperation ... generated among the imperialists by a sharp sense of the failure of their international policies." Such moods of desperation could grow if the imperialists met growing resistance; on the other hand, the collapse of the democratic forces, occasioned by the enactment of antilabor legislation or a "big Republican victory ... in 1948," could also make for a sudden danger of war.

In the Dennis report, all these contradictory themes were repeated. Dennis praised Foster for his insight that the imperialists might grow more desperate as they were thwarted, and hailed the evidence that the imperialists were in fact being thwarted. "The approaching economic crisis" was stated as a certainty, with the corollary that the monopolies would seek "a more desperate and reactionary way out of the crisis." The "fascist danger" was evoked with reference to Dimitrov's analysis of 1935, as though implying that what had happened in Germany was taking place in the United States.

Yet something else stood out in the Dennis report — a warning against countermeasures of desperation by the Communists and their closest allies. Struggle decides everything, Dennis declared, but Communists "must not confuse mass struggle with adventurous, desperate and sectarian actions." The left wing, he argued, "must not permit itself to be forced into the position of throwing itself single-handedly into abortive or ill-timed actions." Dennis returned to those themes which had preoccupied him earlier. He inveighed against the tendency to indulge in self-defeating invective against the opponents of the C.P., the Walter Reuthers or John L. Lewises "and now a little more frequently against the Murrays."

That "the Murray forces [had] capitulated on a number of key questions to all sorts of reactionary pressures," Dennis granted. The C.I.O.'s president had not broken with the Truman administration and had sometimes abetted attacks on the left wing leadership of particular unions. "But it is a fact," Dennis warned, that "the Murray forces do not desire to see the C.I.O. destroyed; that in their own way, inadequate as it may be, they opposed the passage of the Taft-Hartley Bill and they are fighting for its nullification today." Although the left wing had to oppose anti-Communism, it was "equally clear that a halt must be brought to existing tendencies to resolve differences within the C.I.O. by adopting, advertently or otherwise, a go-it-alone policy, e.g., by seceding from the C.I.O. or by breaking relations in one way or another with the Murray forces."

Turning to the pressing issue of political strategy, Dennis was even more explicit than Gates. The problem was to relate the third-party movement to the struggle within the Democratic Party, and thus to disprove the arguments of those trade unionists who opposed a third party on the grounds that it would serve to elect a Republican. As Dennis phrased it: "We must drive home the understanding that it is possible, actually possible, for a third-party movement to facilitate the election of a progressive presidential ticket in 1948. Such a victory will be possible if this movement is so organized and so broadened as to bring about a situation in which there can be a coalition candidate, backed by the independent and third-party forces, *running as a Democrat.* To put it realistically, no matter how theoretical it may sound, this is the *only* way for the third-party and pro-Roosevelt forces to ensure the defeat of the G.O.P. candidate in 1948" (italics in the original).[10]

Thus, the Party's general secretary envisaged in mid-1947 an attempt to win the Democratic Party for a progressive candidate, building a third party locally but only for the purpose of aiding this attempt.

### The Contradictions of a Critical Autumn

It now becomes essential to project the film of history and try to pinpoint exactly how the American Communist Party's most fateful decision was taken, bearing in mind that the Party was by no means the only actor in the drama, and keeping within our analytical grasp all the elements of contradiction in Party policy and all the activity which had gone into preparing the American Communists for battle. The screen must necessarily be as panoramic and stereoscopic as possible. It must simultaneously span events from California to Massachusetts, the decisions of Henry Wallace and his closest advisors, the behavior of the Party's influentials within the C.I.O., and of the chief leaders of American labor. It must account for the impact of a meeting in an obscure village in Poland where the Communist Information Bureau (Cominform) was established. It must include hidden history, involving meetings of the Party leaders with their supporters in the labor movement a few days after

Mr. Wallace made his decision and a few days before he announced it.

An ideologically motivated group of people had come to a moment of truth. They were trying to square their perception of American realities with their conception of their international duties. They were trying to make some kind of historical leap which would overcome their inner weaknesses. They were trying to force the historical process on the assumption that this is what Marxism-Leninism demanded of them. They exhibited, at this moment, the full impact upon themselves of the two tendencies which had been operative within them for a long time, and which continued to operate even though they had presumably overcome the damage which (so they had been told and so they had persuaded themselves) their Browderite policies had inflicted. Ten years later they were to lament what had been done without recounting the details. It is useful now to establish the most essential details.

After the Progressive Citizens of America had met in Chicago in the last days of June 1947, two West Coast figures returned home from its sessions. One was Robert W. Kenny, who had just assumed the co-chairmanship of the P.C.A., a man whose political roots were deep in California Democratic Party politics. He had been attorney-general until 1946 and had lost the gubernatorial nomination to Earl Warren on both the Democratic and Republican lines; but he had remained a political power, with important connections in all walks of life. Although not a Communist, he was quite infatuated with the California left wing, from which he drew personal friendships and political support. Kenny now issued a call that "Democrats for Wallace" meet at Fresno on July 19. Three hundred and fifty delegates from the state's twenty-three congressional districts attended. Together with Wallace's personal aide, Harold Young of Texas, Kenny began to build an all-Western bloc for Wallace *within* the Democratic Party (Kenny was at that time the head of the Hollywood Democratic Committee).

Simultaneously, Hugh Bryson, who had risen the previous year to the presidency of the Marine Cooks and Stewards Union, returned from Chicago with a proposal that an independent political party be formed in California.[11] The essential argument of Bryson and his friends was that progressives could not wait in California for the Democratic primaries on June 1, 1948.

If Wallace did not win the primary, he would not have an instrument available to support an independent candidacy, since in California such a body had to be created before March 1948. It could be created, however, in two ways: if 27,597 Democratic voters changed their registration or if 275,970 voters of any affiliation signed up for a new party.

The former method which would have been relatively easy, might, however, deprive the Democratic Party of a substantial group of its most advanced supporters. To collect several hundred thousand signatures would have the advantage of throwing pro-Wallace supporters into contact with the electorate, giving them an opportunity to proselytize on the issues. It would also mean an extraordinary burden on California's "progressives." Only a disciplined group like the California Communist Party, small as it was, could undertake such a drive with any prospect of success.

Bryson insisted that building an Independent Progressive Party (I.P.P.) did not preclude the success of Kenny's strategy. He argued that California needed something like the American Labor Party of New York which could, as a distinct entity, throw its weight on the Democratic line if necessary. Bryson's friends decided to use the occasion of the California Legislative Conference that August to launch the I.P.P.[12]

Behind the scenes Kenny was sufficiently distraught by the Bryson initiative to voice his concern to the top Communist leader Foster, who was touring the West Coast that summer speaking at meetings from Los Angeles to Seattle. Sometime late in August, a meeting between Foster and Kenny was arranged. By then the Los Angeles Communists, under the direction of Nemmy Sparks, one of their most eminent leaders, had thrown themselves into the signature campaign. Kenny argued that the left wing's tactics were suicidal. Sparks, who arrived at the Foster-Kenny meeting late, almost came to blows with Kenny. Foster was, however, impressed with the argument that much more could be accomplished by a mobilization of Democrats for Wallace than by an independent party, valuable as such an agency might be in the future.[13] In the Foster speeches, as reported in the San Francisco *Daily People's World* in late August and early September, an emphasis on the danger of a Republican victory stood out. All his references to a third party were couched in terms of a project for the future — as an eventual development, not an immediate prospect.

What was happening elsewhere in the meantime? Abroad, the Soviet delegation had come to the conference in Paris to discuss the Marshall Plan but obviously for no other purpose than to denounce it. Henry Wallace, at that time editor of the *New Republic*, did not oppose the Marshall Plan. He viewed it as a confirmation of his own proposals and saw the Marshall idea as a criticism of the Truman Doctrine. The prospect of American assistance to war-shattered Europe appealed to him, although he urged that this take place through the United Nations. He expressed fear that Secretary Marshall's initiative might polarize relations with the Soviet Union beyond repair. On the other hand, the decision of the Council of Foreign Ministers to meet in the autumn of 1947 to continue discussions on German reparations was a ray of hope.

It is of crucial significance, however, that Henry Wallace *resisted the formation of a third party* all through the summer and early autumn of 1947. Both his public speeches and his *New Republic* articles make this plain. Reporting in the June 2, 1947, issue of this magazine on his cross-country tour, Wallace wrote: "Throughout this journey I have found sentiment for a third party strong among many groups, so strong I have tried to emphasize that the first problem now is to create, not a third, but a second party." In his August 4, 1947, editorial, Wallace lamented the "varied and conflicting voices" among liberals and argued that "if all these voices were united in concentrating on immediate issues, the form of the instruments for progress would almost take shape of itself." Increasingly, Wallace accepted the tactic of trying to set the Democratic Party straight while welcoming "independents" who would "meet the varied legal requirements of the different states for a third party as a hedge against the complete sell-out of the present Democratic leadership." In his September 1, 1947 editorial, Wallace was much sharper with the Truman administration. Yet he clung to the strategy of "winning control of the Democratic convention." At a Labor Day rally in Cadillac Square, Detroit, his approach was more ambivalent. "If we don't make the Democratic Party into a party of peace and prosperity we shall build a new party." On the other hand, in a radio interview with Leland Stowe on September 10, 1947, Wallace was asked whether his remarks meant he intended to stay in the Democratic Party and reform it. He replied: "Yes, that is exactly what it does mean."[14]

Throughout October the formulas of the Wallace campaign varied between stress on the redeemability of the Democrats and the need to build a third party if they proved irredeemable. Although the detailed study by Curtis MacDougall shows that Wallace decided to be a candidate on December 2, 1947 (at a meeting in the studio of the sculptor, Jo Davidson), the precise character of the decision he was making was still so unclear in Wallace's own mind that *two days later*, on December 4, 1947, he told an American Labor Party meeting in Brooklyn: "Tonight I speak as a Democrat — as a Democrat who is grateful for the contributions the A.L.P. has made to the victories of my party in times past." As late as mid-December, having already given assurances to his P.C.A. friends, Wallace was still telling an audience in Albany, New York, that he was pleased Democratic chairman Howard McGrath had said that the Democrats would accept Wallace's support. "That was a hopeful sign. I interpret it to mean that there is a chance for a change. I want to assure Senator McGrath that I would certainly support every progressive Democratic candidate for Congress. I shall also hope that there will be valid reasons for me to support the entire Democratic ticket in 1948."[15]

Thus, at the very last moment, Wallace had difficulty deciding whether he would run as a Democrat with independent support, or as an independent with a third party behind him.[16] Between the two conceptions, there was a world of political difference.

What was taking place in the labor movement, especially in the C.I.O.'s left wing, during this same summer and autumn? Although Bryson and other left wingers were supporting a local third party in California, the left wing as a whole was not enamored of a third party. Harry Bridges, president of the I.L.W.U., was at that time the regional representative of the C.I.O. in the West. His union's executive board reportedly backed Robert Kenny's proposal that progressives "should rally around the fight to revitalize the Democratic Party."[17] At the state C.I.O. meeting, Richard Lynden — a left winger who headed the Warehousemen's division of the I.L.W.U. — opposed his fellow left wingers on the third party proposition.[18] At this meeting, Clifford T. McAvoy, then assistant to the national director of the

C.I.O.'s Political Action Committee, indicated that national C.I.O. policy did not include support for a third party at all. In a Labor Day speech, Harry Bridges straddled the two tactics that were being advanced in California. "We will support the progressive forces in the Democratic Party led by Henry Wallace and other Roosevelt New Deal Democrats," he said and then added: "The time has come to decide that the evils of the two-party system cannot be tolerated for the rest of our lives."[19] As late as November 23, at a Santa Cruz session of the state C.I.O., the I.L.W.U. delegates did not support the third party proposition, which produced complete deadlock.

Nor was the California experience peculiar to that state. Evidence from New York is equally persuasive about the lack of labor support for a third party. The New York State C.I.O. was scheduled to meet in Saratoga Springs over the Labor Day weekend, 1947. On the eve of that meeting, its chairman, Louis Hollander of the Amalgamated Clothing Workers, was visited by three left wing labor leaders — Irving Potash, manager of the Furriers' Joint Council; Ruth Young, of the United Electrical Workers; and Saul Mills, at that time secretary of the Greater New York C.I.O. Council. As Hollander related this incident, the left wing leaders asked whether any controversial issues were to be expected.[20] Hollander said he saw none, unless a third party resolution was proposed, and added: "If there is anyone who introduces a resolution on a third party, it will be opposed and I will be one of those to oppose it." In Hollander's recollection, Potash replied suavely: "We have no intention of proposing a third party. What for?" The state C.I.O. convention went smoothly, with the alliance of the left and the center maintained. Thus, both Wallace himself and the American Communists (as well as their trade union influentials) were quite undecided as late as October-November 1947.

At the Boston convention of the National C.I.O., late in October, the left wing did not make an issue of foreign policy. No battle royal developed over the Marshall Plan proposals. Even though Philip Murray invited Secretary of State George C. Marshall to speak at the gathering — this was the first time that a secretary of state had ever addressed the C.I.O. — no significant division took place over this issue. The left wing was still attempting to maintain its center-left alliance. An innocuous resolution on foreign policy affirming that the C.I.O. stood for rehabilitating war-devastated areas, thus fulfilling Roosevelt's objectives, was adopted almost unanimously. The "resent-and-reject" resolution against Communist Party interference in the labor movement was also reaffirmed.[21]

But this attempt to hold the left-center alliance together was being undone by other considerations and events. One element of change in the relationship of forces took place within the C.I.O. as the result of the definitive rupture between the left wing and the president of the National Maritime Union, Joseph Curran, that autumn. One of the key elements in this breakdown was the left wing's ambitious attempt to coordinate the activities of seamen, longshoremen, and radio operators in a movement known as the Committee for Maritime Unity. Curran, who had been feuding for two years with two different Communist groups within his union, came to the conclusion that the Committee for Maritime Unity was a roundabout way for the left wingers to undermine his position. More important, however, was the changed balance in a decisive component of the C.I.O. — the United Automobile Workers. Since May 1946, President Walter Reuther had been obliged to function with an executive board that opposed him by fifteen to seven; the C.P., through alliance with the faction led by George Addes and R. J. Thomas, could hold Reuther in check. In November 1947, at the U.A.W.'s Atlantic City convention, Reuther succeeded in routing the Addes-Thomas forces upon whom the Communists had depended. Having swept the executive board, Reuther announced immediately that he would sign the Taft-Hartley affidavit. He moved with equal speed to serve notice on Communists, pro-Communists, and all other anti-Reuther men in local and national offices that their services would be dispensed with. This development shattered the national C.I.O. balance. Commentators speculated that Reuther could be the successor to Philip Murray.[22]

Even these defeats might not have been decisive, given the Communist Party's desire to maintain its relations with Murray, were it not for the evolution of the affidavit issue. In the previous summer, all wings of labor appeared to be united in refusing to sign the Taft-Hartley affidavits. Forty labor lawyers counseled such a refusal. The United Steelworkers (President Murray's union) entered a suit to invalidate provision 9H. In the A.F.L., John L. Lewis thundered that the very notion of labor leaders having to swear they were non-Communists was demeaning and insulting. By the end of the summer, however, the atmosphere was changing. In October 1947, there was a trend toward compliance. The C.I.O. decided that the matter would be left to the autonomous decision of the constituent unions — a move which was extremely dangerous to the left wing. If it had to face the problem of compliance without national C.I.O. support, the left was in great difficulty. At the end of September, the vice-president of the International Woodworkers, Karley Larsen, an admitted Communist Party member, resigned from his union on the grounds that he did not wish his personal politics to jeopardize the union's fortunes.[23] In mid-October 1947, John L. Lewis withdrew the Mine Workers from the A.F.L. at the latter's San Francisco convention because its leaders refused to meet the issue of the Taft-Hartley affidavit head-on.[24]

In the first days of October, the chairman of the National Labor Relations Board, Robert Denham, handed down a ruling which affirmed that the top C.I.O. leaders need not file oaths but that the leaders of constituent and local unions would have to do so if they wished to avail themselves of the N.R.L.B. machinery. On the surface this was something of a C.I.O. victory. In reality, it was a body blow to the left wing. To refuse compliance was possible only where the rank and file was sufficiently behind its leaders and sufficiently in control of local plant situations to bypass the Labor Board. To comply, however, meant to disclose affiliations which had hitherto been concealed or denied.

Several political developments — both abroad and at home — must now be examined. They are part of the story of how and why the Communist leaders (together with some influentials) suddenly changed their tactics and supported a third party. The November 4, 1947, congressional and local elections played a distinct part, notably the balloting for judicial nominees in Chicago. An independent movement to change the way in which judges were selected swept through Illinois that fall; a nonpartisan ticket of black and white jurists was placed on the ballot, independently of the traditional machines. This was not a third party in the image of the I.P.P. in California. It was a civic reform movement attracting voters who could not necessarily be counted on to support Mr. Wallace either in the Democratic column or as an independent.[25] Yet the fact that the Chicago Progressive Party — the label under which Wallace would run next year — polled over 300,000 votes, 40 percent of the total, for its top candidate, had a distinct influence on both Wallace and the Communists. In many other states, the left wing was impressed with the power of local progressive candidates. In San Francisco, congressman Frank Havenner got 101,400 votes for mayor, only 15,000 less than the winner. The Communist candidate for San Francisco's school board, Oleta O'Connor Yates, received 37,000 votes, or 37 percent of the total. An equally unprecedented Communist vote for local offices was recorded in Oakland, across the bay, and in several other cities.

Yet the most important political event was the announcement on October 5, 1947, that representatives of nine Communist parties had met in Poland to exchange opinions and set up an Information Bureau. This was the famous Cominform. Its headquarters were to be in Belgrade, and it was to publish a journal for the exchange of news and views. In the chief speech at this meeting, the Soviet leader Andrei Zhdanov did not rule out better relations with the United States nor disavow peaceful coexistence. In fact, the Cominform's statement decried the "noise about another war" and specifically noted the "big gap between the desire of the imperialists for a new war and the possibility of organizing one." But it did constitute a ringing call for the Communist parties to undertake a vigorous counteroffensive against what was described as the offensive of American imperialism. At this meeting the Yugoslav delegates criticized both the Italian and French parties for not having seized power in 1944, and for having failed to maintain their leadership in the liberation movements.[26]

The American Communist Party's National Board expressed solidarity with the nine founding members of the Cominform and at the same time declared: "The present political situation in the United States is such that the Communist Party should not affiliate."[27] Two things were strange about this declaration. First, it did not come until November 2, almost a month after the news of the Cominform was made public. Second, the American Communists were expressing their regrets at their inability to affiliate with the Cominform, *although there is no evidence at all that they were ever invited to do so.* The Cominform's membership was selective. Important European parties, such as the comparatively powerful Finns and the embattled Greeks, were not invited to join. The Spanish Party and all the Scandinavians were also absent as were the Albanians and East Germans. The American Communist chiefs were so passionately involved with the idea of authoritative leadership from abroad that they assumed implicitly that they *ought* to formally accept such leadership by joining a body like the Cominform. They realized neither the incongruity of their statement nor the selective and limited character of the Cominform.

The establishment of the Cominform must have meant to them that a period of indecision and conflicting views within the international movement had been brought to a close. Foster, who had been puzzled the previous year by the discrepancy between his own view of an increasing war danger and Stalin's, and who had been rebuked by Duclos in March, could only feel relieved by the emphasis on the menace of U.S. imperialism. The Zhdanov speech, which was published on October 22, 1947, in *Pravda*, and the apparent endorsement of the Yugoslav views in general, meant that the world movement was at last coming around to Foster's way of looking at things.[28]

A year later, at the Party's 14th National Convention, in August 1948, he was to boast of this quite frankly. "The formation of the Information Bureau affirmed the correctness of our line, especially on the all-important question of the role of American imperialism and the danger of war and fascism connected with it. Of course, there was much for us to learn from the Nine-Party conference. I may add that we would have learned these lessons faster had we not taken a rather complacent attitude toward the conference precisely because we saw that our general line agreed with that of the conference."[29]

The last phrase in this statement is most revealing for the purpose of our present inquiry. In what sense could the American Communist leaders feel they had been guilty of complacency? Only in the sense of having hesitated to precipitate a third party and in clinging to the center-left alliance with the C.I.O. What happened in November and December constituted, in effect, a reversal of policy. It was a sudden decision, intended to overcome what was later judged as complacency. More exactly, the Party leaders saw in the Cominform's existence and in Zhdanov's advice not to underestimate the capacity of the working class for struggle against imperialism, all the ingredients of a critique of their hesitation and a signal to go all-out.

From mid-November into December 1947, the American Communist leaders underwent a convulsive change. Their underestimation of the necessity for "decisive action" had now put them out of step with the world movement. In the American context, the change was from support for the Wallace movement as an independent candidacy on the Democratic ticket, to support for a distinct third party headed by Wallace, even if this meant foregoing the chance of remaining a serious factor within the Democratic Party. The difference between these two positions also determined Party strategy within the C.I.O. at a moment when the over-all position of the left wing had become perilous. To have supported Wallace as a Democrat would not necessarily have entailed a rupture within the C.I.O., but to build a third party did.

Important left wingers wanted to remain within the labor movement at all costs. Others, however, believed it was possible to use their positions within the labor movement to help build a third party which would give them a political arena if they lost their positions in the labor movement in the process. These were tactical differences which reflected, at bottom, distinct strategic perceptions. Dennis had for a year polemicized with the latter group, but by mid-November 1947, Dennis had yielded to the same tendencies he had been opposing. He could not resist the power of the argument, now supported by the existence of the Cominform, that a cautious course meant underestimating the readiness of the working class to struggle, and overestimating the power of imperialism. The Cominform's entry on the scene was thus the key catalyst in the change of Party policy (although there were other powerful arguments for this change).[30]

Another event which had a catalytic effect must be taken into account. On November 7, 1947, the former assistant attorney-general, O. John Rogge, solemnly charged that the Department of Justice was planning a "dramatic round-up of dozens of Communist leaders and alleged fellow-travellers."[31] This roundup was predicted for November 17. Rogge, who had been ousted from the government a year before and had soon staked out a career for himself in the New York State American Labor Party and in the Wallace movement generally, was in effect predicting something in the nature of the Palmer Raids. (In 1919-1920, thousands of left wingers had been rounded up in dramatic raids instigated by A. Mitchell Palmer, the attorney-general of that time — an event which was crucial in the coming-of-age of the men who were now leading the American Communist Party.) Rogge's revelation implied that the C.P. might suddenly be unable to function in full legality. Was the Rogge revelation not in harmony with the emphasis on incipient American fascism? Was it not, after all, a premonition of the sudden, cataclysmic events that pervaded all of Foster's perceptions of the war danger?

The foundation for the Communist Party's decision to go underground in 1950-51, began to be laid directly after the Rogge predictions of November 1947 (as will be shown later).[32] If the prospect that the Party might not be able to function normally was worrisome enough to justify the important preparations for an illegal existence that were taken late in 1947, it follows that the prospect of a third party would present itself to the Communist leadership in a new light. A Progressive Party in which Communists could function without being "Red-baited" and in which they could act on all the workaday issues would commend itself, even if it would not be the vanguard party capable of leading the struggle for socialism. The new party could not be Marxist-Leninist, to be sure. For that, an illegal party would be necessary. Yet as a "cover," a "haven," or an "umbrella" for the Communists, a Progressive Party was altogether advisable.

At the February 3-5, 1948, National Committee meeting following Wallace's decision to run, Dennis voiced a variant of this thought. If the "Progressive Party develops we Communists will seek to affiliate with it." Such an idea, voiced in February, must certainly have been current two months before.

A great deal of light is shed on the way the C.P. decided to switch support from a Democratic presidential candidate to a third party, and the way it imparted this decision to the Communist influentials, especially in the labor movement, by the testimony of the Transport Union leader, Michael Quill. Quill's famous statement plays an important part in the literature about the Wallace movement and the C.I.O., as well as in the literature about the internecine conflict within the C.I.O. which ousted the left wing by 1950. There is in Quill's revelation, which became known only in April 1948, when the bitter battle for the C.I.O.'s leadership was basically over, such an authentic account by a man who considered himself a Communist, who had always been consulted by the Party, and who finally had to choose between his private politics and his union position, that the revelation commands close attention.

To appreciate Quill's evidence one must run ahead of the chronology by half a year. On April 28, 1948, C.I.O. President Philip Murray denounced the Wallace movement at the Textile Workers' Union convention and flatly declared: "The Communist Party is directly responsible for the organization of a third party in the United States. There is no question about that." Murray added that the decision had been made at a Party meeting in October 1947. Two weeks later, on May 10, 1948 (at the same Amalgamated Clothing Workers' convention where Louis Hollander, the N.Y. State C.I.O. chairman, expressed himself so bitterly against the left wingers who had changed their minds after Labor Day, 1947) Murray gave further details of his accusations. He spoke of a meeting of Communist officials and left wing labor leaders shortly after the Boston convention (i.e., late in October). A few days later three different newsmen published versions of what had happened, each mentioning Quill.[33] Comparison of their stories suggests that they came from a common source which linked Quill and Murray; clearly a memorandum had been submitted by Michael Quill to Philip Murray, providing the basis for Murray's charges and for his private fury with the left wing.

All three stories agree that high Communist Party officials met with left wing labor leaders directly after the C.I.O. convention. To quote Alfred Friendly's version in the *Washington Post*, which is more elaborate than the others, "there was a long discussion of how to put pressure on the unions and on Congress to defeat the passage of E.R.P. — that is, Marshall Plan legislation." This would be consonant with the Party's aims. Having compromised on this point in Boston, the Party was anxious to have expressions of anti-Marshall Plan opinion. But it did not intend breaking up all relationships within the C.I.O. over this matter (at least this was not its intention late in October). A national third party was not mentioned at all, although there was some reference to local efforts in Illinois and California. There was, however, "discussion of how to get the C.I.O. to reverse its convention stand and to accept the idea of dumping Mr. Truman . . .," which would conform to the Party's general aims. The Communists were not decided on a third party at that moment. Neither was Mr. Wallace himself. Nor were the middle class left wingers in the Progressive Citizens of America. At that point the crucial distinction still operated between rousing public opinion *to go on record* for a third party and the actual organization of a national third party in place of a Democratic presidential ticket.

The Communist National Committee met immediately after this gathering. The next reported meeting between Party and left wing labor leaders is almost two months later. According to Friendly, it took place on December 15, 1947 — the same day that the P.C.A. was in the final throes of its own arguments, and a good ten days after Wallace's decision to run as an independent Democrat with a minimum stress on a national third party. Twenty-six persons were said to have been present at this meeting, with one to three representatives from most of the New York unions. Foster was not present, but Dennis was. Most interestingly, the report at this meeting was not given by Dennis, although he was responsible for the Party's electoral policy as a whole, but by the New York state chairman, Robert Thompson.

Thompson is reported to have affirmed that a decision to create a third party had been made, and all union leaders should support Mr. Wallace's candidacy, which would be announced within two weeks, and that every effort should be made to bring about the national C.I.O.'s endorsement, despite all the unfavorable prospects for such a step. Michael Quill asked who had made the decision. Thompson replied, according to the Friendly story, that "the Central Committee" had done so.[34] Quill then shouted that the Party's Central Committee could not tell him or his union what to do. The proposed action, Quill continued, would split the C.I.O. Thompson is reported to have replied that the movement to endorse Wallace and build a third party would have to be pressed "even if it splits the C.I.O. right down the middle."

Such a position was entirely new. It could only be interpreted as a profound and decisive change in Party policy. It is perhaps significant that Thompson made the report, suggesting that the most dynamic wing of the Communist leadership had by this time taken over. It is hard to imagine Dennis talking so glibly about a C.I.O. split, although it was not all out of character for Dennis to stand by while such things were being said. It was also entirely in character that Quill should have retorted: "To hell with you and your Central Committee!" In the Friendly version, he is supposed to have added that he wanted Thompson to relay his, Quill's, opinions, to that "crack-pot, Foster."[35] To Quill, the great achievement of the left wing — and of the unavowed Communists like himself — had been the building of the C.I.O. and the union movement generally. Quill, it will be recalled, had been the chairman of the subcommittee of the C.I.O.'s Executive Board which had in 1946 brought in the "resent-and-reject" resolution. All the contradictions of the American Communist Party's policy bore on the role and behavior of a man like Quill. If what was now being proposed was the splitting of the C.I.O. — already divided on many other issues — over a purely political matter, Quill would maintain his career in the labor movement. rather than leave the C.I.O. with the Communists. He was voicing publicly what hundreds of left wing labor leaders were to express privately by "voting with their feet" against the Party.

The Friendly report also tells a good deal about the mood of the Party at that moment. Thompson is reported to have given the situation in Western Europe as a further argument for the National Committee's decision. He is quoted as saying that "the Communist parties in France and Italy were making their decisions and there would be revolutions in both countries within two weeks." Such a precise prediction on the part of either Thompson or his fellow Party leaders cannot be documented independently. But from what is known of them, it is reasonable to suppose that the American leaders were deeply impressed by the magnitude of the strike actions in Western Europe. It is not farfetched to assume that Thompson expected a cataclysmic showdown of some kind. All the more reason, then, that the Party do something big and decisive of a comparable character in the United States, namely, gamble everything on a political action such as building a third party.

It is also significant that, according to Friendly, the December 15 meeting included a wide-ranging discussion about the merits of Mr. Wallace as a candidate. Many participants expressed their doubts that Wallace was a reliable standard-bearer for the third party movement. Some remembered his ambiguous Madison Square Garden speech in September 1946. Thompson made a characteristic reply. The Communists were not supporting Wallace because of any illusions about his differences with the

Party on ideological matters. The chief guarantee of the new party's success would be the degree of mass pressure that could be exerted on Wallace.[36] Thus, the concept of coalition did not involve, in Thompson's eyes, any genuine understanding either with Wallace as an individual or with his ideas. The Communist Party was retaining its freedom of action and was supporting the Wallace candidacy as the necessary instrument of its larger strategy.

### The 1948 Campaign: Hallucinations and Disappointments

In dealing with the tumultuous, picturesque and tragic concatenation of events which led the Henry Wallace movement from a point of high hopes and great political leverage to bitter defeat, our chief concern cannot be to recount the campaign itself. There is already an impressive body of literature, both historical and analytical, on the campaign.[37] What must concern us is whether the Communist Party's attempt to resolve the contradictions facing it by opting for a third party was successful, or whether these contradictions were exacerbated.

Only if the Communist Party's behavior is seen as an unsuccessful but determined attempt to overcome internal contradictions can some of the mysteries surrounding Party policy on the Wallace movement be dispelled. The essential weakness of the conventional anti-Communist argument (as advanced, for example, by the Americans for Democratic Action), that the Wallace movement originated with and was guided throughout by the Communists, is that it overlooks precisely the contradictions ravaging the Communists.[38] It is also the weakness of MacDougall and those Wallace leaders who were not anti-Communist. Their treatment of the Party's role is fragmentary and essentially puzzling because they, too, did not understand the nature of the ally with whom they acted in concert.

Since early 1946 and even late 1945 the American Communists had projected a new strategic orientation. Browder's heresy resided in his view that the prevention of war and the achievement of coexistence with the Soviet Union and the world's revolutionary forces depended on moving what he called the "decisive sections" of monopoly capitalism. In the interests of achieving this objective, Browder proposed that the Party be turned into a left-wing lobby. It would eschew independent politics in its own name in the interests of uniting with a wide body of independent voters who expressed themselves within the two-party system without being bound by party affiliations. In the ancillary premise of Browder's thought, the Political Association would also make it possible to overcome the historic gap between the Communist leadership and its most effective cadres, its concealed influentials.

Foster's strategic orientation rested on another concept. The prevention of war depended on building an antimonopoly coalition of diverse elements, led by the organized working class, with the Communist Party as the vanguard. The Party would not only operate electorally in its own name, but would also build a larger coalition because it could not hope, by itself, to decide key issues in the foreseeable future. This coalition would once and for all end the straitjacket of the two-party system. Such a coalition was also expected to give shelter and refuge to the Communists and presumably to legitimatize the political activity of the hitherto-concealed Party influentials.

Browder's view was not only "revisionist" but "post-revisionist." It was a new conception of Communist tactics applied to an American electoral structure quite different from the European. Foster's view was a peculiar amalgam — a return to the Populist devices of the 1890's and the La Follette experience of 1924 plus the *Front Populaire* conceptions borrowed from the 1930's and the wartime Resistance.[39] Foster tried to emulate other Communists while returning to his own past. Browder was anticipating other Communist parties in trying to learn what *not* to repeat from his own past.

Yet the Wallace movement was hardly the antimonopoly coalition which the Communists had projected. It did not conform to what Foster himself had enunciated as essential; namely, that a third-party movement would have to be led by the organized working class, and enter into firm alliances with the organized farmers, the Negro people, and the progressive middle class. No major labor leader, no labor federation, no prominent Negro organizations (but many important *local* leaders), and very few of the spokesmen for the middle class previously associated with the New Deal supported the Wallace movement once it took shape as a third party.

The Communists were aware of this reality. Instead of admitting that no real coalition had been built, however, they rationalized their plight by drawing upon an earlier arsenal of ideas

and experiences. They evoked the "united front from below" —
a concept derived from the twenties which served them until
they abandoned it in the midthirties.[40] At the February 3-5,
1948, National Committee meeting, Dennis voiced a retrospective criticism which was in strong contrast to most earlier views.
It showed how easily the Communist leaders could rationalize
what they decided to be necessary, and how easily their doctrine
could be made to serve policy. "In connection with the development of the Wallace peace campaign and the third party movement, our generally correct political orientation and line was
considerably weakened for a time by our failure to wage an adequate and sharp enough struggle against a host of sectarian and
opportunist tendencies. We were much too slow in combatting
the erroneous views of certain party leaders and district organi-
gations, as well as many of our trade union cadres who, up till
the announcement of Wallace's candidacy, expressed doubts as
to the advisability of an independent Presidential ticket and
confused the maneuverings and treacherous position of most of
Labor's top officials with the position being taken by the rank
and file."[41]

But did the united front from below work out either? Perhaps
the important reality of the Wallace campaign was the inability
of the left wing labor leaders who supported it to mobilize their
rank-and-file. The same left wing leaders who, as has been
shown, were motivated both by their own deep-rooted inclina-
tions and by Party discipline to take part in the Wallace movement were also the ones who gave it rather token support. As
Curtis MacDougall notes, "no new support was recruited among
the higher echelons of organized labor" after the C.I.O.'s January 22, 1948, vote of thirty-three to eleven against the Wallace
party. "No one not already known as a Wallaceite was converted
during the campaign. Rather, most of the avowed Progressives
among union officials at all levels merely sat on their hands, doing little or nothing to line up their mass memberships as participants in the movement."[42]

The inner rift between the Party and its influentials was
actually widened by the 1948 campaign. Those who had left the
labor movement to run as Wallace candidates or who gambled
their positions in so doing were among a larger body that turned
against the Party's policies in subsequent years. Those who followed the Party afterward did so most reluctantly. Their 1948

experience was to create in them an ever-greater doubt as to the Party's wisdom. This doubt increased the practical gap between the Party and their own behavior. Others, like Quill (and many who did not achieve his notoriety), refused to follow the Party. They increased their distance from everything which had to do with Communism.

Curtis MacDougall put the matter flatly and philosophically: "Even the international presidents, members of the C.I.O. national executive board who had voted in January [1948] against condemning the Wallace movement, and in August against endorsing Truman, were mostly unable to persuade their unions to endorse the Progressive Party. Or if that was achieved, they could not make their members put forward vigorous efforts in the P.P.'s behalf."[43]

Much the same point can be made with regard to other classes and parts of classes that had been expected to become the natural constituency of the antimonopoly coalition. The only exception, and a limited one, concerns the Negro people. The Wallace candidacy generated an exceptional response within the black community. Wallace himself entered the South, accompanied by black and white figures of prestige and importance.[44] He insisted upon speaking at desegregated meetings in the South, a political demonstration without precedent. It is estimated that more than forty-five blacks ran for office on the Progressive Party ticket, "the largest number of Negro candidates ever picked to run on a single ticket since the days of Thaddeus Stevens."[45] As MacDougall notes, "the Progressive Party nominated proportionately more Negro candidates than did the other parties; and it nominated them for offices to which Negroes had never been named by either major party.[46]

But the Negro people declined to fulfill their role as a component of the antimonopoly coalition in the terms conceived by the Communists. Although the 1948 campaign became the point of departure for a much more conscious participation in the real politics of the country, blacks expressed their grasp of the "national question" *not* in terms of revolutionary, or extra-parliamentary change, but in terms of taking part in bargaining for democratization within the limits of American life. Appreciating Henry Wallace for his fine sentiments and sympathy, blacks turned to the Democratic Party; they took advantage of the difficulty in which Harry Truman found himself to win specific things in the course of the campaign.[47] Truman not only accepted the sweeping civil rights proposals at the Democratic convention but also issued his famous executive order in September 1948 outlawing discrimination in the armed forces and establishing fair practices procedures throughout the federal government.

Truman, moreover, ended the Democratic Party's reliance on the most "Bourbon" parts of the Solid South. This was something which all progressives, including the Communists, had talked about for a generation. It will be remembered that the 1948 campaign was unprecedented in the sense that it was a four-way race: the States' Rights party took a bloc of southern states out of the Democratic column. The average black voter grasped that this was the beginning of the breakdown of those political relationships that had long been the obstacle to the realization of his most pressing needs. To use the Communist language, the Negro vote for Truman was an expression of self-determination — an objective which the Communists championed and tried in vain to realize within the confines of an illusory and elusive antimonopoly coalition.

Neither the farmers nor the smaller capitalists rallied to the Wallace movement, although Wallace himself was both an outstanding farmer and a successful businessman. The Progressive Party candidate had been identified for a generation with agricultural problems.[48] His grandfather's journal, *Wallace's Farmer*, had been a Midwestern institution of great prestige. The president of the National Farmer's Union (N.F.U.), James R. Patton, was one of the many New Deal liberals who urged Wallace not to form a third party, but Patton sympathized with the idea of trying to get him the Democratic nomination. The N.F.U. remained neutral during the campaign. Those local bodies — as in Iowa and the East — which supported Wallace were not penalized. But the simple fact remained, as MacDougall has noted, that "no agrarian revolt" coincided with the Wallace movement. Wallace's farm vote was "negligible." This in itself placed the 1948 Progressive Party in contradistinction to the Populist party and the La Follette movement.

As for professional people and businessmen, Wallace did have their support in many localities. Detailed studies of his campaign reveal, however, that these circles were repelled by the amateurishness of the Progressive Party and by the obtrusiveness of Communist participation; they were among the first to leave. They responded to Wallace because of his foreign policy position, not because of his career as a successful corngrower, and surely not because they were conscious of their role as part of a class within the antimonopoly coalition.

It is ironic that the most radical, the most socialist-minded, plank in the Wallace program came out of a group known as the Conference for the Preservation and Advancement of Independent Business, which met in Philadelphia on July 22, 1948, just as the P.P.'s platform committee was meeting. At this conference, two independent socialists, Paul Sweezy, onetime professor of economics at Harvard, and Leo Huberman, the well-known publicist, introduced a motion calling for the nationalization of the basic industries. (Frederick L. Schuman, a government professor, unsuccessfully opposed the resolution on the grounds that this fetish of the earlier era of populist and socialist agitation had little to do with postwar realities.) Working through the businessman's conference, Sweezy and Huberman contributed the most radical plank in the Progressive Party program and then largely abstained from that party's campaign on the ground that it was insufficiently socialist in character.[49]

The greatest paradox of the 1948 campaign was the way in which it operated to exacerbate one of the most fundamental problems of the time — the relations between Communists and non-Communists. Outwardly rather impressive as a popular front, the Wallace movement was inwardly beset with disharmony, suspicion, recrimination, and a conflict of conceptions; only this reality explains the subsequent political eclipse of all the elements in this uneasy alliance. At the close of 1947, Wallace's leverage in American politics was at its height. He was credited with being able to attract anywhere from five to ten million votes. In profound despondency, his onetime liberal-labor friends in the Americans for Democratic Action were aghast at the prospect of supporting Mr. Truman; they became involved in a feverish search for alternatives which led them throughout the first months of 1948 to woo none other than General Dwight D. Eisenhower. At the same moment, the Communist Party achieved its highest postwar membership, its greatest battle readiness and its largest number of connections with other real movements. It appeared so important that even opponents were unwilling to ostracize it. Nothing seemed more favorable to the Party than the fact that a dynamic movement headed by a prestigious figure, a former vice-president, was willing to defend its right to participate in American political life.

Within a few months, the underlying reality manifested itself in a shattering fashion. The great untold story of the 1948 campaign was Wallace's antagonism toward the Communists and their own total inability to overcome it. The moment of their greatest apparent strength also revealed their greatest weakness. By the inexorable mathematics of American politics, the weakness of one movement when multiplied by the weakness of another did not add up to strength; it weakened both movements. The alliance between Wallace and the Communists helped neither of them to resolve basic problems because it was not an alliance at all. It functioned within a supposed coalition that was no coalition at all.[50]

What Henry Wallace wanted of the Communists was not an alliance but an illicit and discreet liaison in which the Communists would do the work that his own associates could not do. Verbally, Wallace defended the right of the Communists to be acknowledged as a political force under the protection of the Constitution. He viewed them as wrong in their perception of the world but defended their right to be wrong. And in this he stood almost alone in American life. Among his former friends the conception of Communism as a conspiracy had gained ground and was to dominate their thought for two decades. In practice, however, Wallace feared the stigma of association with Communism.

Wallace's discomfiture came to a head in mid-June 1948. In an interview with Edward R. Murrow, on the eve of a mass meeting in Albuquerque, New Mexico, Wallace said: "According to the newspapers, I'm getting a lot of support from the Communists, and the Communist leaders seem to think they have to endorse me every day or so. There's no question that this sort of thing is a political liability." Then Wallace added what had become his characteristic position. "I will not repudiate any support which comes to me on the basis of interest in peace. . . If you accept the idea that Communists have no right to express their opinions, then you don't believe in democracy. And if you accept the notion that is is impossible to live in a world with sharply differing opinions, then you accept the inevitability of war. I don't believe in the inevitability of war. I do believe in democracy."[51]

But, a few days later, in Burlington, Vermont, Wallace indicated how greatly the problem of relations with the Communists preyed upon him and blurted out: "If the Communists would have a ticket of their own, the New Party would lose 100,000 votes but gain four million." At a gathering in Center Sandwich, New Hampshire, immediately after the Burlington statement, Wallace returned to this idea, as though it might be a way out of his dilemma. "I'm never going to say anything in the nature of Red-baiting. But I must say this: if the Communists would run a ticket of their own this year, we might lose 100,000 votes but we would gain three million. I know if the Communists really wanted to help us, they would run their own ticket this year and let us get those extra votes."[52]

Thus, Wallace wanted to believe that the Communists would do the work of building the Progressive Party without being obtrusive. When this liaison, because it was indiscreet, began to be costly and many supporters of Wallace found themselves ill at ease with the Communist presence, Wallace made a desperate appeal to the Party. He placed himself in the contradictory position of asking in public for a divorce, or more exactly, for the end of a liaison which he had never acknowledged. Refusing to join in the hysteria against the Communists, he nevertheless sought some gimmick, some device, that would make clear that his common-law relationship with them was never intended to have the sanctity of marriage.

Wallace's extreme discomfort with the Communists, his desire to include them and to use them, his unwillingness to disavow them, and yet his hope that they would remain unobtrusive or actually help him by running an independent candidacy could only have the effect of making both him and his closest associates uneasy, suspicious, and bitter. Wanting to use the Communists, Wallace, inevitably felt that he and his friends were being used.

On August 19, 1948, after having served as the P.P. platform committee chairman, Rexford Guy Tugwell gave a famous interview to Howard Norton of the *Baltimore Sun*, suggesting that he Tugwell, was "an uneasy member of the Progressive Party" and that he was thinking of leaving it if "the wrong people get control." When asked whether by the phrase "wrong people" he meant the Communists, Tugwell gave an answer which illuminated quite precisely the dilemma which the Communist Party's own policy and the unavowed character of its key supporters imposed on movements with which the C.P. wanted to cooperate. "Who can say whether they are or not? I certainly don't know whether they are Communists, but they act as though they are."

After this interview, on Auguest 24 in Louisville, Kentucky, Henry Wallace finally made his strongest statement. He came as close to a declaration that he did not want Communist interference as he ever had, but *six months after* such a statement might have helped him. "I solemnly pledge that when I am elected President neither the Communists nor the Fascists nor any other group will control my policies." Six months before, newspapermen had reminded him that Franklin D. Roosevelt had systematically disavowed Communist support. Wallace had professed not to know this. Trying to remain true to his conception of nonostracism of the Party and trying, as we have seen, to get the Party to help him by opposing him, Wallace finally wound up saying things which contradicted his initial tactics.

In an interview with Edwin A. Lahey, in the *Chicago Daily News* for March 31, 1951 — after he had abandoned the wreckage of the Progressives — Wallace declared: "You know, I didn't actually realize how strong the Communists were in the Progressive Party. I think now that they were out to knife me." By contrast, the New York C.P. leader, Robert Thompson, called Wallace a traitor because of his break with the Progressive Party in June 1950, over the Korean war. Characteristically, an illicit liaison begun in such auspicious circumstances, ended in mutual cries of treachery.

To the Communists, the basic decision to make a third party out of what had been a dissident and powerful movement within the Democratic Party was influenced in large part by the conviction that the historic moment had arrived to accomplish a double objective: to legitimize the Communist Party (at the same time giving it a possible shield against illegality), and to make some tangible contribution to the initiative of the Cominform in the belief that a worldwide showdown in the Cold War was approaching.

At a Lenin anniversary meeting on January 15, 1948, Eugene Dennis tried to formulate what the Communists believed the Wallace movement to be. "This trend toward an historical breakaway from the two-party system does not follow the pattern anticipated by advanced workers years ago. It did not arise from a severe economic crisis, but was born in the course of a people's crusade for peace and civil liberty. It is not a labor party, nor even a farmer-labor party. It is a new type of people's anti-war and anti-imperialist and democratic people's coalition, which is being created within the United States and reflects in its own way the struggle between the world camps of progress and reaction."[53] Unable to define the coalition, the Communists were nevertheless sure they had one. Uppermost in their minds was the notion that this movement would be their contribution to the "struggle between the [two] world camps."

It would not be fair to say that the Communists wanted to dominate the Progressive Party. At last here was a movement far larger than their own in which they could function without disavowal and yet discharge their "leading role." On the other hand, without the fullest deployment of the Communist members the Progressive Party could not accomplish the tasks which it had set for itself. The C.P. was caught in a dilemma. The more it threw its own forces in to compensate for the weakness of the Progressives, the greater the problems within the Progressive Party as its hesitant supporters withdrew in proportion as the Communists came in.[54] On the other hand as summer soldiers among the Progressives withdrew, the Communists felt compelled to increase their own mobilization on behalf of the Progressives. In this process, however, the C.P. itself was undergoing a certain disintegration. Many of its own cadres seized on the existence of a Progressive Party as an alternate terrain for political activity. They had been dissatisfied with their own anonymity and the insecurity of being concealed Communists or sympathizers. A great many unionists who were losing their positions in the labor movement turned to the Progressive Party as a new arena for activity and many onetime Communists, people who had become inactive during the war, saw in the Progressives a safe and respectable forum; this was especially true in the middle class. The radical language which Frederick L. Schuman noted among the businessmen reflected a new trend. The onetime left wingers who had once manned the W.P.A. picket lines, but who had prospered during the war or in the post war boom (despite their own predictions of capitalism's imminent doom) now were able to attend dinners for Wallace and applaud nostalgic evocations of the revolutionary past. The Party exercised less discipline and authority over all these trends than non-Communists supposed. The differentiation within the Party's orbit and the *de facto* distintegration of its influence at the moment of its outward strength coincided with the political need of the Wallace-ites. But this need for power could not be satisfied. The Communist movement was succumbing to the multiple pressures of three years of traumatic political difficulty. It could no longer "deliver."

Yet Wallace's appeal for a tactical departure by the Commuist Party that would help him out did not go unheeded in Party circles. The Communists knew what Wallace wanted, and they must have given it serious consideration. Speaking at the August 3-6, 1948, National Convention, Dennis repeated Wallace's Center Sandwich statement without mentioning Wallace's name, and then said: "Granting that this spokesman is most sincere in his motive, his prognostication is at best wishful thinking. It also unwittingly reflects the pressure of the anti-Communists." This was a remarkable judgment. Dennis was saying that Wallace was kidding himself if he believed he could get an extra three or four million votes if the Communists ran independently. The fact that an independent party would at last take shape, whatever the number of its votes, was to the Communists most important. By telling Wallace that his plea reflected the "pressure of the anti-Communists," whereas in fact it was the pressure of the Communists within the Progressive Party that was worrying Wallace, the Communist general secretary eliminated any alternatives, such as an independent C.P. campaign. "In so far as the C.P. is concerned," he said rather imperiously, "it gives or withholds support to mass movements for principled reasons." The Party would not run its own presidential candidate, but it would advance its socialist program while supporting the Progressive Party. Dennis was thus acting as if a coalition existed, which it did not. He was "making believe" in a situation where make-believe was exasperating those closest to him. Dennis was using words, that is, propaganda on behalf of socialism, which presumably were meant to signal to Americans that the C.P. was something distinct from and beyond the P.P., while refusing to make the concrete and simple gesture that would have been more persuasive to millions of Americans than all the abstract doctrinal distinctions.

Was this simply ineptitude or stubbornness? Was there some obscure consideration which inhibited Eugene Dennis from accepting Wallace's proposal that the Communists run an independent candidate? Wallace himself did not know; Dennis did. The tactic which Wallace proposed was the tactic that Browder had carried out in 1936. It was the device of using the Party as a lightning rod to draw off the "Communist" charges against Roosevelt, while deploying its real strength for specific political activity on Roosevelt's behalf. The Communists in 1948 were hardly in a mood to repeat a tactic which Browder had used, even if he had done so as long ago as 1936, when his supposedly revisionist proclivities were by no means full-blown, and when his decision had been argued out in Moscow and upheld.

Too many Communist leaders had come to believe — by that peculiar penchant for giving every new historical decision a retroactive justification — that nothing under Browder's regime was worth emulating. Having decided that Browder had been guilty of hiding the Party's light under a bushel in 1944, the post-Browder leadership was hardly able to mount a Browder-type campaign in 1948 even though this might have been most helpful. They contented themselves with ideological dissociation and polite remonstration. In practice, they tried furiously to bail out an increasingly storm-tossed vessel which they had helped to make unseaworthy.

Even at the last moment, Wallace himself rejected a chance to make for a safe harbor. The most sensational but largely unknown aspect of the 1948 campaign is that as late as July 1948 the Democratic High Command, intensely worried over the prospect that Wallace votes would succeed in defeating Mr. Truman, *offered to negotiate with Wallace himself.* This offer was rejected.

It has already been noted that the Democratic Party's chairman, J. Howard McGrath, had been extremely reluctant to read Wallace out of the Democratic Party in the early weeks of 1948. When by the end of February 1948 the Progressives received an enormous lift in the shape of American Labor Party candidate Leo Isacson's victory in a New York congressional by-election, powerful Democratic political figures were deeply alarmed. Wallace's standing increased and so did his leverage. At that moment, Truman's fortunes were at their lowest. When the President announced to a Democratic Party dinner in mid-February 1948 that he would be the next president, this was widely viewed as whistling in the dark. By July a great many of the forces who were later to rally to Truman — after the Democratic convention and his dramatic moves on civil rights — had not given him any support. The C.I.O., for example, was systematically taking measures to oust the third party adherents from the city-wide and state wide union councils; but not until the end of August 1948 did the C.I.O. leadership decide to support Truman. In July 1948, when the Philadelphia convention of the Progressive Party received unprecedented national attention, Oscar Chapman, Truman's Secretary of the Interior, approached C.B. Baldwin in the hope of making a deal with the Wallace movement; similar approaches were made to Rexford Guy Tugwell.

The evidence that emissaries of Truman and the Democratic Party chairman, J. Howard McGrath, approached the Progressives not once but several times is found in MacDougall's account, although he does not realize its implications. "The Democrats, on the other hand, worked on Tugwell. As late as the night before the Progressive Party convention formally opened in Philadelphia, he received a call from Oscar Chapman, Secretary of the Interior and the leading liberal left figure in Truman's cabinet. He also heard from Robert Straus, brother of Michael Straus, Federal Reclamation Director and a Wallace supporter in Maryland. Almost simultaneously Ed Hart, a Washington radio commentator, got in touch with 'Beanie' Baldwin, giving the impression that he was speaking with the knowledge of Demoocratic National Committee chairman, J. Howard McGrath, to suggest that a meeting be arranged between Truman and Wallace. To all these overtures, the Progressive leaders turned a deaf ear. Wallace sent word to Truman, through Baldwin and via McGrath and Hart, that only an about-face by the Administration on foreign policy could cause him to call off his venture."[55]

Thus, in July, the Progressives could have negotiated with Truman, and refused. What part the Communists played in this refusal is unknown. But they must have been aware that a negotiation was possible. Half a year later, Tugwell — whose erratic behavior mirrors the contradictions of those who wanted to save Wallace from himself and yet could not influence him — lamented that Truman had won the election because of a shift of seven to ten million Progressives and asked that Truman pay his political debts by inviting Wallace back into the fold. This time, Truman spurned the offer.

It is conceivable that by trading off a third party (which was in any case in severe difficulties), Wallace could have materially altered the nature of the Democratic Party's campaign. This might easily have included a relaxation of the pressure on the Communist Party. If the grand jury indictments under the Smith Act could not have been halted, at least the Department of Justice could have decided that the Smith Act was indefensible under the terms of the First Amendment.

Once the election returns were in, both the Progressive Party spokesman, C.B. Baldwin, and the Communist Party's spokesman, Eugene Dennis, argued that the 1948 campaign had been worthwhile because it had compelled Mr. Truman to take a leftward course, to make positive moves toward easing the cold war (such as the proposed Vinson mission to Moscow). There was some truth in this argument, but as a rationalization for Gideon's Army, it was also pathetic. Mr. Truman as victor, was far less inclined to pay any price whatsoever to those who had done their utmost to imperil his victory. He might very well have paid a considerable price in advance to make certain of the victory. The Progressives might have been in a much stronger position to enforce their claim to a share in the Democratic victory if they had in fact shifted their support voluntarily to Truman in August. Instead, they argued in November that they had a share in the victory because their audience had turned from them.[56]

In substance, the 1948 campaign destroyed both for the friends and opponents of American Communism its carefully nurtured reputation of exceptional political expertise which it had traded on for a decade. The Party's combination of a supposed mastery of Marxism-Leninism with the capacity of its members to ring door bells, collect money, and devote themselves single-mindedly to a cause no longer gave them the leverage in American political life which they had painfully acquired. Exactly at the moment when all these attributes were put to the severest test, they proved illusory. Standing alone, without the support of significant allies, the C.P. revealed a weakness which ten years of hard work had served to conceal. This weakness invited attack, and the attack contributed to further weakness.

Henceforth, the American Communists were to be pilloried and gored with a vindictive ruthlessness by the liberal-labor antagonists whom they had exasperated. These attacks did not come to an end when the fuller expression of this political assault in the McCarthy era began to endanger this liberal-labor coalition. The fury of the anti-Communist assault was equaled only by the Party's capacity to pillory and gore its own adherents. From this point on, the American Communist Party became at least a case in civil liberties, at best an object of sympathy, but no longer a power.[57]

One final consideration must enter into this analysis of the year 1948 — the impact of developments in the world Communist movement upon American Communism. As has been shown, the C.P.U.S.A. conceived of itself as making a vital contribution to a world wide coalition, whose existence was assumed to be a factor contributing to its strength. Throughout both the Browder and Foster regimes, it was axiomatic that the American Communist Party had to contribute, even at cost to itself, to the tactical orientations of world Communism as defined by its leading force, the Soviet Communists. Presumably, the American C.P. would share in the rewards, as it had during the war. Events of 1948 shattered this delusion of reciprocity.

The world Communist movement underwent decisive changes without any indication whatsoever that the American Party's needs were being taken into consideration. The C.P.U.S.A., although at its peak of influence and the architect of a political movement which Stalin respected sufficiently to exchange letters with Henry Wallace, nevertheless was considered by Moscow quite expendable. There is no sign that the tempo .of Stalin's mobilization for the Cold War, which had begun the previous summer, was in any way adjusted to take into account the internal American scene.

The trend of events in Europe and Asia worked unfavorably for the C.P.U.S.A. In February 1948, at precisely the moment when the American Communists were postulating a long-term united front with Wallace and what he presumably represented, the most impressive united front in Eastern Europe broke down completely. The Czechoslovak Communists seized power for themselves at the expense of those Czechs and Slovaks with whom they had solemnly entered into coalition, President Eduard Benes and Foreign Minister Jan Masaryk. By June 1948, the expulsion of Tito's Yugoslavia from the Communist bloc on the grounds that, among other things, Tito had mismanaged relations with non-Communists, could only signify that the era of building long-term relationships with non-Communists had come to a close.[58]

The only way in which U.S. Communists could carry any conviction that their cooperation with non-Communists in America would be different from what was happening in Eastern Europe would have been to dissociate themselves from the Cominform. At least they might have entered a quiet dissent. They did neither, however. The American comrades were driven by their own conceptions to march stridently into the anti-Yugoslav campaign, accepting with a quasi-military discipline the implications of their political commitment. Even Browder, as has been noted, applied for readmission to the Party in August 1948 on the unconvincing ground that the crisis of the international movement following the Cominform's action required his participation in the C.P.U.S.A., although he was at that moment formulating critiques of the Party's basic course.[59]

Throughout 1948, the Cold War intensified, chiefly as a result of Communist initiatives. By 1948 is could hardly be claimed that the posture of the Soviet Union was defensive or simply a function of American bellicosity as Americans had believed in 1946 and 1947. It could be argued that Stalin was coordinating the Eastern European states (and with them the Communist parties of Western Europe) because any other policy held out dangers to the Soviet Union and perhaps even to Communism. It could be argued that in achieving this coordination Stalin was attempting to take maximum advantage of the impact of the Chinese Revolution which was then approaching a final victory. Yet such arguments undermined the simple Communist position that the easing of international tensions depended essentially on the United States. The events of 1948 undermined Henry Wallace's chief argument, that an American-Soviet settlement required only a change in political power in Washington. Even to those who placed *initial* responsibility for the Cold War on the United States, the Cold War was a two-way process by 1948 and a reciprocal responsibility. It was clearly being escalated *on both sides*, no matter how one determined it had begun.

Wallace was so deeply a prisoner of the conceptions which he had advanced two years earlier — at a time when they appeared to have credibility — that he did not attempt to prevent one of the most damaging events at the Progressive Party's convention — the passage of the famous "Vermont resolution." Near the end of the Progressive Party's founding convention, three delegates from Vermont submitted the following innocuous resolution as an amendment to the P.P.'s platform. "Although we are critical of the present foreign policy of the United States, it is not our intention to give blanket endorsement to the foreign policy of any nation."[60] The convention record shows that the debate on this declaration was desultory. Few delegates seemed to realize what was at stake. The chief opponent of this resolution, former congressman Hugh De Lacy, argued vigorously that the platform already adopted was a sound basis for American-Soviet friendship and that "unless the Progressive Party was willing to take a position and fight for it and hold it and not back it up with some kind of phoney declaration that didn't mean anything" the entire Progressive Party crusade would come to naught. None of the other left wingers took part in this debate. The Vermont resolution was defeated, but neither the Wallace-ites nor the Communists seemed to be clear as to what they were doing.

The Progressive Party's defeat, however, was very much bound up with the Vermont resolution. The opposition to this resolution was not an instance of militant Communist defense of Soviet policy and the unwillingness of non-Communists to disagree. Everyone in the Progressive Party was apparently "inoculated" against any criticism of the Soviet Union; even a hint of a *mutual* responsibility for the Cold War was widely viewed as a concession to "Red-baiting." The entire question of mutual responsibility was passed over. By midsummer of 1948, a euphoric, insensitive mood permeated all wings of the Progressive Party.

The fate of the Vermont resolution became the *cause célébre* of the press in reporting the convention, even though almost all the convention leaders were quite bewildered as to why this was so.[61] The defeat of the resolution was taken as proof that the Progressives had become dominated by the Communists, which was true but not the point at all. In reality, the defeat of the Vermont resolution proved only that the Progressives were the victims of the way in which the Cold War was being conducted. Because the Truman administration acted as though it desired a settlement with the Soviet Union, millions of Americans voted to reelect the President, while those who believed that no responsibility attached to the Soviet Union lost votes by the millions.

The most ambitious, most costly, most energetic effort of a wide variety of Americans of progressive persuasion to halt the Cold War via a third party came to defeat. The American public grasped that the Cold War could not be halted by any movement which could not even approve the Vermont resolution and was largely unaware of its significance. In this complete misreading of both the American mood and the realities abroad, the American Communists were no more perspicacious than the coalition which they had fostered and which — in the end — failed them.

# 8 INCOHERENCE
# AND AGONY

The American Communist Party did not collapse after 1948; it staggered. Punch-drunk but determined to stay its course, the movement gave every sign of incoherence, of suppressed inner conflict, and of a capacity for hallucinatory political adventures for which the only precedents lay in its very beginnings as an underground sect. In staggering, the Party managed to keep most of its cadres, and, at least until 1951, a large part of its postwar membership. It came no closer, however, to a fundamental reappraisal of its course than at any of the earlier points of bewilderment since 1945. There is little evidence that any significant number of leaders or members asked whether the setbacks and defeats had deep historical reasons. Many individuals had questions, but the directing group did not question that the Party's line must be pursued. Half a dozen years were to go by before the roots of Communism's dilemma were exposed. Because it was delayed, the outburst of 1956 was all the more profound and spectacular.

This state of affairs — a living organism staggering to its doom without being able to probe the premises of its own action — appears inexplicable only to those who do not realize the momentum generated by intense ideological commitments.[1] Although the Party professed "scientific socialism," it did not act like an organization engaged in pragmatic experiments in which results could be measured, experience could be evaluated, and premises could be discarded. Ostensibly rational, the Party was pervaded by a deep irrationality. The ideological block to self-examination and self-correction was at one and the same time the guarantee of the Party's capacity to continue under adverse circumstances and the quality that complicated these very circumstances. "The mentality of a person who lives in a closed system of thought, Communist or other," says Arthur Koestler in his remarkable autobiographical study, "can be summed up in a single formula: he can prove anything he believes and he believes everything he can prove. The closed system sharpens the faculties of the mind, like an over-efficient grindstone, to a brittle edge; it produces a scholastic, Talmudic, hair-splitting brand of cleverness which affords no protection against committing the crudest imbecilities."[2]

The Party's propensity to imbecilities was accentuated by increasing governmental and public repression of the Party, and by the feverish search for heresy within the international Communist movement. McCarthyism was not only an American phenomenon but also a Communist one, even if the latter was sanctified by Stalin himself. The U.S. Communists had to endure both forms of McCarthyism.

The outward expression of the increasing governmental and extragovernmental repression was the Smith Act trial (at Foley Square in New York) of the eleven members of the Party's highest body, the National Board, which went on throughout 1949. The verdict in this trial set a precedent and laid the basis for arrests and prosecutions of the second-echelon leaders. Because of the nature of the American appeals system, the top leaders had several years of freedom after the verdict, and the Supreme Court did not uphold the sentence until mid-1951. But the repressive atmosphere went beyond the legal issues and quickly affected tens of thousands of rank and filers, both members of the Party and those who could be considered as being within its orbit, or who were accused of so being. In those years the House Committee on Un-American Activities and the Internal Security Committee in the Senate specialized in calling witnesses before them, ostensibly to answer questions concerning Communism and, indeed, anything that could be claimed to be connected with Communism. These witnesses were confronted with the choice of either answering such questions, which usually involved the naming of other individuals and carried with it the danger of prosecution, or refusing to testify at all. In the latter case, a witness could evade a "contempt of Congress" citation (for refusing to cooperate with the committees) only by taking the Fifth Amendment.[3] By then the Supreme Court had denied witnesses the protection of the First Amendment.[4]

The most repressive aspect of these procedures was not the jeopardy to the individuals involved, nor the stigma attached to the use of constitutional amendments to avoid inquiry and prosecution, but the public atmosphere created. Thousands of men and women of left wing views, some having a genuine and others a remote affiliation with Communist organizations, soon found that unless they cooperated abjectly with these committees they faced not only prosecution but also ostracism. It soon became customary to oust these people from their jobs, whether in factories, in colleges, in government, or in business. This repression spread to a point where hostile witnesses and persons accused of Communist connections were ousted from trade unions, churches, professional societies, neighborhood groups, and were refused rentals of apartments and even insurance policies.[5] Communists, and anyone accused of any association with causes or groups said to be Communist controlled, found themselves pariahs. The tolerated status they had enjoyed for two or three years after the war had suddenly and mercilessly been reversed. Near-hysteria gripped the nation.

A large segment of the labor-liberal world joined in this hysteria. Encouraged by the political defeat of Henry Wallace, the labor-liberal forces mounted an intense campaign to rout and isolate everyone who could now be considered a misguided member, not of a mistaken political movement, but of a conspiracy.[6] In such an atmosphere, many Party members quietly retired from political activity. This tendency was even more pronounced on the part of sympathizers. Those members who remained placed a greater premium than ever before on loyalty and on defiance of the "establishment" and of anyone conceivably connected with it. The Party reacted by consolidating its ranks and preparing itself for greater tribulations. More and more, its members looked abroad where Communism appeared to be advancing, and justified their behavior at home on the grounds that reverses were temporary. The concept that America was but one sector of a world front took on new meaning. This new dependence on international Communism in turn intensified all the moods of leftism within the C.P. and all the inherent tendencies to imitate the world movement. An inner cycle of self-justification developed which militated against any re-examination within the Party's ranks. Re-examination could easily be equated with doubt and weakness. For members of an ideologically bound community the greatest crime is disloyalty when that community appears in danger. Disloyalty could easily be attributed to anyone seeking to pause and take stock.

As the American Communists staggered, they turned inward, The cause of policy dilemmas came to be sought not in the policies themselves but in the make-up, behavior, and capability of

Party members. Unable to evaluate their policies objectively, Communists began to measure each other for deviations and heresies. Thus the strange paradox: *in the name of defying the witchhunt against them, the American Communists complemented it by engaging in a witchhunt of their own. Beleagured from without, they went through agony from within.*

The American Communist Party's internal witchhunt formed part of the search for heresy that swept the international movement after the Yugoslav Communist defiance of Stalin. Not only were the accusations against Tito and his comrades taken as gospel truth, but the conclusion was drawn that if the treachery of such hitherto-revered men had been possible within the European Communist family, among such powerful states and parties — and the trials in Hungary, Bulgaria, and later Czechoslovakia "confirmed" the treachery — then surely such treachery was possible in as inexperienced and vulnerable a party as the American. One consequence was the search for heretics in high places, to which reference will be made shortly. The other was a total transposition of Eastern Europe political standards to America. Many sympathizers who had been viewed as friends of the Party now became suspect on the sole ground that they refused to break their ties with the Yugoslavs.[7] Because they were dissatisfied with the orthodox explanations and expressed curiosity about the Yugoslav-Soviet issue these one-time friends became suspect. At the moment when the American Communists badly needed allies, they began to draw the line against anyone who did not concur with the Soviet version of the Yugoslav affair. It now became simple to assimilate the phenomenon of Browderism to Titoism. In 1945-46, Browder had been viewed as stubbornly misguided. His cordial reception in Moscow had been perplexing. At the 14th National Convention in August 1948, his application for readmission, if taken literally, meant that he was still capable of redemption.[8] But after 1948, the "ism" which had become associated with his name was equated with Titoism. Some of the bitterest Party polemics against him date from this period despite his own professions of support for Moscow at that time (and — in private — for several more years).[9]

Probably the most symptomatic example of this "turning inward" was the 1949-1953 campaign against "white chauvinism." This was a veritable paroxysm that reflected far more than the ostensible issue of the Party's relations with the Negro movement. No single experience is remembered in retrospect with such dismay, even fifteen years later, by thousands of former Communists and their progressive sympathizers. Not a few have asked themselves: if they were capable of such cruelties to each other when they were a small handful of people bound by sacred ideals, what might they have done if they had been in power? The white chauvinism experience helped a great many understand the later revelations about Stalinism. The underground adventure was to affect only a few thousand, but the struggle against white chauvinism wracked the lives of tens of thousands. This frenzy marks one of the many points at which the experience of the American Communists two decades ago offers a parallel and a precedent to the trauma affecting the new left in the late 1960's on the same issue — black-white relations.

The campaign began with a seemingly routine article by the chairman of the Party's Negro Commission, Pettis Perry.[10] To meet the challenge of reaction and to be worthy of the new levels and potentials of the Negro liberation movement, Perry believed the Party had to take the offensive against chauvinist moods and themes within its own ranks and among its sympathizers. Much of this had been heard before. The Communists had always believed that part of the fight for civil rights involved self-purification and self-liberation from anti-Negro prejudice. But within a short time, a demonstrative campaign was under way. Important Party leaders were demoted from their posts for real or alleged insults to black members.[11] Some accepted the criticism. Others did not and were punished. Grievances of every sort, some real and many imaginary, were aired in local and state meetings.

The Communists began to examine everyday language for signs of racism. Words like "whitewash" were deemed chauvinism in reverse. The term, "black sheep" was deemed chauvinist in its essence. Howard Fast apologized because in an old novel of his, one character used racist language and dialect, although this use was quite in keeping with the story. The search for heresy soon affected the left led trade unions at the moment that they were facing expulsion from the C.I.O.[12] It spilled over into the American Labor Party and the Progressive Party. Trials began to take place of prominent trade union leaders, some of whom resented the fact that the Party deemed itself the arbiter of their affairs. Within a few months the left wing, which had prided it-

self for over twenty years on having built an integrated movement and had shown its devotion to Negro rights by exemplary
acts, underwent a striking internal change. A bitter internecine
battle ravaged every organization.

Increasingly motivations became blurred. Both whites and
blacks began to take advantage of the enormous weapon which
the charge of "white chauvinism" gave them to settle scores, to
climb organizational ladders, to fight for jobs and to express
personality conflicts which, by Communist definition, were never
supposed to predominate over political objectivity.

This internal witchhunt brought to the surface extremely interesting theories which questioned fundamental doctrine. As
has been emphasized, the traditional socialist view was that the
solution of the American Negro question lay within the scope of
the struggle of the working class as a whole for a new social
order. Workers, both white and black, were assumed to constitute the revolutionary force whose unity was essential to confront
common exploitation.

The Communists had introduced a new element into this traditional view. They had urged that the Negro people constituted
a nation, or at least an emergent nation, and that their struggle
was auxiliary to that of the working class; that they were allies
of a special kind. As a national struggle, however, the fight for
Negro self-determination had a basic ambiguity about it. National struggles were after all part of the process of democracy;
civil rights was a democratic demand attainable within the
framework of capitalism, as history had shown. National self-
determination could be presocialist in character, and not necessarily postcapitalist. This had been the stand of Dr. Doxey Wilkerson. Other Communist theorists, it will be recalled, had been
critical of his assumption that Negro equality could be realized
under conditions of monopoly capitalism. Harry Haywood, one
of the pioneers of the self-determination concept, had argued
strongly that U.S. imperialism could not possibly satisfy the agrarian, national, and political revolution implied by the emergent Negro nation's struggle, and that therefore this struggle
constituted the "Achilles heel" of the whole system.

In 1949, Party differences on the Negro question complicated
the white chauvinism campaign. The Negro people's movement
was said to be assuming such militant forms, in contrast to the
comparative weakness of the white working class (especially in

view of the crisis of the left wing in every field), that it was over-shadowing the working class. Moreover, the rise of "national liberation" movements abroad by the end of the forties — notably the successful Chinese revolution and harbingers of similar movements in Africa — led to the view that the American Negro struggle was not simply a democratic one, that it was incapable of being contained within the framework of the system and that it was not presocialist in character. Instead, the view developed that this struggle was replacing the struggle of the working class as a whole *as the true revolutionary force.*

The Communists found themselves with a new theoretical position, emanating from their most prestigious leaders, which held that the vanguard of the battle against imperialism was no longer the working class as a whole but *the black component of it.* From this it was only a short step to asserting that whites were incapable of understanding blacks and could not work in the same organizations. Within the Party and its orbit the whites had to move out of the way so as to enable the blacks to take over.

On the most prosaic level, the struggle signified a contest for power within a dwindling movement. It expressed the agony of many hundreds of black left wingers who had been attracted to the Communist movement as a vehicle for the realization of Negro aims, and were now confronted with the error of their calculation and the collapse of their investment.[13] In the trauma of this realization, these blacks asked the white left wing to re-place by acts of self-purification what had been lost. The priority of the Negro struggle was given a theoretical justification: the colonial and semicolonial upheaval was outdistancing the working class as such. Here lay the prefiguration of a major doctrinal issue at the heart of the Sino-Soviet schism. The resulting campaign against white chauvinism produced profound chaos until the campaign had run its course.[14]

There were also other signs of the Party's failure to maintain a coherent policy. In the trade union movement, the left wing of the C.I.O., which had invested so heavily in the Progressive Party and lost, found itself faced by a vindictive campaign on the part of its opponents. The gamble of the Americans for Democratic Action on Harry Truman had been won, much to their own surprise. The opportunity now presented itself to rout the pro-Communist left; the so-called center, personified by Philip Murray, was no longer a restraining force. A bitter vendetta against the left wing swept through the unions it had done so much to build. The left was soon isolated and helpless in the U.A.W., and its members faced physical attack in the Steel Workers' Union. In the Transport Workers Union and the National Maritime Union the onetime friends of the Party knew whom to oust and how to go about it. And by the end of 1949, proceedings were under way for the formal expulsion of the eleven left-led unions that had opposed official C.I.O. policy the year before.

With the Taft-Hartley Act functioning, left wingers either resigned from local posts in the A.F.L. and the C.I.O. or faced perjury proceedings. Only in rare cases did local leaders have the support among the rank and file to admit Party membership and still maintain their positions. Very shortly, important union leaders whose Communist affiliation or sympathies had never been concealed felt obliged to resign from the Party to hold on to their posts. The resignation of Ben Gold of the Furriers' Union was one of the bitterest pills for American Communism to swallow.[15]

Simultaneously, left-led unions underwent a process of defensive consolidation at the moment they were facing raids by right-led unions. The weaker left-led unions were absorbed into other left-led unions — the Food, Agricultural and Tobacco Workers into the Distributive Workers; and the Marine Cooks and Stewards into the International Longshoremen and Warehousemen's Union. This process caused severe strains, since jobs of officials were involved.[16] Political kinship hardly softened the blows which the leaders of the left wing inflicted on one another, although there were many cases of mutual assistance. The prestige of the Party with its own influentials continued to diminish. The most striking instance came over the policy of the U.E. — the United Electrical Workers — which was perhaps the best of the left wing unions, the largest and the most dynamic. The leaders of the U.E. decided not to wait for expulsion from the C.I.O., especially after a rival union — the I.U.E. — was chartered in Washington. Unlike the ten other unions, it was never expelled. It walked out, but it did so largely against the Party's own advice, which at that time was to engage in the most effective possible rearguard action. Communists were thus divided with regard to U.E. policy. Within a short time, the U.E. leaders, who managed to maintain a union of some power, had little but contempt for the

Party's emissaries and did not hesitate to show it. This contempt, felt by most influentials, was intensified when in 1952 the foremost Communist leaders called from the underground for a return of the left wing to the mainstream of American labor.[17] The term, "mainstream," had by then become an epithet and a mark of derision in those left wing labor circles which had survived shifts of Party policy.

The incoherence, exaggeration, blind faith, and collapse of cohesion which characterized those years are illustrated by other examples, some of them of political importance. Mention has been made of Foster's own contributions to economic theory, consisting of an all-out attack on the theory of Lord Keynes, as though this were a major intellectual issue. One finds in the pages of the *Daily Worker* as well as *Political Affairs* a wholesale onslaught against psychoanalysis and, indeed, against all schools of psychological thought except Pavlov's. Once the theories of Trofim Lysenko with respect to genetics were enthroned in the Soviet Union, American biologists and geneticists (who happened to include a few outstanding Marxists) were treated to a campaign on behalf of Lysenko. Anti-Mendelian theories of genetics became the test of Marxian orthodoxy. Biologists and psychoanalysts of left wing persuasion found themselves at loggerheads with the Party leadership. Committees and subcommittees multiplied. Representations were made to the highest Party authorities. Learned papers were prepared. The average Party member was entirely mystified, while Party members with any knowledge or the ideas of Freud or Mendel were appalled.[18]

As in the campaign against white chauvinism, long-time Party leaders were not spared. One example was the destruction of the political career of Avrom Landy, a Communist since his early twenties, with long service in directing Party work among ethnic groups. In 1945, Landy published an interesting volume, *Marxism and the Democratic Tradition*, one of the most ambitious attempts to relate Marxism to the democratic movement of the nineteenth century and present its premises as part of the heritage both of the American democratic mainstream and of Western democracy as a whole.[19] Landy was assailed by the long-time specialist in organizational affairs, one of those unhappy people whose neuroses find political expression, Betty Gannett. No Party leader contradicted her assault on Landy's work even though it came at a moment when American Communism needed badly to affirm its continuity with the democratic heritage — the thesis that was defended without success in the Smith Act trial.

Two events in 1949 appear to have little connection with Communist policy as such; nevertheless, they throw light on the Party's collapse. One had to do with Anna Louise Strong, the other with the inauguration of the independent socialist magazine, *Monthly Review*. "Anna Louise," as she was widely known, had been one of the most persuasive figures in popularizing Soviet developments. Her infatuation with Russia stemmed not only from her early experience with the Nansen relief mission but also from her own origins as an authentic radical of the American Northwest.[20] Few experts found as much acceptance in a wide variety of church and civic groups as Miss Strong did. She also had unusual access to the Department of State and other Washington agencies, where her eyewitness testimony on both Soviet Russia and Chinese Communist developments was received with respect and attention.[21] Nor was she without credit of another kind in Moscow: she had served with Borodin on the *Moscow News* and her Russian husband had sufficient standing in Comintern circles to have been sent to the United States on Communist business.[22] One day in 1949, entirely without warning, Anna Louise Strong was declared *persona non grata* in Moscow and labeled by high Soviet authorities as a "notorious spy." No further explanation was given. Miss Strong's self-defense soon appeared in the *New York Herald-Tribune* and then in the *National Guardian*. Most remarkable in our context was the failure of anyone in the American Communist movement, or in organizations such as the National Council for American-Soviet Friendship (under whose auspices she had often spoken), to make any public reservations about the Soviet action. No protest was made by the U.S. Communists. No inquiry was made even in private, so far as those who were in a position to know could judge. The frame-up of "Anna Louise" was one of the costliest burdens of the American left at a time when it needed friends badly, and one of the heaviest blows to Soviet prestige in the United States at a critical moment of the Cold War. The left's audience was astonished. The only periodical on the left which gave Miss Strong a hearing was the *National Guardian*, whose editors were for this reason (as well as for others) viewed with suspicion. "Anna Louise," whose articles on China had been appearing in the *Daily Worker* in January and February 1949 and were then abruptly discontinued, became an "unperson." Her contribution to the defense fund of the Smith Act victims was returned by the Civil Rights Congress as "tainted money" (the words of Eugene Dennis).[23]

*Monthly Review* was founded in 1949 by the independent socialists, Paul Sweezy, one-time professor of economics at Harvard, and Leo Huberman, the labor publicist who had worked in the National Maritime Union's educational department in the heydey of Communist control. (The third founder, who left *Monthly Review* almost immediately, was Otto Nathan, a German-born economist and, later, the executor of Albert Einstein's estate.) Avowing a faith in socialism, the magazine's first issue made it clear that it had little reverence for political iconography. Its editors intended to discuss foreign affairs, including the policies of the Soviet Union, without the assumption which animated the American Communists. Little attention was paid in Communist circles to *Monthly Review* in its first two years. The National Committee's library did not even subscribe to it. A proposal by its editors that a member of the Party's national staff participate in a symposium on the Yugoslav issue was brusquely vetoed. Yet the magazine continued to gain readers. It quickly found an audience in circles close to the Party, especially among trade unionists and academics who were by then disillusioned with the Party's leadership without, however, quite knowing why.

In the May 1951 issue of *Political Affairs*, the Party's chief theoretician, Alexander Bittelman, let loose an intemperate blast at *Monthly Review*, altogether oblivious to the overriding problem, which at that moment was particularly acute, of how to win friends and influence people. *Monthly Review* never replied to the attack. So far as is known, no letters appeared in the Communist press questioning this behavior. No apologies were ever made to Sweezy and Huberman (with one exception — an apology was made in 1956 after the Party's entire course had come up for review, and then only by one who had already left the Communist ranks).[24]

### Legal Problems and the Peace Campaign

Two other aspects of Party policy in the post-1948 period require analysis. The first is its legal and political defense, and the second is the attempt to build a "peace movement," the activity which preoccupied all Communist parties at the height of the Cold War.

In the conduct of the Foley Square trial, the Party's legal moves were at the outset tactical and educational. An elaborate presentation was made challenging the jury system on the interesting grounds that discrimination against Negroes violated the 14th Amendment. This recalled the effort of Dennis to disqualify the "contempt of Congress" charge against him in 1947 on the grounds that members of Congress who had voted to ask the Department of Justice to prosecute were seated in the House illegally, in violation of the same Amendment. These were, in their way, pioneer challenges. Once these opening moves made no headway, the Party was faced with the more fundamental challenge — how to conduct itself in order to win both a legal and political victory.[25] Under the Smith Act provisions, the reconstitution of the Party on the basis of Marxism-Leninism in 1945 was held to have been a conspiracy; the Act provided that the "teaching and advocating" of Marxism-Leninism meant *ipso facto* the advocacy of violent overthrow of the government.

Two paths were open to the Communist leaders. They could either proclaim their revolutionary faith, asserting that they meant to achieve radical change by constitutional means but appealing to the revolutionary traditions in the American experience, and hence insisting that prosecution for advocacy violated the First Amendment. Or else, they could make an elaborate defense of Marxism-Leninism, explaining the complex history of their movement. The first option meant at minimum a disavowal of those obscure chapters in the Party's history which were inexplicable — and indefensible — to a wide audience. It also could have meant the opportunity for frank self-criticism. This was the type of defense which Clarence Darrow had made in the Communist cases in 1919.[26] If the Party adopted such a strategy, the trial might be brief. The risk was that the verdict would be negative, and even with appeals to higher courts the sentences would go into effect relatively quickly. The second course involved a defense of doctrine, and discussion of the labyrinthine history of the Communist International. Much of this was hardly understandable either to the jury or the public. This course ran the risk of encountering the tides of doctrinal change which were mounting with the Stalinization of the international movement.

The U.S. Communists straddled the challenge. They asserted their right to advocate whatever they pleased, and combined this with a most elaborate presentation of their doctrinal position, centering heavily on the changes brought about by the Seventh Congress of the International in 1935. The key document in this regard was a deposition by William Z. Foster (who had been severed from the case on the grounds of poor health); he argued that a constitutional and peaceful road to socialism had become Communist doctrine after the Seventh Congress. But the Communist leaders were not convincing. They could not make a believable case that, in ousting Browder and reconstituting the Party, they were still operating within the framework of the American system of constitutional change. No element of self-criticism entered into their statements. Indeed, any cogent clarification of the 1944-45 days would be a Pandora's box that could hardly be opened before a jury. There was at least one difficulty with Foster's assertion that his Party believed in a peaceful, American path to socialism, an assertion intended to disprove the government's charge that the reconstitution of the party constituted a commitment to violence. *By early 1949 the ideas of peaceful evolution were being disavowed internationally.* At the December 1948 Congress of the Polish Workers Party, the Soviet and Eastern European parties had interred the very ideas which Foster was putting forward.[27] Thus in the June 1950 *Political Affairs* Foster made an explicit self-criticism of his own deposition. He now found that, in essence, socialism meant the "defeat of the capitalist class and the establishment of the dictatorship of the proletariat." Although he still believed that a democratically elected government of transition from capitalism to socialism was possible, Communists could "only conditionally presuppose the election of such a government," he declared, and then added: "One would be naive to speak of a peaceful election under such circumstances of sharp political struggle; it would be equally silly in the face of the organized violence of the big capitalists to think that it would be simply a parliamentary election struggle."[28]

Thus, in the midst of the appeals to higher courts from the Foley Square verdict, the American Communists were admitting that the entire basis of their case was faulty. They had not used the Smith Act indictment to admit they had been mistaken in the past. Nor had they distinguished their own political circumstances from Communist perspectives in other countries. Instead, they had aligned themselves once again with the international movement, even though its terrain, tactics, and compulsions were different from their own.[29]

In subsequent years, when second-echelon leaders were tried in other parts of the country, efforts were made to take another tack, to forego an elaborate defense of the world movement and to defend — under American constitutional procedures — the right of Americans to be Communists. This was done notably in California, where the defendants ultimately won an acquittal. It was attempted in Washington State, despite pressure from the National Office to make the trial in Seattle a replica of the New York trial; the attempt was only partly successful and had its own tragedies.[30]

But the problem of a credible stance by the left arose not only in the Smith Act trials. The entire left, not only the Communists, made a crucial decision when the Fifth Amendment, a perfectly valid constitutional protection, began to be employed in place of the First Amendment, an equally valid protection which did not, however, give any assurance that a witness who used it might not go to jail. Numerous witnesses were cited for "contempt of Congress" because they refused on First Amendment grounds to answer questions by Congressional committees. It soon became obvious that merely asserting one's protection under the First Amendment would not deter the Department of Justice from prosecution.

On the other hand, in the *Blau* case the Supreme Court ruled that a witness could refuse to answer questions by asserting his rights against self-incrimination under the Fifth Amendment only if he did so consistently. In this way, a witness might gain freedom from jail only to face a still greater penalty in the realm of politics. Historically and legally the use of the Fifth Amendment did not imply that the witness was guilty, or that in asserting his right not to testify against himself he had anything to hide. At a time when the government was asserting that Communism was a conspiracy and advocacy of unpopular ideas was akin to crime, however, the witness who found himself refusing to testify on the grounds that self-incrimination might be involved did in fact incriminate himself in the eyes of the public.[31] Years later it was acknowledged that this type of defense was altogether within the framework of the American system. In the meantime much political damage had been done.

Should left wingers and Communists have gone to jail in large numbers? Might they not have been better off *politically*, in terms of their *image*, to assert their affiliations, to proclaim them instead of asserting their right to keep them private, to explain the issues as they saw them, and to take the consequences? The widespread use of the Fifth Amendment became a device of dubious value. It gave immunity from imprisonment, but it condemned the left wing to failure through self-defeating accommodation.

The U.S. Communist Party suffered from similar dilemmas in the major area of its activity, or what was supposed to become the major area — the building of a peace movement. The defeat of Wallace and the crisis of the left wing in the labor movement coincided with the full unfolding of the Cold War. The international Communist movement began mobilizing what it believed to be world peace sentiment; simultaneously, Stalin appeared to be making those moves which would give him time and gain him leverage for some ultimate bargain with the West. In 1948 Stalin had orchestrated a series of events, from the coup in Prague to the blockade of Berlin; upheavals shook Asia from Indonesia to Burma — coinciding with Chinese Communist offensives in the Yangtse valley. In early 1949 Stalin's tactics took another form. A political offensive was mounted in which the prospect of a peaceful settlement was held out to the West while the Communist parties were given an issue around which to overcome their isolation and gain political mileage.[32]

Early in January 1949, the veteran Communist leader, Marcel Cachin, travelled to Rome in his official capacity as president of the French National Assembly to be received by the Italian Chamber of Deputies. Cachin voiced the view that a *détente* in the tense international situation was entirely possible. This was taken as a serious peace feeler in the West. It was followed, not long after, by the end of the Berlin blockade. At almost the same time, both Palmiro Togliatti, secretary of the Italian Communist Party, and Maurice Thorez, holding a comparable position in France, jointly declaring that if in the course of repelling aggression in Western Europe the Soviet armies were obliged to come into Italy and France, the peoples of those countries would not regard the Soviet armies as aggressors and would not resist their advance. This was a plain enough threat of civil war in Western Europe in the event of an American-Soviet conflict. It coincided with the crystallization of the North Atlantic Treaty Organization and was obviously intended to nullify N.A.T.O. in advance. To be sure, the Italian and French Communists were presumptuous in speaking for their peoples as a whole; but the

Togliatti-Thorez initiative touched the nerves of war weariness, of neutralism, and of remaining pro-Soviet sympathy. Within this context it was formidable enough.

The initiative soon spread to other European parties. Then, as though on signal, it was taken up in Latin America and even in far-off corners of the world such as Australia. Despite the improbability of the Soviet armies ever coming to Australia to repel aggression, the Communist Party chairman there dutifully repeated the *mot d'ordre* from Western Europe.[33] What had been planned as a careful and potent move to influence the Western European balance became a worldwide campaign in defiance of the United States and a gesture of solidarity with the Soviet Union, (and perhaps also an exultation at the approaching climax in China).

The American Communist leaders did not repeat verbatim the Togliatti-Thorez formulations, but they did endorse them even though they came at the delicate moment when the Foley Square trial had just begun.[34] What American Communists would do in case of war between the United States and the Soviet Union had been a major question before the American public for a generation. The C.P. had never offered a politically persuasive answer. The day after the Foster-Dennis endorsement, President Harry Truman denounced them as traitors, which further inflamed the atmosphere.Truman had seized on a moment when he, too, could revenge himself on men who had done their utmost to deny him the presidency. Had Foster and Dennis paused to consider whether their stance was really obligatory? Were conditions in the United States at all comparable with the atmosphere in Italy and France? There is no evidence that such questions were ever asked.

The problem of participating in the worldwide Communist initiative was peculiarly complex for the American Communists. The credibility of the Party's peace policy, as of its other policies, was open to doubt. The credibility gap, however, was as much an internal matter as a public one. As has been shown, the American Party's problem was not merely organizational. Despite the failure of the Wallace campaign, there were resources on the left for building a peace movement, as the Independent Citizens Committee of the Arts and Sciences showed by its famous conference at the Waldorf-Astoria in New York in March 1949. The real problem was ideological. The American Communists had come to the following conclusion, put forward by Foster in the August 1948

*Political Affairs.* "American Big Business has undoubtedly resolved upon throwing our country into war against the U.S.S.R." The war danger was said to be growing, whether the "peace camp" was growing stronger or not. American imperialism had been defined in such terms that if it had its way in the world it would take the path of war, and if it were blocked it would take the path of war out of desperation. Hence, Foster had argued, "the American people will have to accept the logic of the situation."[35]

On the other hand, the building of a peace movement required a refusal to "accept the logic of the situation." Quasi-Calvinist conceptions of ever-imminent doom and fundamental perdition could not energize a peace movement. Moreover, in the specific condition of prevailing American opinion, a peace movement would have to include all those Americans, a majority of the population, who did not consider the Soviet Union blameless in the world deadlock and who might be hostile to both the Soviet Union and the American Communists, but who nevertheless were determined that there was a way out of the deadlock.

In brief, the building of a peace movement raised the ghost of the Vermont resolution which the left wing had contemptuously dismissed the year before. Throughout 1949 and 1950 the Party feverishly exhorted its members to realize that a peace movement *could* be built, and argued repeatedly in articles in *Political Affairs* that peace was possible, even though the Party line emphasized that without curbing or even overthrowing monopoly capitalism, peace was a Browderist illusion. Throughout these articles and in reports to the 15th National Convention in December 1950, left-sectarian moods and practices were criticized as inhibiting the Party's work.[36] At the same time, the C.P.U.S.A. was faced with intensified pressure from abroad to produce important results within the United States.[37] Although some of the results achieved in 1949-1950 were impressive under the circumstances, the inherent contradiction in policy was never overcome.[38]

The most dramatic and poignant case of the dilemma in which the American left found itself — the personification of its dedication and its mistaken course — involved the most famous baritone of the generation, Paul Robeson. Outstanding student at Rutgers, football star, and actor, he was internationally acclaimed by the late twenties. During a sojourn in England he was among the most sought-after American artists. Returning to the United States, he was hailed by the leading organizations of the Negro world as one "of the tallest trees in the forest." The N.A.A.C.P. awarded him its Spingarn medal. He was included naturally in National Citizens' P.A.C. during the 1944 campaign. By 1947 he had renounced the concert stage to devote himself to the civil rights movement. He took an active part in the formation of the Progressive Party, and his prestige had much to do with the support Wallace received from a large number of Negro figures. Robeson moved increasingly to the left and became associated in 1948 with Dr. W. E. B. DuBois (who had by then broken with the N.A.A.C.P., which he had helped found fifty years earlier) to form the Council on African Affairs. This body soon became the operational center for the association of left-minded Negro figures. Robeson's preoccupation had an increasingly global cast, with a strong pan-African emphasis. His sense of world mission, stemming from his position as a "world citizen," tended to blur the specific situation in the United States in his own mind. It was natural that he should appear with a predominantly left wing U.S. delegation at the first gathering of the World Committee of the Partisans of Peace in Paris, the agency which became the vehicle of the 1949 peace campaign.

Here Robeson made his famous declaration to the effect that in case of war between the United States and the Soviet Union, American Negroes could not be counted on to fight for their own country. This was the precise counterpart of the Togliatti-Thorez initiative. Whereas other Communist parties as such had made analogous statements, in Robeson's case an individual presumed to speak for an entire people. It was the turning point in Robeson's career. He was immediately disavowed by the major Negro organizations on the grounds that his statement was both presumptuous and unpatriotic. In the autumn of 1949 what would have been a routine left wing picnic in Peekskill, New York, became a bloody riot as American Legionnaires assaulted the gathering because Robeson was scheduled to sing. The left wing responded by assembling its own war veterans; on a second Sunday, a potentially even bloodier encounter was narrowly averted.[39] For the first time in the degeneration of the left wing's postwar position, it now faced organized physical violence by an activated right wing, with the labor-liberal world passively hostile or indifferent.

Robeson soon became a pariah, vindictively punished by the Department of State by the cancellation of his passport. For the next six years he roamed the country, singing to left wing banquets, attempting to return to the concert stage, trying a find his audience in the Negro churches. He annually visited the country's outer limit, the Peace Arch Bridge at the Canadian-United States border north of Seattle, to sing for a mixed Canadian-U.S. audience, mainly hardrock miners and lumber workers, in diminishing but loyal numbers.

Coinciding as it did with the paroxysm of the white chauvinism campaign, the Robeson case became the measuring-rod of all left wing relationships with other groups. Many such groups were less and less prepared to engage in common actions with left wingers if what appeared to them as the separate, though deplorable, issue of Robeson's right to travel became the condition of cooperation. Those who thought Robeson was being treated harshly nevertheless found it compromising to share a common platform with him. A hero to the left wing throughout the world, Robeson stood his ground at home, virtually enchained and on increasingly narrow ground. (All this coincided with the time when he was losing his voice.) Increasingly Robeson came to see himself as a world citizen for the very reason that his own land, including a large proportion of his own people, did not give him support.

His was the most striking example of the impossibility of an American political strategy that tried to keep in step with — and serve — the strategy of Communism abroad. And he personified the profligate waste of talent of which the American Communists were capable, their capacity for devaluing their own political currency and destroying themselves in the process.[40]

# 9  HOW THE DIE WAS CAST,

# AND OTHER SKELETONS

Two decisions shaped the American Communist Party's course in 1951 and were to effect its subsequent evolution. Both decisions involved matters of the greatest secrecy. Most of the leadership was not privy to them. The membership had no share in making them. It was the nature of democratic centralism that a small group of leaders could make decisions which had crucial, sometimes fatal, consequences for large groups of followers including the influentials. In making these decisions, the leaders also decided their own fate.

The first of these events was the American Communist Party's first contact with the Soviet Communist Party since before the war, intended to be the beginning of systematic consultation. The second (not directly connected with the former) involved the decision by the top leaders that several of their number should evade the prison sentences under the Smith Act. This was to be the signal for an ambitious project to direct Party work from an underground. Preparations for this experiment in dual leadership had been under way since 1947.

The initiative for the contact between the American and the Soviet parties came from Moscow; this in itself raises stimulating political speculation. Not since their Comintern days had the U.S. leaders had any formal tie with Moscow in the sense of a mechanism for policy formulation and a thorough exchange of views. The periodic visit of key leaders had come to a halt with the war. Since the thirties, the American Communists had maintained their allegiance to the international movement by a form of political telepathy, a sort of transatlantic Couéism, or — to use the concept that was so popular in those days — a type of Pavlovian response to stimuli. Browder had in 1939 sought to maintain contact by setting up a shortwave radio on Long Island, but after one contact with Dimitrov this method was abandoned. Now they were invited to consult.[1]

Just why Moscow felt this need was not clear at the time. In retrospect, it may be relevant that by 1951 the men in the Kremlin took an active interest in the Communist Parties of three major capitalist countries — Japan, Britain and the United States. It may be that the Cold War had by then presented problems which gave these Parties greater importance than they had had before. The basic course of the Cold War had been decided in 1947-48. Moscow had concentrated first on the Eastern European Parties, obliging them to stand together with the Cominform and then to stand against the Yugoslavs. In 1949, emphasis was placed on stimulating the peace campaign whose greatest impact was felt in Western Europe. In 1950, both the British and Japanese Parties came under scrutiny. The British C.P. formulated a New Program, stressing the possibility of a peaceful and parliamentary path to a socialist Britain — an emphasis quite out of keeping with the main trend elsewhere. Early in that same year, during Mao Tse-tung's first visit to Moscow, where the Sino-Soviet alliance was signed, severe criticism was leveled in the Cominform's paper against the Japanese Communists; this sent them into confrontation with the U.S. occupation authorities, a round of clandestine activity, and a break with the Japanese Socialists — a political move from which they were not to recover for a decade. (The main target of the critique was Sanzo Nosaka, the veteran Communist leader who had functioned in the Comintern under the name of Okano; in the late thirties he had resided in Yenan.) The Japanese Communists were accused of mistakenly believing they could continue to prosper under the U.S. occupation policies of that time, as indeed they had. Because the North Korean adventure must have been prepared for months before it broke forth in June 1950, it is probable that Stalin and/or Mao Tse-tung (whether they acted jointly or independently in the Korean affair does not affect the main point) wanted to alert the Japanese Communists to their responsibilities. Japan, after all, would be the major staging center for American operations if the North Korean challenge were accepted.

In inviting contact with the U.S. Party — and this came half a year after the Korean crisis — Stalin may have been thinking both in "British" and "Japanese" terms. He may have wished to consider what new path the American Party might take to emerge from the incoherence of its post-1948 crisis. Possibly the British pattern held some relevance for America in Stalin's eyes. At the same time, the Russians may have wished to judge what useful role the U.S. Party might play if the Cold War intensified or diminished. This could have been the Russians' intention whether or not Stalin's last document, *Economic Problems of Socialism*, presented on the eve of the 19th C.P.S.U. Congress in 1952, foreshadowed an easing of Soviet Cold War tactics. Scholars have differed over Stalin's intentions, but it does seem clear that major Soviet discussions had been going on since the previous winter in an attempt to judge United States policy and the outlook for war or peace.[2]

Exactly how the Communist Party interpreted the Soviet overture is not clear; no discussion of the overture was made available at the time even to the emissary selected to consummate the contact. But early in February 1951, I was briefed by two of the top leaders — Gilbert Green and Gus Hall — and given a series of questions to place before the Soviet leaders. (At that time I was a member of the Party's staff and in charge of its peace activities.) These questions were the most astonishing phase of the entire episode. The questions themselves suggested how parochially the American Communists regarded this exchange of views. The inquiry was, on the American side, almost entirely technical, dealing with matters that seemed insignificant. For example, Moscow was asked whether the American Communists could abandon their defense of the Lenin School, which had figured so luridly in the Smith Act trial. The Lenin School had been founded in 1926; all the major Communist leaders who came of age in the late twenties and were sent to Moscow studied at the school. It was discontinued in 1937 but continued to figure in all anti-Communist propaganda and investigations, supposedly because of its quasi-military curriculum and courses on sabotage. It was revealing that the U.S. Party leaders felt this ancient institution a burden and yet did not feel that they could, of their own decision, disavow it. *They had to ask permission of those who had originally been their "schoolmasters."* The "old school tie" proved all-powerful even though the school no longer existed.

I broached two questions, however, which I had not been authorized to raise. One dealt with the British Party's New Program; the other with the controversial and pregnant question of the war danger. On the authority of Georgi Malenkov (one of the Soviet interlocutors — Boris Ponomarev was the other), it was established that the British C.P. had consulted Moscow in formulating its Program; the stress on peaceful and constitutional roads to socialism, even though at variance with what was being stressed elsewhere, had Soviet support. The American Communists were asked whether they did not think the time had come for them to prepare a New Program of their own, to make some new initiatives to win public support.[3] As for the war danger, I commented on a declaration by Stalin which was then being repeated widely, a statement in which he had declared that the peace could be saved if the peoples of the world "took up the cause of peace" and defended it "to the very end." Malenkov was asked whether this phrase "to the very end" did not imply that the Soviet leaders really had little confidence that peace could be maintained. Did it not suggest that an early showdown with the West was at hand? By putting the matter negatively and dealing with a subject which had agitated the American Communist leadership for a decade, the attempt was made — outside the original instructions — to generate a discussion on political perspectives, and to elicit from the Russians some clear and unequivocal view of the international crisis. Malenkov was quick, even eager, to emphasize that the Soviet Party did not believe that the prospects for peace were as grim as the question implied. Stalin's statement should in no sense be interpreted as suggesting that war was inevitable or imminent, Malenkov explained. The day after this encounter in the Kremlin, two subordinates of the Soviet Politburo were sent to continue the discussion on this very point. Both of them took great pains to stress that there was nothing in the C.P.S.U.'s outlook which could be construed as lacking confidence in the possibility of avoiding war.

Late in February 1951, the substance of these conversations was transmitted to the American Party leaders who had originated the mission. Provisions were also made for continuing contacts; what came of these further contacts is difficult to determine. Within a few months decisions were to be taken which entirely changed the way the Party's leadership was to function for the next four years. It can be established without any doubt that in making these decisions the key U.S. Communist leaders were aware that the views which had governed their behavior up until then were not shared by the Soviet Communists, at least as regards the international outlook.[4] One immediate consequence of this mission was that a letter which Foster had prepared sharply attacking the British Communist Party's Program was never sent. Foster, like Browder before him, had come to feel responsibility for leadership among Communists in the Anglo-Saxon world, and perhaps in Latin America as well. Foster was about to "correct" his British comrades, but was kept from doing so by the arrival of the news that the British C.P.'s new, quasi-revisionist course had Soviet sanction.

Another ancillary consequence of this "mission to Moscow" was the macabre and famous "Lautner affair." The allegation of treachery in high places which swept Eastern Europe in the wake of the Yugoslav ouster from the Cominform had its repercussions in the U.S. Communist Party. A complete "verification" of its cadres had been carried out. Each one had been required to fill out a comprehensive, searching questionnaire. The most trusted men and women were being selected for the underground in a general mood of vigilance. The name of one of the C.P.U.S.A.'s most trusted cadres, John Lautner, had been mentioned at the Rajk trial in Hungary; a minor witness against the Hungarian leader Laszlo Rajk suggested that Lautner's wartime services in the O.S.S. made him suspect. Throughout the thirties, Lautner had served in secondary C.P. posts, and like many other Communists had been employed by the O.S.S. This activity was not, in American Communist eyes, a basis for suspicion. In 1949 Lautner became head of the New York State Cadre and Review Commission, a position of great responsibility. Louis Weinstock, who had headed the New York District Council of the A.F.L. Painters for many years, visited Hungary in the spring of 1949 and brought back the report that Lautner had been "implicated" by Rajk trial testimony.[5] The American Party leadership, on the basis of Weinstock's report from Budapest, decided that Lautner had been a government agent. He was lured to Cleveland, confronted with the charge, threatened with a revolver, and interrogated at length by a group of the most trusted figures in the Party's security apparatus, but he continued to deny his guilt. Thereafter he was expelled. He was publicly charged with treachery and suffered total ostracism. Lautner's wife left him — more faithful to the Party's dictates than to her husband. One of the items on my agenda during my visit to Moscow in February 1951 was to learn what I could about the Lautner matter.[6] While waiting in Czechoslovakia for admission to the Soviet Union, I visited Budapest and was received by Matyas Rakosi, then general secretary of the Hungarian Working People's Party. Rakosi was pressed to elaborate on what evidence there had been for the charge against Lautner. It turned out that the only evidence was the testimony of a minor figure in the Rajk trial; Lautner's O.S.S. service was incomprehensible and suspicious to the Hungarians. Rakosi confirmed that all this had been explained to Weinstock. Then Rakosi volunteered his opinion that Weinstock, too, was a government agent! When pressed to give evidence for this charge, the Hungarian Communist leader explained that it had been noted that after Weinstock's visit, his wife had come to Hungary as well, and there was an old Hungarian saying: "When you don't have a horse, send an ass. . . ."

Thus, as early as February 1951, the C.P. leaders knew they had been misled by the extraordinary paranoia then prevailing in Hungary, for who was prepared to suspect Weinstock? It also followed that if Weinstock could be named as a traitor with such capriciousness in Budapest then Lautner had been "framed." Having been treated as a pariah, Lautner began testifying against American Communists at innumerable trials and proceedings. He had not been a government agent, but his own comrades made him one.[7]

### The Time of Troubles

Intellectual and political changes of the first order would have been necessary to challenge the premises on which the decision to set up the underground was taken. However, there was some vacillation over this decision. During the latter part of 1950, after the passage of the McCarran Act, which proposed to prosecute the Party as a "foreign agent," an atmosphere of near-panic had gripped the American Communists. Offices had been closed down. Public activity had diminished and in some areas ceased. Important cadres had disappeared. In December 1950 at the 15th National Convention these moods were criticized in the chief report by the acting general secretary, Gus Hall. Yet the leadership was fully involved in plans which fed the apocalyptic mood. The top leaders were debating which of them should appear for sentencing if the Supreme Court upheld the Smith Act convictions; attempting to brake the mood of panic, the chief Party leaders nevertheless continued to prepare for what would be the signal to go underground.

In the early spring of 1951, one of the most trusted figures preparing the entire project visited Foster, then vacationing in San Francisco, and brought back Foster's considered judgment on three points.[8] The Party's chairman believed that war between

America and Russia was inevitable. He also believed that the Party would inevitably be declared illegal, but he did not share the view of others that fascism was inevitable. With this authoritative judgment, the Communists went forward with the project to build an operational structure capable of withstanding quasi-fascist repression. The five-minutes-to-midnight signal came on June 4, 1951, when the Supreme Court in its last sitting for that period upheld jail sentences for the eleven convicted Communist leaders. This meant that within one month, by July 4, 1951, they had to enter prison. On that day not all of them appeared. The absentees were: Gilbert Green, secretary for Illinois; Henry Winston, the organizational secretary; Robert Thompson, the secretary for New York State; and Gus Hall, acting general secretary in the previous year (while Dennis served almost a year in prison on a "contempt of Congress" charge). Several weeks before, in a declaration denouncing the Supreme Court's June 4 decision, Foster and Dennis had evoked the experience of the Italian and the Japanese parties which, they recalled, had endured all manner of trials and tribulations and had emerged triumphant like a phoenix from the ashes.[9] No image more plainly mirrored the outlook of the foremost figures of American Communism than this comparison with Italy and Japan.

The precise structure and the inner history of the underground cannot be documented in all its detail. Even fifteen years later it is remembered by the several thousands cadres who took part in it as the most traumatic period of their lives. This book has chronicled the contradictions of Party policy and practice, from 1948 to 1951. The C.P.U.S.A. sustained itself in subsequent years only because the underground both heightened these contradictions and made it impossible to deal with them. The organism which had boasted an exceptional unity and had suppressed the divergence arising from its own past over the previous ten years now experienced its most profound disorganization. Having saved U.S. Communism from its supposed dissolution in 1945, the same leadership which had reconstituted the Party now dissolved it. The experience of 1951 to 1956 was a *de facto* dissolution, but at the same time it was an elaborate design for enabling the Party to function under the most adverse conditions.

In part, this dissolution was real. Early in July 1951, the organizational department of the Party announced publicly that all those members who had not re-registered would be dropped from membership. A great many loyal although inactive members were in effect expelled. They were considered unreliable merely because they had not reasserted their party ties. This action was part of a theory that the American C.P. could only function in the years to come as a "cadre-organization," a skeletal force, because only such a force could withstand further repression.

In its organizational pattern, the underground involved three different categories of cadres. One category was known as the "deep freeze." It consisted of the men who had evaded jail and who were now to go into prolonged hiding.[10] Also in this category were several of the second echelon leaders who faced indictment under the Smith Act but did not show up for the trials, as well as several hundred men and women who were not under indictment at all. The latter group had been selected because of their knowledge of the Party, their experience, and the expectation that they might at some time be indicted. The second category was known as the "deep, deep freeze." It consisted of trusted cadres who had not necessarily been prominent but who were viewed as an ultimate source of leadership and responsibility in case all other levels of leadership had been discovered and arrested. Many of these had been sent abroad — to Mexico, Europe and Canada. They were under instructions to change their lives completely. They were not intended to engage in any direct or immediate activity. The third category was known as the "O.B.U.," the "operative but unavailable" leadership, consisting of cadres who moved about the country, often disguised; this group attempted to conduct the liaison between the open and formal party (which was never made illegal at all) and the men in the "deep freeze" category.

The American Communist Party continued as an open and public organization, with many of its spokesmen remaining at their posts, but it was guided by a shadow leadership. The National board, that is, the leadership elected at the 1948 and 1950 conventions, attempted by letters and through visits from family members to make suggestions and offer advice; most of these men were in different prisons. Their views were sometimes in complete contradiction to the opinions of the leaders at other levels.

This extraordinary apparatus was not only cumbersome: it took an enormous political, financial and personal toll. Several thousand cadres were separated from their families. Husband and wife often did not see each other except in the most furtive ways.

Children grew up without quite understanding what had happened to their parents. In some cases, even the death of a father or a brother did not mean that close kin would appear for the ceremonies if they happened to be part of the O.B.U. category. Vast sums of money, probably running into  millions of dollars, were expended for the lodging, the transportation, and the conclaves of different cadres. Complex systems of couriers were set up. Attempts were made to study the techniques of the several thousand F.B.I. agents who were involved in trying to keep track of this entirely new structure which the Party had adopted. Conflict broke out in determining the authority of the different echelons; factions quickly formed as the normal restraint on Party behavior disappeared. It took some time for Foster and those who remained in public view to acknowledge that the directing O.B.U. cadres constituted the leadership; all public statements, even many newspaper articles, had to be cleared through these cadres. Differences of opinion soon appeared. In *Political Affairs* for those years articles appear under a wide variety of pseudonyms, names that were unknown before 1951, and do not appear after 1956. In these articles, it is not difficult to find different policy formulations on all of the issues which made up the Party line.[11]

The underground adventure was also shattering in unexpected ways. Thousands of the cadres who had sustained the Party since the war (including some who were veterans of its relative successes prior to the war) suddenly found themselves torn out of their customary routine. Some were "colonized" to work in plants and at occupations they had not tried before. Many went into business.[12] All of them were separated from families. New personal liaisons often developed, some fugitive, some more lasting. The self-imposed isolation almost immediately caused profound soul searching, and in most cases, a political re-evaluation. Some had imagined themselves "Bolsheviks," and had looked forward to this supreme test of their revolutionary fiber. They now found they could not take the experience of loneliness; scores of nervous and mental breakdowns occurred. It quickly became evident that the F.B.I. was well aware of this underground, and was following it closely although none of it was *ipso facto* illegal. It was often unnerving to a good cadre to be confronted by an F.B.I. man who asked what these maneuvers were all about. The fact that government agents seemed to know all about it utterly undermined its credibility.

Members of this underground began to have the most profound doubts about the whole course of American Communism. Thrown upon their own resources and separated from their accustomed paths, they began for the first time to question some of the most sacred premises of the Party. Many began to read books that they hitherto had been persuaded to ignore. Whether abroad or within the United States, tested and seasoned C.P. cadres felt the impossibility of trying to manage a political movement in this fashion.[13] They would not leave the Party of their own volition, however. They stayed until 1955 and 1956, inwardly disenchanted not always with their original ideals but almost always with themselves.

This situation explains in part the force of the 1956 upheaval. It explains also why virtually everyone who had anything to do with the underground left the American Communist movement between mid-1956 and mid-1957; some did so after the 16th National Convention in February 1957 and many without waiting for it. The difficulty of renovating the American Communist Party in 1956 reinforced the conviction that even if such a renovation were achieved in words it would be futile in practice. When the leaders of international Communism, at the Soviet Party's 20th Congress (and even the year before during the Yugoslav-Soviet reconciliation), began to revive propositions about the possibilities of coexistence and peaceful roads to socialism according to national peculiarities, the cadres of the American C.P. felt humiliated. They had devoted themselves stubbornly during the previous ten years to rejecting these propositions and had endured every kind of vicissitude in doing so. Yesterday's unorthodoxy had now become orthodox. Khrushchev was now advancing views which his predecessors had held to be anathema.

A minor party in a major country had been through all this for a dozen years. This is why the explosion following the Soviet Party's 20th Congress took such spectacular forms in the C.P.U.S.A., and why its full implications were felt half a decade earlier in the United States than in other parts of the world movement. Communists in other countries never comprehended what was happening in the United States, because they were largely unaware of the hidden history of the American movement.

# 10    FROM BREAKDOWN

# TO BREAKUP, 1956-57

The American Communist Party's disintegration had the quality of an inexorable process independent of the will of the actors involved. It appears in retrospect (and was perceived by many at the time) as but an epilogue to a tormented history. To some, however, the bitter battle to save the Party by adopting an independent course and re-examining the past appeared as the climactic moment, the high point of their careers.[1] No other period of American Communist history received such an immediate and rather sympathetic treatment by a varied group of commentators.[2] And it is true that the American Communists, in their upheaval of 1956-57 — climaxing in the 16th National Convention — were far ahead of the international movement in their independent thinking, their desire for a national form, and their search for a new kind of Marxism-Leninism. Twelve years before the Czechoslovak "spring" and the search for a "socialism with a human visage," the American Communists went through an analogous process. As at other stages of its history, this small movement had a precocious and advanced experience. All this is reflected in the Dennis report of April 1956, which was a sweeping self-criticism, and in the Draft Resolution of September 13, 1956, which laid the basis for the unusual convention of February 9-12, 1957.[3]

One of the new elements in the 1956-57 crisis was itself the product of the prolonged incubation of this crisis — tens of thousands of members as well as leaders refused to stay in the Party and take part in the preconvention debates. Nor did the Party's influentials and fellow travellers show any passionate interest in its crisis. An emotional and intellectual exhaustion appeared to affect almost all the participants. Attempts were made to give a new essence to the movement by new formulas, by state and national conventions at which for the first time majority and minority reports were legitimized, and by a declaration of independence from Moscow, but none of these attempts could revive the Party. The chief figures among the dramatis personae realized that the American Communist movement was afflicted with a mortal illness.[4]

Twenty years of experiences that contradicted tenaciously held concepts had taken this movement from a sect to a considerable force and were returning it to a sect. At the moment of its most daring insight into its whole course, American Communism seemed paralyzed.

The central dilemma of 1956 lay in the American Communist Party's continued dependence on the international constellation of parties of which it still wanted to be part. The Party's own re-examination which had begun several years earlier, as has been shown, was overtaken and intertwined with the much more sensational upheaval generated by Nikita Khrushchev's secret speech at the Soviet Party's 20th Congress. Knowledge of details of the secret speech remained limited to the small leadership body at the April 28-May 1 National Committee meeting, where, it was later admitted by one leading participant, the full implications of this speech were not comprehended.[5] But the shock of it went deep, whatever the details. The revelations of what Stalinism had cost the Russians, the allegations about Stalin's tyrannical and paranoid character, and the mortal challenge which this information presented to the very foundations of the Leninist heritage galvanized and accelerated the American Party's upheaval. Yet the 20th Congress speech and the upheavals following it also deflected the purely American character of the re-examination under way. Despite the new determination to apply Marxist-Leninist propositions in a bold, fresh fashion to the specific nature of the American scene, the American Communists now found themselves discussing their own problems within the context of what had happened elsewhere. The opportunity to make an independent self-evaluation was therefore undercut. The American Communists found themselves once again trying to keep pace with bewildering events of a world movement from which they could not dissociate even though they knew — and now boldly confirmed — that a one-sided association with international Communism had been the seedbed of their disasters.

They attempted vainly to keep pace with the crisis that had broken out abroad, without altogether comprehending the dynamics of this crisis. Suddenly, a sanction had come whence it had always been sought, namely Moscow; but the scope of this sanction was not easy to judge, even for experienced Moscow-watchers, Lenin School graduates, and veterans of the Comintern. Eventually Moscow's sanction turned out to be limited. The summer of

1956 witnessed a convulsive Soviet effort to minimize the implications of the 20th Congress and to master the disturbances throughout Communism, which took the form of an uprising in Poland and a catastrophic clash between Russian armed forces and Hungary's revolution. By early January 1957, Khrushchev was praising Stalin once again,[6] but with little conviction. Yet something important and in contradistinction to the past did sweep the C.P. The *Daily Worker*[7] and the *Party Voice* (bulletin of the New York State organization)[8] now became forums for an astonishingly vigorous free-for-all. Defenders of orthodoxy were criticized and critics were denounced. Strong as this process was, the basic tropism of many leaders and members toward Moscow operated to defeat what had earlier appeared as a unified new course. In April 1956 the American Communists reached the conviction that left-sectarianism had been the cause of the Party's failures in the previous decade, and that this deviation had its roots in the imitation of foreign Communists. This consensus was repeated in the September 13 Draft Resolution. By autumn, this consensus had been undermined. In April, Party chairman William Z. Foster had stood alone and discredited; even Benjamin J. Davis, Jr., who had so ruthlessly exploited Foster's authority, abandoned his mentor. Early in September, Foster supported the Draft Resolution "with qualifications"; in October, he changed his mind and opposed it.[9] Foster's opposition should have obliged Eugene Dennis to stand behind his own resolution, but this required a willingness to take part in a "polycentrism" that was beyond Dennis' experience. By then, Dennis could hardly mistake the Soviet warnings, which were becoming increasingly blatant. At that moment, Irving Potash, who had accepted deportation to his native Poland after his Smith Act sentence, returned to the United States via Canada; before serving a one-year term for so doing, he re-emphasized the Soviet attitude. That attitude was being signaled also by another deportee, John Williamson, the onetime organizational secretary, then in Britain. In late June Soviet press had published an article by Dennis on the Khrushchev revelations; in this way the Soviet public came to know of the secret speech.[10] But this article, which may have appeared in the international context to be a rather bold delineation of the issues, was, in its American context, a very cautious one. In fact, just as the Dennis article was being republished in Moscow it was being superseded in Rome by a very much stronger statement by Palmiro Togliatti in an interview with *Nuovi Argumenti*.[11] Dennis thus realized that Moscow had favored his article for the very reason that it was cautious. To him, with his training, this spoke volumes. In the initial stages of the upheaval, the majority of the Party supporting re-examination had everything in its favor — the Party press, whose editors both in New York and San Francisco supported strong changes,[12] and the sympathy of most members, especially in the largest state organizations. The intense desire to make a drastic departure "in the name and form," to find a better mechanism than "democratic centralism," to somehow shake off the past and start afresh — this mood made the 16th Convention exceptional in Communist annals.[13] Yet Moscow's refusal to tolerate this change in the American C.P. (even though Soviet leaders knew that only such a revamping could give the American Communist a chance) doomed the re-examination. Moscow preferred the pale shadow of the C.P.U.S.A. to anything "revisionist." It is striking to what lengths the Russians went to intervene in the affairs of the hapless American Communists.[14]

The ultimate defeat of the "re-examinationist" majority did not come about because of Russian maneuvers or even because the centrist leaders like Dennis recoiled before the logic of their own self-critique. Basically, it occurred because the bottom dropped out of the whole enterprise. The American Communist movement disintegrated and those who wanted a re-examination were inevitably the chief losers. They had the votes and won the argument, but their Party disappeared. The orthodox wing led by Foster (soon rejoined by Dennis) did not have the votes and did not win the argument. They had no Party left, either, but they held the franchise. To them that was all that mattered. By staying within the organization while the departure of thousands emptied it of meaning, the orthodox group increased its relative importance. Even veteran leaders of the twenties whose names are found in the 1956 discussion disappeared from view.[15] The cadres shaped by the experience of the thirties (to whom the prospect of a factional battle was especially repulsive, because such battles were among the worst features of their history) refused to take part. They "voted with their feet."[16] They doubted whether their views could ultimately convince anyone, least of all the diehards. These cadres no longer wished either to coexist with the diehards, to argue with them, or to be led by them. The re-examinationist victory of the 16th National Convention was thus entirely Pyrrhic even though it is important in the annals of Communism.[17]

In 1958 no regeneration of the C.P. seemed probable despite the resolutions of the 16th National Convention, and no "mass party of socialism" seemed probable even in the distant future. In this respect, again, the experience of 1956-57 was distinctive. The C.P. did not undergo a factional fight nor did the majority which left the shell of a movement to the quarrels of Foster, Dennis, and others try to build any opposing force. The whole problem of Marxism in America required re-examination before any quick organizational solutions to the crisis of the left could be found.

It has already been suggested that another distinctive feature of the 1956-57 upheaval was the virtual absence in the Party's debates of its own influentials. This, too, was a sharp contrast with the events of 1944 and 1945. The left wing trade unionists who had drawn their sustenance from Communism were by then either immersed in trying to integrate themselves into those unions which had accepted them, or were standing defiant in separate formations; they were by then thoroughly contemptuous of the Party's advice. Some were totally occupied with fending off political persecution and interunion membership raids, as in the Rocky Mountain area. Others, on the West Coast, had developed the view that a left wing could operate only as a quasi-guerrilla formation, each group "doing its thing." Whether this view was a rationale for political irresponsibility or simply the recognition of a harsh reality, it resulted in aloofness from the Party's agony. The quarrels among once-prestigious leaders seemed remote. Some of the Party's influentials were compassionate toward the leaders; others were intensely critical on the assumption that they knew the answers and had kept the revolutionary faith (in private). But the reality remained: the Party no longer had the participation, even indirectly, of those whom it considered its most valuable supporters.

No other political force on the left had any impact on the Communist Party's ultimate crisis; no other wing of the left could inherit those who could not remain Communists. None of American Communism's ideological kinfolk benefited from the debacle, although hopes rose in different sects and groups. The Trotskyist movement attracted some of the former fellow travellers to its perennial election campaigns, especially in New York after the American Labor Party finally dissolved in 1956. Former Communists in the Northwest, especially those who remembered their heyday in the Commonwealth Federation, were likewise attracted to the Socialist Workers Party. But no significant number of former Stalinists became adherents of the Trotskyist groups. The Socialist Party, led by Norman Thomas, made some effort to attract former Communists, but except for a cordial dialogue on the underlying problems, nothing came of such efforts. Earl Browder, who had dismissed the Party's crisis in the spring of 1956 with a contemptuous remark ("I am not interested in microbiology"), was encouraged for a brief moment by the way his name and record were being evoked in the inner-Party debate.[18] On October 15, 1956, Browder met with his old opponent, Norman Thomas, and proposed that the latter take the leadership in revitalizing the left. As Browder put it, Norman Thomas had "over the years won a special moral authority among large masses," and had "always stood superior to faction and spoke for one of the main currents when the Left was strong."[19] There is no record that anything came of the initiative. A letter written by "George Benjamin" appeared in the *Nation* urging the Communists to dissolve on the grounds that this would clear the way for a radical revival. Few replies came to this letter.[20]

Perhaps the most ambitious effort to revive the left was made by the veteran pacifist, A. J. Muste, who had once before, in the midthirties, tried to build bridges among dissident radicals. He had sought then, in his American Workers' Party, to create some sort of viable non-Communist radicalism. Twenty years later, he was still trying. In May 1957, Muste and his closest associates launched The American Forum for Socialist Education. It was not intended to be a party but simply an arena for discussion.[21] It proposed a debate about the issues without the exclusion of Communists, but without focusing on them in particular. This group remained essentially a letterhead organization. It spent one "lost weekend" that summer with a wide variety of radicals present on Saturday and virtually no one on Sunday. Several pamphlets were published,[22] and forums were held in Detroit and Chicago under its auspices. But it was viewed with suspicion on all sides. The editors of *Dissent* were opposed to any contact with Communists and essentially mistrustful of ex-Communists. The orthodox wing of the C.P. was contemptuous; J. Edgar

Hoover was watchful and took the Forum most seriously as still another "Communist front" which, of course, it was not.

Neither the C.P.'s strict adherence to Marxism-Leninism over a decade nor its acceptance of revisionism for the second time in a decade enabled it to maintain political momentum. Nor did the C.P. recover from the debacle once the revisionists of 1956-57 had withdrawn. Within a few years most of the older leaders were to pass away, after obscure, internecine battles. What remained of the Communist Party has played a most inconsequential role in the sixties. The new left is a phenomenon which owes little to Communism, does not understand its lessons, and does not seem to care.

Numerically, the former Communists make up the largest part of the older radical tradition. They number more than a million, but nothing is gained by adding the figures. No political mathematics exists to account for the post-Party activities of this extraordinary group of individuals with such a complex experience. Many have remained alienated from politics. For the thousands who could not stay in the Party after 1956, as distinct from the hundreds of thousands who departed earlier, the problems of personal realization, of professional achievement, in many cases simply of earning a living, have been considerable. Not all those who left necessarily comprehend what happened to them. Few of them feel that *everything* they did was necessarily harmful. Some feel they did their greatest harm to themselves, not to others. A great many have digested or repressed the experience so well that its discussion cannot be attractive. Insofar as any of this generation has contributed to the great issues or the new trends in American life their past experience was both limiting and illuminating. They can only say, as Aeneas does, in Homer's *Iliad*, that they lived through great events and also mean ones, "all of which I saw and a great part of which I was."

### Second Thoughts in Summation

From the narrative in the preceding pages it seems clear that the American Communist movement cannot be explained by the conventional wisdom that says it was altogether alien to American life as a consequence of its international attachment. The American Communist Party was not a "conspiracy in the service of a foreign power" if such a conspiracy is defined as a body of men and women who consciously take part in what they know to be someone else's service, act according to someone else's design, and are prepared to take the consequences.[23]

All the evidence suggests that the C.P. leaders never really *knew* what either the Soviet Union or the international movement wanted of them — except for them to keep in step at every turn. The evidence also suggests that neither the Soviet nor the international leaders knew very much of any importance about the United States, although they knew details about the C.P.U.S.A. itself. They were not equipped to make the essential distinctions about the terrain of American radicalism which might have made their orders, or even their advice, relevant. Moscow acknowledged the loyalties of the American Communists. It wanted those loyalties essentially because it could not tolerate any suggestion that the evolution of American society was not in keeping with the simple, all-embracing contours of Marxist-Leninist doctrine.[24] To the American Communists, who wanted so much to believe in a world revolutionary movement, Moscow gave little advice, basically because it had no advice to give. If the Soviet leaders *ever* concerted their own policies with any parties whose support they wanted, and evidence that they did is rather sparse, certainly they did not concert them with the U.S. Party, which supposedly had been "entrusted by history with tasks of decisive importance." Soviet policies were not weighed in terms of their effect on the Communist Party in the most important capitalist country. Moscow had become accustomed to domination over a world movement by "waving the baton" (in the phrase of the Chinese Communists). The Soviet Party waved the baton, and all parties responded whether or not the music was appropriate to the occasion.

The American Communists, proceeding from their universalism and a conviction that they could succeed only as part of a world movement, were essentially unable to follow the world movement. Even had they been more skillful, it is doubtful that they could have done so. Perhaps the real point was that no common line of world political and historical development was really possible. Perhaps this is why there has never been a genuine world Communist alliance, in the sense of a movement which weighs the specific needs and the differing potentials of different sectors, and articulates different policies for those sectors in the orchestration of a general strategy. Thus, the American Communists were neither allies nor agents of the Soviet Communists.

In their later years, they lived in what can only be called "a mental Comintern," imagining themselves part of something which did not exist. Seen in the best light, they were a species of self-proclaimed guerrillas, operating in what they believed to be a world battle, but having no significant contact with any "main force" and without a perception of the battle plan. They resorted essentially to zodiac signs for guidance. Because they dared not analyze Soviet aims in terms of the hard realities of power, they could not appraise Soviet policy either pragmatically or cynically. Nor would they admit the profound crisis within Soviet life and in other parts of the Communist movement, an admission which might have made for rational understanding. When this admission finally came, it was much too late. The American Communists not only were viewed by others as expendable, but they also expended themselves — in a noble or pathetic fashion, depending on one's point of view. Their international commitment was thus a species of drug, contracting the mind as it expanded the illusions of the mind.

Is there some theory which explains the American Communist experience as a whole? To Irving Howe and Lewis Coser, the explanation of the fate of the Party lies in the nature of Stalinism. They put forward a summation which is elusive and enigmatic. "It may be that Stalinism, like all totalitarian movements in which terror and irrationality play so great a role, really had no ultimate end which could be related significantly to its activity."[25] Yet terror played a small role in the American Party's drama, excepting intellectual terror, and at all times a struggle for rationality was at work. Howe and Coser view the Communists as riding a treadmill which got them nowhere but which they could not dismount; its continued functioning became the end in itself.

Theodore Draper's view is less sweeping. He locates the Party's dilemma in the contradiction between struggling for immediate demands and expecting this struggle necessarily to give the Party leadership in revolutionary change. In a sense, this is another way of stating Gabriel Almond's distinction between the "esoteric Party" with its "steeled inner core," remaining true to revolutionary objectives at whatever cost, and the "exoteric" Party composed of members who respond to simple appeals and can leave just as simply as they joined. Almond, taking off from Max Weber, puts the matter in these terms:

"Any advocate of fundamental human and social reconstruction must make a hard choice if he is to avoid the most serious distortion of his purposes. If he operates outside the framework of politics and influences his fellow men through sermons and exemplary behavior, he limits his effectiveness but keeps his ethical mission pure." Once involved in the struggle for political power, "the ethical absolutist is confronted by the most serious temptation. Here in politics he has an instrumentality of enormous and problematic force. It is not possible that by striking one blow, so to speak, he can hit an ethical jackpot which will in retrospect make these costs seem trivial and bring the worlds of aspiration and reality once and for all together? The Socialists confronted this tempation and indefinitely postponed their decision. They could not avoid the anguish and guilt which always arises when there are serious discrepancies between an absolute calling and the mixed choices of the market place. But if they did not save the world, at least they saved their souls. The Leninists seized this temptation and let loose forces which swept them beyond humane anchorage."[26]

Daniel Bell has taken this same thought and restated it in terms of Martin Luther's conception of his own Church, which the great Protestant reformer believed to be "*in* the world but *not of it*." Much of what has been recounted here fits well into the paradigm which Bell uses to analyze the prewar Socialist Party, the modern American labor movement, and the Communists.[27]

The Socialists were like Luther's church — that is, "*in* the world but *not of it*" — in the sense that they advocated change which amounted to reforms but accepted no responsibility for the society as such. This position turned them into a sect, although they had an important influence in fostering reform. The modern American labor movement was both "*in* and *of* the world." By accepting American capitalism, it also helped to transform "some of the values of the society." Using this paradigm, Bell finds that the American Communist Party "lived *neither in* the world *nor of* it, but sought to *encapsulate* itself as a world of its own" (italics added). In such a movement, "there was inevitably a peculiar problem of cohesion." The Communists, "living in the society while seeking to promote a revolutionary movement" against it, were under the compulsion to maintain their zeal by "establishing a psychological distance from the society . . . and by instilling a combat posture in their adherents."[28]

Bell's view, with its rich insight, can be elaborated as follows: the American Communists constituted themselves as a fraternal community of like-minded people conscious that they must remake themselves in order to be worthy and capable of the revolutionary transformation they espoused. Rejecting the process of gaining converts by revelation or education as the futile path of a sect, they sought to activate the masses, to gain leadership in the stage-by-stage struggle through example and sacrifice. The assumption was made that when the masses had reached the point of acknowledging the ineluctability of revolutionary change, they would simultaneously acknowledge the vanguard which had known this truth all along, and had proven its worth by works. The Communists thus sought to overcome the shortcomings of the two traditions from which they sprang, the reformist socialist and the revolutionary syndicalist.[29]

It is easy to argue that in attempting to create such a revolutionary community, with such dual tasks, the Communists were very imperfect. There is much evidence that the leadership they sought to give *"in* the world" had crucial defects. This argument could be admitted by Communists without invalidating the project in their eyes. They did not claim to have achieved, a priori, a perfected, encapsulated world of their own. They could only engage in what Nathan Glazer has called a continual "human alchemy," trying to remake themselves. Their answer was *action*, not contemplation or self-correction derived from some absolute moral standard. Admitting their shortcomings, these were attributed not to ideals but to the inadequate realization of these ideals, the corruptions *"of* the world."

Every manner of reply was available to every manner of criticism, so long as it could be assumed that society required a total change, and that only a revolutionary elite could achieve such change. If the Communists were indicted as an unrepresentative force in a land where their pretensions was so vast, they replied that they were as adequate a channel of the process of acculturation as could be found. If they attracted the insecure, the rebellious, the lonely, or the authoritarian personalities, they promised to remold them all and to a certain degree succeeded. As Almond has observed, America is a land where the "general social consensus itself is insecure. One of the consequences of a 'melting pot' society is that it takes generations before the various ingredients are assimilated to each other."[30] Nathan Glazer has shown that the American Party was not uniquely or disproportionately a group of misfits, and recruited an impressive cross-section of both industrial and white-collar workers, as well as intellectuals, at least through 1948. To those who, in Daniel Bell's phrase, recoiled at the "*Schwärmerei* and grubbiness" of the Communist milieu, the answer could be made that competing radicals movements were not free of the same vices. The sanctimoniousness of the Party could be indicted, but its validity to its adherents was not thereby undermined. For all those who left it because their "God had failed" there were others who came in search of comradeship, and found it.[31] Not intended to be a family but a quasi-military elite, forged for stern historical tasks, it was in fact a family to many.[32] Kenneth Boulding has insisted that the Communists lost out in mass movements because they were found guilty of exploiting them for ulterior aims.[33] The Communists resented the charge on the grounds that their aims were not in fact ulterior; the final aim had stimulated their activity in building worthwhile movements. Thus, at most, it could be said that their aims were premature. The Communists believed they would someday be recognized by those whom the Party served. The argument could oscillate indefinitely between the purity of the aim and the reality of Communist practice, as well as their disloyalty to their own achievements. Those who lamented the hierarchical leadership, the intolerance of dissent, and the "war mentality," all of which alienated potential allies, were always reminded that replacing capitalism involved the class war, in which no quarter was given. This argument had a certain force. Almond has written that "the fully-initiated Communist clings to the Party even though he is deeply troubled by its actions," and this loyalty had its continuous self-justification. The troubled Communist could argue, and contemporary political science from Michels to Deutsch confirms the point, that life in any political organization has its *grandeurs et misères*. The Party was not unique in the contradiction of ends and means.[34]

Even if the American Communist granted the Soviet Union's imperfections — although this was hazardous — he could point to the differentiation which was at work by the forties between his own experience and the Russian one; he could argue that, thanks to the lessons of Soviet difficulties, the way forward in America might be different. Given comparative success at home, this sophisticated approach could give the movement some mileage.

Moreover, the argument could be turned against those who had not "fought the good fight." The critics of the Communists on the left were charged with having been ineffectual themselves. This convenient and powerful *non sequitur* was satisfying to Party members, and it kept them from appreciating the fruitful explorations which socialists, Trotskyists, and liberals were making of Communism's impasse and of the changing dynamics of capitalism.

But one must return to the key question. Suppose society's ills did not require a *total* change? Suppose change did not proceed by *total* means without becoming totalitarian? Perhaps the adaptability of American capitalism and the flexibility of democracy were greater than the Communists realized. Perhaps the contradictions *were* soluble, and the differences between America and Europe were not superficial but basic. If quantitative accretions of reform could result in important changes in quality, then the fundamental Communist assumption broke down. World politics might very well be operating like a chemical reaction which did not have to go to completion. The idea of a political Gibbs' law, a concept of equilibrium, of synthesis, of osmosis, or of interaction which goes forward in such a way *as to alter the terms of the political reaction process itself*, was ruled out by doctrine. But if some world equilibrium were being established, then the doctrine and its entire organizational architecture was outmoded.

What if the limits of capitalism were more elastic than theory allowed? What if this elasticity *had increased* as a consequence of the very changes to which the revolutionaries could claim, not without justice, that they had contributed? What if the missionary community, estranged from the world yet striving to remake it, was becoming obsolete not because it was a total failure but because it was a partial success? For this possibility, the Communists were unprepared. And this unpreparedness was at the root of their own self-destruction.

After the Second World War, the American Communist movement had two courses open to it. It could become a force for radical reform, militantly seeking to extend the system's elasticity. This course would imply revisions in ideology, behavior, and structure. It could be justified as a variant of Leninism only to a point; it would have to seek a justification which made Leninism historical, not eternal. The other course was to conduct a protracted struggle, postponing the inner contradiction by prolonging it. Such a course was more suitable to less mobile and less fluid societies, where precapitalist rigidities and undemocratic vestiges made radical subcultures possible. To speed up the protracted struggle, the American Communists would have to make the voluntaristic attempt to force the recalcitrance of historical reality by some extraordinary leap, to turn the "locomotive of history" onto the rails it had not taken. For this, too, Leninism gave sanction. In the American context, however, the penalty of failure was self-destruction.

The American Communists did not choose either alternative: *their story resides in having tried both* within a single decade (and at times simultaneously) and having succeeded at neither.

# NOTES, BIBLIOGRAPHY, AND INDEX

# NOTES

## CHAPTER 1. THE HARD LOOK BACKWARD

1. Eugene Dennis, *The Communists Take a New Look* (New York: New Century Publishers, 1956). Unless otherwise noted, all of the quotations from Dennis in this chapter are from this report.

2. The Smith Act proscribed the teaching and advocacy of violent overthrow of the government. The indictment of 1948 under which the C.P. leaders were tried and convicted charged that the Party's reconstitution in 1945 amounted to conspiracy to overthrow the United States government. The Party's National Board was tried in 1949, and on June 4, 1951, the Supreme Court upheld the conviction of ten of its eleven members. William Z. Foster's case had been severed because of his heart condition. Trials took place in California, Ohio, Connecticut, New York, Pennsylvania and Maryland in 1952. There was also a clause in the Smith Act making individual Party membership punishable. Although several Party leaders were indicted under this clause, only one, Junius Scales of North Carolina, was tried. He was convicted and served part of his term *after his departure from the Party*. He was freed by President Kennedy in 1962. The other indictments were dropped. *Fortune* magazine asserted in February 1957 that 108 "top leaders" of the C.P.U.S.A. had been convicted under the Smith Act. Most of these either did not serve their sentences, or served brief ones, or won their cases on appeal. For a discussion of the issues in the Smith Act trials, see John Somerville, *The Communist Trials and the American Tradition,* (New York: Cameron Associates, 1956).

3. See Theodore Draper, *The Roots of American Communism* (New York: Viking Press, 1957), chapter 12.

4. Winston and Green "came out" later in 1956. But they had to serve their original terms plus penalties, and were not at liberty until 1961. Winston, currently the Party's chairman (1971), lost his eyesight because of neglect in prison. Both men paid the price of nearly a decade of isolation. Two other leaders absent in April 1956 were Irving Potash and John Williamson, neither of them U. S. citizens, who opted for voluntary deportation, in the first case to Poland, in the second to England. Potash returned to this country via Canada after travels to Moscow and Peking, and served a year in 1957 for illegal entry. Williamson, active in British Communist politics, now directs the Marx Memorial Library in London.

5. Hall was captured in Mexico in October 1951, after his attempted departure for Moscow was bungled, partly because his aides underestimated F.B.I. penetration of their network in Mexico, partly because the Soviet agents there were rank amateurs. Thompson was

found in a California mountain hideout in August 1953. In addition to the absence of six of the original Smith Act defendants, it should be noted that Elizabeth Gurley Flynn was not present; as a "second string" Smith Act victim she was then in jail, as was another veteran leader, Alexander Bittelman.

6. A fuller treatment of this underground will be found in chapter 9. The cadres who went underground were expected, as Gilbert Green put it to me in 1951, "to reconstruct the Party if it were smashed." This statement is revealing of the expectations of the leadership at that time.

7. Eugene Dennis, *Letters from Prison* (New York: International Publishers, 1956).

8. John Gates, *The Story of an American Communist* (New York: Thomas Nelson's, 1958), p. 142.

9. In a private communication to me, Gates revealed that many of his associates could not understand his failure to mention the Soviet Union and its problems. See the *Daily Worker*, January 21, 1956, for details of the meeting.

10. The chief leaders knew of Khrushchev's speech at the April 28-May 1 meeting. Dennis had received an abbreviated version which his personal secretary presented to the meeting as though it had come "from Britain"; the audience assumed that this meant it had been sent by John Williamson although it may have come to Dennis via the Canadian Communists. Max Weiss, who reported on the 20th Congress to this meeting and whose report was later published, had not been made privy to this abbreviated version and his remarks show no trace of the document. When the State Department made the full text of the speech public early in June, the *Daily Worker* reprinted it. What gave its editor, Gates, confidence in doing so was his knowledge of the version which Dennis gave the meeting in April. The *Daily Worker* was, however, the only Communist paper in the world to credit the State Department's text, and the only daily, I believe, ever to publish the full text. The *Canadian Tribune*, a Toronto weekly, also published the text as a special supplement. See N. 5, Chapter 10, for Weiss' comment.

11. Joseph Clark, who returned in 1953 from three years as *Daily Worker* editor in Moscow, broached these problems in a memorandum to Foster in 1954. This nearly cost Clark his political neck. The memorandum was similar to letters which I, as the same paper's European editor, had been sending since 1951 from Paris, Rome, and Peking, taking issue with Party policy. Foster (in *Political Affairs*, October 1956) disclosed that Clark and Starobin had challenged the Party line and caused "serious disruption." In this context, my own book, *Paris to Peking* (New York: Cameron Associates, 1955), was part of a veiled

attempt to conduct a campaign for a Party's change of course, prior to the 20th Congress. See "A Communication," *Political Affairs,* Jan. 1957.

12. The California defendants went free later in 1956.

13. Foster had published a series of articles in *Political Affairs,* beginning in 1946, which made the theories of John Maynard Keynes the chief object of scorn on the grounds that Keynes had been trying to prop up an outmoded capitalist system. For a rebuttal to Foster, see the privately printed pamphlet by Earl Browder, *Keynes, Foster and Marx,* Parts I and II (1950).

14. Green's search for some formulation which would connect the Communists with support of the welfare state was criticized on the grounds that it suggested solutions for the ailments of the society short of the complete victory of socialism. It is interesting that this quest for a less doctrinaire position rose again in other forms. Alexander Bittelman, the Party's chief economic expert and ideological mainstay of those years, claims that he broached variations of Green's slogan several times in the early fifties. Bittelman's last effort, in the form of a full-length manuscript, came at the end of the fifties. The manuscript, which the Party refused to publish, roused the ire of Foster, Dennis, and Hall, and led to Bittelman's expulsion from the Party in 1959, after having served it for forty years. Bittelman subsequently published this manuscript privately and despite the Party's ban, under the title *A Communist Views America's Future,* in 1960.

15. The split among the left wing unionists and the refusal of important unions and union leaders to follow the Party's advice to return to the main body of the labor movement was one of the shattering facts of the early fifties. It had been foreshadowed in the 1948 election campaign and had its roots in the peculiar relation between the Party and its union cadres (see chapter 2). In the early fifties the publication, *March of Labor,* edited by John Steuben, a long-time Party stalwart in the unions, mirrored the effort of the left wing unionists to stand together. Nothing came of many attempts to interest John L. Lewis in the fate of these unions, or in some kind of independent center. A decade earlier he had accepted the Communist cadres as an asset in the building of the C.I.O. Now he declined to give them shelter in their adversity. They offered him little.

16. Walter Reuther and in particular his secretary-treasurer, Emil Mazey, were increasingly critical of government policy after 1955 and, by implication, of the policies represented by George Meany and his chief advisor, the onetime Communist, Jay Lovestone.

17. The A.L.P. was formally dissolved in mid-1956, twenty years after its formation. For a very biased but informative study of the A.L.P., see David J. Saposs, *Communism in American Politics* (Washington, D. C.; Public Affairs Press, 1960); also, Kenneth J. Waltzer,

"The American Labor Party of New York," a Ph.D. thesis in preparation at Harvard University. See also the pamphlet "Selected Readings on Coalition Politics and Electoral Problems," (New York: Jefferson School of Social Science, October 1954) which gives citations of C.P. writings from 1936 to 1950 on the A.L.P. and data on the decline of the A.L.P.

18. Marcantonio stayed on with the A.L.P. and discovered quite belatedly its domination by the Communist Party. Before he could unfold a strategy for returning to conventional politics, he was stricken by a heart attack and died in 1954. For an account of Marcantonio's relations with the American Labor Party and the Communist Party in 1953-54, see Annette T. Rubinstein, ed., *I Vote My Conscience* (New York: The Vito Marcantonio Memorial, 1956).

19. Dennis' real name, Francis Waldron, was revealed in the 1949 Smith Act trial. For additional details of his early career, in particular why Dennis disappeared from California in 1930, see a letter by Peggy Dennis, *San Francisco People's World*, March 13, 1971.

20. Eugene Dennis, *Ideas They Cannot Jail* (New York: International Publishers, 1950). See also pp. 190-191. At the cadre meeting on May 2, 1950, Dennis disclosed, for the first time to my knowledge, his presence among the Chinese Communists at Shanghai in 1934. The year before he had shown great difficulty in explaining this part of his past. Dennis attracted national attention when he refused to answer questions by the House Committee on un-American Activities, claiming protection of the First Amendment and charging that, because of discrimination against Negroes, one Southern member of HUAC held his seat illegally and hence the Committee was improperly constituted. This challenge still echoes in Mississippi politics. Bert Andrews, of the Washington press corps, was impressed and invited Dennis to speak with reporters. But when asked why he had gone to China, Dennis replied stiffly: "I was serving the American people." He could not be brought to elaborate on this answer or to make his presence in China less mysterious. His sophisticated audience walked out, much to the mortification of the *Daily Worker's* own correspondent at that time, who saw this as proof of the Party's leader's ineptitude.

21. Nathan Glazer, *The Social Basis of American Communism* (New York: Harcourt, Brace & World, 1961), p. 216, cites a report on American developments by "Tim Ryan" in the Comintern weekly, *Inprecorr,* for 1937. This had been Dennis' name in Moscow, and he passed this name to a son who was born there and who, for unknown reasons, did not accompany his American parents to the United States. The young "Tim Ryan" became a Soviet citizen; he is now Professor

Timur Timofeyev, a prominent Soviet political scientist and head of the Institute for the Study of the World Labor Movement.

22. See Gates, *Story of an American Communist*, pp. 142, 145, on his experience with Dennis while in prison. One of my own experiences with Dennis, with whom I had had a particularly close relationship from 1949 to 1951, resulted in the same impression of indecisiveness and hesitation in the extreme. Although I had refused to re-register in the Party in 1954, partly in protest against Foster's proposal to expel me because of differences over the "war danger," I remained accessible to the Party leadership, and Dennis sought me out during his parole in mid-1955 for long discussions on my experience in Europe and China. He did so again in June 1956, at a point when he was scheduled to speak in a Carnegie Hall symposium with Norman Thomas, A. J. Muste, and W. E. B. DuBois, the first occasion for the presentation of the Party's views following the 20th Congress of the C.P.S.U. Dennis, who was ill, asked me to prepare a draft of a speech for him. The next day, he had revised the ideas and the language of this draft back to the old, familiar, and hackneyed, but he was himself conscious that this would not do for the occasion. I submitted a new draft, and again Dennis started reworking it back to the "safe" and the familiar. Each day he was more ill than the last. After three days, I gave up the effort. I did not attend the Carnegie Hall meeting and did not see Dennis again. By the summer of 1956 the conviction that Dennis could never lead the renovation of American Communism was widespread in Party circles. One *Daily Worker* writer made a quip to the effect that "Comrade Dennis does not have the guts even for a *peaceful* transition to socialism ... " See my own article, "1956 A Memoir," in *Problems of Communism*, November-December 1966.

23. William Z. Foster, in *Political Affairs*, October 1956.

24. Dennis, *The Communists Take a New Look* (New York: New Century Publishers, 1956), p. 21. This is one of the few references to the impact on the U.S. Party of its subordination to Soviet policy.

25. Much of the inner party struggle in the C.P.U.S.A. revolved around the "war danger" judgment. This was also true in the Communist countries. See Imre Nagy's letter to the Hungarian Party's Central Committee, in his *On Communism* (New York: Praeger, 1957): "In the years 1949 to 1952, incorrect evaluations of the international situation, *overemphasis of the war danger, and the actions resulting from these assumptions,* played a very serious part in those grave mistakes that were made by our Party leadership" (italics in the original).

26. See William Z. Foster, "Is There a War Danger?" *Daily Worker*, April 8, 1955. At this late date in the thaw, Foster was still affirming a war danger in the same language as he had used since 1946.

27. The Vinson decision was the Supreme Court's final statement upholding the Smith Act, refusing the Party's appeal. The National Committee's reply was a declaration by Foster and Dennis, evoking the heroism of the Italian and Japanese parties during the fascist period. This could only imply that the American Party would have to arise as a Phoenix from the ashes of fascism and war. (*Daily Worker,* June 5, 1951).

28. Organizational secretary Henry Winston announced a drastic reduction in Party rolls in the summer of 1951 on the grounds that those who were not immediately re-registering were to be considered as having been "dropped." Party headquarters and offices in many areas (except California) were closed by the Party. If the membership in 1956 was 17,000, as reported by Gates (*Story of an American Communist,* p. 173), this suggests that 8,000 members had been "dissolved" in the 1951 hysteria. The most characteristic act of that time was the evasion of prison by Robert Thompson, who had been given only a three-year (rather than five-year) sentence, in view of his DSC in the war. He would have been free in eighteen months, given time off for good behavior. His personal decision to "go underground" was thus a judgment that the C.P. could not be functioning normally within eighteen months. Thompson is known to have justified his action in joining the unavailables on the grounds that his experience in guerrilla warfare would be useful, and that such warfare would inevitably come in the wake of war and fascism. Yet Thompson was caught in the Sierras without resistance.

29. At this point Dennis again referred to the American Party's dependence on economic estimates from abroad, although it was just as true that foreign Communist analysts had been misled by the Americans. For instance, a conference in May 1949 at the Jefferson School produced a book by James S. Allen and Doxey A. Wilkerson, eds., *The Economic Crisis and the Cold War,* with an introduction by Foster (New York: New Century, 1949), which received wide currency abroad; the economic judgments of this book proved entirely erroneous, but were accepted as accurate in many foreign Communist circles.

30. Dennis touched here on sensitive matters, which are elaborated in chapter 7. Important Wallace supporters, such as the former attorney general of California, Robert W. Kenny, had opposed a separate Wallace party. Moreover, many Communist leaders had doubted the strategy as late as the summer of 1947. They had yielded in part to the pressure from among the C.P.'s own influentials. They had misread the meaning of the first meeting of the Cominform, taking the formation of that body to mean that the political polarization taking place in Europe had to be duplicated in the United States.

31. In 1946, a strong leftist current manifested itself, pressuring Foster to make a clean sweep of the former Browder men. Foster had prided himself on his ability to steer a proper middle course. Speaking to the National Committee meeting on July 16-18, 1946, he had said: "At the Convention a year ago, as the comrades will recall, we laid great stress upon the danger that, in correcting our line from the revisionism of Browder, we might, so to speak, over-correct it, and make a swing to 'Left' sectarianism. Such swings have happened before in correcting a wrong line, not only in the history of our Party but of other Parties as well. It can be said, however, that in the course of this past year we have, by and large, avoided this mistake." *Political Affairs,* August 1946, p. 773. It was exactly this judgment that Dennis now challenged, ten years too late.

## CHAPTER 2. REMEMBRANCE OF THINGS PAST

1. Theodore Draper, *American Communism and Soviet Russia* (New York: Viking, 1960), gives an excellent description of the Party's older generation, its quarrels and its trauma. See also Draper's earlier work, *The Roots of American Communism* (New York: Viking, 1957).

2. Leon Festinger et al., *When Prophecy Fails* (Minneapolis: University of Minneapolis Press, 1956), is exceptionally stimulating for its analysis of those sects who believe in political astrology, and of what happens when predictions fail.

3. The most exhaustive study of the kinds of people who come to Communism, even though based on a limited sampling, is by Gabriel Almond et al., *The Appeals of Communism* (Princeton: Princeton University Press, 1954). Its bibliography on the cleavages within Communist parties, pp. 183-184, is especially useful. See also Robert E. Lane, *Political Life* (New York: The Free Press, 1960), and the same author's "Notes on a Theory of Democratic Personality," *Political Ideology* (New York: The Free Press, 1962).

4. In addition to Draper's books, two studies from rather differing angles of vision give good portraits of the C.P.'s rise and its transformation. These are: Irving Howe and Lewis Coser, *The American Communist Party* rev. ed. (New York: Praeger, 1962); Earl Latham, *The Communist Controversy in Washington* (Cambridge: Harvard University Press, 1966). Howe and Coser speculate that "several hundred thousand" Americans came into and left the C.P.U.S.A. They consider too high the figure of 750,000 given by Morris Ernst and David Loth, *Report on the American Communist* (New York: Holt, 1952). Howe and Coser (p. 225) agree with the 7,000 figure for 1930. Earl Browder, *Communism in the United States* (New York: International Publish-

ers 1935), p. 66, given a figure of 7,545 members as of June 1930.

5. David A. Shannon, *The Socialist Party of America* (New York: Macmillan, 1955).

6. Daniel Bell, *Marxian Socialism in the United States,* rev. ed. (Princeton: Princeton University Press, 1968), gives a detailed picture of the internecine battles among the Socialists as they declined, of their attempts to digest the Trotskyists who had joined them, and of the Reverend A. J. Muste's unifying efforts. As long ago as January 14, 1931, in the *New Republic,* Edmund Wilson had projected the need to "take Communism away from the Communists." He wanted a radical movement, rooted in American circumstances and idiom, free of the Stalinist fixations and ties. My own recollection is that few young Communists who joined the Party in the very early thirties knew much about the origins of the Lovestone and Cannon groups, and about subsequent splits among the Trotskyists. This was not only because the Party's past seemed irrelevant and contact with the heretics was taboo, but also because these groups seemed unimportant by contrast with the Party's relative successes. Granville Hicks expressed the same recollection after quitting the Communists: "We did not understand the fine points of Marxist doctrine over which the Party fought the Trotskyites and other factions, and we were not interested in them. It was enough for us that Marxism was in general right, and that the Communist Party was in general Marxist." See his essay in I. D. Talmadge, ed., *Whose Revolution?* (New York: Howell, Soskin, 1941).

7. Among the recruits to the Communists were Mrs. Meta Berger, widow of the Socialist onetime congressman from Milwaukee, Victor Berger. At least three prominent figures were recruited from the Industrial Workers of the World (I.W.W.) — Elizabeth Gurley Flynn, Harrison George, and Vern Smith. The most prominent of the Musteites were Louis F. Budenz, who quit Communism in 1945, and Arnold Johnson, who has remained with the Communists to the present.

8. Figures on the shift from foreign-born to native-born are given in detail by Nathan Glazer, *The Social Basis of American Communism* (New York: Harcourt, Brace & World, 1961), pp. 90, 100. Glazer notes (p. 74) that "the industrial workingclass in America in the twenties and in declining proportions in the thirties, was foreign-born: if the party was less 'American' for being in such large measure an immigrant party, it was by the same token more 'workingclass'. Small as it was the party during the twenties was really a working class organization." This continued to be true in the thirties and forties, despite the entry of new, native-born strata, including white-collar workers, professionals and even business men. On the other hand, it was not difficult to cite the Eastern European origin of many of the Party's leaders and second-echelon cadres into the late forties. See the report of At-

torney General Tom Clark, in 1952, to the U. S. Congress, Senate, Committee on the Judiciary, Subcommittee on Immigration and Nationalization, *Hearings on S. 1832,* 81st Cong. 1st sess., pt. 1, p. 318.

9. Almond, *Appeals of Communism,* pp. 204-206, discusses the growth of the American Communist Party as a phenomenon in the "acculturation" of its different elements. Unfortunately, he hardly deals either with its Negro members or with those of "old American stock," whose adaptation to change via the Party was part of the same process. See my article in *Polemic,* a student journal published at Western Reserve University, 1959, which made the same point, but before my reading of Almond.

10. Glazer, *The Social Basis,* p. 144, on the influx of non-working class members during the war.

11. Williamson's analysis of Party composition is found in *The Communist,* October 1943, pp. 922-933. His figure for membership of blacks corresponds with the data of Wilson Record, *The Negro and the Communist Party* (Chapel Hill: University of North Carolina, 1951). It is interesting that despite the Party's opposition to A. Philip Randolph's "March on Washington" movement in 1942, which was judged an interference in the war effort, and the later self-criticism in 1945 that the "Browder" line had operated to repel potential Negro members, comparatively large numbers did join in 1943.

12. John Williamson, *Political Affairs,* January 1945, p. 49.

13. John Williamson, *Political Affairs,* April 1945, pp. 365-366.

14. New Century Publishers, the Party's pamphlet-issuing agency, had replaced the older Workers Library Publishers, and year after year printed several million copies of brochures, broadsides, and pamphlets.

15. Sections of the International Workers Order acquired an influence during the war beyond their own ranks. The South Slavs, for example, gained control of the Croatian Fraternal Union. The Jewish People's Fraternal Order (formerly part of the I.W.O. and later an autonomous body) was accepted into the American Jewish Congress in 1942. Through the I.W.O., left wingers acquired influence in the American Slav Congress, headed by the Socialist union leader, Leo Krzycki. Among the older cadres who had been active in Party affairs, Boleslaw Gebert, well known as a steel workers organizer, and Michael Salerno, long active among Italian workers, held positions in the I.W.O. before returning to their native Poland and Italy. The tie between the Party's financial apparatus and the I.W.O. was maintained through William Weiner, who was for a time both the Party's treasurer and an official of the Jewish People's Fraternal Order. While direct contributions from the I.W.O. to the Party can hardly be proven, no secret was made of contributions to the *Daily Worker*'s sustaining fund

drives. Max Bedacht, the head of the International Workers Order, had been a major Communist leader in the twenties; he was acting secretary of the Party in the interim between the expulsion of Lovestone and the establishment of the secretariat (of which he was a member) which led the Party until Browder's pre-eminence was acknowledged in 1934. Bedacht remained a Party leader of stature, although the specific preoccupations of running his own organization, a substantial enterprise in itself, kept him at a discreet distance from the centers of power. It is significant that with the mounting Party crisis in the late forties, Bedacht could not restrain himself from criticizing the Party's course. He was one of the many old-timers who were expelled as "leftists" during the Foster-Dennis regime. For details on Bedacht's differences with the Party which centered on the character of C.P. support to the Progressive Party as well as on the "Jewish question," see his appeal to the 14th National Convention, August 1948, in the oppositional *Manhattan Communist Bulletin,* No. 3 (April 1949).

16. Davis and Cacchione had each rolled up some 107,000 first-choice votes in November 1943. During the same wartime period, Arnold Johnson received 47,000 votes as candidate for the Cleveland, Ohio, school board, and Oleta O'Connor Yates, in the San Francisco mayoralty race, got 40,000 votes.

17. Draper, *The Roots of American Communism,* in the chapter appropriately entitled "The Manipulated Revolution," explains how this strategy came about. For an acidulous but well reasoned view of the C.P., a view which has been very influential on the new left, see Dr. Gabriel Kolko, "The Decline of American Radicalism," *Studies on the Left,* September-October 1966. In Kolko's judgment, the participation of the Communists in movements for democratic reform proved their undoing. But he does not explain how they could have avoided such participation, unless they adopted his position that a truly revolutionary course entails abstinence from day-to-day politics. This is elaborated in his *Triumph of American Conservatism* (New York: The Free Press, 1963), in which the whole evolution of American society is made to appear as a spiteful frustration of revolutionaries by reformers. This leads Kolko to the logical conclusion, again popular on the new left, that "rational hopes for the 20th century now rest outside of America, and in spite of it." This view makes American radicals either impotent victims, bystanders, or imitators. For a cogent reply to the Kolko thesis, as well as a good summary of the C.P.'s strength and weakness, see Max Gordon in *New Left Notes,* August 5, 1966, replying to Stanley Aronowitz in the same periodical, June 10, 1966.

18. Daniel Bell, *Marxian Socialism,* p. 16, argues that the party's

impact was that it "provided an unmatched political sophistication to a generation that went through its ranks and gave an easygoing, tolerant, sprawling America a lesson in organizational manipulation, and hard-bitten ideological devotion which this country, because of its tradition and temperament, found hard to understand. . . . "

19. During the second half of the twenties, the Communists had great difficulty with the problem that the United States, as a consequence of its exceptional development, could not be analyzed in the same way as the European or Asian countries, and hence required revolutionary strategy and tactics different from what may have been applicable elsewhere. It was one of the nails in Lovestone's political coffin that he had been an "American exceptionalist." Even Foster, though an opponent of Lovestone's in the period 1927-1929, had at times been deemed guilty of seeing something quite exceptional in U.S. capitalism, something which required trade union tactics that did not fit what the international movement found proper. Browder, coming to power after Lovestone's debacle and Foster's impotence, was fiercely "anti-exceptionalist." Yet he developed concepts about the relation between American Communism and the international movement which stressed the distinctively different problems of this country. However much Browder, too, tried to make his answers to these problems mesh with the needs of Moscow and the world movement, he became an exceptionalist. By 1956, after fighting Browder's version of exceptionalism for a decade, the Dennis report was obliged, as has been shown, to try to differentiate the American scene from the postulates of the world movement. See Draper, *American Communism and Soviet Russia*, chapter 12. See also my chapters 3 and 4.

20. Earl Browder, in his memoir for the Columbia University Oral History Project, gave the figure of five million for the American League's membership. Browder claimed that the League's influence was so great that at the time of the Munich crisis, when Winston Churchill found himself standing almost alone, he considered having the League sponsor a tour by him of the United States. See Browder's article in *Harper's* March 1960. See also Howe and Coser, *American Communist Party*, p. 353. For a comprehensive view of how Browder saw the C.P.'s ramifications during his leadership, see *I. F. Stone's Weekly*, October 18, 1954.

21. Probably the best single recent book on Spain is by Hugh Thomas, *The Spanish Civil War* (New York: Harper & Row, 1961). *The Heart of Spain,* edited by Alvah Bessie and published in 1952 by the Veterans of the Abraham Lincoln Brigade, is a collection from varied European and American authors, warmly evoking the Spanish experience.

22. On the Abraham Lincoln Brigade, as well as on the Interna-

tional Brigade as a whole, see Vincent Brome, *The International Brigades* (New York: William Morrow, 1966); Cecil Eby, *Between the Bullet and the Lie* (New York: Holt Rinehart & Winston, 1969); William Herrick, *¡Hermanos!* (New York, Simon & Schuster, 1969); Robert A. Rosenstone, *Crusade of the Left* (New York: Pegasus, 1969); and Arthur H. Landis, *The Abraham Lincoln Brigade* (New York: Citadel Press, 1967). In all of these books, as in the reminiscences of Gates (in *The Story of an American Communist* [New York: Thomas Nelson's, 1958]), the initiating role of the American Communists and their contribution to the Spanish effort stands out.

23. For the complex, bizarre origins of the "Negro question," Draper's *The Roots of American Communism,* chapter 15, is essential, as is his recent book, *Origins of Black Nationalism* (New York: Viking, 1970). See also Howe and Coser, *American Communist Party,* pp. 355-358. Very useful is the running critique by Harold Cruse, *The Crisis of the Negro Intellectual* (New York: William Morrow, 1967), although its main importance lies in its reflection, not of the upswing of the thirties, but of the crisis of the fifties. (See below: chapter 6). See also John W. Van Zanten, "Communist Theory and the American Negro Question," *Review of Politics,* October 1967 (a chapter from a Ph.D. dissertation at Yale), and Joseph C. Mouledous, "From Browderism to Peaceful Coexistence," *Phylon,* vol. XXV, no. 1 (Spring 1964).

24. Wilson Record, *Race and Radicalism: the N.A.A.C.P. and the Communist Party in Conflict* (Ithaca: Cornell University Press, 1964) has some of the major data on the National Negro Congress. On p. 156, Record mentions that "perhaps the most incisive evaluation of the first meeting of the Congress is contained in Ralph Bunche's 'Programs, Ideologies, Tactics and Achievements of Negro Betterment and Interracial Organizations'." A limited part of Bunche's monograph was used in Gunnar Myrdal's classic, *An American Dilemma* (New York: Harper, 1949).

25. During my own trip throughout the South in the spring of 1956, I heard many non-Communist figures of the southern liberal-radical tradition recall with compassion their contacts with the southern Communists. For example, Dean Brazeal, of Morehouse College in Atlanta, Mrs. Grace Hamilton, of the Urban League in that same city, and Myles Horton, head of the very influential Highlander Folk School (then in its original location in Monteagle, Tennessee). All told me they had wanted to listen to the southern Communists, black and white, and had wanted to help them, although they had at the same time been repelled by their dogmatism. There is a small irony in the fact that in the criticism of the Browder era, during the summer of 1945, the alleged influence of southern white liberals upon Browder

was held responsible for the transformation of the Communist Party in the South into a series of "people's educational institutes"; this attempt to give the Party a form more suitable and influential in the South was viewed as heresy. Yet the same Southern Conference for Human Welfare which the Party contemptuously treated as "liberal" in 1945 was attacked as a "Communist-front" by the McCarthyites half a dozen years later.

26. Daniel Aaron, *Writers on the Left* (New York: Harcourt, Brace & World, 1961), is perhaps the best survey of the Party's "cultural" sweep, its achievements and contradictions. It forms a complement to Eugene Lyons, *The Red Decade* (Indianapolis: Bobbs, Merrill, 1941). See also, Albert Halper, *Goodbye Union Square* (Chicago: Quadrangle Books, 1970), Edward Dahlberg, *The Confessions of Edward Dahlberg* (New York: George Braziller, 1970), and Nathan Glazer, *The Social Basis.*

27. "For the discontented magazine writer, the guilty Hollywood scenarist, the aggrieved university instructor, the unpaid high school teacher, the politically inexperienced scientist, the intelligent clerk, the culturally aspiring dentist — as well as for a diminishing number of genuinely creative people — Marxism as a system of explanation and consolation carried great appeal." Arthur Schlesinger, Jr., *The Age of Roosevelt: The Politics of Upheaval* (Boston: Houghton, Mifflin, 1960), p. 165.

28. Murray Kempton, *Part of our Time* (New York: Simon and Schuster, 1955). Fifteen years later, in two *New Yorker* articles, February 20 and 27, 1971, on the career of Orson Welles as "Citizen Kane," Pauline Kael returns to the problem of the left wing writers in Hollywood during their heyday. For a portrait of the inveterate and indefatigable fellow-traveller, including glimpses of Hollywood, see Ella Winter, *And Not To Yield* (New York: Harcourt, Brace & World, 1963).

29. Daniel J. Leab, *A Union of Individuals: the Formation of the American Newspaper Guild* (New York: Columbia University Press, 1970).

30. Harold Clurman, *The Fervent Years: the Story of the Group Theatre and the Thirties* (New York: A. A. Knopf, 1945).

31. William O'Neill, *Echoes of Revolt: The Masses* (Chicago: Quadrangle Books, 1966).

32. Joseph Freeman was probably the Communist Party's most talented intellectual. His autobiographical *An American Testament* (New York: Farrar & Rinehart, Inc., 1936) made a great impression on the youth of the thirties, and was one of the few American radical memoirs to echo abroad, where Victor Gollancz' *Left Book Club* reprinted it. Freeman, who started *Partisan Review* (it was originally

sponsored by the John Reed Clubs) was editor of *New Masses* during the Moscow Trials; he made the mistake of allowing his correspondent in the Soviet Union, Joshua Kunitz, leeway to voice doubts about what was happening. A blast from the Comintern attacked Freeman's book as disrespectful to Stalin, among other sins. Freeman was quietly ousted from the Party in 1939. Freeman's own interpretation of the crisis within Communism will be found in his psychological novel, set in a Nazi concentration camp. *Never Call Retreat* (New York: Farrar, Rinehart, 1943). This book was scheduled to be made into a wartime motion picture when the project was scotched — according to Freeman's account, by Howard Fast and left wingers on the West Coast, who refused to give a "renegade" his chance in Hollywood. In this ironic way, Eugene Lyon's charges of a C.P. dictatorship in communications were confirmed. Freeman, in later years, became a genial friend both of his onetime social-democratic and *Partisan Review* opponents as well as of Earl Browder, who had expelled him half a dozen years before the latter's own expulsion. One of my most memorable recollections was an evening in the late fifties at my home in which Kunitz, Granville Hicks, and Herman Michelson (who had left a top position on the old *New York World* to become Freeman's successor on *New Masses*), met again for the first time in nearly twenty years. Freeman's papers, a gold mine about the left spanning several decades, are now at Columbia University. Part of them are also in the files which Daniel Aaron, at Smith College, Northhampton, Mass., used for *Writers on the Left.*

33. Aaron, *Writers,* p. 347, mentions the remarkable group of American intellectuals who signed the famous "Culture and the Crisis" statement on behalf of the candidacy of Foster and Ford on the Communist ticket in 1932. Everybody who was anybody took that stand. The pro-Communist galaxy of American intellectuals grew until the period of the Trials and the Pact, after which intellectuals began to turn away from the Party. Granville Hicks, in his *Where We Came Out* (New York: Viking, 1954), says that five of the original fifty-two signers of the "Culture and the Crisis" statement had become anti-Communist before 1939. Ten years later, only nine of the original fifty-two supported the Waldorf-Astoria Peace Conference.

34. Joseph P. Lash and James A. Wechsler, *War Our Heritage* (New York: International Publishers, 1936), give a vivid picture of the antiwar movement as seen by two leaders of the American Student Union at its high point.

35. Leslie A. Gould, *American Youth Today* (New York: Random House, 1940), describes the Youth Congress and what it wanted. For the origins of the Youth Congress, see the unpublished manuscript by George P. Rawick, at Oakland University, Michigan, prepared for the

Fund for the Republic and used in part by Hal Draper in Rita James
Simon, ed., *As We Saw the Thirties* (Urbana: University of Illinois
Press, 1967). For a picture of the problems of Mrs. Roosevelt, sponsor
of the American Youth Congress but perplexed by the fact that so
many of her proteges were concealed Communists and did not explain
their behavior to her, see Joseph P. Lash, *Eleanor Roosevelt: a
Friend's Memoir* (Garden City: Doubleday, 1964). The rationale of
dissolving the Young Communist League during the war and building
a new organization, American Youth for Democracy, is given by Carl
Ross and James West, *The Communist,* April 1944, pp. 336-346. See
also, Max Weiss, *The Communist,* September 1943, in an article entitled "Toward a New Anti-Fascist Youth Organization."

36. John Williamson, *Political Affairs,* January 1945. p. 359.

37. Stevan Dedijer, the older brother of the famous Yugoslav,
Vladimir Dedijer, studied at Princeton and was a member of the
American Communist Party, for a while editing its Serb newspaper in
Pittsburgh. During the war, Stevan became General Maxwell Taylor's
bodyguard. Now a professor of the history of science at the University
of Lund, Sweden, Dedijer recounted to me during a visit in June 1965
how utterly amazed General Taylor was when he discovered Dedijer's
political background. The anecdote was told to me when I noted an
autographed picture of the general on Dedijer's mantlepiece.

38. Robert Thompson, *Political Affairs,* January 1946, p. 49.

39. The A.L.P.'s original scope is indicated by its support for
Thomas E. Dewey, later the Republican presidential candidate, in
local New York elections. By the close of the war, the A.L.P. had two
New York city councilman, Michael Quill and Eugene Connolly. For
the problems of A.L.P.-Communist relations, see above, chapter 4.
Early in the war, the International Ladies Garment Workers Union
split away from the A.L.P. to form the nucleus of the Liberal Party,
which remained for the next decade a weaker factor than the A.L.P.
For a picture of Communist influence within the Democratic Party,
see U.S., Congress, House, Committee on Un-American Activities,
*Investigation of Communist Activities in Seattle, Wash. Area,* 84th
Cong., 1st sess., 1955.

40. Browder, in his Columbia University Oral History Project
memoir, recounts that when he and Foster came to the Communist
International's Executive Committee early in 1936 to discuss the U.S.
Party's electoral tactics, Foster proposed that the Communists endorse Roosevelt. For a while this view seemed to get Comintern
approval until Browder won out with the alternate strategy of an independent C.P. candidacy that would direct the main fire at Roosevelt's
opponent. This event has a bearing on the Party's dilemma in the 1948
campaign.

41. Earl Browder's report to the June 17-20, 1937, Central Committee meeting. *The Communist*, July 1937, p. 597.

42. Some members of the left bloc in the House were Jerry O'Connell, Democrat of Montana; John Bernard, Democrat-Farmer-Labor of Minnesota; Hugh De Lacy, Democrat of Washington, and of course Vito Marcantonio, of New York. In the Senate, Elbert Thomas, Democrat of Utah, and Harley Kilgore, Democrat of West Virginia were among those to whom the left had access.

43. One of the milestones of the U.S. Communist Party's fight for legitimacy during the war was the Supreme Court decision that the Party's secretary of California, William Schneiderman, could not be deported although he had not been a citizen upon joining the organization many years earlier. The Court held that the Party's advocacy of socialism fell within the purview of the First Amendment; this contrasted with the Court's decision in the Smith Act case in 1951. Wendell Willkie, the Republican candidate for the presidency in 1940, argued the Communist case before the Court. Another milestone was President Roosevelt's pardon, "in the interests of national unity" for Earl Browder in May 1942; the Party's general secretary had been jailed the year before on an old charge of passport violation which the Department of Justice had not pressed throughout the thirties, but had revived in the "phoney war" period. Browder himself, under repeated query by me and others, denies that he ever met Roosevelt, at the White House or elsewhere. But there is no question that an artist of old New England stock, Josephine Truslow Adams, who had been instrumental in persuading Roosevelt to free Browder in 1942, often carried Browder's opinions on political matters back to the White House. Browder does say, in his Columbia University Oral History Project memoirs, that he met early in 1944 with Wendell Willkie, who was at that time engaged in discussions with Roosevelt on a realignment of liberals and conservatives in the two parties.

44. Nathan Glazer, *The Social Basis*, p. 107. For a vivid portrait of how the C.I.O. came into being and how the left wing was finally defeated, plus anecdotal observations about its internal balances, see Len DeCaux, *Labor Radical: from the Wobblies to the C.I.O.* (Boston: Beacon Press, 1970). DeCaux, a New Zealander educated in the best British schools and active in the British left wing, came to the United States early in the twenties. He worked in a variety of unions, belonged to various radical factions, and then became the editor of the *C.I.O. News* in its hey day; he was ousted after the purge of the left in 1948. For other insights on the great change in U.S. labor, see Louis Stark (once labor editor of the N.Y. *Times*) in the symposium, *America Now* (New York: Literary Guild, 1938). See also Sidney Lens, *Left, Right and Center* (Hinsdale, Ill.: H. Regnery,

1949), and *Crisis of American Labor* (New York: Sagamore Press, 1959). The important point that the Communists had been aided in their organizing of the mass production industries by their earlier experience building cadres in the unemployed movement is made by Bernard Karsh and Phillips J. Gorman in their essay "The Impact of the Political Left" for the volume by Milton Derber and Edwin Young, *Labor and the New Deal*, (Madison: University of Wisconsin Press, 1957).

45. Arthur Goldberg, *A.F.L.-C.I.O.: Labor United* (New York: McGraw Hill, 1956), pp. 174-196, quotes an authority on labor at the University of Chicago, Dr. Joel Seidman, as believing that the Communists led unions with one-third of the C.I.O.'s membership. Arnold Beichman, in the *Christian Science Monitor,* October 16, 1956, recalled the time "a decade ago when, by universal admission, it [the C.P.] controlled C.I.O. unions with 20 per cent of the C.I.O.'s membership." Beichman was also the author of a policy memorandum of the Research Institute of America, March 28, 1946, which tried to assess the left influence in all wings of U.S. labor. For an anti-Communist, but insightful, view, see Merlyn S. Pitzele, "Can American Labor Defeat the Communists?" *Atlantic Monthly,* March 1947.

46. Aliens were dropped from the Party's rolls after 1940, essentially to protect them from prosecution under the Voorhis Act. This Act was also the reason for the Party's disaffiliation from the International. The Party continued to support the civil rights of aliens, mainly through the effective American Committee for the Protection of Foreign Born. Some exceptions were made to the rule excluding aliens from Party membership, and these were pointed out to me by Roy Hudson, the onetime Political Committee member, in an interview in San Francisco in July 1967. He noted somewhat bitterly that both John Williamson and Irving Potash had remained in the top leadership although they were aliens. When I pressed him, Hudson implied that both men had some higher sanction for their presence in the uppermost ranks.

47. The best-known analyses of Communist Party organization are found in Philip Selznick, *The Organizational Weapon* (New York: McGraw Hill, 1952), and Frank S. Meyer, *The Moulding of Communists* (New York: Harcourt, Brace & World, 1961). Both authors drew heavily on *The Communist Party, a Manual on Organization,* by J. Peters (New York: Workers Library, 1935), one of those mysterious and ubiquitous Hungarians who was active in the Party's inner structure in the early thirties. A strong reply to the major premises of Selznick's analysis was made by Earl Browder, in a memorandum in the files of the Fund for the Republic.

48. Almond, *Appeals of Communism,* p. 158, noted a "real plane of

cleavage in the party between the inner core and the members operating in trade unions, youth organizations and similar 'transmission belts.' Inner core people frequently tend to have an almost trained incapacity to be effective with non-party groups. Workers in mass organizations have to avoid full assimilation in the party, if their capacity for effective communication and mass leadership is to be maintained." Elaboration of the same point is found on p. 170.

49. Ella Winter, in *Not to Yield*, p. 255, recalls a visit to the White House early in 1945, during which she was entertained at tea. "Just before I left, Mrs. Roosevelt had talked about how much she resented the lies told her by young radicals and Communists she had invited to the White House a year or so before. 'I didn't mind their being Communists, if they'd told me,' she said 'I minded being lied to, and finding out afterward from the F.B.I.' "

50. An interesting instance of the conflict between the Party and its influentials is found in the Earl Browder papers in Syracuse University. Among these is a copy of a letter (dated January 29, 1945) from Clifford McAvoy, at that time Washington representative of the United Electrical Workers to Louis Budenz, then editor of the *Daily Worker*. McAvoy notes the paper's support of Representative May's compulsory service bill "with some astonishment." He cites a conference of eight C.I.O. unions on January 13, 1945, opposing May's plan for compulsory labor and military service. The Communists, as part of their 1944 line, were supporting such projects. Unions closest to them were not.

51. The best example of this type of influential is Harry Bridges, leader of the West Coast longshoremen, who, although he was close to anarcho-syndicalism and never a Communist, enjoyed intimate ties with the Party, usually on his own terms. In the mid-fifties, during the Party's agony and re-examination, Bridges talked freely, at private dinner parties, of quitting his union (he has in fact stayed as its president long beyond his retirement age) in order to form a "real" Communist Party. Bridges always found, in his infatuations with overseas Communists, evidence of how much wiser they were than the Americans with whom he had cooperated closely and who had, in a large sense, enabled him to become a foremost radical unionist.

52. Roy Hudson, in the pamphlet published in the 1944 discussion, *Shall the Communist Party Change Its Name?*, made the following argument for a change in name (p. 14). "It has not always been possible for Communists in some industries to fully make their influence felt *as* Communists. Under these conditions, to have emphasized the fact that they were Communists would only have been to help those who sought to attack Labor and disrupt its ranks. However, if the change of name . . . helps us to achieve those changes in our relation-

ship with broader Labor forces, it will also soon — and very soon — create those conditions where every Communist trade unionist will be able to contribute a maximum in helping to determine our policies, in helping more directly lead our movement, build it, and increase its influence among the masses. And if this comes about, if the trade unionists have greater opportunity to make their contribution in the direct work and leadership of our movement, it will be very important indeed."

53. The mood of wonder over the success of the Russian Revolution was widespread among American radicals, including prominent Socialists. Even those who soon became disillusioned with the Bolsheviks, for example two such diverse figures as Morris Hillquit and Eugene Victor Debs, avowed their support for the Soviets well into the twenties. See *The Impact of the Russian Revolution, 1917-1967* (London: Oxford University Press, 1967). See also, Philip S. Foner, *The Bolshevik Revolution: its Impact on American Radicals, Liberals and Labor* (New York: International Publishers, 1967).

54. See V. I. Lenin, "Report of the Fourth Congress of the Communist International", November 13, 1922, *Selected Works*, vol. X (New York: International Publishers, 1938), p. 332. "At the Third Congress in 1921, we adopted a resolution on the organizational structure of the Communist Parties and on the methods and content of their work. The resolution is an excellent one, but it is almost thoroughly Russian, that is to say, everything is taken from Russian conditions. I have the impression that we made a big mistake with this resolution, namely that we have blocked our own road to further success. . . . The resolution is too Russian; it reflects Russian experience. That is why it is quite unintelligible to foreigners. But they cannot be content with hanging it in a corner like an icon and praying to it."

55. For details on the Comintern's financial assistance to the U.S. Communists in the twenties, see Draper, *American Communism and Soviet Russia*, pp. 202, 204 and 480. For the thirties, Browder's comment on sources of Party funds, in his March 5, 1956, memorandum to William Goldsmith of the Fund for the Republic, has some interest. The former C.P. general secretary said that private business ventures, with an investment of perhaps three hundred thousand dollars, were built under his leadership. He estimated the profit from these enterprises at 10 percent per year. Browder insisted that such investments were not really different from funds available from business sources to other political parties. He also argued that this money was "of considerably less economic importance than the contributions to the *Daily Worker,* or even less than direct donations of individuals to the Party." "Outside these general characteristics, I would not care to discuss it," Browder concluded.

56. J. B. S. Hardman, himself a former Communist and later distinguished for his writings on American labor, in a series for the *New Republic,* August-September 1930, quoted a onetime Comintern "rep" as saying: "Granted that the American Party is plainly crazy, still we must work with the material at hand." Hardman also quoted the views of Karl Radek in 1922 that the American Party was a *"narrenhaus"* ("house of fools"). The Comintern representative cited was Valetski (Walecki), a Polish mathematician who entered the United States via Canada in July 1922. See William Rodney, *Soldiers of the International: a History of the Communist Party of Canada, 1919-1929* (Toronto: University of Toronto Press, 1968), p. 54.

57. *The Communist,* June 1930. Quoted by William Z. Foster, *A History of the Communist Party of the United States* (New York: International Publishers, 1952), p. 570.

58. Apart from important Latin American and Canadian Communists who moved across U.S. borders with comparative ease, the United States in those years was a haven for many European and Asian Communists. During the thirties it was a safer place for many of them than the Soviet Union, whose foreign Communist refugees "disappeared" by the hundreds in the purges. Many who found themselves in the U.S. received direct help from the American Communists. Many were to return to their own countries after the war and achieve prominence there. Among those in this category were: Chi Chao-ting, foreign trade expert of People's China in the fifties; Chang Han-fu, who became a deputy foreign minister in Peking; Tang Ming-chao, a leader of China's Peace Committee who has specialized in Peking's nongovernmental contacts abroad; Ambrogio Donini, a Communist senator in the postwar years and one of Italy's ambassadors to Poland; Giuseppe Berti, the Italian Communist Party's *responsable* in Paris before coming to the United States, and later a specialist in the Italian party's historical research, notably on the Angelo Tasca papers; his wife, Dina Berti, a Communist senator; Serge Prica, Yugoslav ambassador in London, Paris, and Rome between the fifties and seventies; Boleslaw Gebert, onetime trade union leader in Warsaw, later Poland's delegate to the World Federation of Trade Unions, and also in the Polish diplomatic service; George Pirinsky, prominent in Bulgarian public life; Lajos Bebrits, who, together with J. Peters, returned to Hungary; and Albert Norden, a spokesman of the German Democratic Republic and a leader of that country's Socialist Unity Party. Finally, there was Gerhart Eisler, the German Communist whose flight from a jail sentence in the United States caused a sensation in 1949.

59. The last lines of the *Internationale* originally were as follows: "The Internationale shall be the human race." Written by Eugene Pottier in 1871, at the time of the Paris Commune, the song later

became a worldwide radical anthem. After the Russian Revolution the words "International Soviet shall be the human race" came into use. By returning to the original version, the American Communists were emphasizing that they did not envisage an "international Soviet". This was consonant with their new policies, but made the song more difficult to sing.

60. The slogan "Communism is 20th Century Americanism" was evidently criticized in Moscow where this idea caused a certain bewilderment. That Communism was being equated with Americanism was too much. See *The Communist,* December 1938, for an attempted explanation of why the slogan was abandoned.

61. The Executive Committee of the Communist International, in its final statement of May 1943, credited the "fundamental differences of the historical development of the separate countries of the world" and noted that these were apparent even before the war. This was a curious, retrospective admission that the C.I. *even before the war,* had not been soundly based. The U.S. Party's departure from the organization was also noted as a sign that the International had become outmoded. The document added that Communists "never were advocates of the preservation of outmoded historical forms." See Kermit E. McKenzie, *Comintern and World Revolution* (New York: Columbia University Press, 1964).

62. Granville Hicks, *I Like America* (New York: Modern Age Books, 1938).

63. In San Francisco in July 1966, I went through the files of the *Farmer's Weekly* in the home of a friend who had once taken part in the Party's "ag-work" (agricultural work). Few experiences in preparing this study were so painful. For details of the crisis in the U.S. farm belt during the thirties, see John L. Shover, *Cornbelt Rebellion: the Farmers' Holiday Association* (Urbana: University of Illinois Press, 1965).

## CHAPTER 3. TWO LEADERS FACE THE UNKNOWN

1. Only one other prominent Party leader, Sam Darcy in Philadelphia, opposed Browder's course in 1944. Foster, who demurred and then remained silent, did not support Darcy when the latter persisted and was expelled. In fact, Foster headed the committee that ousted his only prominent supporter.

2. *Pages from a Worker's Life* (New York: International Publishers, 1939).

3. James Oneal, *American Communism* (New York: E. P. Dutton, 1947). Oneal, a Socialist, locates one of the main impulses of Foster's career in his syndicalist beginnings (p. 31).

4. William Z. Foster, *The Great Steel Strike* (New York: Huebsch, 1920). Cf. David Brody, *Labor in Crisis: the Great Steel Strike of 1919* (New York: Lippincott, 1965).

5. For a sharply critical and yet appreciative evocation of Foster, his organizing skill, and his drive for power by any means, see James Cannon, "Foster and Browder," *Fourth International*, Fall, 1955. Cannon, who worked closely with both men in the Kansas City and Chicago union movements and then in the Communist Party, became the leader of American Trotskyism. His essay was written as a memorandum to Theodore Draper during the latter's research on the C.P.U.S.A.

6. The Trade Union Education League (T.U.E.L.), founded in 1920, must be distinguished in its origins from the Trade Union Unity League (T.U.U.L.), a dual-union effort founded in 1929. The T.U.E.L. tried to radicalize the labor movement from within while the T.U.U.L., using the prestige of the earlier movement, tried to build industrial unions of its own.

7. Cannon, *"Foster and Browder,"* uses the word "clerk" in speaking of Browder. Benjamin Gitlow, *I Confess* (New York: E. P. Dutton, 1940), p. 173, uses the term "man-Friday." Bertram Wolfe, in conversations with me at Stanford University in August 1966, confirmed that Browder's contemporaries in those early years looked upon him as a secondary figure. It is not without significance that even in May 1944, at the inaugural convention of the Communist Political Association, of which Foster became chairman, he introduced its president, Browder, as "one of the finest agitators and educators in the labor movement" — which in Party parlance was not an especially high order of appreciation. Foster's secretary in the postwar period, Carl Dorfman, has told me that when Foster referred to Browder in Foster's close family circle it was always as "that schoolboy" — a characteristic deprecation and also anti-intellectualism of Foster's.

8. Robert Minor, *The Heritage of the Communist Political Association* (New York: New Century Publishers, 1944). For a full treatment of the factions which wracked the C.P. in the twenties, see Theodore Draper, *American Communist and Soviet Russia*.

9. The dependence of the American party on the Comintern, which constantly recalled leaders from New York, and heard appeals from these leaders, is evoked in J. Lovestone's famous wisecrack: "Why is the American Party like the Brooklyn Bridge? Because it is suspended at both ends by cables." Lovestone's joke was a wry comment on himself as well as on his colleagues. It was told to me by the Canadian former Communist, J. B. Salsberg, in Toronto, March 29, 1969.

10. Edmund Wilson, in his preface to *The American Earthquake*

(Garden City: Doubleday, 1958) muses on "why I should have been so stirred by Foster's appearance before a Congressional committee" in 1930 (and clearly he was stirred by Foster's strong, single-minded demeanor). But in *The New Republic,* December 24, 1930, Wilson mingled his admiration with the observation that "an element appears in his language which is quite alien to anything which has hitherto been characteristic of the militant American workingman — it is the idiom of Russian Communism."

11. Browder, in *Harper's,* March 1960, said that Dimitrov, then head of the Comintern, had urged Foster's removal from the Party leadership in 1938. In Browder's recollections for Columbia University's Oral History Project he asserts that during consultations with the Comintern early in 1936 Foster urged that the American Party support Roosevelt directly. Browder demurred on the grounds that such support would prejudice Roosevelt's campaign and lead to a disavowal of the Communists. Browder persuaded the Comintern chiefs that if the Party ran its own presidential ticket but directed the main burden of its attack against the Republicans, this would accomplish the purpose of supporting F.D.R. without endorsing him. In the private papers of Philip J. Jaffe will be found the minutes of the Party's Political Bureau in the autumn of 1939, showing that serious differences between Foster and Browder occupied several sessions. Echoes of these differences were heard during the first days of the Duclos article discussions in May 1945.

12. For a very inadequate biography of Minor, see Joseph North's *Robert Minor: Artist and Crusader* (New York: International Publishers, 1956). In deference to Lydia Gibson Minor, this book manages to avoid the fact that Minor had been previously married to the independent radical, Mary Heaton Vorse. The name of Browder does not appear at all.

13. Roy Hudson, one of the few original veterans of American Communism still alive at this writing, told me in July 1966 in San Francisco that Foster gave the trade union cadres little guidance whereas "from Browder you could get answers." This same appreciation was made by Stewart Smith, the onetime leading figure of the Canadian Communist movement, in discussions at Toronto in December 1968.

14. At a banquet honoring Foster's birthday, on March 17 1941, Browder recalled his first meetings with his colleague in 1912, but carefully restricted the scope of the lessons learned from Foster to trade union matters. See *The Path of Browder and Foster* (New York: Workers Library Publishers, 1941).

15. William Z. Foster, *The Twilight of World Capitalism* (New York: International Publishers, 1949) laments his lack of education.

In the ensuing years, Foster published half a dozen books, each of them compendia of a feverish reading and replete with unanalyzed generalizations. The dwindling Party audience of that time bought these books and then discarded them during the McCarthy days. John Gates, in his *The Story of an American Communist* (New York: Thomas Nelson's, 1958), recounts that at the April 1956 National Committee meeting Foster was rebuked for having written tomes which few Americans read. Foster replied that this mattered little since the books had been reprinted abroad and widely circulated in the Communist countries. Gates comments: "It did not seem to matter that few Americans were influenced by his work, so long as foreign Communists held him in high repute , or so he believed. He saw himself a world figure. He lived in a 'make believe' world of his own and though more typically 'American' than most Party leaders, he was also strangely remote from his own land and his own people" (p. 166).

16. In his address to the Party's Emergency convention, on July 26, 1945, Foster catalogued Browder's shortcomings as a "reverence for the spoken word. He is a talker, not a mass fighter. He has had very little experience in, or understanding of, the need to back up his word with action. Especially of recent years has this trend become manifest as Browder, poisoned by our sickly adulation, developed more and more of an inflated idea of the importance of his speeches. He eventually got to the point where he seemed to believe that all that was necessary in the case of a given issue was for him to make a speech, for the Party to scatter huge quantities of it throughout the country and all would be well" (*Political Affairs*, September 1945, p. 794). In his valedictory remarks on July 28, Browder made his rebuttal: "The strangest result of the resolution [the draft document which the convention was debating] and the Duclos article is to bring forward Comrade Foster as the foremost Marxist. Whatever his qualities in other respects, it is well known to all who have had extended collaboration with Comrade Foster that he has never understood Marxism, that this is not his strong side. Comrade Foster is an eclectic, subject to all sorts of theoretical influences; and in addition he suffers from fear of responsibility; he is by character irresolute and wavering on principle." The word "eclectic" and some of the same nuances appear in Cannon's portrait of Foster ten years later (Cannon, "Foster and Browder").

17. Earl Browder, *Victory and After* (New York: International Publishers, 1942).

18. Earl Browder, *Teheran and America* (New York: Workers Library Publishers, January 1944), p. 14. This pamphlet was the text of his National Committee report, January 7-9, 1944. His subsequent

book, *Teheran*, was a full-fledged elaboration, but with many new concepts.

19. *Ibid.*, p. 19.

20. *Ibid.*, p. 19.

21. *Ibid.*, p. 24.

22. *Ibid.*, p. 25.

23. Irving Howe and B. J. Widick, *The U.A.W. and Walter Reuther* (New York: Random House, 1949). See also Joel Seidman, "Labor Policy of the Communist Party during World War II," *Industrial and Labor Relations Review*, vol. IV (October 1950).

24. Browder was not unique in these postwar concerns: liberal and conservative economists and business leaders were discussing the same problem. The original aspect of Browder's preoccupation lay in the fact that, whereas Communists in the past had insisted that capitalism could not solve its problems, he was at least accentuating the positive and projecting programs short of abolishing the system. Lewis Lorwin in his *Post-war Plans of the United Nations* (New York: Twentieth Century Fund, 1942) cited studies of the Committee for Economic Development which spoke of the urgency to reach an output of 135-150 billion at 1941 prices: "This output must be reached quickly — at most within two years after peace comes — and employment must be increased by half a million jobs per year in subsequent years to take care of normal increases in available manpower." Eric Johnston, head of the Chamber of Commerce, had declared on April 27, 1943, that mass distribution of industrial goods was no longer a "pious wish" but a "concrete necessity." Beardsley Ruml put it this way before the American Retail Federation on February 29, 1944: "Today most business men agree that the elimination of mass unemployment is the first requirement for the postwar period. . . . Unless mass unemployment can be eliminated under a system of private business enterprise [it] will be supplanted by some other arrangement."

25. Earl Browder, *Teheran and America*, p. 28.

26. In Chicago and Detroit, Browder had spoken late in 1943 on the basic character of the Party. See *A Talk About the Communist Party* (New York: Workers' Library Publishers, 1943). In his address to the January 7-9, 1944, meeting, he alluded to the "permanent features of any such organization, whatever may be its name or immediate tasks. Such an organization, we are sure, must be maintained in the United States and must be built even stronger."

27. In Columbia University's collection of the Robert Minor Papers will be found a memorandum with twenty variants of the new name, apparently listed at the time of these discussions. The proposed name, American Communist Political Association, received sixteen votes,

and American Communist Association fourteen votes, with four votes for American Communist League and a scattering of two votes each for six other variations. Curiously, the word "American" was left off the proposal with the highest number of votes. "Communist Political Association" came to be the new name, although the word "American" was supposed to precede it.

28. Browder, *Teheran and America*, p. 40.

29. *Ibid.,* p. 41.

30. *Ibid.,* p. 47.

31. It is interesting to compare Browder's unwillingness to make a full-scale re-examination of capitalism with the contrasting behavior of Lewis Corey, whose wartime volume, *The Unfinished Task* (New York: Viking, 1942) does exactly that. Corey's insights were not essentially original; they had been anticipated by Adolph Berle and many others. But his abandonment of Marxist concepts was all the more dramatic because he had been, under his real name, Louis Fraina, one of the founders of American Communism. For the valuable reconstruction of the Fraina-Corey transformation, see Theodore Draper, *The Roots of American Communism* (New York: Viking, 1957).

32. Foster told the C.P.'s 14th national convention in August 1948: "By indicating the world drive of American imperialism, with its implications of fascism and war, as we did very definitely and clearly in our 1945 resolution, it appears to me that we did some international pioneering. In fact, our Party was among the first, if not the very first Party, to speak out clearly on the world drive of American imperialism and its accompanying dangers." *Political Affairs,* September 1948, p. 823. Browder had struck the same note in 1944-45. (See Browder, *Teheran and America.*)

33. Earl Browder, *Teheran and America,* pp. 43-45.

34. In talking with Darcy in February 1967, I had access to the stenotype of the January 7-9, 1944, meeting, but was not given a copy. Darcy's remarks appear in the minutes of the meeting in the private files of Philip J. Jaffe.

35. William Z. Foster, *World Capitalism and World Socialism* (New York: Workers' Library Publishers, 1941), p. 18. In his deposition at the Smith Act trial in 1949, Foster alluded to this pamphlet to show the continuity of his own thought and the fact that before the Party's reconstitution in 1945 he had seen, in 1941, the main characteristics (as he believed them to be) of the postwar period.

36. Foster's letter was published in *Political Affairs,* July 1945, pp. 640-655.

37. *Ibid.,* p. 645.

38. *Ibid.,* pp. 640-655.

CHAPTER 4. SANCTION FROM DIMITROV AND DOOM
BY DUCLOS

1. Interview with Earl Browder by Harold Lavine, in *PM*, March 26, 27, and 28, 1944.

2. Arnold Johnson, in *The Communist*, April 1944, pp. 319-326. See a similar report by Doxey A. Wilkerson, in *The Communist*, May 1944, on the results of the "enlightenment campaign" in the Baltimore, Maryland, and Washington, D.C. areas.

3. This was to be one of Browder's chief arguments in the debates of May 1945, justifying the transformation of the C.P.U.S.A. into the C.P.A.

4. Important Republican commentators, such as Walter Lippmann and Dorothy Thompson, and many who had been fervent supporters of Wendell Willkie in 1940, supported F.D.R. on the grounds that Dewey could not possibly be a reliable negotiator with both Stalin and Churchill. Early in 1944 Willkie himself negotiated with Roosevelt for a realignment of both parties to make their definition as liberals and conservatives clear. Browder was involved in these negotiations, having discussed these matters with the Republican leader. Whether Browder met with Roosevelt is difficult to ascertain. He himself always denied any direct encounter with F.D.R. Another sign of the great esteem in which the Communists under Browder held Wendell Willkie was the C.P.A.'s gift of $5,000 to the Freedom House Building Fund in honor of Willkie shortly after his death. The gift was made in March 1945.

5. For example, Adam Lapin, *Daily Worker*, July 24, 1944. See also the editorial of July 23, 1944.

6. Excerpts from Foster's address on the CBS nationwide radio hookup appear in the *Daily Worker*, January 10, 1944.

7. From the transcript of the February 8, 1944, meeting in the files of Philip J. Jaffe. Darcy's attempt to separate the politics and economics of the Teheran line received special denunciation as "unprincipled" from the veteran Party leader, Robert Minor, who said: "I believe that the responsible leaders of the trade union movement who are here are entitled to be informed that it is not usual for the Political Committee to be the occasion for such speeches as Comrade Darcy has made."

8. Frederick Woltman, in the *New York World-Telegram* for May 9, 1944, reported a "bitter clash" between Foster and Browder in the American Party's hierarchy, to which Foster replied in the *Daily Worker*, May 10, 1944, expressing indignation "at the florid imagination of writers on certain New York newspapers in conjuring up imaginary struggles within the leadership of the Communist Party."

9. The *Daily Worker* for April 5, 1944, announced Darcy's expulsion briefly but refused to publish his own letter of explanation. Darcy himself did not return to Communism even after his vindication in 1945, although he contemplated this for a time, and continued to have political influence throughout 1946. When asked twenty years later why he had given up at the point of his vindication, Darcy had no answer except to say that perhaps it was because of "some weakness" on his part. See N. 21, Chapter 5, and N. 24, Chapter 4.

10. Very sharp words were exchanged between Browder and Foster at the February 8, 1944, meeting. Foster believed that Browder was "now in the process of making a mistake" and needed "to be kept in check and controlled by the Political Committee." Browder said: "Comrade Foster is terribly confused, tragically confused. I think he has lost his way and the world has become too complex for him." Browder continued that there were "no wet nurses around here to take care of leaders" and spoke grimly of the "necessity of dealing with this question after tonight." Browder added: "We are not a friendly debating society, not a friendly club. We are a political army engaged in a struggle for the world. . . . " For the transcript of this exchange see Philip Jaffe's collection.

11. For Marty's letter, which was written in English on the stationery of the Assemblee Consultative Provisoire, Algiers, see Earl Browder's pamphlet, *Answer to Vronsky* (privately published, May 1948). Browder's prestige and the confidence which the Comintern leaders had in his leadership are confirmed by an anecdote told to me by the former Canadian Communist, J. B. Salsberg (March 28, 1969). Salsberg said that in the late thirties, Dimitrov had advised Canadian Party leaders, in case they had any problems, to consult with Browder, whom the Comintern leaders considered to be "the foremost Marxist in the English-speaking world."

12. Browder, in the Oral History Project, Columbia University, 1965.

13. See Herbert Feis, *Churchill, Roosevelt and Stalin* (Princeton: Princeton University Press, 1957), pp. 441-453.

14. Joseph Stalin, *For Victory and Enduring Peace* (New York: Workers' Library Publishers, 1944), p. 13.

15. Minor led the field in this oversimplification with his columns in the *Daily Worker*. His course at the Jefferson School of Social Science, the outlines for which are found in his Papers now at the Columbia University Library, show very clearly the petrification of a political projection into dogma.

16. *Daily Worker* columns by James S. Allen and myself in this

period suggest the conflict between the Teheran ideal and realities. In one column, I made so bold as to suggest that postwar problems "could not be resolved by rubbing an Aladdin's Lamp called Teheran." Yet both Allen and myself, together with Gilbert Green and Max Gordon, wrote a series of articles for *The Worker*, trying to define the theory of Teheran in terms we were later to regret. For the articles which theorized "boldly" on the Teheran conceptions see: James S. Allen, "Can There Be a Lasting Peace?" *The Worker*, March 11, 1945; Max Gordon, "Is Full Employment Possible?" *The Worker,* March 25, 1945; Joseph Starobin, "Preview of a New Europe," *The Worker,* April 1, 1945; Gilbert Green, "Imperialism and the New Epoch," *The Worker,* April 8, 1945. Green's article was intellectually the most ambitious.

17. One of the great complications which arose for the C.P. leaders when the Duclos article arrived was that both Hudson and Browder were reviewing trade union policy whereas Foster — kept at a distance from their discussions — published in the June 1945 *Political Affairs* a long, rather "Browderist" article hailing the formation of the World Federation of Trade Unions, upholding the idea of a profund division in American ruling circles, and suggesting that strikes should be minimized as far as possible in the postwar period. Foster therefore had difficulty blaming Browder for the postwar no-strike pledge idea. It is also interesting that Bridges went beyond Party policy, as the subsequent debates in the C.P.A. National Board revealed. Only those who simplify the relation between left wing labor leaders such as Bridges, and the Party itself will be surprised at this fact.

18. Correspondents on the special train provided by the State Department for travel to San Francisco in mid-April 1945 (of whom I was one) realized quickly that Ambassador Harriman was briefing selected commentators in a very anti-Soviet sense. Harriman was reported to have told an off-the-record group of which the publisher, Roy Howard, was a member that "the interests of the U.S.A. and the U.S.S.R. are irreconcilable." Howard exclaimed that if this were true, "the United States should be helping Japan, instead of urging Russia to enter the way against Japan."

19. Browder, in his Columbia University Oral History project interview, declares that John Abt, who as general counsel of the Amalgamated Clothing Workers had participated in the preparatory meetings of the W.F.T.U., told him early in 1945 that the French Communists were critical of American Communist policy. But Browder did not take this seriously, perhaps because of his confidence that he could pursue an autonomous policy, different from the French.

20. The article arrived at the *Daily Worker* office in New York in

the first days of May 1945 and was translated for the Party leadership by a member of the paper's foreign department. By then I was at the San Francisco conference.

21. I am using the translation which appeared in the *Daily Worker*, May 24, 1945, and which formed the text of the Communist Party's discussion. The original article by Jacques Duclos was entitled "A propos de la dissolution du P.C.A.," *Les Cahiers du Communisme*, Nouvelle Serie, no. 6 (April 1945), pp. 21-38.

22. To appreciate the genuine tendency of foreign Communists at that time to hold different views, it is revealing to contrast Italian and British reactions. Two important Italian Communists, Giuseppe Berti and Ambrogio Donini, were living in the United States as political refugees; mention of them has been made earlier. The former had been second in command to Togliatti himself during their prewar years in France. In May, 1945, both men immediately set out to square themselves away in the face of the Duclos article, and began to publish a newspaper, *Italia d'Oggi* [Italy today] in both English and Italian, signed by themselves as the "Delegation of the Italian Communist Party in North America," a formation which had not been heard of before. They berated the American Communists for failing to appreciate the import of the Duclos article. Their views had a significant circulation in American Communist ranks and a strong influence. Browder was incensed at their behavior. He considered it an interference in the autonomy of the American Communists. At the May 23, 1945, National Board meeting, Browder even charged them with having given the Duclos article to the *New York World-Telegram*, where the article appeared on May 22, 1945, before it did in the *Daily Worker*. When Berti and Donini returned to Italy they were severely criticized, among other reasons, for their attempt to influence the American Party's affairs. Togliatti was not enamored of the *mission civilisatrice* that the French Communists displayed toward many other C.P.'s throughout the forties.

On the other hand, the British Communists who had disagreed in private correspondence with Browder's line and especially his projection of it to the British scene, did not view the Duclos article as a conclusive reflection of Soviet policy even as late as December 1945. For example, in the daily bulletin of the British C.P. Congress in that month, the following reply is made by the general secretary, Harry Pollitt, to critics in his own ranks. "On the question of Browder, I only want to make one or two points," Pollitt declared. "When the Communist International was dissolved in 1942 [sic] we were all unanimously in support of the decision because of the political maturity of every section of the Communist Party. No one knew in this country anything of Foster's disagreement with Browder's line until the appearance of the Duclos article. That is a statement of fact. We expressed our disagreement with Browder's line, and in my opinion correctly at that moment and in that situation. The American comrades were in profound disagreement with the policy of our Party. We refused to publish Browder's book in this country because we disagreed with its contents and the American comrades were made aware of that. If you consider that it is Communist leadership that we tip you all off about circumstances of that description, in the most difficult stages of winning the war against Fascism, so far as I am concerned you have another think coming. Browder's policy was endorsed in January, 1944. It was not criticized by Comrade Duclos of the French Communist Party until April, 1945. And it may well be that a Party with a million members will have its views listened to with more respect than a party of 50,000. And finally, to those of you who are so worried about this problem, I must draw your attention to the fact that I have not yet seen any criticism of Browder in any of the theoretical organs of the Communist Party of the Soviet Union — not an unimportant Party of this world!"

The degree to which an embryonic polycentrism had emerged in the course of the war and the degree to which different parties took differing views of the Browder thesis *during* the war is striking. It is also striking that, whereas the Italian Communists in the U.S. saw the Duclos article as an act emanating from the highest international sources, Pollitt did not. My own subsequent talks with former Polish and German Communists suggest that Pollitt was not alone in this failure to grasp Moscow's role in the matter. Seweryn Bialer, now professor at Columbia University, confirmed to me that the Duclos article got no attention in Polish circles. Wolfgang Leonhard, a secretary to Walter Ulbricht when the German Communists returned to Berlin from Moscow, has made the same point in personal conversations. Neither the Polish nor German Communists pursued the "Duclos line" in 1945 or 1946.

23. Browder, in Columbia University's Oral History Project, refers to this meeting with Benoit Frachon and François Billoux, both P.C.F. Political Bureau members. As Browder recalls it, both men admitted that the Duclos article had not been discussed in advance within the P.C.F. leadership, which suggested that the whole thing originated outside the French Party's ranks. When Browder expostulated that in effect the French "were calling for [his] expulsion," both Billoux and Frachon were silent. Thus, Browder realized the high stakes involved in the Duclos criticism. It is a minor detail in this entire matter that the American party membership — and most of the leaders — were never informed that Browder, Foster, and Dennis had met with such authoritative figures from France. In July, when Browder's

article referring to this was published, it was made to appear that he had met with "two trade unionists," the implication being that he had consulted with Americans, not Frenchmen. Incidentally, this encounter in Washington gives the lie to Louis Budenz, who, after leaving the party in October 1945, alleged that the news of the Duclos article was brought to the American Communists by Dmitri Manuilski, who came to the San Francisco meeting of the United Nations as the foreign minister of the Ukraine and who was supposed to have told me of the Duclos article. The "Starobin letter," supposedly transmitting this information to New York, figured in the Smith Act trial in 1949. I met Manuilski in San Francisco, but never discussed Duclos with him. My superiors in the C.P. leadership learned about the Duclos article *before* I met anyone at all in San Francisco.

24. Browder's introduction to the Duclos article, published in the *Daily Worker,* May 24, 1945, was suave. It took the view that American Marxists always realized the end of the war in Europe would confront them with the need for reappraising aspects of their policy. Duclos was presented as a prominent European Marxist who had simply initiated a long overdue discussion. Browder attempted, in short, to make of the Duclos article little more than a contribution to a debate which, he implied, the American Communists had been undertaking on their own initiative. During my interview with Samuel Adams Darcy, December 13, 1966, the later recounted that the *New York World-Telegram* had first called him, Darcy, and he had telephoned Foster, urging Foster to press for the earliest publication of the article to avoid being "scooped." In Darcy's recollection, Foster was disoriented by the turn of events. Thus, Darcy was trying to help the man who had expelled him, even after Darcy had been vindicated. Yet as Darcy recalled these events, his dismay at Foster's hesitation when the Duclos article arrived also confirms that Foster did not expect the Duclos criticism and had no hand in bringing it about.

25. My information about this meeting comes from the stenogram in the collection of Philip J. Jaffe.

26. *The Writings and Speeches of Earl Browder, May-July 1945* (privately published).

27. This phrase came from an article in *LIFE* by the former ambassador to the USSR, William Bullitt, advocating a policy of both inducement and pressure in U.S. relations with Moscow.

28. Browder, *Writings and Speeches.*

29. It is interesting that within fifteen years of this discussion, American exports did exceed the fifty billion dollar mark. Even if corrected for the inflation of currency, gross national product by the midsixties far exceeded what the American Communists deemed it possible to project in 1945.

30. Elizabeth Gurley Flynn said: "I confess I realize that I have a certain inadequacy in dealing with some of these problems. I came into the C.P. from the top, and there is a great honor to that, but at the same time the great disadvantage of not having the background and experience and the solid foundation of having worked through the organization and having the experience that comes from that to make it easier to formulate an opinion."

31. The tendency of left wing unionists to go further than Party policy, as expressed in this instance, suggests the importance of the inner duality within this movement which would in later years be the key to the alienation of the influentials from the Party. A study of the articles in the newspaper, *PM*, for May 1944 throws a good deal of light on the divergence of Bridges' views from the Party position. The Bridges declaration was made at his own Local #6, and did not commit the entire I.L.W.U. Louis Weinstock, one of the few avowed Communist unionists at that time, is quoted in *PM* on May 30, 1944, as saying that unless the employers found some new way of satisfying the demands of the workers, the left wing would not abandon the strike weapon. This gave an "escape clause" to the flat proposal by Bridges that the strike weapon would not be needed in the post war era.

32. Hudson was to make an abject apology at a later stage for his abstention. Throughout the forties, however, this abstention was held against him. The California secretary, William Schneiderman, who arrived late and was not recorded as voting for the draft resolution, subsequently voted 'yes' with the majority.

33. Browder's address to the June 2, 1945, National Board meeting appeared in *The Worker* for June 10, 1945.

34. Mrs. Eleanor Roosevelt's syndicated columns of June 9 and June 11, 1945, expressed alarm that the Communists were now returning to conceptions of "world revolution" which contrasted with their wartime conduct. Westbrook Pegler, also syndicated in the Scripps-Howard press, called for a general offensive against the American Communists. The *Chicago Tribune* on June 12, 1945, noted that if Browder had been right the year before and was now considered wrong, then the boast that Marxism-Leninism constituted "a science" had now been revealed as hollow indeed.

35. In two interviews with me in January and March 1968, Bittelman emphasized his effort to bring Browder to the meeting and confirmed that Browder by his stubbornness had in effect forfeited the leadership; he was not even making a fight for it.

36. Minor's abject, overnight flip-flop exasperated Bella Dodd and Ben Gold, both trade unionists, the latter a veteran Communist, the former a newcomer. Ben Gold exclaimed that Minor had been heard to say at a Jefferson School gathering *after* the Duclos article:

"God Bless Earl Browder!," which contrasted with his denunciation of his former hero within a few weeks. Minor equivocated: This was "not true, but almost true." Gold revealed the contempt with which many Communists regarded Minor thereafter. See Bella Dodd's account in her *School of Darkness* (New York: P. J. Kenedy, 1954).

37. Pat Toohey's judgment in 1945 should be compared with an effusive letter by him to Browder in 1937, written from Moscow, full of glowing praise for Browder's "Americanization" of the C.P.U.S.A. The letter will be found in the University of Syracuse collection of Browder's personal papers.

38. The Communists were aware that they ought not, by the standards of their cause, to idolize their leaders because to do so could only corrupt followers and leaders. It is curious that in this exchange about the idolization of Browder and Foster no one broached the matter of Stalin.

39. One of the more emotional statements was made by "Fred M." who, from the internal evidence of his remarks, was the leader of a maritime union. Without discussing any of the issues at stake, he hailed William Z. Foster as a true proletarian and recalled the influence of Foster during a meeting many years before in Seattle, which had inspired Fred M.'s adherence to Communism. This was apparently the same Fred M. who, in the February 1944 discussions when Browder threatened Foster with his political life, had assured the enlarged National Committee meetings that the Communists in the maritime industry had complete faith in Earl Browder.

40. Bella Dodd's compassion for Browder was held against her by the leadership that was to take over the New York state organization under Robert Thompson. Her inability to renounce Browder without regrets and her deeply felt associations with the non-Communists in the American Labor Party were the causes of her expulsion in 1946. Bella Dodd's reference to "leather jackets and low heels" which disappeared in Browder's time evoked the bohemianism of an earlier day, and constituted praise for the fact that the Party had gone beyond those times. The Communists had lost their earlier "strange" and "foreign" air. See her own book, *School of Darkness,* and the comments about her case in George Charney's recollections, *A Long Journey* (Chicago: Quadrangle, 1968).

41. Davis had by then enrolled in the local Tammany Club. On July 20, 1945, he was endorsed by the Democrats, and a substantial movement was growing in Harlem to gain Davis the A.L.P. and Republican endorsements as well. Four days later, the city Democratic leadership under William O'Dwyer withdrew the endorsement of Davis, partly because of an article he had published in the *Daily Worker* that weekend wholeheartedly siding with Foster in the intra-

Communist debate and projecting the Negro question as a "national question" (a return to the prewar position). That November, Davis was re-elected to the Council on the Communist line. The A.L.P. gained another councilman, Eugene Connolly, but he was always at loggerheads with the C.P. elements in the A.L.P. O'Dwyer became mayor in November — with C.P. aid.

42. Comprehensive data on membership was not given again until the report of Henry Winston, Williamson's successor, to the 14th national convention in August 1948.

43. John Williamson, in the *Daily Worker,* July 1, 1945.

44. Elizabeth Gurley Flynn's contribution to the discussion in the July 23, 1945, *Worker* is preoccupied with the mood of rebellion in the ranks but reveals the still-lingering hope that Browder might yet give his former colleagues assistance. "Our collective duty is to get our ship back on its charted course with as few fatalities as possible. The captain may jump overboard (at present he remains in his cabin and his intentions are obscure) but should we demand the crew jump overboard, too? The captain is determined apparently to follow the old course even if he goes alone. The crew are agreed it is not the right one. Before removing the crew we'd better be certain we have others ready and equipped to take their places and to face the stormy seas ahead."

45. This secretariat, with the addition of Robert Thompson in August 1945, guided the reconstituted Party for the next year, until Dennis was named general secretary in July 1946. At that time Henry Winston was added to make a secretariat of five members.

46. For a review of all the state conventions which had by then upheld the Draft Resolution, see an interview with John Williamson in the *Daily Worker,* July 25, 1945.

47. Browder's contradictory course is indicated by an exchange between himself and the Emergency Convention's presiding committee on July 28, 1945, in which he professed to see a "consolidation of [the Party's] ranks on the foundation of correct Marxist-Leninist concepts." On August 3, the National Board replied noting that he had not repudiated his views and asking flatly whether he accepted the Convention decisions. (See the *Daily Worker,* August 4, 1945.) The question was never really answered except by Browder's expulsion in February 1946. For more on Browder's strange gyrations from 1946 to 1949, see chapter 6, and in particular footnote 20 in that chapter. Also N. 59 in Chapter 7 and N. 8 in Chapter 8.

48. An abbreviated version of this exchange was made public in the *Daily Worker,* July 28, 1945. The full text is found in Browder, *Writings and Speeches,* p. 66.

49. Among the many greetings to the Emergency Convention that

reconstituted the Communist Party was one from the Communist Party of China. It was published in the *Daily Worker,* July 22, 1945, but with an interesting omission. The full Chinese Communist message contained a reference to Earl Browder, noting his errors but also recalling his services to the working class and the international movement. The second half of this reference did not appear in the American Communist paper and its audience had no knowledge of it. But the full text was published in the *People's Daily* in far-off Yenan. It is reprinted in full in Stuart Schram's, *The Political Thought of Mao Tse-tung* (New York: Praeger, 1963). On the other hand, the original greetings with favorable references to Browder, appearing in the Chinese edition of Mao Tse-tung's *Collected Works,* were omitted from editions after 1961. Thus, the Chinese expression of sympathy for Browder's contribution — the only such expression he received from any Party — was twice censored, once for the American Communist audience in 1945 by Browder's closest coworkers, and sixteen years later when someone in Peking revised the original edition of Mao's Works and decided that one passage in the Chinese C.P.'s 1945 greetings should no longer be available in China.

## CHAPTER 5. THE PARTY RESTORED

1. Robert C. Morlan, *Prairie Fire:the Story of the Non-Partisan League* (Minneapolis: University of Minnesota Press, 1958).

2. Raymond Gram Swing, *Forerunners of American Fascism* (New York: J. Messner, 1935).

3. See, for example, Joyce Kornbluth, *Voices of Revolt* (Chicago: Quadrangle Books, 1966). Also, Melvyn Dubofsky, *We Shall Be All: a History of the I.W.W.* (Chicago, Quadrangle Books, 1969).

4. The demobilization was speeded by demonstrations of soldiers, from the Philippines to central Europe. Many left wingers out of the youth movement of the late thirties led these actions. Some of them were later to distinguish themselves in the trade unions.

5. Of the 318 candidates supported by the C.I.O.'s Political Action Committee in the November 5, 1946, elections, only seventy-five were elected. Part of the G.O.P. sweep in Congress stemmed from a massive abstention in Democratic ranks. Only three-eighths of the eligible electorate voted; the total Democratic vote dropped from twenty-five million to fifteen million, while the Republican vote fell only from twenty-two million to eighteen million.

6. Although Truman vetoed the Case bill in 1946 and his veto was sustained, the Senate did not uphold his veto of the Taft-Hartley Act the next year. Many observers felt that Truman could have mobilized

more support in the Senate if he had wished to; the veto failed by a single vote.

7. *Political Affairs,* June 1946, p. 494. Simon had left an important post in the U.E. as a Washington representative (he had also been a member of the Regional War Labor Board) to become the New York state trade union expert for the Communist Party. (Conversation of May 16, 1966.)

8. Nathan Glazer, *The Social Basis of American Communism* (New York: Harcourt, Brace & World, 1961), notes the increasing proportion of white-collar members in the C.P.U.S.A. and particularly the penchant of social workers to join it.

9. Clifton Brock, *Americans for Democratic Action* (Washington, D.C.: Americans for Democratic Action, 1962).

10. For example, Philip Murray, head of the C.I.O., in 1946 publicly opposed any witch hunt of Communists. See Curtis D. MacDougall, *Gideon's Army* (New York: Marzani & Munsell, 1965) vol. I, p. 109.

11. As David A. Shannon in his *Decline of American Communism* (New York: Harcourt, Brace, 1959), p. 253, points out, the American Communists showed a comparatively high vote in some areas in the 1946 and 1947 elections. Apart from New York City, where the Party had two councilmen, there was a contest for the nonpartisan Cleveland school board election in 1947 where A. R. Krchmarek, a well-known Communist, polled 64,264 votes. In 1946, the Negro leader, William Harrison, received 3,124 votes, or one-sixth of the total, in a race for the Massachusetts legislature. Anne Burke in Richmond, Virginia, also fared well that year; and Archie Brown, in San Francisco, received 22,206 votes in a write-in campaign for the California governorship in 1946. As late as 1950, a Communist candidate, Bernadette Doyle, received 605,393 votes for the post of school superintendent in California, but undoubtedly this surprising figure is explained in part by the fact that most voters liked her name and demeanor and did not necessarily know her political views. See Shannon, *Decline of American Communism,* pp. 91-101. See N. 16 in Chapter 2.

12. Dean Acheson, in his *A Democrat Looks at His Party* (New York: Harper, 1955), regrets the loyalty decrees as opening the way to McCarthyism.

13. Report on Organization to the 14th National Convention, August 1948, in Political Affairs, September 1948.

14. Eugene Dennis, *What America Faces* (New York: New Century Publishers, March 1946). It will be recalled that the Duclos article had erroneously reported a membership decline in 1944. It can

be argued that the decline in 1945 was itself proof that Duclos was in error with regard to 1944.

15. N. Ross, in *Political Affairs,* March 1946, p. 264.

16. N. Ross, in *Political Affairs,* October 1947, p. 926.

17. Henry Winston, in *Political Affairs,* September 1948, pp. 834-856.

18. Gilbert Green, in *Political Affairs,* July 1948, p. 737.

19. For a comprehensive picture of the role of factions in the C.P.'s past, see Theodore Draper, *American Communism and Soviet Russia* (New York: Viking, 1960). Also, Daniel Bell, *Marxian Socialism in the United States* (Princeton: Princeton University Press, 1968).

20. Mention has already been made of Browder's curious trajectory throughout 1946. His own Party club in Yonkers hesitated to expel him. This same hesitation was evident on the Westchester County level, whereupon the National Office stepped in and forced his ouster in February 1946. The chief reason given was that Browder had persisted in publishing an unauthorized bulletin, *Distributors' Guide,* late in 1945. Shortly after, Browder received a visa from the Soviet Embassy and traveled to Moscow in May 1946 where he was received with interest and cordiality — much to the astonishment of his former American comrades who denounced his action as a provocation. Browder's departure from Moscow was delayed at the express request of the foreign minister, Vyacheslav Molotov, then at a meeting in Paris, and who later heard out Browder's views at length. Such treatment for a deposed Communist leader was unprecedented. Browder took up a post as a distributor of Soviet scientific literature in the United States and wrote widely in 1946 on behalf of the proposition that an American-Soviet understanding remained possible. His Moscow trip was well reported. *The New Republic* published a series by him, beginning August 5, 1946, much of which then appeared in his book *War or Peace with Russia?* (New York: A.A. Wyn, 1947). His views were also widely circulated by the North American Newspaper Alliance. As late as August 1948, Browder still believed in the chance of a political comeback. He appealed to the C.P.'s 14th National Convention for reinstatement on the curious ground that the Tito heresy confronted the world movement with a grave challenge, and hence his own return to the Party was necessary. In mid-1949 he abandoned the post as distributor of Soviet books, but his personal papers at the University of Syracuse indicate his continued loyalty to socialism and to the Soviet Union; the final letter in that collection of papers asks that he be remembered warmly to those who gave him the post. From 1948 until well into 1950, Browder privately published a revealing series of pamphlets. He argued about the C.P.'s problems as though the Party's audience were important to him. And he evidently clung

to the hope of some change in the world movement that would justify him. For example, in the privately published pamphlet *Modern Resurrections and Miracles,* p. 50, he said: "The crisis in the American party had only been a by-product, an indirect and distorted expression of a much more profound crisis in certain parts of the international Communist movement. It was impossible for the American problem to be solved from abroad, except as part of the solution of the whole international crisis which continues." He was thus pinpointing a deeper dilemma of Communism. In this period, he worked for Michael Quill, leader of the Transport Workers Union (who was then breaking with Communism), and used this post to appeal to the Western European Communists against Foster. Browder's private papers at the University of Syracuse show that his friend during those years, A. A. Heller, a long-time "financial angel" of the Party and founder of International Publishers, talked with Maurice Thorez in Paris on behalf of Browder and Browder's views as late as 1949. At another point in this same period, Browder negotiated with the defense lawyers in the Smith Act trial, offering to defend the Party's policies prior to 1945; the negotiations finally broke down. Browder's own definitive break with Communism coincided with the illness in 1952 of his wife, Raissa, whom the Justice Department was attempting to deport as she lay dying of cancer. Browder was thus intellectually active with respect to the C.P.U.S.A. but never formed an opposition, perhaps because he would not have been able to, perhaps because he hoped until the early 1950's to make an eventual return. See the privately printed booklet, *Contempt of Congress: The Trial of Earl Browder,* 1951, the story of his self-defense before the Tydings committee. This is useful for many details of his war-time maneuvers, and shows that as late as 1950-51, he was trying to prove to his former colleagues what an effective Marxist he held himself to be.

21. In two interviews with me (February and December 1966), Darcy recounted his warm welcome at the National Office on the heels of the Duclos article, but also his falling-out with Williamson and Dennis. The latter insisted that Darcy make available the manuscript of a book he had been writing in 1944. Because of this issue, as well as because of Darcy's indignation that former Browder men were dominant in the mid-1945 upheaval, his candidacy for a high post, perhaps in the Party's secretariat, came to naught. He then became a successful furniture merchant, altogether avoiding politics. But the passion and detail with which, twenty years later, he recounted the episodes of the period suggests how deep and lasting his emotional commitment was. See Ns. 9 and 24 in chapter 4.

22. Harrison George, in his privately published pamphlet, *The Crisis in the C.P.U.S.A.* (December 1947), gives a revealing account

of the period with rich details on the California Party and on the dubious role of Foster. For the Party's explanation of the expulsion of Dunne and others, see the National Board statement of September 29, 1946, in *Political Affairs,* November 1946, pp. 1011-1015. See also Oleta O'Connor Yates, in *Political Affairs,* December 1946.

23. Winston was, with Green, Thompson, and Hall, among the top leaders convicted under the Smith Act who evaded jail from 1951 onwards and did not re-emerge until 1956. Serving additional time for contempt, Winston lost another few years in prison, and also lost his eyesight after an operation by prison doctors. He spent subsequent years in Moscow and succeeded Elizabeth Gurley Flynn (after her death in 1964) as the Party chairman.

24. Gates has recounted his evolution as a Communist (and in the late fifties as the chief "revisionist") in his *The Story of an American Communist* (New York: Thomas Nelson & Sons, 1958).

25. Steuben, who was to edit *March of Labor* in the early fifties, broke with Communism shortly before his death in 1959. See A. H. Raskin, in the New York *Times,* January 19, 1957.

26. For Sentner's story, see *Fortune,* November 1943. This article entitled "A Yaleman and a Communist" describes Sentner's relations with Stuart Symington, at that time a prominent St. Louis industrialist and later Democratic senator.

27. In 1966 and 1967 I interviewed Hudson in San Francisco; he was working there as a housepainter. It was, Hudson said, the first time in fifteen years that anyone from his past had looked him up. His former wife, of Hungarian descent, against whom accusations of disloyalty were probably most unfair, retired from politics to become a devout Catholic.

28. Hall fled from his political career in 1957, virtually in a state of personal and political paralysis.

29. For Stachel's earlier history in the Lovestone crisis, see the biting characterization in Theodore Draper *American Communism and Soviet Russia* (New York: Viking, 1960), p. 433.

30. According to an interview I had with the leading California Communist, Dorothy Healy, in August 1966, Thompson admitted his complete inadequacy for the New York assignment, an asssignment which required a sophistication and experience entirely beyond Thompson. No self-criticism of his role there was ever formally made. According to Carl Dorfman, who was Foster's personal secretary (interview of April 16, 1969), Foster "loved Thompson like a son." There was unquestionably a personal bond between the two men which explains in large measure Thompson's dynamic role as the main motive force of the leftist line in the late forties.

31. Returning to leadership under the Gus Hall regime in the early

sixties, Green was increasingly disturbed by aspects of the Communist movement, especially by events abroad — the Sino-Soviet schism and the Czechoslovak affair. Thus, he experienced a decade later what most of his friends of the thirties had experienced long before. Green is known to have had profound differences with Hall, the Party's leader in the sixties and at this writing, but exactly what these may be is unclear. He was a member of the C.P.'s National Committee as late as September 1970.

32. See below, chapter 9.

33. Both the contact between Dennis and Katz-Suchy and the National Board's meeting with Courtade took place in my home.

## CHAPTER 6. QUESTIONS IN SEARCH OF ANSWERS, 1946-47

1. Perhaps the one exception was a book by James S. Allen, *World Monopoly and Peace* (New York: International Publishers, 1946), written in the winter of 1945-46. It advanced some of the concepts of state monopoly capitalism as a new phase of the imperialist system which the Soviet authority, Eugene Varga, elaborated independently. Allen criticized himself, however, in the spring of 1948, after the Soviet writer, Kuzminov, took exception to all implications that state monopoly capitalism in any way invalidated Leninist propositions on the necessity of revolutionary change.

2. The *Daily Worker*, September 19, 1945.

3. *Political Affairs*, February 1946, pp. 99-109. On the anniversary of Lenin's birth, Communist leaders usually wrote long-range, *theoretical* (as opposed to purely topical) articles. Browder had done this in the February 1945 *Political Affairs*, seeking justification in Lenin's theory for his coexistence line. Foster did it a year later. The contrast between the two positions was pointed up in the introduction to Foster's February 1946 article by the magazine's editor, V. J. Jerome.

4. Foster, in *Political Affairs*, February 1946, p. 102.

5. *Ibid*, p. 105

6. Eugene Dennis, *What America Faces* (New York: New Century Publishers, 1946), p. 32.

7. Joseph Starobin, "The Foreign Ministers' Conference," *Political Affairs*, August 1946.

8. Foster, in *Political Affairs*, August 1946, pp. 686-695.

9. *Ibid.*, p. 691.

10. Speaking in the July 16, 1946, plenary session of the National Committee, Foster expressed great pride in what he believed was his pioneering role in Marxist-Leninist prognosis. Two years before, Earl Browder had also expressed pride at what he believed was the

pioneering of American Marxists in the pursuit of the "Teheran Line." Both C.P.U.S.A. leaders, opposed in all other ways, shared this characteristically American need to make their weight felt in the international Communist movement, despite the insignificant power of their own party. Both of them wanted the world Communist movement to recognize their unique contributions to world strategy.

11. On Bittelman's history and role, see Theodore Draper, *American Communism and Soviet Russia* (New York: Viking, 1957), p. 432.

12. *Political Affairs,* January 1946, p. 58.

13. *Political Affairs,* November 1946, p. 1008.

14. *Ibid.,* p. 1008.

15. Dennis, "Remarks on the Discussion," *Political Affairs,* January 1947, p. 18.

16. For example, the *Daily Worker* report of March 1, 1947, on the Conference of the Communist Parties of the British Empire countries has the British Communist Party secretary, Harry Pollitt saying that "the United States, while boasting and glorifying her free enterprise, is heading for an economic crisis which will break out either at the end of this year or the beginning of 1948." It is possible that the coincidence between the Dennis prediction and Varga's opinion was due, indirectly, to Bittelman himself. He was one of the few American C.P. leaders who could read Russian and he followed *Pravda* regularly. The story is told (perhaps it is apocryphal) that Bittelman's economic analyses would be picked up and printed in the Soviet press, whereupon Bittelman would cite this fact as proof that his views had Soviet backing; thus, the Soviet stamp of approval was used to validate analyses which originated in the United States to further the conviction of the American Communists that their views were sound. In this circuitous fashion, the American comrades misled their Soviet mentors and were in turn misled by them. For a most perceptive analysis of the Soviet image of U.S. reality, which also bears on the Allen-Kuzminov effort to define state-monopoly capitalism (n. 1), see two unpublished papers by the University of Toronto professor, Franklyn Griffiths, for the Canadian Political Science Association, June 1971, and the American Political Science Association, September 1971.

17. Beginning with an article by Claudia Jones, in the January 1946 *Political Affairs,* which opened the discussion, almost every issue of this most authoritative magazine throughout that year and into the first months of 1947 featured a contribution by one or another Communist leader on the Negro question.

18. Howe and Widick, *The U.A.W. and Walter Reuther* (New York: Random House, 1949), show that Reuther as late as 1947 opposed a black vice-president in the U.A.W. on the typically Socialist grounds that this would be discrimination.

19. See Draper, *American Communism and Soviet Russia,* chapter 15. Also, his article in *Commentary,* July 1969, and his *The Rediscovery of Black Nationalism* (New York: Viking, 1970).

20. Robert Minor, as his collected papers in the Columbia University archives show, was involved in the Party's overtures to the Garvey movement. Minor was to emphasize in later years that this sensitivity to the Negro question as a "national question" *antedated* the Comintern's stand in 1928-1930.

21. Stalin's definition was that "a nation is a historically-evolved, stable community of language, territory, economic life and psychological make-up manifested in a community of culture." See his *Marxism and the National and Colonial Question* (New York: International Publishers, 1942).

22. Harry Haywood, in *Political Affairs,* October 1946, pp. 938-939. Haywood wrote *Negro Liberation* (New York: International Publishers, 1938). He was one of the two brothers whose role in the early development of the self-determination concept is discussed by Draper, *American Communism and Soviet Russia,* chapter 15.

23. Wilson Record, whose two books, *The Negro and the Communist Party* (Chapel Hill: University of North Carolina Press, 1951) and *Race and Radicalism* (Ithaca: Cornell University Press, 1964) are major sources on the Negro question, credits the Party with having been attractive enough so that in the early forties 10 percent of its members were black.

24. *Political Affairs,* July 1946, pp. 652-668.

25. *Political Affairs,* May 1946, pp. 438-456. Although accused in this debate of Browderist tendencies, Franklin was expelled later in 1946 as a member of the leftist grouping.

26. *Political Affairs,* November and December 1946. Allen, who had been an instructor of history at the University of Pennsylvania before entering Communist fulltime activity in the late twenties, served in the early thirties as a Comintern representative in the Philippines, doing some of the basic academic study of that country. A vendetta with Eugene Dennis, evidently stemming from their Comintern experiences, kept him from becoming a political power, although his work ranged from the editorship of the first Communist Party newspaper in the South in the early thirties to writings on economic affairs and international relations; in the forties he was the foreign editor of the *Daily Worker* for a time and later of its Sunday edition, *The Worker.* One of the Party's best minds, unshaken by its tribulations, he is now head of *International Publishers.* In the 1959 debates, he completely disavowed his 1946 position and the whole premise of C.P. policy since 1929. Whether the rise of black power has caused him to reverse earlier reversals is unclear.

27. *Political Affairs,* May 1946, pp. 457-478. Weiss, a student leader in the early thirties, rapidly became a Young Communist official, residing in Moscow at the end of the decade in the Young Communist International's service. A staunch Browder man, he became an equally staunch anti-Browder man and was entrusted in the late forties with some of the Party's most important assignments. He was also a key figure in the underground of the early fifties, and then became a most outspoken critic of previous policy as soon as the 20th Congress gave sanction to such criticism. But he was evidently alienated from the Dennis-Hall-Foster leadership. Not in the "revisionist" movement of 1957, he seems to have dropped out of all visible activity after 1958.

28. *Political Affairs,* January 1947, p. 9. The resolution itself and remarks on it by the Negro commission's chairman, Benjamin J. Davis, Jr., appear in the February 1947 *Political Affairs.*

29. *Political Affairs,* January 1947, pp. 54-58.

30. *New Masses,* October 23, 1954. On the milieu from which Schneider came, see Malcolm Cowley's *Exile's Return* (New York: W. W. Norton, 1924), Samuel Putnam's *Paris Was Our Mistress* (New York: Viking Press, 1947), and Matthew Josephson, *Infidel in the Temple* (New York: A. A. Knopf, 1967).

31. *Daily Worker,* February 12, 1946. See also *Daily Worker,* March 2, 1946. Gold's penchant for a simplistic answer to every problem had been noted before by Josephine Herbst, whose controversy with Gold was an earlier edition of the Maltz affair. (See *New Masses,* February 18 and March 10, 1936). See also Harold Cruse, *The Crisis of the Negro Intellectual* (New York: William Morrow, 1967), pp. 49-51.

32. For Maltz's recantation, see *New Masses,* April 19, 1946. See also his message to the symposium which was held on Party policy, *Daily Worker,* April 18, 1946. William Z. Foster took part in the symposium.

33. Probably the foremost of those who left the Party's orbit because of the implications of the Maltz affair was the playwright Arthur Miller. The most useful summaries of the Maltz affair are found in Irving Howe and Lewis Coser, *The American Communist Party* (New York: Praeger, 1962) and in Daniel Aaron, *Writers on the Left* (New York: Harcourt, Brace & World, 1961).

34. In *Political Affairs,* September 1946, p. 781, the issue which carried the Dennis remarks, he is quoted as saying that the American monopolists were "hell-bent on building an Ango-American axis," and the "extreme war-mongers, intoxicated with the atom bomb" were "oriented on provoking, at the earliest possible date, a new world war — a military conflict between the Anglo-Saxon powers and the U.S.S.R." In light of the self-criticism of ten years later, this statement reveals

how closely Dennis hewed to Foster's views. Yet the thrust of his warnings against the Party's isolation was not in consonance with Foster at all, and in part a hidden polemic with him.

35. *Political Affairs*, September 1946, p. 795.

36. *Ibid.*, p. 795

37. Robert W. Kenny, Attorney-General of California, who ran for the gubernatorial nomination in the June 1946 primary and was defeated by Earl Warren, told me in the late fifties that he, Kenny had been defeated not by Warren but "by a Frenchman named Duclos." This was Kenny's way of criticising the California Communists on whose activity he depended for many of his votes.

38. *Political Affairs*, September 1946, p. 796.

39. *Ibid.*, p. 797.

40. *Ibid.*, p. 798.

41. *Ibid.*, p. 806.

42. For details of the Wallace-Truman break, see Curtis D. MacDougall, *Gideon's Army* (New York: Marzani & Munsell, 1965), vol. I, pp. 54-80.

43. The United Automobile Workers Union was dominated for most of the forties by a combination of rather routine factions and the Communists. The president before Reuther was R. J. Thomas, who depended heavily on his secretary-treasurer, George Addes.

44. For a useful discussion of the "party-missionary type" in the labor movement, see Harold L. Wilensky, *Intellectuals in Labor Unions* (Glencoe: The Free Press, 1956). See also Len DeCaux, *Labor Radical* (Boston: Beacon Press, 1970).

45. *Labor and Socialism*, privately published in September 1948 by Americus, a pseudonym for Earl Browder, gives a historical review. See also Browder's *The Decline of the Left Wing of American Labor*, (privately published, December 1948). For greater historical perspective, see Louis S. Reed, *The Labor Philosophy of Samuel Gompers* (New York: Prentice Hall, 1951). See also, J.B.S. Hardman and Maurice F. Neufeld, *The House of Labor* (New York: Columbia University Press, 1930).

46. Daniel Bell in his *Marxian Socialism in the United States* (Princeton: Princeton University Press, 1968) — written during Bell's tenure as labor editor of *Fortune* — cites a rise of union membership from three million to fourteen million by the war's end.

47. For details on the aborted Conference of Progressives, see MacDougall, *Gideon's Army*, vol. I, pp. 105-106.

48. MacDougall, *Gideon's Army*, vol. I, p. 109. It is useful to compare Max Kampelman's *The Communist Party and the C.I.O.* (New York: Praeger, 1957) which indicates plainly how impatient the Social-Democratic and A.C.T.U. leaders were with Murray's reluctance to start a witch hunt against the left.

49. On the eve of my Latin American visit Dennis was most anxious that Party leaders in the hemisphere be aware of why the Party entertained and supported the "resent and reject" declaration. Dennis assumed that everyone was watching the U.S. Party. More important, he was sensitive to the underlying issue.

50. Bridges, the most effective of the left wing leaders and relatively the most powerful of them in terms of his position as West Coast regional director of the C.I.O. and head of a critically important union, had been molded in the I.W.W. long before his contact with the Communists. His syndicalism also was part of his Australian heritage. Anyone who knew Bridges well in the fifties, after the Party's collapse, realized how deeply he was affected by syndicalist conceptions of Party and union: he often spoke of the I.L.W.U. as a surrogate party on the West Coast and in Hawaii. This was more of a boast than a reality. See N. 51, Chapter 2 and N. 17, Chapter 4.

51. This speech is often viewed by students of Soviet policy as a milestone in the Cold War. Dennis cited it early in 1946 as confirmation of the American Party's course, but there was much in Soviet policy at the time which contradicts this view.

52. *Political Affairs,* November 1946, p. 868.

53. *Ibid.,* p. 968.

54. This revelation, which shows that the Thompson-Davis faction had formed as early as 1946, was coupled with the news that the National Board had been obliged the previous July to criticize the New York Party for a leftist and sectarian line of conduct, a criticism which had been accepted, at least formally. Max Gordon, the *Daily Worker's* editor for N.Y. state politics and a member of the Party's State Board at that time, told me in a letter of February, 1971 that the Dennis criticism of the N.Y. leadership arose from a statement by Robert Thompson that if the "Hillman leaders" of the American Labor Party would not split with the Truman administration, the Communists "would break with Hillman within the A.L.P." Thompson denied this statement. But there was enough evidence of "leftist" moods in New York that the National Board censured the state leadership. Gordon adds that "Morris Childs (then the paper's editor) and I were under constant pressure and criticism from Thompson and others for the way we handled political and electoral developments."

55. *Political Affairs,* January 1947, pp. 15-16.


CHAPTER 7. DUBIOUS BATTLES AND CRUCIAL
DECISIONS, 1947-48

1. William Z. Foster, *The New Europe* (New York: International Publishers, 1947).

2. Many years later, John Gates recalled that Foster told his col-

leagues what he, Foster, had told the Europeans but did not spell out what the Europeans had said by way of rebuttal.

3. *Political Affairs,* September 1948, p. 823.

4. Tim Buck, *Europe's Rebirth* (Toronto: Progress Books, 1947), p. 97.

5. For a vivid picture of Wallace's impact in the spring and summer of 1947, see chapter 8 of Curtis MacDougall's *Gideon's Army* (New York: Marzani & Munsell, 1965), vol. I.

6. See Williamson's report to the June 1947 plenary session of the Party's National Committee in *Political Affairs,* August, 1947, pp. 701-715.

7. For the precise evolution of the third party decision, the most valuable record is volume I of Curtis MacDougall's *Gideon's Army,* chapters 9 and 10. See also Karl Schmidt, *Henry A. Wallace, Quixotic Crusader* (Syracuse, Syracuse University Press, 1960). Angus Cameron, in 1947 an editor of Little, Brown, the Boston publishing house, and a leader of the Progressive Citizens of America in Massachusetts (later chairman of the Massachusetts Progressive Party), recalled that early in 1947, after his circles had begun to organize for a third party, the Communists in Boston suddenly indicated their resistance to it. Discussing this experience with me twenty years later, Cameron said that he could not comprehend the Party's effort to put brakes on a movement which it had earlier stimulated and was to support so feverishly within the year. Cameron was, of course, unaware of what was going on among the Communists.

8. For the full text of Gates' report to the June 27-30 National Committee meeting, see *Political Affairs,* August 1947, p. 728. The Gates report, like the statements by Dennis, reflected what Morris Childs, editor of the *Daily Worker,* brought back from his visit to Moscow just prior to the June meeting. According to Philip Jaffe, Childs spent a long hour with the prominent Soviet Communist, Solomon Lozovsky, who had followed the American C.P.'s doings since the early twenties and had in that period been one of Browder's mentors. (Lozovsky, head of the Soviet Information Bureau during the war, was purged by the early fifties). The weight of Lozovsky's views was that a third world war was not in the cards. As regards a third party in the United States, Lozovsky saw plainly that it would ruin the American C.P.'s position in the labor movement, and he told Childs, "In trade union tactics it is not the job of a labor leader to cooperate with the more radical political leaders but it is the job of the radical political leaders to cooperate with the labor leaders." Also according to Jaffe, Childs met with Jacques Duclos in Paris and asked the French Communist leader whether another "letter" to the American C.P. might not be helpful as the first one had been two years

before. Duclos is supposed to have replied: "Look at what you did with the last one."

9. William Z. Foster, *Political Affairs,* August, 1947, pp. 675-687.

10. Dennis, "Concluding Remarks at the Plenum," *Political Affairs,* August 1947, pp. 688-700. It should be noted that in the September 1947 *Political Affairs,* Jack Stachel stressed the same themes and flatly declared: "It can be accepted as a fact that the Communists alone, and even with them the Left supporters in the labor and people's movement will not and cannot organize a third party." The authoritative commentator, A. B. Magil, whose polemics the previous winter against premature third party tendencies have been cited, declared in *New Masses,* September 23, 1947: "It remains true that without the active participation of a substantial section of the trade union movement and without the support of a large number of Democratic voters, no serious new party can be formed."

11. Bryson was tried in the early fifties on the charge of perjury in signing the Taft-Hartley non-Communist affidavit, and served a prison sentence. During that time, his union fell apart (as did many of the smaller left-led unions); most of it was absorbed by the I.L.W.U. When I interviewed Bryson in July 1967, the latter was unable to recall any of the details of the third-party movement.

12. The California Legislative Conference, an established institution since World War II, brought together every variety of organization to discuss statewide legislative problems. At its August 24, 1947, meeting, 1214 delegates were present, representing union locals, Townsend clubs, youth organizations, and including prominent Democrats, Republicans and independents. The Bryson caucus for an independent party met Sunday afternoon, one hour after the Legislative Conference dispersed. Kenny, who was to debate Bryson at the conference, had been called East to substitute on a radio program for Fiorello La Guardia, the former mayor of New York, who was seriously ill. But the two proposed tactics were presented, with Bryson arguing strongly that an Independent Progressive Party (as it came to be called) would help, not hinder, the Democrats-for-Wallace.

13. The details of this encounter were first told to me in July 1966, by Mrs. Eleanor Abewitz, Kenny's secretary in the Hollywood Democratic Party Committee twenty years earlier. The meeting was confirmed by Kenny himself on July 23, 1967. Kenny remembers that the meeting took place after the Legislative Conference (hence late in August or early September 1947). "I shook him up," Kenny declared about his impact on Foster, but he "must have gotten unshook afterwards." Kenny himself, now a municipal judge and no longer a power in Democratic circles in California, was seriously shaken by the Wallace adventure. In response to my question as to why he did not fight

for a Wallace candidacy in the Democratic Party more strongly, Kenny replied that he did not quite know the answer himself. Looking back on the matter, he felt (in 1967) that twenty years before he had been in a dilemma. So many prominent liberals were resigning from organizations in which the left was involved that he, Kenny, did not wish to follow their pattern. On the other hand, he had become something of a *papier-maché* figure, he felt, lending his prestige to left causes but unable to influence their course. Kenny tried all during the autumn of 1947 to dissuade Wallace from announcing an independent party. As late as the spring of 1948 (Kenny said in 1967) he had "half-persuaded" Wallace's running mate, Senator Glen Taylor of Idaho, that Wallace ought to enter the California Democratic primary and turn to the Democratic convention, but Wallace himself "was too far gone." After supporting Wallace's decision at the end of 1947, Kenny increasingly despaired of Wallace's 1948 prospects and toward the close of the campaign was one of the many who dissociated himself from Wallace. Curtis MacDougall, *Gideon's Army,* vol. I, p. 191, quotes a "post-mortem" letter from Kenny: "We needed a third party here like a hole in the head. We had control of a second party and might have remained in control had it not been for this alien doctrine which came in from the East and dictated that the Left Wing sever itself from the Democratic Party and go into seclusion as a separate Independent Progressive Party. Such a move might have been wise in Pennsylvania but it was utter folly in California."

14. On September 11, President Truman rebuked the Democratic chairman, Gael Sullivan, for suggesting that neither Senator Claude Pepper nor Henry Wallace would be welcome to speak for the Democratic campaign. The President was not ready to rule out some relationship with Wallace and his closest supporters.

15. MacDougall, *Gideon's Army,* vol. I, pp. 228, 239.

16. Probably the most fascinating example of how uncertain Henry Wallace was about his decision to run as an independent, and whether it was wise at all, is to be found in MacDougall's revelation that even after the December 2 and December 5, 1947, meetings of the Progressive Citizens of America, at which the decisions were taken, some of Wallace's closest friends were dubious. Thus, still another meeting was called on December 15, 1947 — this time, a meeting of the board of the Progressive Citizens of America. MacDougall (*Gideon's Army,* vol. I, p. 236) reveals that "at this stage Beanie Baldwin was working 'tooth and nail' to get Henry Wallace to commit himself and was taking no chances on being exposed to any influences which might delay or distract him in making up his mind. The charge that he [Baldwin] acted in a highhanded fashion as regards to P.C.A. was, I believe, justified." Two days later, Wallace met with some of his

close friends at the Hotel McAlpin. As MacDougall reports it, "although he had already given his consent to run," Wallace "expressed concern about the new party's potential labor support. He looked around the room and declared that it looked as though the movement would be almost entirely a middle-class one." This was also the concern of Alfred K. Stern, a close friend of Wallace who proposed the next day that "the announcement of Wallace's candidacy be delayed until a nationwide canvass could be made of the sentiment of local labor leaders." Baldwin is reported to have "severely chastised" Stern. The same day labor delegations from left wing unions began to descend on Wallace assuring him of support. On the same day also, student groups came to reassure Wallace. Thus, as late as December 18 — and that date is quite important, as will be shown later — there was profound indecision in Wallace's own camp on the vital matter of whether he would run as an independent Democrat or on a third party ticket. On December 29, 1947, Wallace finally declared himself publicly for a third party.

17. *Daily People's World,* July 26, 1947. The argument between supporters of the I.P.P. and those who wanted Wallace to run as a Democrat can best be followed in the West Coast Communist paper throughout this period. Bryson's position took prominent place in that paper's Labor Day supplement. Its most astute columnist, Adam Lapin, reflected in his articles all the disagreements among progressives, and also the strong doubt in Communist ranks about a third party.

18. *Daily People's World,* August 4, 1947.

19. *Daily People's World,* September 3, 1947.

20. Hollander related this incident to the Amalgamated Clothing Workers convention at Atlantic City, N. J., on May 14, 1948, by which time the left wing had broken even with their previous allies, the Murray-Hillman forces. Hollander's account is contained in Curtis MacDougall, *Gideon's Army,* vol. I, pp. 250-251. In the same book (p. 258), Ruth Young and Saul Mills are quoted as denying Hollander's report, arguing that it was "an attempt to bolster his own sinking morale." MacDougall cites conversations with another prominent labor leader who also had drinks with Potash at Saratoga Springs and who is reported to believe that Potash was himself very favorable to a third party at that time. But if Stachel's strictures against a third party that did not include the Amalgamated, and Magil's articles in the same vein in August-September 1947 are recalled, the original Hollander account seems believable. The point is not that the Communists did not want a third party; they had wanted it since late in 1945. The point is that they hesitated throughout 1947, fearing its consequences for their position in the labor movement.

21. George Morris, the *Daily Worker's* labor editor, reporting the Boston convention (*Daily People's World,* October 20, 1947), indicates plainly the Party's desperate effort to maintain the left-center alliance. "There is no group in the C.I.O. that could take a convention majority by itself. Even the Rights and Lefts are coalitions, and they in turn are making bids for the middle-of-the-roaders. So you are bound to have compromises in resolutions and decisions. . . . I am not suggesting that Murray wants it that way. He wants to maintain some sort of teamwork in the C.I.O. and this is his way of pulling together the groups within it. He is doing it despite his own inclination. I don't know of another man sitting in this convention who would be more successful in such an effort." As late as October 20, Murray was viewed as trying to hold his organization together despite his own views. In effect the Communists were conceding that agreement with Murray was possible unless a move to break this area of agreement came as a result of new issues on which the C.I.O.'s president would have to be irreconcilable. See also John Williamson's call for "re-establishing the Center-Left alliance" in his summary of the complex events in the labor movement, *Daily People's World,* September 26, 1947.

22. Stewart Alsop, in his column of November 16, 1947, wrote: "It is difficult to overestimate the meaning of Walter Reuther's overwhelming victory at the United Automobile Worker's convention in Atlantic City this week. For the Communists have lost their last chance to dominate or deeply influence an important segment of the American labor movement. . . . In doing so they have lost their last chance to dominate or deeply influence the whole American political Left." Alsop speculated in this column that Lee Pressman's position as the C.I.O.'s general counsel would be jeopardized and that the United Electrical Workers would be subject to raiding. "Thus, the whole internal balance of power in the C.I.O. has been overturned and will be overturned still further."

23. Larsen was among the few trade unionists who faced the Smith Act trials in the early 1950's. Larsen was acquitted, after conducting his defense independently of the Communist Party officials in the State of Washington.

24. Lewis' action undoubtedly contributed to the left wing's decision to exacerbate relations within the C.I.O., since so many of its leaders had come to power under Lewis' wing in the thirties. Many of these leaders were to continue seeking the will-o'-the-wisp of a "third labor federation," together with Lewis, after the eleven Communist-dominated unions were expelled. See the left wing monthly, *March of Labor,* in the early fifties. See also N. 15, Chapter 1.

25. Gilbert Green, the Illinois Communist leader, writing in the *Daily Worker* of December 9, 1947, (pp. 1112-1119) was very circum-

spect in treating the judicial elections, and warned: "It would be highly dangerous to exaggerate what took place." He noted that the election contained "certain peculiarities that will not repeat themselves in the same way or form." Thus Green reflected the characteristic caution about a national third party. Yet undeniably the Chicago results influenced and encouraged Wallace's friends in Illinois. See MacDougall, *Gideon's Army,* vol. I, pp. 193-195.

26. For the Cominform background, see Adam Ulam, *Titoism and the Cominform* (Cambridge: Harvard University Press, 1952). See also Eugenio Reale, *Avec Jacques Duclos au Banc des Accusés* (Paris: Mondadori, 1958).

27. *Political Affairs,* December 1947, pp. 1141-1142, gives the full text.

28. As has been noted earlier, the Yugoslav Party secretary, Edvard Kardelj, had expressed the opinion the previous winter that "no temporary stabilization of capitalism" was probable. See *Political Affairs,* June 1947. Foster was thus closer to the Yugoslav view (that is, to the left within international Communism) at that time than any other.

29. *Political Affairs,* September 1948, p. 824.

30. Michael Straight, then editor of the *New Republic,* who accompanied Henry Wallace on a quick visit to Palestine in the first days of October 1947, is reported by Curtis MacDougall (*Gideon's Army,* vol. I, p. 264) to have recognized that the announcement of the Cominform would have the effect of forcing the American left wing to press for a third party. I questioned Mr. Straight, twenty years later, in an interview on May 16, 1967, and he confirmed this recollection. He could not explain why, but he remembered feeling that the Cominform's establishment would end indecision in the Wallace entourage.

31. MacDougall, *Gideon's Army,* vol. I, p. 213.

32. The importance of the Rogge revelation in changing the American Party's attitude was first suggested to me by George Watt. (See chapter 9.) Watt, who was secretary of the National Cadre and Review Commission and played a vital part in the 1950-1953 events (he was in charge of the ill-fated attempt by Gus Hall to go abroad via Mexico) indicated to me in two conversations (January 27, and December 26, 1968) that the underground preparations had begun late in 1947 and had continued to occupy Watt throughout much of 1948.

33. The three news reports came from Alfred Friendly, in the *Washington Post* of May 2, 1948; Victor Riesel, in the *New York Post,* May 7, and Edwin Lahey, in the *Chicago Daily News,* May 17. Extensive quotations from all these reports, plus commentaries, are found in Curtis MacDougall, *Gideon's Army,* vol. I, pp. 251-263.

34. Use of the term "Central Committee" is one of the details which gives this account authenticity. To Quill, who had been working with

the Party for twenty years, the use of the older term, "Central Committee," instead of the modern term, "National Committee," would have been altogether appropriate. Thompson, as a younger man and a Party official, might not have used the term "Central Committee." But Quill, in reporting Thompson's speech, almost certainly would have done so.

35. The phrase "crack-pot Foster" is another detail which authenticates the Quill document. On April 15, 1948, Quill sent a letter to Communist leaders abroad explaining the crisis of the American left. He did so on Transport Workers' Union stationery. A draft of this document will be found in the personal papers of Earl Browder at the University of Syracuse. Browder, who was on Quill's payroll in 1948, undoubtedly had a hand in this letter, in which the same derogatory phrase — "crack-pot-Foster" — appears. Whether this was Michael Quill's language or Browder's, it surely coincides with the strong feelings of Browder against Foster. That Quill was being coached by Browder or was collaborating with him is suggestive of Browder's "anti-Party" activity in this period; it casts doubt on his integrity in applying for reinstatement in the Party a few months later. Browder did not, as we have seen, try to form a faction in the Party, but he did try to influence Party policy through his ties with the Party's influentials.

36. At first Quill went along with the C.P.'s policy despite his misgivings. He joined the Labor Committee for Wallace, argued at the January 22, 1948, C.I.O. Executive Board meeting on Wallace's behalf, and did not break with his friends in the New York labor movement and within the Transport Workers' Union until April 1948. MacDougall is puzzled by this fact. But it is entirely consistent with the behavior of dissidents within a Communist movement. Dissidents rarely break cleanly or immediately. They tend to give the Party the benefit of the doubt while arguing their case. In the Quill instance, there is evidence from his testimony at the I.L.W.U. trial in 1950 that he went to see Foster and even sought out the onetime Comintern "rep," Gerhart Eisler, to plead against the Party's line. It is this very inconsistency in his behavior — strange to students who have no experience with Communism — which authenticates the Quill memorandum. He broke with the Party in a traumatic frame of mind after much soul searching and maneuvering. He continued to feel both self-justification and guilt, as is clear from the ouster of his old friends who had built the T.W.U. with him and some of whom he later returned to power. In the fifties Quill was often to propose "a Labor Party" at the C.I.O. conventions. Curiously, even the men against whom he testified, such as Harry Bridges, were to become cordial to Quill in his last years. Bridges told me in the summer of 1966 that he had given Quill advice on the New York subway strike earlier that year.

37. Reference has already been made to the comprehensive and sympathetic study by Curtis MacDougall, *Gideon's Army,* and the discussion by Karl Schmidt for the Syracuse University Press. A contrasting view is found in the unpublished doctoral dissertation of John Cotton Brown entitled: "The 1948 Progressive Campaign: a Scientific Approach" in the library of the University of Chicago. Brown's professor, Rexford Guy Tugwell, presided over the P.P.'s Platform Committee, and Brown had access to its proceedings as Tugwell's assistant. Mention has also been made of an analysis by Harvey Brandt for Columbia University and a firsthand account of the Progressives in California which became Merrill Raymond Moreman's master's essay for Stanford University. Rexford Guy Tugwell's postmortem discussion in the April 1949 *Progressive* is essential for an understanding of the Wallace movement. Irwin Ross' study of the Truman candidacy, *The Loneliest Campaign* (New York: New American Library, 1968), is also useful, as are the polemical contemporary writings of Dwight Macdonald and James A. Wechsler. See also I. F. Stone's contemporary view, his column of August 25, 1948, which forms an essay in his *The Truman Era* (New York: Monthly Review Press, 1953); Samuel Lubell's *The Future of American Politics,* rev. ed. (New York: Anchor, 1956) and Eric Goldman's *The Crucial Decade: America, 1945-1955* (New York: Knopf, 1956).

38. See the A.D.A.'s propaganda throughout 1948 that the idea of the third party originated with the C.P. and even with Jacques Duclos' article. Dorothy Thompson and others also sought to establish this without ever exploring the matter in any depth. See MacDougall, *Gideon's Army,* vol. I, chapter 13; and vol. III, chapter 35. See also the A.D.A.'s mimeographed report, *Henry A. Wallace: The First Three Months,* cited by MacDougall, *Gideon's Army,* vol. I, pp. 272-273.

39. It is one of the peculiarities of Communist conduct (and perhaps of all human conduct) that in facing new problems the past is evoked as though it holds the answer. Even when people have had a bitter experience with past policies and have criticized themselves for it, they tend to return to the past for guidance. They rarely return to the immediate past generation. They skip a generation and go back to their grandfathers. Foster went back to the 1890s and 1912 just as the new left today skips the Communist experience to go back to the anarcho-syndicalism of pre-Communist days.

40. In the *Daily Worker,* December 27, 1947, Dennis answered questions about a third party — on the eve of Wallace's announcement — and used the term "united front from below," a throwback to the period *prior* to the People's Front.

41. *Political Affairs,* March 1948, p. 217.

42. MacDougall, *Gideon's Army,* vol. III, p. 612.

43. MacDougall, *Gideon's Army*, vol. III, p. 613. Only a few left-led unions endorsed Wallace — the Food and Tobacco Workers, the Furniture Workers, the Fur Workers, the Marine Cooks and Stewards, and the Mine, Mill and Smelter Workers. Within larger unions, such as the I.L.W.U. and the U.E., the issue was left to the autonomous decision of local unions and individual conscience. The chairman of the National Labor Committee for Wallace, Albert J. Fitzgerald, president of the United Electrical Workers, discovered at the U.E.'s convention in September 1948 that if he and his associates pressed for endorsement of Wallace, the union would be split wide open. Therefore, they left the entire issue up to individual choice. Harry Bridges, as MacDougall notes, did not campaign actively for Wallace, apart from chairing a Wallace meeting in San Francisco. In the autumn of 1948 the longshoremen were engaged in a bitter 99-day strike. Bridges was thus able to concentrate on union matters and leave politics alone — a course of action which coincided with his anarcho-syndicalist background and temperament. Even in California, where the I.P.P. had been launched by a trade union committee, only a brief list of local unions finally rallied to its support. In New York, the Wallace issue caused the Amalgamated Clothing Workers to withdraw from the American Labor Party. Throughout the C.I.O. the local industrial union councils controlled by the left wing were taken over or dissolved or competitive groups were established if these left-led councils failed to back away from the Wallace endorsement as demanded by the national C.I.O. Whatever else may be said of the million votes for Wallace, it was not primarily a labor vote.

44. Wallace was accompanied in the South and on most of his tours before black audiences by Charles P. Howard, of Iowa, well-known figure in Republican and Negro fraternal organizations, and by Clark Foreman, a white New Dealer who had been the key figure in the Southern Conference of Human Welfare, the grouping of progressive Southerners so helpful to F. D. R. In addition, W. E. B. DuBois and Paul Robeson, the outstanding artist, supported Wallace. Locally, such prestigious figures as Larkin Marshall, of Georgia; Roscoe Dunjee, editor of the *Oklahoma Black Dispatch;* and Earl Dickerson, the outstanding Chicago attorney, worked for Wallace. Joe Louis, the boxing champion, and Canada Lee, the actor, were also in Wallace's corner. Excellent organizers worked in the Wallace headquarters, such as Louis Burnham, who had won his spurs in the Southern Negro Youth Congress, and George P. Murphy, Jr., whose family controlled the *Baltimore Afro-American.*

45. George P. Murphy, Jr., in *The Crisis,* October 1948.

46. MacDougall, *Gideon's Army,* vol. III, p. 664.

47. MacDougall points out that on May 3, 1948, the Supreme Court outlawed restrictive real estate covenants and on April 19, 1948, up-

held the Waring decision prohibiting South Carolina's attempt to restrict Negro voting in Democratic primaries. Barney Conal, the Progressive Party's vote analyst, estimated that if Wallace had run in the early 1948 primaries, he would have had 85 percent of the Negro vote. Henry L. Moon, the N.A.A.C.P.'s director of research, is quoted by MacDougall as saying that, although the Wallace vote was higher among Negroes than among other sectors of the population, 69 percent of the black vote went to Truman.

48. Wallace had been Secretary of Agriculture from the first Roosevelt cabinet until 1940, when he became vice-president. C. B. Baldwin, his 1948 campaign manager, had been his key aide as head of the Farm Security Administration. Rexford Guy Tugwell, onetime professor of economics at Columbia, had become Wallace's chief assistant in agricultural affairs and in 1948 was chairman of the Progressive Party's platform committee. Many of the key "brains" of the campaign had served Wallace in the Department of Agriculture (e.g., Charles Kramer).

49. It will be recalled that in 1947 Dennis had broached the need for popularizing the idea of nationalization on the assumption that to do so raised the independent and third party tendencies to a higher level of political consciousness. The idea was reflected in the May 1948 "draft resolutions" for the Communist Party's August 1948 convention. But the Sweezy-Huberman initiative within the Wallace movement was quite independent of the C.P. Both men had little regard for the Communists and derived their socialism from a different tradition.

50. It is interesting that the Communist Party made no appearance before the Progressive Party's platform committee, although many other organizations, including the Americans for Democratic Action, did so. The C.P. could have appeared and used the occasion to underline the distinction between itself and Wallace, an act which might have helped him.

51. MacDougall, *Gideon's Army*, vol. II, p. 423.

52. MacDougall's detailed study of the campaign shows the evolution of this crucial idea. See *Gideon's Army*, vol. II, pp. 423, 426, and 427.

53. *Daily Worker*, January 16, 1948.

54. Serious problems arose in getting the Progressive Party under way in a variety of states partly because onetime Communists came to the surface in its organization. They were easily exposed in the press, and yet appeared for a time to be quite indispensable. (See MacDougall's account of the problems in Pennsylvania, Colorado, Ohio, and Nebraska.) In some cases, former unionists closely associated with the Party were called upon to do the organizational work. They were often more intractable in relations with non-Communists

than they might have been if under Party discipline. In the instance of the Colorado Progressive Party, which MacDougall describes in detail, the conflicts between different C.P. factions served to alienate non-Communist liberals and give them an easy excuse to step away from the movement they had themselves started and whose prospects were by mid-1948 so poor that they wanted to disavow it.

55. MacDougall, *Gideon's Army*, vol. II, p. 545.

56. As MacDougall says (*Gideon's Army*, vol. III, p. 866) the quixotic behavior of the non-Communists around Wallace cost them heavily. "It is not mere rationalization for many of them to believe today that it would have been better to have remained within the Democratic Party." Very few of the Progressives ever participated thereafter in recognizable roles within the Democratic Party, except perhaps for Paul O'Dwyer in New York, whose renaissance has come only recently. C. B. Baldwin, whose reputation for political expertise was great, was ignored when he announced himself for Adlai Stevenson in 1952. Baldwin broke with the remnants of "Gideon's Army" in 1952 and played no part in the 1952 Hallinan-Bass campaign, but was accepted only as a "private" in Stevenson's campaign.

57. It is not without ironic interest that the organization which set itself the most explicit anti-Communist tasks, the Americans for Democratic Action, prospered after a faltering start in 1947, by the technique of becoming a lobby but not a party. It became the mirror image in organizational terms of what Browder had envisaged for the Communist Political Association. Once the ban on labor participation in the A.D.A. was lifted early in 1948 — Philip Murray had tried to avert a schism within his own movement by vetoing labor participation in either the A.D.A. or the P.C.A. — the Americans for Democratic Action became an important non-party force.

58. Alvarez del Vayo, the exiled foreign minister of the Spanish Republic and believer to the end that coalition with the Communists was desirable, wrote in the *Nation*, on July 10, 1948, that the expulsion of the Yugoslavs could only mean a "revision of the Communist position in relation to other left groups and workingclass parties." V. J. Jerome, in *Political Affairs* for August 1948, took issue with Del Vayo's pregnant foreboding without admitting its relevance to the American Communist Party's tactics in the Wallace movement.

59. Earl Browder's application for return to party membership was brusquely turned down at the 14th National Convention. He then proceeded to analyze this Convention in a series of privately published pamphlets, *Labor and Socialism in America, The Decline of the Left Wing of American Labor,* and *Where Do We Go from Here?* All three pamphlets are caustic rebuttals of Foster's course and confirmations that Browder would hardly have been at home in the Party in 1948-1949. The Tito heresy, which Browder defended several years

later and then only briefly, was thus exploited by him in a most futile fashion. He did not recognize to what extent his own course had been the forerunner of the centrifugal forces at work in Communism. He clung to orthodoxy long after his career in Communism had ended and any hope of a return to it was foreclosed.

60. MacDougall, *Gideon's Army,* vol. II, p. 571. For the full text of the convention debate see pp. 571-578. A preview of this attempt to hold both the U.S. and the U.S.S.R. responsible for the Cold War had come to the Platform Committee. A motion to this effect by Frederick L. Schuman was opposed by the Progressive Party's vice-presidential candidate, Senator Glen Taylor (see MacDougall, *Gideon's Army,* vol. II, p. 566) and was changed to make ending the threat of war the joint responsibility of both the U.S. and the U.S.S.R.

61. The Vermont resolution continued to echo in the campaign, notably in California. At the Independent Progressive Party's convention in Sacramento, on August 7, 1948, the brother of Senator Glen Taylor, who was also a local candidate, had to "pace the floor to cool off" after a local version of the Vermont resolution was defeated. As a result of this defeat, twelve members of the San Mateo Progressive Club resigned, among them Robert C. North, who was to become a professor of political science at Stanford University. North called my attention to this episode as proof of how non-Communist progressives could not get along in a movement with "persons who sounded like Communists" and whose reply to people like North was that "we can get along without the liberals" — a rejoinder that has a modern ring today. North, whose conversations with me took place in the summer of 1966, seems to have been the major source for the Stanford University master's essay, "The Independent Progressive Party in California, 1948," by Merrill Raymond Moreman.

### CHAPTER 8. INCOHERENCE AND AGONY

1. Hans Toch, *The Social Psychology of Social Movements* (Indianapolis: Bobbs-Merrill, 1965), throws some light on these phenomena.

2. Arthur Koestler, *Arrow in the Blue* (New York: Macmillan, 1961), p. 288.

3. In the *Blau* case, the Supreme Court held that a witness who took the Fifth Amendment on any question had to continue to use it throughout the interrogation. This led to testimony which became utterly unintelligible to the lay public, involving refusal even to acknowledge one's name.

4. In the *Dennis* case and again in the instance of the Hollywood Writers, the use of the First Amendment had not been enough to avoid jail sentences for contempt.

5. For example, I found in 1953 that my name was on a blacklist. No insurance company would underwrite a policy of any kind until half a decade later.

6. In the fascinating symposium by prominent anti-Communist liberals and radicals in *Commentary*, September 1967, this complicity of the labor-liberal element in McCarthyism is evaded. That evasion makes much of the symposium rather hollow.

7. Among these was the playwright Lillian Hellman. The lawyer O. John Rogge, active in Progressive Party affairs, became suspect because of his work for the Yugoslav interests in the United States. William Gailmor, the "pitchman" in the Wallace campaign, was castigated for visiting Belgrade and writing about the Yugoslavs sympathetically in the *New York Post*. Louis Adamic, the writer, sided with Tito and lost standing among those who considered him a progressive.

8. In resigning from his post as distributor of Soviet scientific books, Browder (letter to Moscow of June 13, 1949) said that he remained an "unshakeable partisan of Socialist construction in the USSR" and asked that this stance be indicated to "responsible personalities in the USSR upon whose advice "he originally accepted the position" he was "now forced to resign." See Browder's private papers, in the Syracuse University Library.

9. For example, see the bitter attack by John Gates in *Political Affairs*, June 1949, and by Gilbert Green, in the October and November 1949, and March 1950 issues.

10. For a sympathetic portrait of Perry (who, like Foster and E. G. Flynn, died in Moscow in the early sixties), see Richard O. Boyer, *Pettis Perry: the Story of a Working Class Leader* (New York: Self-Defense Committee of the 17 Smith Act Victims, 1952). Perry's *Political Affairs* article appeared in October 1949.

11. This happened to Isadore Begun, the Party's Bronx, New York, leader, and Fred Bassett Blair, secretary for Wisconsin.

12. Robert Thompson, "Strengthen the Struggle against White Chauvinism," *Political Affairs*, June 1949. See also Pettis Perry, "Press Forward the Fight Against White Chauvinism," *Political Affairs*, May 1950. See Shannon, *Decline of American Communism* (New York: Harcourt, Brace & World, 1959), chapter 7.

13. Only this background explains the present thinking of Harold Cruse, whose *Crisis of the Negro Intellectual* (New York: William Morrow, 1967) is currently popular. Cruse worked on the *Daily Worker* and was active in left wing Negro circles at the time of the disintegration, of which the "white chauvinism" campaign was one sign. He is the product of the late forties and early fifties, which explains what he learned and what never left him.

14. It took the article by William Z. Foster, "Left-Sectarianism in the Fight for Negro Rights and Against White Chauvinism," *Political*

*Affairs,* July 1953, to bring the Party's paroxysm to a close. See Shannon's treatment of its impact on the unions, especially the impact of the attack on District 65 of the Distributive, Processing and Office Workers' Union by "Alexander Kendrick" in the June 1953, *Political Affairs,* the second part of which never appeared. "Kendrick" was the underground pseudonym of Robert Thompson, whose conflicts with unionists have already been noted above. (See the Quill affair, chapter 7, above.)

15. Gold's resignation from the Party was followed a few years later by his ouster as president of the Furriers, with whom he had so long been identified. This was part of the price for the merger of the Furriers with the Amalgamated Meat Cutters and Butcher Workmen, an A.F.L. union headed by the onetime Socialist, Patrick Gorman. Gold's regime in the Furriers was a "cult of personality," and left a legacy of bitterness against him. He has remained a rank and file worker.

16. One victim of these changes, Donald Henderson, soon disappeared from the field. Hugh Bryson, convicted in the early fifties for perjury, was virtually abandoned by his I.L.W.U. friends. Frederick N. Myers, the famous "Blackie" of the Maritime Union, had great difficulty finding work in San Francisco. These were but the most prominent cases of outstanding men whom the left helped very little.

17. See the articles by "John Swift," the pseudonym of Gilbert Green, in *Political Affairs,* April and May 1952. See also *Political Affairs,* February 1953.

18. At one gathering, political commissars discussed the Lysenko ideas with the editors of *Science and Society,* the scholarly Marxist periodical then edited by the late Dr. Bernhard Stern, of Columbia University. Stern resisted the commissars, who felt that Lysenko's genetic theory had to be upheld simply because it had become orthodoxy in Moscow.

19. A. Landy, *Marxism and the Democratic Tradition* (New York: International, 1948). See Miss Gannett's article in *Political Affairs,* April 1951.

20. Miss Strong's book, *I Change Worlds* (New York: Holt, 1935) — a title characteristic of her generation of radicals — gives a vivid picture of how she came to confuse the frontier radicalism in which she was reared with the Soviet "experiment."

21. A characteristic tribute to Miss Strong's authenticity as a reporter is found in the moving self-defense of Owen Lattimore, *Ordeal by Slander* (Boston: Little, Brown, 1950), p. 163.

22. According to Earl Browder's account, in Columbia University's Oral History Project, Miss Strong's husband was the last Communist International "rep" in the U.S.

23. See Shannon, *Decline of American Communism,* pp. 234-235.

So far as I know, the only remonstrance by an American Communist came in the form of a private protest by Robert W. Dunn, of the Labor Research Association, to the Soviet Embassy in Washington. It is not known whether this letter was ever answered. My own behavior in this matter was nothing that I can be proud of. At the time of the accusations against her, "Anna Louise" sought me out, having read that I had been placed in charge of the Party's united front activities. I declined to see her. A year later, I did greet her at a San Francisco meeting, at which she sat forlorn and ostracized, and heard out her story that she had been mistreated by the Russians because she had tried to go to the Communist areas of China via Soviet transport at a moment when China's revolution was near its climax and the Moscow authorities felt this would embarrass them. But I did nothing to help her. It was not until 1956, when she was "rehabilitated," that C.P. people would associate with her. Many continued even then to believe the original charges.

24. I apologized to *Monthly Review* after I had left the Communist movement and at a time when efforts were being made by A. J. Muste to bring together diverse forces on the left, including the Communists, in the short-lived American Forum for Socialist Education. Sweezy and Huberman, whose distinctive brand of socialist thought has already been referred to in discussing the tribulations of the Progressive Party's convention in July 1948, continued to publish a lively and informative magazine. They continued to seek some variant of socialist thought that would distinguish them from the Communists, toward whom they had very mixed feelings. Both had cooperated at times with the Party, but neither had ever joined it. By the early sixties *Monthly Review* was undergoing intellectual upheavals of its own. It welcomed the Castro revolution in Cuba fervently. When the Sino-Soviet dispute came to the surface, it first supported the Soviet side and then abruptly decided that the Chinese were right, after all. In its March 1961 issue, *Monthly Review* paid tribute to William Z. Foster on the occasion of his death. Foster was the only American Communist leader for whom the editors appeared to have any regard, perhaps for the very reason that he symbolized the radical workingman of a by-gone time, with "fundamentalist" views that anticipated their own pro-Maoist orientation. In 1958, the late Paul Baran, professor of economics at Stanford University, opened a discussion of the crisis of Marxist thought, to which I contributed a piece critical of Baran's approach. Baran's past was mysterious. It was reported that at one time he had been an active functionary of the Young Communist International, had left his native Moscow for Berlin, then had come to the United States, where he met Paul Sweezy and worked for the O.S.S. Until the late fifties he was entirely unknown on the American left, but made an impression with his *Political Economy of Growth* (New

York: Monthly Review Press, 1957). In his reply to various contributions, Baran was extraordinarily contemptuous. He read me out of the socialist movement in a manner entirely reminiscent of Bittelman's assault on *Monthly Review*. It was the performance of a Stalinist *manqué*. In its evolution in the sixties *Monthly Review* has in many ways anticipated the ideas of the new left while retaining the allegiance of former influentials, people who had been in the Communist Party without ever accepting responsibility either for its successes or for its catastrophes. The magazine represented a trend which might be called "parisitism lost."

25. William Schneiderman, the California Communist leader, who was for a brief time national secretary and in charge of Party defense, put the matter this way: "We must so conduct the struggle that large masses of non-Communists will vigorously take the position that while they may disagree with the C.P. on this or that issue, they will fight for the civil rights of the Communists to advocate their program. With few exceptions, we have up to now not been conducting that kind of fight. . . . " (*Political Affairs,* October 1949, p. 121.)

26. Irving Stone, *Clarence Darrow for the Defense* (Garden City: Doubleday, Doran, 1941).

27. The Polish Workers Party Congress in December 1948 attracted a wide representation from the nonruling parties: it was in fact a turning point, the occasion for a general ideological mobilization of the international movement.

28. William Z. Foster, *Political Affairs,* June 1950, pp. 14-31. In a memorial booklet on the occasion of Foster's 70th birthday, February 25, 1951, published by the Educational Department of the N.Y. State Communist Party, Thompson singled out the June 1950 article as an example of Foster's capacity for self-criticism. This made it clear that the deposition at the Smith Act trial had been modified.

29. Throughout 1950 the American Communists wrestled with these matters and this helps explain their bewilderment at the British Party's new program. See chapter 9.

30. In his interview with me (November 16, 1966), John Caughlan, the Seattle attorney who defended the Washington State Communists, confirmed that they were under intense pressure from New York. This pressure was one of the reasons, he believed, for the suicide during the trial of the popular leader of the Washington Pension Union, William Pennock. The latter was a charismatic figure, an influential in the Northwest, who suddenly found himself obliged to defend abstruse, recondite political matters quite unrelated to the simple issue of pensions for the aged on which he had built, as an unavowed Communist, a powerful organization. Seattle also produced the ony case of a defendant becoming a government witness, Barbara Hartle.

31. For a study of the use of the Fifth Amendment and its problems,

see Daniel H. Pollitt, "The Fifth Amendment Plea Before Congressional Committees Investigating Subversion: Motives and Justifiable Presumption — a Survey of 120 Witnesses." *University of Pennsylvania Law Review*, 106 (1958) pp. 1117-1137.

32. Marshall Shulman's *Stalin's Foreign Policy Reappraised* (Cambridge: Harvard University Press, 1963) is useful for an overview of the peace campaign.

33. Lance Sharkey, the Australian C.P. leader at that time, served a year in jail for his declaration.

34. The Foster-Dennis statement said: "If, despite efforts of the peace camp of America and the world, Wall Street should succeed in plunging the world into war, we would oppose it as an unjust, aggressive, imperialist war, as an undemocratic and anti-Socialist war, destructive of the deepest interests of the American people and all humanity." The pledge was made to "defeat the war aims of U. S. imperialism and bring the war to a speedy conclusion on the basis of a democratic peace." See *Political Affairs*, April 1949, pp. 1-4.

35. It would be fascinating to compare Foster's views with those of, say, James Forrestal in the same period. See *The Forrestal Diaries*, ed. Walter Millis (New York: Viking, 1951). Forrestal, Truman's secretary of the navy and a prominent financier, appears to have resolved the intense contradiction within himself by suicide; Foster brought about the suicide of the American Communist Party, then climaxed the achievement by going to Moscow on his deathbed. I have pointed out the fact that Foster was given a solemn funeral by Soviet leaders although he had by then adopted the Maoist view of the world quite explicitly and had praised Mao as the foremost Marxist after Stalin, in my article in *International Communism after Khrushchev*, ed. Leo Labedz (Cambridge: M.I.T.-Wiley, 1965).

36. *Political Affairs*, February 1949, carried articles by Joseph Clark and George Siskind in which the concept of peaceful coexistence was for the first time given substantial treatment. In the October 1949 *Political Affairs*, Fred Fine attacked the "mischievous speculation" on the "imminence of war." In the May 1950 *Political Affairs* a letter by Foster to the March 23-25, 1950, National Committee meeting lamented as "tragic" the fact that "huge masses" of Americans, "perhaps the majority have been convinced by the liars of Wall Street that the U.S. is quite innocent, that the Soviet Union is completely to blame for the present dangerous cold war situation." But, he reaffirmed, the "war danger will last as long as capitalism does, and we must orientate upon this realization." By August 1950, Alexander Bittelman had begun to speak of the peace issue as the essential link in creating the approaches for new transitions to socialism. In May 1951, a letter from Dennis discussing the ouster of General Douglas MacArthur managed to combine the view that the differences between

Truman and his general were insubstantial with a lament that the Party was "creating so-called united front peace organizations and campaigns in [its] own image, with an advanced program, the immediate program of [the] Party, with forms of organization and activity" that involved "at best only a narrow circle of workers and progressives already under the Party's influence."

37. The Cominform had in November 1949 passed a special resolution urging all parties to "subordinate their entire activity to this," that is, the peace movement, which was "now the central task," and to "proceed from the concrete conditions in each country." The American Party at this time sent a draft of its "theses" for the preconvention discussion of 1950 to Paris via Pierre Courtade, *L'Humanite's* foreign editor. He brought back word that Jacques Duclos wondered why the concept of peaceful coexistence played virtually no part in the document.

38. The most impressive Party-sponsored activity was the Stockholm Peace Pledge campaign of early 1950 and the delegation to the World Peace Council congress in Warsaw in November 1950, at which non-Communists presented a "peaceful coexistence" view that was in some contrast to what had been heard before. The Party also participated discreetly in the Mid-Century Conference in Chicago called by the Committee for Peaceful Alternatives, a group of Chicago-based professors.

39. Howard Fast, *Peekskill* (New York: New Century Publishers, 1950).

40. It is not without relevance that the American Communists received in 1949 an implied rebuke from Gerhart Eisler, a German Communist who had worked closely with them in the more hopeful moments of the thirties and who had happened to find himself quite by accident among them in the forties. The full story of Eisler's sojourn in the United States has never been told. Eisler, at loggerheads with his own party in 1929 and called to Moscow by Stalin because of his "rightist" line, came to know the C.P.U.S.A. leaders in the Comintern's Anglo-American Commission at their nadir in 1929-1930. Some years later, after working for the Communist International in China, he came to the States. He was a factor in the relative successes of that time. He then returned to Western Europe. When the Nazis over-ran France, he left for Mexico, but the ship on which he and his wife embarked was diverted to New York under the Neutrality Act regulations. To the U.S. Communist leaders, he was thus a ghost from the past. He lived quietly, contributing occasional articles to the Communist press. In 1946 as he was preparing to return to Germany, he was arrested and accused of being the "top Communist International agent" in the United States. He conducted a largely one-man fight on his own behalf, receiving little help from the C.P.U.S.A. Facing a

five-year jail sentence on insubstantial charges, he stowed away on the Polish vessel, the Batory, in April 1949, and successfully evaded U.S. authorities. On the face of it, Eisler left the country because he wanted to return to Germany, after a lifetime of wandering, and to participate in its reconstruction. But his behavior also reflected a certain nonconfidence in his American comrades. He had conducted his self-defense campaign in a manner which was, in effect, a criticisim of them. By taking off in a spectacular manner he was demonstrating that he did not want to stay and live through the coming debacle.

## CHAPTER 9. HOW THE DIE WAS CAST, AND OTHER SKELETONS

1. Browder is the source of the knowledge that this shortwave radio was set up. (See his testimony in Columbia University's Oral History Project.) The late Rudy Blum, who worked with Browder in the Orient and was active in the C.P.U.S.A. under the name of Rudy Nelson, was in charge of this project. Browder says that contact with Dimitrov was made only once, in the fall of 1939.

2. In Rome in the autumn of 1951, I talked at length with Palmiro Togliatti, largely on the war danger. The Italian Communist Party leader was interested in the differences within the C.P.U.S.A. on this subject, and he indicated to me that the Soviet debate was in fact international in scope. Togliatti seemed most impressed by my view that the Cold War was not being pressed by any important section of U.S. capitalism to the point of a military showdown. The fact that he seemed to concur in this judgment was reported to my colleagues in New York, and played a part in the Party's underground debates in 1952.

3. This was the origin of the New Program issued in 1954. The belief that it might be useful was resisted by the leaders of the Foster-Thompson-Davis faction for several years. The 1954 Program was, as Dennis complained in his April 1956 re-examination, ambivalent in many crucial ways. It bore the marks of contradictory concepts and of the inner-Party struggle that was raging at the time in the underground. For the full text, see *The American Way to Jobs, Democracy and Peace* (New York: New Century Publishers, 1954).

4. The Soviet Communist Party's leadership expressed many doubts about C.P.U.S.A. policy to me in my last visit to Moscow in July 1953, even suggesting that some new overture in Browder's direction be made. Top Soviet figures seemed to be very well informed about the American Communists. For example, in June 1955 I encountered the Soviet foreign minister, Vyacheslav Molotov, at a United Nations gathering, and was asked why, "if you have failed to change things in one way, you do not try another way?" This was a reference to the bit-

ter, but secret struggle within the U.S. Communist Party. I was astonished that Molotov seemed to know of it. He knew also that I had refused to register in the C.P.U.S.A. the year before.

5. David A. Shannon, *Decline of America Communism* (New York: Harcourt, Brace & World, 1959).

6. The Lautner story is told by George Charney in his *A Long Journey* (Chicago: Quadrangle Books, 1968). Until Charney's book in 1968 few knew the implications of the Lautner affair, except for the top C.P. leaders, who had known of their unfair and self-damaging treatment of Lautner since 1951.

7. In Herbert L. Packard's study, *Ex-Communist Witnesses* (Stanford: Stanford University Press, 1965) the witness against Communism who comes off best in a careful examination of veracity and consistency is Lautner. So far as is known, the American C.P. has never moved to "rehabilitate" Lautner. At a conference convened by the Institute of International Studies, University of South Carolina, in September 1969, John Gates encountered Lautner for the first time in nearly twenty years. Without excusing Lautner's service to the government, Gates nonetheless apologized for his part in the treatment of Lautner in 1951.

8. Interview with George Watt, at that time secretary of the National Cadre and Review Commission, January 27, 1966, and December 26, 1968.

9. *Daily Worker*, June 5, 1951.

10. In a communication to me (October 12, 1970) John Gates gives the following picture of the crisis within the C.P. top leadership over the decision as to who should go underground. "As on every other question, there was a big fight on the matter. Some, such as Carl Winter and Elizabeth Gurley Flynn, took the position that no one should go underground, and that each of the Smith Act defendants should serve their prison terms. They pointed out that the Party had many other leaders, quite capable of replacing them. They evoked the case of "Big Bill" Haywood, whose skipping bail in the early twenties had a bad effect on the I.W.W. But Foster, Davis and Thompson demanded that everyone should go underground, arguing that the United States was in for a long fascist-like period and once we all went into prison, none of us would come out. Others argued for a compromise, that some leaders go into prison and that others do not. The argument was that a period of reaction should be distinguished from fascism, and the Party should be prepared to function both legally and illegally. In their view, the leadership had to set an example, some going to jail and others into the underground. In the same way, the secondary cadres would function legally while some went into the underground. This position was accepted by a majority vote. Then Foster proposed that anyone of the leaders who want-

ed to skip bail should be allowed to do so. This, too, was rejected. It was finally decided so that the ones who did skip bail — Green, Hall, Winston and Thompson — were the ones who were supposed to. But Eugene Dennis was also included. It was felt that for the head of the Party to be unavailable would be a signal to the Party that the main emphasis was on its illegal work. Dennis was personally opposed to this decision, but had been placed in the position of appearing to be a coward if he refused. When the time came, there was a snafu in his case. Later, this was investigated and judged to have been a legitimate snafu, with no responsibility for it resting on Dennis himself. It is not true that Thompson was not supposed to skip bail. The decision included him, mainly because of his strenuous insistence. Davis and I were in the category of those who should surrender and serve our jail terms (as we did) mainly because of our positions. Davis was a New York councilman and it was felt his political future might be jeopardized if he jumped bail. As editor of the *Daily Worker,* I was chosen to serve the term on the argument that the paper's legality might be in danger if I did not."

11. Names such as Andrew Stevens, Joseph Rockman, Hugh Bradley, Alexander Kendrick, John Swift appear and then disappear. A careful reading of these articles shows emergent differences of opinion and conflicts on the major issues.

12. Perhaps this is one of the reasons why so many succeeded in business ventures after they left the Communist Party. One of the untold stories of the U.S. economic boom of the sixties is the part played in it by former Communists.

13. Some of the most searching questions arose for those who had been assigned to far-off places, from Paris to Prague and Moscow to Peking. For example, the *Daily Worker's* correspondent in Moscow, Joseph Clark, pressed his views in a private memorandum, in 1954, challenging the "war danger concept," and discovered that similar challenges were being made from the underground. Both Clark and myself would have been expelled by Foster, Betty Gannett, and Pettis Perry directly upon our return from abroad in the second half of 1953 had not the O.B.U. intervened. Both of us were raising questions that had also arisen for the "unavailables."

## CHAPTER 10. THE BREAKDOWN AND THE BREAKUP, 1956-57

1. See George Charney, *A Long Journey* (Chicago: Quadrangle Books, 1968) and John Gates, *The Story of an American Communist* (New York: Thomas Nelson's 1958).

2. The sheer volume of periodical articles on the 1956-57 events is impressive. See the American Jewish Committee, *Memorandum on the American Communists,* December 23, 1956; Daniel Seligman,

"Dilemma in New York,"*Fortune,* February 1957; Gus Tyler, director of the Training Institute of the International Ladies Garment Workers' Union, in *A.D.A. World,* March 1957; Louis Jay Herman, "Turmoil in U.S. Communism," the *New Leader,* January 21, 1957; Robert Bendiner, "The U.S. Communists — Rebellion in a Microcosm," the *Reporter,* December 13, 1956; Maurice J. Goldbloom, "The American Communists Today," *Commentary,* February 1957 and Bert Cochran, "The Communist Convention," the *American Socialist,* March 1957. This issue of the *American Socialist* also contains a comment by me in the article "Toward a Socialist Revival." See also, H.W. Benson, "The C.P. at the Crossroads," the *New International,* Fall 1956. Cf. U.S. Congress, Senate Committee on the Judiciary, a statement by J. Edgar Hoover, March 12, 1957; and *ibid.,* "The 16th National Convention of the Communist Party, U.S.A.," June 13, 1957. Of the widespread newspaper coverage of the period, Joseph P. Lash, the *New York Post,* July 22, 1956, had a special importance because he revealed to the Party membership the existence of hitherto concealed opposing groups in the C.P. leadership. *The Anti-Stalin Campaign and International Communism,* a selection of documents, edited by the Russian Institute, Columbia University (New York: Columbia University Press, 1956) has particular value.

3. *Draft Resolution for the 16th National Convention of the Communist Party, U.S.A.* (New York: New Century Publishers, 1956.)

4. Fred Fine, the Party's organizational secretary, made the following assessment of the Party's situation, in the *Worker,* July 1, 1956. "The Party is at the most critical juncture of its development. It is at a crossroads which can lead to its becoming an impotent sect. Furthermore, there is among the membership a confusion and lack of confidence in the Party that go far deeper than anything I have seen in over twenty years of experience." See Fine's earlier article, in the *Worker,* June 24, 1956.

5. Max Weiss is quoted in the American Jewish Committee, *Memorandum on the American Communists,* as saying: "The disclosure of the mistakes made under Stalin's leadership came as a stunning surprise to our Party leadership and membership. We have not been prepared for this depite the attention paid to all the political preparations for the 20th Congress. Neither did we grasp the full extent of the mistakes made even when Khrushchev's report was made available." See N. 10, Chapter 1.

6. See *New York Times,* report of Khrushchev's remarks at the New Year's Eve party, December 31, 1956.

7. The *Daily Worker,* from March 13, 1956, onwards and beginning with a column by its managing editor, Alan Max, began to comment on the crisis. For the next year, the paper mirrored with exceptional

clarity an extraordinary upheaval, performing a function entirely un-usual for a Communist newspaper.

8. *Party Voice,* a magazine-type bulletin, was issued for several years, prior to 1956. With its No. 3 issue of June 1956, it became the foremost vehicle for some of the most serious Communist reappraisals.

9. Foster's change of heart came a few days after *Pravda* conve-niently decided to review a book of his on Negro history which had been published a year earlier in Moscow. The *New York Times,* September 24, 1956 reported that *Pravda's* review praised Foster as a "noted theoretician and Marxist historian."

10. For the full text, see Russian Institute, Columbia University, *The Anti-Stalin Campaign and International Communism,* pp. 148-165. See the observations by the editor that the Dennis article "was the first criticism by a foreign Communist to be acknowledged in the Soviet press prior to the Central Committee resolution of June 30. It was likewise carried by the satellite presses." (p. 148).

11. For full text, see *ibid.,* pp. 97-139.

12. The West Coast *People's World,* which had been compelled to change to a weekly early in February 1956 after nineteen years as a daily, supported the re-examinationist view. So did the Party's re-maining foreign-language papers. The most important, the *Morning Freiheit,* played a leading part in facing up to the revelations about the repression of Soviet Jewish culture.

13. The proposal to consider a change in "name and form" came in an article by John Gates in *Political Affairs* October 1956. It was attacked as revisionist by Foster in the same issue. The New York State organization, both its members and its leaders, were intensely impatient with the national leaders. This impatience was reflected in a report to the State Committee by its organizational secretary, Nor-man Schrank, in May 1956. This report went much further in its candor and passion than most other state reports. In December 1956, the New York State Committee voted twenty-five to eight in favor of discarding "democratic centralism" and "monolithic unity" and returning to a concept of "a political action association." This was the strongest example of the trend to face squarely the experience of the Browder era. Also, the September 1956 *Party Voice,* the State Committee's bulletin, published an extended reappraisal of the Brow-der period, "Sources of our Dilemma," by a rank and file member, "Chick Mason." Mason's article is one of the most interesting docu-ments of that period. Mason told me early in 1969 that he had had no contact with Browder himself. The ideas in the article were his own.

14. Having bolstered Dennis in July and signaled to Foster in September, the Soviet press then turned on the *Daily Worker,* first in

an article in *Komunist,* November 1956, with respect to Hungary and then on the eve of the 16th National Convention. *Sovietskaya Rossiya* was reported in the *New York Times* for February 4, 1957, as having assailed the *Daily Worker* foreign editor, Joseph Clark, for having championed the idea that Leninism was "a specifically Russian phenomenon" and asserting that it was "obsolete and inapplicable" in the United States. The Soviet writer believed that Clark was trying to "separate Marxism from Leninism" and to "deny the universal character of the basic principles of Marxism-Leninism." This was viewed as a species of "national communism" and was said to be, in the Soviet paper, a "subtle form of bourgeois nationalism in 'communist' trappings." The *New York Times* also reported a critique of the American Party's rightists by the Soviet paper *Partinaya Zhizn.* Immediately following the 16th Convention, *Pravda* hailed its decisions as having achieved the "unity, preservation and consolidation" of the U.S. Party and having remained true to Marxism-Leninism (*New York Times,* February 17, 1956). Most American newspapers, by contrast, stressed that the convention had achieved the C.P.U.S.A.'s independence from Moscow. Perhaps this is what *Pravda* did not wish to tell its own readers.

15. Veterans of the Communist movement such as Max Weiss, Steve Nelson, and William Schneiderman appear early in the 1956 debate with re-examinationist views, and then fall silent. Others — Albert Blumberg, Fred Fine, Sidney Stein, Howard Johnson, Norman Schrank, A. B. Magil, and Max Gordon — appear in the debates and persevere into 1957 and then are not heard from again. Joseph Clark's letter of resignation appeared in the *Daily Worker* for September 9, 1957. John Gates resigned on January 10, 1958, publishing a series of articles which began the following week in the *New York Post.* By this time, a truly factional situation had developed. The *Daily Worker* was forced to suspend publication because opponents of Gates, who still controlled the funds entrusted to them in the underground period, refused to support the paper so long as Gates remained editor. What happened to the funds remains a minor mystery. Peggy Dennis, widow of the onetime general secretary, confirmed all this twelve years later in a letter to *People's World,* San Francisco, October 19, 1968. "The *Daily Worker,*" she wrote, "was a casualty of the [inner-Party] struggle as a result of both the Right that controlled the paper and alienated many of its readers, but also by the factional Left that withheld financial support to the paper because it opened its pages to a free-wheeling debate by all viewpoints."

16. *Party Voice,* no. 4 (July 1956), estimated that at the August 1948 convention the New York State organization had 36,500 members of whom two-thirds had left by mid-1956. No more than one-third of the remaining members attended meetings or engaged in sustained

activity, it was reported, and two-thirds of the remaining members were over forty years of age. In an interview with Stephen A. Hart, of Harvard University, late in 1966, Gates claimed that the entire Party had 12,000 members before the 1956 debates began and 5,000 two years later.

17. One of the minor ironies of the 16th National Convention was the reappearance of Jacques Duclos with a second message that, as in 1945, warned the C.P.U.S.A. not to be misled by the wiles of revisionism. The *Daily Worker* report of February 13, 1957, reported that "Steve Nelson roused applause when, in reply to Jacques Duclos' criticism of 'dangerous' departures from Marxism-Leninism in the U.S. Party, he declared: 'This convention will make its own interpretations.' " The full text of the Duclos letter, dated January 21, 1957, appears in the Interim Report of the subcommittee of the Senate's Committee on the Judiciary, *ibid.* Although Yves Moreau, *L'Humanité* correspondent, was in New York at that time, no mention of the rebuke to Duclos appeared in the French Communist press. Nor was it mentioned in the TASS reports. The memoirs of Duclos make no mention whatever of his role in regard to the American Communists.

18. Browder did seem to hold some hope for the Party's revival, and perhaps for his return to it. He told the Yonkers, N.Y. *Herald-Statesman*, August 24, 1956, that "when a patient is sick with high fever, the fever may portend the patient's demise or quite feasibly, his recovery." When asked whether he would be reconciled to the Party if it altered its attitude toward him and his views, he replied: "It's impossible to answer that. It presumes too much."

19. Joseph P. Lash, the *New York Post*, October 15, 1956. Browder's initiative was reported in the *Daily Worker*, October 16, 1956.

20. The *Nation*, July 28, 1956. "George Benjamin" turned out to be the pseudonym of a prominent economist and onetime Communist. I replied in the August 25, 1956, issue of the same magazine, revealing my own dissociation from the American Party and discussing its dilemma. There was no point urging the Communists to dissolve, my reply argued, but the Party had to be superseded by a new and much broader left formation. I entertained the illusion that this was possible for a while, as had former Communists of an earlier vintage. Granville Hicks in *Where We Came Out* (New York: Viking Press, 1954), p. 75, cites his own efforts in the same direction in 1939-1940. Hicks expressed the wish for "a League of ex-Communists devoted neither to repentance nor self-justification, but to the establishment of the truth . . ." (pp. 203-204).

21. Letter to the *New York Times*, May 23, 1957.

22. A. J. Muste, *Where Are We Now?* (privately published, evidently in 1956); Sidney Lens, *Questions for the Left*, November 1957, and *What is Socialism?*, a six page mimeographed essay.

23. I have left out any discussion of espionage, not because some Americans who called themselves Communists were not involved in this form of service to the Soviet Union, nor even because I believe no C.P. leaders were engaged in it, but because the American Party's dilemmas were not, in my view, related to this matter. The Party's subordination to the world movement was of a different character. Espionage was unrelated to the problem of policy-making, with which this study has been concerned. In retrospect, I believe that an inner ring of men responsible to the Soviet secret police probably operated within the American Communist movement, but their activity had more to do with finances, dissemination of literature, and dispatch of delegations of fellow travellers to Europe than with fundamental issues of high policy as regards either the U.S. scene or the world as a whole. The U.S. Party's image before the public suffered from the espionage charge, but this was not the main cause of its debacle. See Earl Latham, *The Communist Controversy in Washington* (Cambridge: Harvard University Press, 1966).

24. Mention has been made earlier (chapter 2, note 56) of the negative views of the C.P.U.S.A. in Comintern circles. It is interesting that as late as 1956, Pierre Courtade, a member of the French Communist Party's Central Committee, and foreign editor of *L'Humanite,* wrote me deploring my separation from the American Party, saying, "the Party is needed as a banner, as a standard round which to rally, were it a hundred times more stupid than yours. . . ." His letter made the worst possible impression. My reply was that a stupid Party could not be maintained simply to satisfy the needs of Communists abroad, who gained nothing at all from a nonexistent or futile American movement.

25. Irving Howe and Lewis Coser, *The American Communist Party* rev. ed. (New York: Praeger, 1962). See their concluding chapter.

26. Gabriel Almond et al, *The Appeals of Communism* (Princeton: Princeton University Press, 1954), pp. 374-375.

27. Daniel Bell, *Marxism Socialism in the United States,* rev. ed. (Princeton: Princeton University Press, 1968).

28. *Ibid.,* p. x of preface.

29. Max Schachtman's reflection on American Communism, in his review of Draper's first book, is a belated acknowledgement of the value of the Socialist tradition and the harm of syndicated assumptions. It is a yearning to return to the days before Bolshevism. See the *New International,* Fall 1957.

30. Almond, *Appeals of Communism,* p. 384.

31. J. Robert Oppenheimer, in *Science and the Common Understanding* (New York: Simon & Schuster, 1954), says: "Each one of us knows how much he has been transcended by the group of which he has been or is a part . . . ." p. 92.

32. Younger scholars have noted that Communism did provide the channels for personal integration and productiveness through which its adherents learned to function outside of it. See Stephen A. Hart's unpublished B.A. thesis, Harvard University, March 1967, which explores "the relations of organization, ideology and personality" in the cases of the former Communists, James Wechsler, Bella Dodd, and John Gates.

33. Kenneth E. Boulding, *The Organizational Revolution* (New York: Harper & Brothers, 1953). "The unforgivable sin of the Communists is that they regard the union as a means to gain their own ends and not as an organization with its own life and purposes" (p. 103).

34. Observers of an earlier period put their finger on the problem; for example, Barrington Moore, Jr., in *American Political Science Review*, February 1945. See also George Soule's chapter on "Radicalism" in *America Now: an Inquiry into Civilization in the United States* (New York: Scribners, 1938). His essay should be contrasted with that of Evelyn Scott on "Communist Mentalities" in the same volume. See also Robert C. Tucker's exploration of the process of de-radicalization in *The American Political Science Review,* June 1967.

# BIBLIOGRAPHY

Aaron, Daniel. *Writers on the Left*. New York: Harcourt, Brace & World, 1961.

Acheson, Dean. *A Democrat Looks at His Party*. New York: Harper, 1955.

Allen, James S. *World Monopoly and Peace*. New York: International Publishers, 1946.

Allen, James S. and Wilkerson, Doxey A. *The Economic Crisis and the Cold War,* New York: New Century Publishers, 1949.

Almond, Gabriel et al. *The Appeals of Communism*. Princeton: Princeton University Press, 1954.

*America Now: An Inquiry into Civilization in the United States*. New York: Scribners, 1938.

American Jewish Committee. *Memorandum on the American Communists*. December 23, 1956.

Bedacht, Max. *Manhattan Communist Bulletin,* no. 3 (April, 1949).

Beichman, Arnold. *Christian Science Monitor,* October 16, 1956.

Bell, Daniel. *Marxian Socialism in the United States*. Rev. ed. Princeton: Princeton University Press, 1968.

Bendiner, Robert. "The U.S. Communists — Rebellion in Microcosm." *Reporter,* December 13, 1956.

Benson, H. W. "The C.P. at the Crossroads." *New International,* Fall 1956.

Bessie, Alvah, ed. *The Heart of Spain*. New York: Veterans of the Abraham Lincoln Brigade, 1952.

Bittelman, Alexander. *A Communist Views America's Future,* 1960. Privately printed.

Boulding, Kenneth E. *The Organizational Revolution*. New York: Harper & Brothers, 1953.

Boyer, Richard O. *Pettis Perry: The Story of a Working Class Leader*. New York: Self-Defense Committee of the 17 Smith Act Victims, 1952.

Brock, Clifton. *Americans for Democratic Action*. Washington, D.C. 1962.

Brody, David. *Labor in Crisis: The Great Steel Strike of 1919*. New York: Lippincott, 1965.

Browder, Earl R. *Communism in the United States*. New York: International Publishers, 1935.

——— Memoirs and Interviews. Oral History Project, Columbia University.

——— Private Papers. University of Syracuse.

———— *Victory and After.* New York: International Publishers, 1942.

———— *Teheran.* New York: International Publishers, 1944.

———— *Teheran and America.* New York: Workers' Library Publishers, 1944.

———— *Writings and Speeches of Earl Browder, May-July 1945.* Privately printed, no date.

———— *War or Peace with Russia?* New York: A. A. Wyn, 1947.

———— *Answer to Vronsky.* Privately printed, 1948.

———— *Decline of the Left Wing of American Labor.* Privately printed, 1948.

———— *Labor and Socialism in America.* Privately printed, 1948.

———— *Where Do We Go from Here?* Privately printed, 1948.

———— *Keynes, Foster and Marx.* Privately printed, 1950.

———— *Modern Resurrections and Miracles.* Privately printed, 1950.

———— *Contempt of Congress. The Trial of Earl Browder.* Privately printed, 1951.

Buck, Tim. *Europe's Rebirth.* Toronto: Progress Books, 1947.

Cannon, James P. "Foster and Browder." *Fourth International,* Fall 1955.

Charney, George. *A Long Journey.* Chicago: Quadrangle Books, 1968.

Claiborne, Robert. "Twilight on the Left." *The Nation,* May 11, 1957.

Clark, Joseph. "A Memorandum on the 'War Danger'." A letter to William Z. Foster, 1954. Private Collection.

Clurman, Harold. *The Fervent Years: The Story of the Group Theatre and the Thirties.* New York: A. A. Knopf, 1945.

Cochran, Bert. "The Communist Convention." *American Socialist,* March 1957.

*Commentary,* "Liberal Anti-Communism Revisited," September 1967.

Communist Party, U.S.A. *The Path of Browder and Foster.* New York: Workers' Library Publishers, 1941.

———— *A Talk about the Communist Party.* New York: Workers' Library Publishers, 1943.

———— "Shall the Communist Party Change Its Name?" Published by the National Committee, May 1944.

———— "Draft Resolution for the 16th National Convention." New York: New Century Publishers, 1956.

———— *The American Way to Jobs, Democracy and Peace.* New York: New Century Publishers, 1950.

Communist Political Association. *The Heritage of the Communist Political Association.* New York: New Century Publishers, 1944.

Corey, Lewis. *The Unfinished Task.* New York: Viking, 1942.

Cowley, Malcolm. *Exile's Return.* New York: W. W. Norton, 1924.

Cruse, Harold. *The Crisis of the Negro Intellectual*. New York: William Morrow, 1967.

DeCaux, Len. *Labor Radical: From the Wobblies to the C.I.O.* Boston: Beacon Press, 1970.

Dennis, Eugene. *What America Faces*. New York: New Century Publishers, 1946.

———— *Ideas They Cannot Jail*. New York: International Publishers, 1950.

———— *The Communists Take a New Look*. New York: New Century Publishers, 1956.

———— *Letters from Prison*. New York: International Publishers, 1956.

Derber, Milton and Young, Edwin. *Labor and the New Deal*. Madison: University of Wisconsin Press, 1957.

Dodd, Bella. *School of Darkness*. New York: P. J. Kenedy, 1954.

Draper, Theodore. *The Roots of American Communism*. New York: Viking, 1957.

———— *American Communism and Soviet Russia*. New York: Viking, 1960.

———— *The Rediscovery of Black Nationalism*, New York: Viking, 1970.

Dubofsky, Melvyn. *We Shall Be All: A History of the I.W.W.* Chicago Quadrangle Books, 1969.

Duclos, Jacques. "A propos de la dissolution du P.C.A." *Les Cahiers du Communisme*, Nouvelle Serie. no. 6 (April, 1945). English translation in the *Daily Worker*, May 24, 1945.

Ernst, Morris and Loth, David. *Report on the American Communist*. New York: Holt, 1952.

Fast, Howard. *Peekskill*. New York: New Century Publishers, 1950.

Feis, Herbert. *Churchill, Roosevelt and Stalin*. Princeton: Princeton University Press, 1957.

Festinger, Leon, et al. *When Prophecy Fails*. Minneapolis: University of Minnesota Press, 1956.

Foner, Philip S. *The Bolshevik Revolution: Its Impact on American Radicals, Liberals and Labor*. New York: International Publishers, 1967.

*Fortune*, "A Yaleman and a Communist," November 1943.

———— "Dilemma in New York," February 1957.

Foster, William Z. *The Great Steel Strike*. New York: Huebsch, 1920.

———— *Towards a Soviet America*. New York: International Publishers, 1932.

———— *From Bryan to Stalin*. New York: International Publishers, 1937.

———— *Pages from a Worker's Life*. New York: International Publishers, 1939.

———— *World Capitalism and World Socialism*. New York: Workers' Library Publishers, 1941.

———— *The New Europe*. New York: International Publishers, 1947.

———— *The Twilight of World Capitalism*. New York: International Publishers, 1949.

———— *History of the Communist Party of the United States*. New York: International Publishers, 1952.

Freeman, Joseph. *An American Testament*. New York: Farrar, Rinehart, 1936.

———— *Never Call Retreat*. New York: Farrar, Rinehart, 1943.

Gates, John. *The Story of an American Communist*. New York: Thomas Nelson's, 1958.

George, Harrison. *The Crisis in the C.P.U.S.A.* Privately printed, December 1947.

Gitlow, Benjamin. *I Confess*. New York: E. P. Dutton, 1940.

Glazer, Nathan. *The Social Basis of American Communism*. New York: Harcourt, Brace & World, 1961.

Gold, Michael. *The Hollow Men*. New York: International Publishers, 1941.

Goldberg, Arthur. *A.F.L.-C.I.O. United*. New York: McGraw-Hill, 1956.

Goldbloom, Maurice J. "The American Communists Today." *Commentary*, February 1957.

Goldman, Eric. *The Crucial Decade: America, 1945-1955*. New York: A. A. Knopf, 1956.

Gordon, Max. Reply to Stanley Aronowitz. *New Left Notes*, June 10, 1966.

Gould, Leslie A. *American Youth Today*. New York: Random House, 1940.

Guthrie, Woody. *Bound for Glory*. Reprint. New York: New American Library, 1970.

Halper, Albert. *Goodbye Union Square*. Chicago: Quadrangle, 1970.

Hardman, J. B. S. *New Republic*, August and September, 1930.

Hardman, J. B. S. and Neufeld, Maurice F. *The House of Labor*. New York: Columbia University Press, 1930.

Haywood, Harry. *Negro Liberation*. New York: International Publishers, 1938.

Hart, Stephen A. A study of "the relations of organization, ideology and personality" in the cases of Bella Dodd, James Wechsler, and John Gates. B.A. thesis, Harvard University, 1967 (unpublished).

Herman, Louis Jay. "Turmoil in U.S. Communism." *New Leader*, January 21, 1957.

Hicks, Granville. *I Like America*. New York: Modern Age, 1938.

———— *Where We Came Out*. New York: Viking, 1954.

Hoover, J. Edgar. A statement to the sub-committee of the Committee on the Judiciary, U.S. Senate, March 12, 1957.

Howe, Irving and Coser, Lewis. *The American Communist Party.* New York: Praeger, 1962.

Howe, Irving and Widick, B. J. *The U.A.W. and Walter Reuther.* New York: Random House, 1949.

*The Impact of the Russian Revolution, 1917-1967.* London: Oxford University Press, 1967.

*Italia d'Oggi.* New York, May and June 1945.

Jacobson, Julius, ed. *The Negro and the American Labor Movement.* Garden City: Anchor Books, 1968.

Jaffe, Philip J. Transcript of the May and June 1945 meetings of the Communist Political Association, Political Committee and National Committee. Private collection of Philip J. Jaffe.

*Jefferson School of Social Science.* "Selected Readings on Coalition Politics and Electoral Problems." October 1954.

Josephson, Matthew. *Infidel in the Temple.* New York: A. A. Knopf, 1967.

———— *Sidney Hillman: Statesman of American Labor.* New York: Doubleday, 1952.

Kampelman, Max. *The Communist Party and the C.I.O.* New York: Praeger, 1957.

Kardelj, Edvard. "Notes on Some Questions of International Development." *Komunist* (Belgrade), January 1947.

Kempton, Murray. *Part of Our Time.* New York: Simon and Schuster, 1955.

Koestler, Arthur. *Arrow in the Blue.* New York: Macmillan, 1961.

Kolko, Gabriel. *The Triumph of American Conservatism.* New York: The Free Press, 1963.

Kornbluth, Joyce. *Voices of Revolt.* Chicago: Quadrangle Books, 1966.

Labedz, Leo, ed. *International Communism after Khrushchev.* Cambridge: M.I.T. — Wiley, 1965.

Landis, Arthur H. *The Abraham Lincoln Brigade.* New York: Citadel Press, 1967.

Lane, Robert E. *Political Ideology.* New York: The Free Press, 1962.

———— *Political Life.* New York: The Free Press, 1969.

Landy, A. *Marxism and the Democratic Tradition.* New York: International Publishers, 1948.

Lardner, Ring. "My Life on the Blacklist." *Saturday Evening Post,* October 14, 1961.

Lash, Joseph P. *New York Post,* July 22, 1956.

———— *Eleanor Roosevelt: A Friend's Memoir.* Garden City: Doubleday, 1964.

Latham, Earl. *The Communist Controversy in Washington.* Cambridge: Harvard University Press, 1966.

Lattimore, Owen. *Ordeal by Slander*. Boston: Little, Brown, 1950.

Lavine, Harold. Interview with Earl Browder. *PM,* March 26, 27, 28, 1944.

Leab, Daniel J. *A Union of Individuals: The Formation of the American Newspaper Guild*. New York: Columbia University Press, 1970.

Lenin, V. I. *Selected Works*. vol. X. New York: International Publishers, 1938.

Lens, Sidney. *Left, Right and Center*. Hinsdale, Illinois: Regnery, 1949.

——— *Questions for the Left*. Privately published, November 1957.

——— *What Is Socialism?* Privately published, 1957.

——— *Crisis of American Labor*. New York: Sagamore Press, 1959.

Lorwin, Lewis. *Post-War Plans of the United Nations*. New York: Twentieth Century Fund, 1942.

Lu, Ting-yi. "The Post-War International Situation." *Emancipation Daily* (Yenan), January 1, 1947.

Lubell, Samuel. *The Future of American Politics*. rev. ed. New York: Anchor, 1956.

Lyons, Eugene. *The Red Decade*. Indianapolis: Bobbs, Merrill, 1941.

MacDougall, Curtis R. *Gideon's Army*. vols. I, II, III. New York: Marzani & Munsell, 1965.

Magil, A. B. *New Masses,* September 23, 1947.

Mao, Tse-tung. *Selected Works,* vol. IV. Peking: 1961.

McKenzie, Kermit E. *Comintern and World Revolution*. New York: Columbia University Press, 1964.

Meyer, Frank S. *The Moulding of Communists*. New York: Harcourt, Brace & World, 1961.

Minor, Robert. Personal and Political Papers, Columbia University.

Moore, Barrington, Jr. *American Political Science Review,* February 1945.

Moreman, Merrill Raymond. "The Independent Progressive Party in California, 1948." Master's essay, Stanford University, (unpublished).

Morlan, Robert C. *Prairie Fire: the Story of the Non-Partisan League*. Minneapolis: University of Minnesota Press, 1958.

Mouledous, Joseph C. "From Browderism to Peaceful Coexistence." *Phylon,* vol. XXV, no. 1 (Spring 1964).

Muste, A. J. *Where Are We Now?* Privately printed, 1956.

Nagy, Imre. *On Communism*. New York: Praeger, 1957.

North, Joseph. *Robert Minor: Artist and Crusader*. New York: International Publishers, 1956.

Oneal, James. *Amercan Communism*. New York: E. P. Dutton, 1947.

O'Neill, William L. *Echoes of Revolt: The Masses*. Chicago: Quadrangle Books, 1966.

Oppenheimer, J. Robert. *Science and the Common Understanding.* New York: Simon and Schuster, 1954.

Packard, Herbert L. *Ex-Communist Witnesses.* Stanford: Stanford University Press, 1965.

Peters, J. *The Communist Party: A Manual on Organization.* New York: Workers' Library Publishers, 1935.

Pitzele, Merlyn S. "Can American Labor Defeat the Communists?" *Atlantic Monthly,* March 1947.

Pollitt, Daniel H. "The Fifth Amendment Plea Before Congressional Committees Investigating Subversion." *University of Pennsylvania Law Review,* 106, 1958.

Putnam, Samuel. *Paris Was Our Mistress.* New York: Viking, 1947.

Rawick, George P. Manuscript on the American Youth Congress, prepared for the Fund for the Republic (unpublished).

Reale, Eugenio. *Avec Jacques Duclos au Banc des Accusés.* Paris: Mondadori, 1958.

Record, Wilson. *Race and Radicalism: The N.A.A.C.P. and the Communist Party in Conflict.* Ithaca: Cornell University Press, 1964.
——— *The Negro and the Communist Party.* Chapel Hill: The University of North Carolina Press, 1951.

Reed, Louis S. *The Labor Philosophy of Samuel Gompers.* New York: Prentice Hall, 1951.

Rodney, William. *Soldiers of the International: A History of the Communist Party in Canada.* Toronto: University of Toronto Press, 1968.

Ross, Irwin. *The Loneliest Campaign.* New York: New American Library, 1968.

Rubenstein, Annette, ed. *I Vote My Conscience.* New York: The Vito Marcantonio Memorial, 1956.

Russian Institute, Columbia University. *The Anti-Stalin Campaign and International Communism.* New York: Columbia University Press, 1956.

Saposs, David J. *Communism in American Politics.* Washington, D. C.: Public Affairs Press, 1960.

Schachtman, Max. *New International,* Fall, 1957.

Schlesinger, Arthur M., Jr. *The Age of Roosevelt: The Politics of Upheaval.* Boston: Houghton, Mifflin, 1960.

Schmidt, Karl. *Henry A. Wallace: Quixotic Crusader.* Syracuse: Syracuse University Press, 1960.

Schram, Stuart. *The Political Thought of Mao Tse-tung.* New York: Praeger, 1963.

Schwartz, Morton. The formation of the World Federation of Trade Unions, Ph.D. diss., Columbia University, 1963 (unpublished).

Seidman, Joel. "Labor Policy of the Communist Party During World

War II." *Industrial and Labor Relations Review,* vol. IV (October 1950).

Selznick, Philip. *The Organizational Weapon.* New York: McGraw-Hill, 1952.

Shannon, David A. *The Socialist Party of America.* New York: Macmillan, 1955.

—— *Decline of American Communism.* New York: Harcourt, Brace & World, 1959.

Shover, John L. *Cornbelt Rebellion: The Farmer's Holiday Association.* Urbana: University of Illinois Press, 1965.

Shulman, Marshall D. *Stalin's Foreign Policy Reappraised.* Cambridge: Harvard University Press, 1963.

Simon, Rita, ed. *As We Saw the Thirties.* Urbana: University of Illinois Press, 1967.

Somerville, John. *The Communist Trials and the American Tradition.* New York: Cameron Associates, 1956.

Stalin, Joseph. *Marxism and the National and Colonial Question.* New York: International Publishers, 1942.

—— *For Victory and Enduring Peace.* New York: Worker's Library Publishers, December 1944.

—— *Economic Problems of Socialism.* New York: International Publishers, 1952.

Starobin, Joseph R. *Paris to Peking.* New York: Cameron Associates, 1955.

—— *Polemic.* Western Reserve University, 1959.

—— "1956 — a Memoir." *Problems of Communism,* November-December 1966.

—— "Origins of the Cold War: the Communist Dimension." *Foreign Affairs,* July 1969.

Stone, I. F. *The Truman Era.* New York: Monthly Review Press, 1953.

Stone, Irving. *Clarence Darrow for the Defense.* Garden City: Doubleday, Doran, 1941.

Strong, Anna Louise. *I Change Worlds.* New York: Holt, 1935.

Swing, Raymond Gram. *Forerunners of American Fascism.* New York: J. Messner, 1935.

Talmadge, I. D., ed. *Whose Revolution?* New York: Howell, Soskin, 1941.

Thomas, Hugh. *The Spanish Civil War.* New York: Harper and Row, 1961.

Toch, Hans. *The Social Psychology of Social Movements.* Indianapolis: Bobbs-Merrill, 1965.

Togliatti, Palmiro. Interview in *Nuovi Argumenti,* Rome, June 16, 1956.

Tucker, Robert C. *The Soviet Political Mind.* New York: Praeger, 1963.

——— *American Political Science Review,* June 1967.

Tugwell, Rexford Guy. *The Progressive,* April 1949.

Tyler, Gus. *A.D.A. World,* March 1957.

Ulam, Adam. *Titoism and the Cominform.* Cambridge: Harvard University Press, 1952.

U.S. Congress, House, Committee on Un-American Activities. *Investigation of Communist Activities in the Seattle, Washington Area.* 84th Cong., 1st sess., 1955.
*on S. 1832,* Part 1.

U.S. Congress, Senate, Committee on the Judiciary. *Report of the Sub-Committee; The 16th National Convention of the Communist Party, U.S.A.* June 13, 1957.

Van Zanten, John W. "Communist Theory and the American Negro Question." *Review of Politics,* October 1967.

Varga, Eugene. *Pravda,* November 27, 1946.

Waltzer, Kenneth J. "The American Labor Party of New York," a Ph.D. diss. in preparation at Harvard University.

Wechsler, James A. *The Age of Suspicion.* New York: Random House, 1953.

Wilensky, Harold L. *Intellectuals in Labor Unions.* Glencoe: The Free Press, 1956.

Wilson, Edmund. *New Republic,* December 24, 1930.

——— *New Republic,* January 14, 1931.

——— *The American Earthquake.* Garden City: Doubleday, 1968.

Winter, Ella. *And Not to Yield.* New York: Harcourt, Brace & World, 1963.

Woltman, Frederick. *New York World-Telegram,* May 9, 1944.

See also the *Communist,* a monthly from 1935 to 1944, and its successor, *Political Affairs,* after 1944. Also, the *Daily Worker* (and its weekend edition, the *Worker*) for the period 1945 to 1957. Also, the left wing magazine, *March of Labor,* in the fifties; *People's World,* a daily in San Francisco, for the references to 1947; and *Party Voice,* magazine of the New York State Communist Party, 1954 through 1956.

# Index

to go underground, 306n; on C.P.
membership decline, 310n;
resignation from C.P., 310n
Gebert, Boleslaw, 249n, 260n
George, Harrison, 115, 248n
Gitlow, Benjamin, 262n
Glazer, Nathan, 23, 31, 37, 234
Gold, Ben, 116, 202, 273n
Gold, Mike, 32, 137, 284n
Goldsmith, William, 259n
Gompers, Samuel, 144
Gordon, Max, 250n, 286n, 310n
Gottwald, Klement, 155
Graham, Frank P., 30
Green, Gilbert, 45, 56, 216, 220;
welfare state ideas, 10, 243n;
reaction to Duclos, 86; in Duclos
debate, 90; vote on Duclos, 92;
rejects Davis demand, 99, 100;
post-Browder career, 118;
emerges from underground, 241n;
rationale for underground, 242n;
and Gus Hall, 280-281n; and
Chicago judicial election, 291n
Griffiths, Franklyn, 282n
Group Theatre, 32

Hall, Gus, 5, 216, 219, 220; 241n
Hall, Rob Fowler, 118
Hallinan, Vincent, 11, 297n
Hamilton, Grace, 252n
Harriman, W. Averell, 78, 269n
Harrison, William, 277n
Hart, Ed, 189
Hartle, Barbara, 302n
Hartley, Fred, 157
Haywood, "Big Bill," 22
Haywood, Harry, 131, 201
Healy, Dorothy, 280n
Heller, A. A., 279n
Hellman, Lillian, 136, 299n
Henderson, Donald, 300n
Hicks, Granville, 46, 248n, 254n,
311n
Hillman, Sidney, 17, 59, 145
Hillquit, Morris, 259n
Hitler, Adolph, 27
Hollander, Louis, 167, 174, 290n
Hollywood Anti-Nazi League, 32
Hollywood Writers Mobilization, 33
Hoover, J. Edgar, 229, 230
Horton, Myles, 252n
Howard, Charles P., 295n
Howard, Roy, 269n

Howe, Irving, 232
Huberman, Leo, 182, 205
Hudson, Roy: on no-strike pledge,
77; reaction to Duclos, 85;
hesitations about Duclos, 91;
abstention on Duclos vote, 92,
273n; and "legalization" of trade
union "influentials," 97; post-
Browder career, 117, 280n; and
alien leaders, 257n; on Browder's
leadership, 263n

Independent Citizens Committee of
the Arts and Sciences, 110
Independent Citizens Committee of
the Arts, Sciences and Profes-
sions, 33, 110, 210
*Inprecorr,* 44
International Federation of Trade
Unions, 144
International Juridical Association,
31
International Ladies Garment
Workers Union, 35
International Publishers, 25
International Typographical Union,
38
International Workers of the
World, 41, 107
International Workers Order,
25, 249n
Isaacson, Leo, 188
*Italia d'Oggi,* 260n, 270n

Jackson, Andrew, 22
Jefferson School of Social Science,
25
Jefferson, Thomas, 22
Jerome, V. J., 297n
Jewish People's Fraternal Order,
249n
John Reed Clubs, 31
Johnson, Arnold, 71, 248n, 250n
Johnson, Howard, 310n
Jones, Claudia, 282n

Kardelj, Edvard, 292n
Katz-Suchy, Juliusz, 120, 281n
Kempton, Murray, 31
Kenny, Robert W., 16, 163, 164;
opposes Progressive Party, 246n,
288n; impact of Duclos article,
285n; meets Foster, 288n
Keynes, John M., 203

BOOKS PUBLISHED UNDER THE AUSPICES OF
THE RESEARCH INSTITUTE ON COMMUNIST AFFAIRS,
COLUMBIA UNIVERSITY

*Diversity in International Communism*, edited by Alexander Dallin. Published in collaboration with the Russian Institute. Columbia University Press, 1963.

*Political Succession in the USSR*, by Myron Rush. Published jointly with the RAND Corporation. Columbia University Press, 1965.

*Marxism in Modern France*, by George Lichtheim. Columbia University Press, 1966.

*Power in the Kremlin*, by Michel Tatu. Viking Press, 1969. First published in 1967 by Bernard Grasset under the title *Le Pouvoir en URSS*, and also in England by William Collins Sons and Co., Ltd., in 1968.

*The Soviet Bloc: Unity and Conflict*, by Zbigniew Brzezinski. Revised and enlarged edition, Harvard University Press, 1967.

*Vietnam Triangle*, by Donald Zagoria. Pegasus Press, 1968.

*Communism in Malaysia and Singapore*, by Justus van der Kroef. Nijhoff Publications, The Hague, 1967.

*Radicalismo Cattolico Brasiliano*, by Ulisse A. Floridi. Istituto Editoriale Del Mediterraneo, 1968.

*Stalin and His Generals*, edited by Seweryn Bialer. Pegasus Press, 1969.

*Marxism and Ethics*, by Eugene Kamenka. Macmillan and St. Martin's Press, 1969.

*Dilemmas of Change in Soviet Politics*, edited by Zbigniew Brzezinski. Columbia University Press, 1969.

*The USSR Arms the Third World: Case Studies in Soviet Foreign Policy*, by Uri Ra'anan. M.I.T. Press, 1969.

*Communists and Their Law*, by John N. Hazard. University of Chicago Press, 1969.

*Fulcrum of Asia*, by Bhabani Sen Gupta. Published jointly with the East Asian Institute. Pegasus Press, 1970.

*Le Conflit Sino-Soviétique et l'Europe de l'Est*, by Jacques Lévesque. Les Presses de l'Université de Montreal, 1970.

*Between Two Ages*, by Zbigniew Brzezinski. Viking Press, 1970.

*Communist China and Latin America, 1959-1967*, by Cecil Johnson. Columbia University Press, 1970.

*The Czechoslovak Experiment 1968-1969*, by Ivan Svitak. Columbia University Press, 1971.

*Les Regimes Politiques de l'U.R.S.S. et de l'Europe de l'Est*, by Michel Lesage. Presses Universitaires de France, 1971.

*Communism and Nationalism in India: M. N. Roy and Comintern Policy, 1920-1939*, by John P. Haithcox. Princeton University Press, 1971.

*American Communism in Crisis, 1943-1957*, by Joseph R. Starobin. Harvard University Press, 1972.